The Ironies of Affirmative Action

Morality and Society
A Series Edited by Alan Wolfe

THE
IRONIES
of
AFFIRMATIVE
ACTION

POLITICS, CULTURE, AND
JUSTICE IN AMERICA

John David Skrentny

—

THE

UNIVERSITY OF CHICAGO PRESS

CHICAGO & LONDON

The University of Chicago Press, Chicago 60637
The University of Chicago Press, Ltd., London
© 1996 by The University of Chicago
All rights reserved. Published 1996
Printed in the United States of America

05 04 03 02 01 00 99 98 97   2 3 4 5

ISBN 0–226–76177–0 (cloth)
ISBN 0–226–76178–9 (ppbk)

Library of Congress Cataloging-in-Publication Data
Skrentny, John David.
   The ironies of affirmative action: Politics, culture, and justice in
America / John David Skrentny.
      p.   cm. — (Morality and society)
   Includes bibliographical references and index.
   1. Affirmative action programs—United States.   I. Title.
II. Series.
HF5549.5.A34S57   1996
331.13′3′0973—dc20   95-36820
                                                                  CIP

♾ The paper used in this publication meets the minimum
requirements of the American National Standard for Information
Sciences—Permanence of Paper for Printed Library Materials, ANSI
Z39.48-1984.

For my parents

CONTENTS

PREFACE

Readers may justifiably expect this book to have a political agenda, either for or against affirmative action, since almost everything written about that controversial policy has such an agenda. This book, however, has no political agenda, unless one considers the desire to question fundamental assumptions on both sides and move tired debates forward to be a political agenda. The goal of the book is to use sociological and historical tools to show why conservatives resist affirmative action and liberals support it. If social scientists can find ideas that will help them better understand or rethink their study of American politics, policy, or law, and if interested individuals on both sides of the issue can find ideas that will help them better understand or rethink their positions on affirmative action, the book will have succeeded.

The topic has long been a sensitive one, and in the beginning stages of my research, I was warned many times of this sensitivity. I ran the risk that many would regard my contribution as yet another ideological tract. I was committed to the research, however, because I was committed to the simple idea that as social scientists go about refining their understandings of the fundamental workings of society and politics, some should remember to study the specific issues that Americans care about in the process of this theoretical refinement. I felt that sensitive issues were precisely the ones which needed study.

I did not come to study affirmative action because I was fascinated with this particular topic; I came to it because I was fascinated with the sources and dynamics of political controversy. In search of a suitable research topic, I was reading widely, simply looking at books and articles on political controversy and change that sounded particularly interesting. It was in Daniel Bell's *The Coming of Post-Industrial Society* (New York: Basic Books, 1973) that I ran across a sentence which I could not forget. It happened to be about affirmative action: "What is extraordinary about this change [to affirmative action] is that, *without public debate,* an entirely new principle of rights has been introduced into the polity (p. 417, emphasis added)." I agreed with Professor Bell that affirmative action represented something new, and I knew that it was very controversial, with public opinion going decidedly against it. But I had not considered that it had become policy without public debate. It was an apparently anomalous policy victory for a group usually assumed to be far from the center of power. How did it happen? It seemed a fantastic sociological puzzle.

I was especially attracted to just this sort of question because, as an undergraduate major in both sociology and philosophy, I had become interested in the relationship between ideas of justice or morality and the social policies that Americans actually support. Every moral philosophy has been thoroughly criticized through logical argument; how was it that modern people could nevertheless be strongly committed to various ideals that were logically full of holes? And what was the relationship, if any, between the ideals of justice and morality that are extolled over and over in political discourse and the policies that are actually enacted and implemented? The puzzle of affirmative action seemed a perfect case for the exploration of these questions. This book is the result of that exploration.

When I began in 1991, the affirmative action debate was showing many signs not of cooling down but of stabilizing. Since late 1969, quotas were decried but racial preferences were politically possible. The issue was debated throughout the 1970s, 1980s, and early 1990s, though there was little movement, and when I sent the final version of the manuscript to Chicago in January of 1995, this was where the debate still stood. In that version, I predicted the new Republican majority in Congress would likely turn their sights onto affirmative action and begin an attack not just on quotas but on preferences.

But I did not think it would happen so *soon*—just a matter of weeks after I sent my manuscript. Though off the radar screen in the congressional races of 1994, the affirmative action issue exploded in February 1995. The news media was abuzz with analyses of affirmative action. Some on the Left pointedly decided to abandon the policy altogether, others remained committed, while sometimes trying to make the beneficiaries of affirmative action seem more deserving, by emphasizing that *women* benefit from the policies (and not just blacks). Still others tried to co-opt the enemy by making angry white males potential beneficiaries of a new class-based affirmative action.

Despite the change in the debate, much has remained drearily the same and the analysis in this book offers insight for better understanding. The arguments on the Right still reflected the utopian assumption that America would be a meritocracy were it not for affirmative action and the incorrect assertion that the government could never support or tolerate preferences. Moral worthiness is the dominant issue, as it was before, and this is still rarely recognized explicitly. The Left still tried to find ways to defend a policy with little knowledge of where the policy came from and little recognition of its political liabilities. Explaining this situation was one of my original objectives and, despite the renewed and changing debate, I made only minor changes to the book.

A great many generous people have helped me in my investigation of the puzzles and ironies of affirmative action (though none, of course, are responsible for any of this book's shortcomings). At Harvard University, Orlando Patterson agreed to supervise the project when it was still in its dissertation stage, and his creativity, constructive criticism, open-mindedness, and intellectual support were essential for the completion of the project. His consistent emphasis on the importance of context in studying social phenomena was a lesson of enduring value. I was fortunate to have Nathan Glazer, one of the most prominent commentators on affirmative action, on my committee, and his ideas and willingness to share his experiences gave the project a sense of history and showed where new work needed to be done.

As I did the research a framework for understanding gradually came into place. It was difficult, however, to link these ideas with the current debates in social and political analysis. Yasemin Soysal showed me that my framework was similar to that of "institutional" perspectives in sociology, and tirelessly answered my questions as I struggled to see where my voice fit into the conversation. As the project went deeper into the workings of American politics, Theda Skocpol was kind enough to provide guidance with regard to the patterns of the politics of social policy. I did not know at the outset that the answers to the puzzle of affirmative action were to be found through study of administration, the courts, and the presidency, but I became fascinated with this aspect of the project, and her renowned expertise was a great resource. Others at Harvard were generous with their time and their insights, especially David Riesman, Daniel Bell, and Jason Kaufman; but also Victoria Alexander, Liah Greenfeld, Randall Kennedy, Martin Kilson, and H. W. Perry. That I critique some of these scholars' views in the pages that follow is testament of the great influence they have had on my own thinking.

One of the most exciting parts of scholarly work is exchanging views with far-flung scholars who share similar interests. Paul Burstein offered crucial early counsel, and Hugh Davis Graham was willing to offer his views on the manuscript. Both shared their expert knowledge on equal employment opportunity legislation and the history and politics of civil rights law. Edward Shils granted me an opportunity to discuss the relationship between tradition and change on a cold winter evening at the University of Chicago. John W. Meyer offered his unique and creative viewpoint in direct comments on the manuscript and through correspondence. John Boli, Paul Frymer, Jennifer Hochschild, and Stephen Skowronek read portions of manuscript and/or gave helpful comments. One of my greatest debts goes to Frank Dobbin, who read two versions of the manuscript and, for over a year, carried on a dialogue with me on the nuances of cultural explanation. His generosity would set an impossible standard for scholarly collegiality. Faculty at Emory University, the University of California at San Diego, Smith College, and Skidmore College, and faculty and students in the 306 Colloquium at Harvard (especially Peter Marsden, Aage Sørensen, Charles Lilly and Joe Rhea) gave much-appreciated comments. My colleagues at the University of Pennsylvania Department of Sociology, as well as Marissa Martino-Golden in Political Science, and Thomas Sugrue in History all offered helpful comments and assistance along the way. I also thank Alfred Blumrosen, Eli Ginzberg, Jack Greenberg, and James E. Jones, Jr. for allowing me to interview them.

Acknowledgement is in order for my mentors at Indiana University, especially David Brain, Donna Eder, and the incomparable Brian Powell, who convinced me I could pursue a career in academia and were always there for much-needed advice. The impact of my parents, Stanley and Marie Skrentny, on my scholarly pursuits has been great. I especially thank my father for orienting me to the vagaries of labor law and for keeping me abreast of legal and political developments. I also owe great thanks to my lovely wife, Stella. Domestic partners commonly give emotional support when the other is embarking on a large scholarly project, but our debate on the merits of cultural analysis versus structural analysis, which lasted several hours and stretched out over two days, was especially significant to me. She says she did not learn anything, but I certainly did.

I must acknowledge the aid, enthusiasm, and assistance of my editor at the University of Chicago Press, Douglas Mitchell, as well as Kathryn Kraynik and Matt Howard. My series editor, Alan Wolfe, suggested half of the title of this book, gave other important advice, and was generally an inspiration. I also want to thank the anonymous readers at the University of Chicago who offered detailed criticisms. Portions of chapter 5 originally appeared in my article, "Pragmatism, Institutionalism, and the Construction of Employment Discrimination," in *Sociological Forum* 9, no. 3 (1994). I gratefully acknowledge Plenum Publishing for permission to use this material here.

Finally, the National Science Foundation supplied a fellowship during my graduate school years that allowed me the time to acquire some valuable grounding in different disciplines. The Mark DeWolfe Howe Fund from the Harvard Law School supplied necessary funding during the research period.

A note on sources: Most historians studying the origins of social policies have to make time-consuming and expensive treks to various presidential libraries. I was fortunate enough to have at Harvard extensive microfilm collections of documents related to civil rights from the Johnson administration (*Civil Rights During the Johnson Administration, 1963–1969,* ed. Steven F. Lawson [Frederick, Md.: University Publications of America, 1984]), and from the Nixon administration (*Civil Rights During the Nixon Administration, 1969–1974,* ed. Hugh Davis

Graham [Bethesda, Md.: University Publications of America, 1989]). Also available were *Papers of the Nixon White House,* ed. Joan Hoff-Wilson (Bethesda, Md.: University Publications of America, 1989) and the multivolume collection of documents related to civil rights from the Truman administration to the Johnson administration, *Civil Rights, the White House, and the Justice Department,* ed. Michal R. Belknap, (New York: Garland Publishing, 1991). I am grateful to the Harvard librarians in Government Documents for helping me to navigate these as well as the other historical sources in their treasure trove. Hugh Graham's prodigiously researched and trail-blazing *The Civil Rights Era* (New York: Oxford University Press, 1990), which I discovered later than I would have liked, offers rich historical detail that is useful to anyone interested in understanding how obscure political actions can have a major impact. The data for this study included these presidential papers, documents of the various administrative agencies, congressional debates and reports, court opinions, *amicus curiae* and other court briefs, news conferences, memoirs, interviews, and various secondary historical sources.

1

The Ironies of Affirmative Action

Another book about affirmative action? It may seem difficult to justify writing a new book on a subject that has been debated and analyzed for three decades by philosophers, legal scholars, social scientists, politicians, journalists, editorial writers, and common citizens. The affirmative action controversy has followed the pattern of other righteous battles in American politics, such as the abortion debate. There are two sides which have never seemed to tire of stating their positions, sustaining points sometimes with reason and sometimes with emotion, and often showing little hesitation in resorting to insults (in the case of affirmative action, "racist" has been a favored term of opprobrium for both sides). The basic arguments are familiar. The Right has told us to resist affirmative action because it is unmeritocratic, leads to reverse discrimination, and is an un-American guarantee of equal results instead of equal opportunity. The Left has told us to support it as compensation for past injustices, a guarantee of a fair share of the economic pie, and because it is a civil right, guaranteed by the Constitution and refined by later statutes.[1] It would seem there is little left to say on the subject, that we must already know what there is to know.

Nevertheless, it is *not* difficult to justify a new contribution to the subject, and the emotion in the debates suggests that justification. Both sides, often lost in passion or focused on the high stakes of the debate, have rarely stopped to question how the controversial issue *ever emerged in the first place*. The national debate on affirmative action has meant taking the current situation as a given ("We have this affirmative action issue"), and then plunging into the task of either trying to eliminate affirmative action or strengthen it, depending on the direction of one's political compass. But why do we have a national debate on affirmative action? How does an unpopular policy designed to assist a *minority* of the population even get a foothold in American politics? Are the Right's resistance and the Left's support really as clear cut as they appear?

There is a need in the affirmative action debate for a careful consideration of the cultural and historical circumstances that gave rise to the affirmative action issue and an explanation for why it happened when it did: during the turbulent period from 1964 to 1971.[2] Put another way, it is time to look back and see how this Right/Left war of words came about. The key to a better understanding, I will argue, is to explore what both sides have taken for granted. This requires understanding the cultural, political, and historical bases of the Right's resistance and the Left's support.

To gain this understanding, we will need to move away from traditional strategies of political analysis. Policymaking is best understood not as a conflict of competing interests, a war of power or money or values, but as the often unreflective negotiation of boundaries of legitimate and illegitimate action. The actions of policymaking elites are best understood in their contexts, where the elites pursue socially constructed goals while following logics of action that are taken for granted. It is a complex analytical frame (though based on simple ideas) made necessary by a complex reality. The Right's resistance, we will see, is rooted not in a plain belief in equal opportunity over equal results nor in a more sound Constitutional ground, but in the peculiar *cultural* logic of an American moral model, which though inconsistent and fraught with double standards, is remarkably stable nevertheless and underlies boundaries of legitimate action that politicians ignore only at their own peril. As we will see, the Left's eventual acceptance was never anyone's plan, but was the result of a set of patterned, interrelated logics of action enacted in a context of race riots, administrative government, grand presidential aspiration, and a Cold War concern with a global morality. Understanding the emergence of affirmative action requires being attuned to a series of ironies and unintended consequences, with unlikely heroes—or villains, depending on one's point of view.

Ironies of Affirmative Action

Several ironies have escaped most of those battling valiantly in the affirmative action arena, but first, a bit of background is necessary.[3] On the Right, we see a zealous demand for adherence to a color-blind, abstract individual model or approach to civil rights enforcement, with merit as the basis of moral desert. This was the dominant view among both mainstream liberals and grudging conservatives as Congress grappled with the language of the historic Civil Rights Act of 1964. Mainstream civil rights groups, such as Martin Luther King, Jr.'s Southern Christian Leadership Conference and Roy Wilkins's National Association for the Advancement of Colored People, supported color blindness.

Though some more radical groups, such as the Congress of Racial Equality, began to advocate proportional racial hiring as early as the winter of 1962–63, notably, this group suddenly withdrew its support from the idea when asked to testify in Congressional hearings for Title VII, the employment section of the Civil Rights Act in 1963. In these tense hearings, the Congress of Racial Equality's national director, James Farmer, repeatedly denied support of quotas in response to frequent baiting.[4] Explaining politics fundamentally on the basis of different groups fighting for their interests (either a fair fight in the pluralist view or unfair in the radical version) would be missing much of the story here: the interests of the mainstream civil rights groups and liberals were peculiarly limited.[5] Presumably, racial preference was in their interests then, as it is presumably in their interests now. Why not demand it in 1964, go for all one can get, and compromise later if necessary?

The problem was that anything beyond color blindness had a strange, taboolike quality. Advocacy of racial preference was one of those "third rails" of American politics: Touch it and you die. In other words, advocate racial preference and lose your legitimacy as a serious player in American politics. As a result, Title VII is color-blind.[6] The effort to ensure color blindness in the Congressional debates is well covered elsewhere, so a simple representative quote will suffice here. The racial preference issue came up repeatedly, and Minnesota Senator Hubert Humphrey tried to put both worried liberals and southern segregationists at ease:

> Contrary to the allegations of some opponents of this title, there is nothing in it that will give any power to the Commission [enforcing Title VII] or to any court to require hiring, firing, or promotion of employees in order to meet a racial "quota" or to achieve a certain racial balance.
>
> That bugaboo has been brought up a dozen times; but it is nonexistent. In fact the very opposite is true. Title VII prohibits discrimination. In effect, it says that race, religion, and national origin are not to be used as the basis for hiring and firing. Title VII is designed to encourage hiring on the basis of ability and qualification, not race or religion.[7]

The Right's position on affirmative action reflects the thrust of Humphrey's view.

The irony is that despite the enthusiasm for equal treatment and merit, we live in a society rife with exceptions to difference blindness, with exceptions to the abstract individual model at the base of the color blindness that dominated Congress in 1964. Law and policies regularly divide Americans.[8] For example, victims of disaster get special consideration, and the family farm is protected with subsidies. Senior citizens, to use an everyday example, are given preference on some urban mass-transit systems, paying a fraction of the rate charged younger patrons. They also receive discounts at many retail stores, regardless of financial need. Shall other groups, perhaps African-Americans, receive a lower subway fare or retail discounts? Exceptions to difference blindness, exceptions to merit, also prevail in employment, though employment is assumed to be a meritocracy by proponents of color blindness. In Chapter 3, we will see the affirmative action employment model in operation for groups other than racial minorities, specifically, for veterans and family relatives. One of the ironies of the affirmative action debate is the tattered condition of the celebrated and supposedly standard merit model of employment justice, despite the Right's spirited defense against racial desecrations.

On the Left, we have the obvious irony that racial employment classifications and preferences overcame their taboolike quality in the 1964 liberal community to become a part of national policy and the liberal agenda. How was it that liberals came to support race consciousness when touching it meant political death in 1964?

It certainly was not the positive force of public opinion that changed Left-leaning minds in Washington. Public opinion had been an important force for the passage of the Civil Rights Act of 1964. Acceptance of the color-blind principle of equal employment opportunity was at an all-time high in 1964; without this, Congress most likely would not have passed the bill. Not so with affirmative action. Thus another irony in the rise of affirmative action is that public opinion does *not* support it, and in fact seems to be rather solidly against it. In other words, the Right's position is the position of most Americans. Affirmative action was so far out of the political mainstream in the late 1960s that it is difficult to find poll data for that formative period. Nevertheless, affirmative action arose and remained a part of policy despite the strong public disapproval shown in poll data since the 1970s. The Gallup poll asked the following question five times between 1977 and 1989: "Some people say that to make up for past discrimination, women and minorities should be given preferential treatment in getting jobs and places in college. Others say that ability as determined by test scores should be the main consideration. Which point of view comes close to how you feel on the subject?" Preferential treatment was rejected by men and women equally in the surveys, with about 10 percent supporting preferential treatment for minorities, and between 81 and 84 percent supporting test-measured ability as the primary factor. Race was controlled for in the 1989 survey, and blacks were found to be more supportive than whites of preferential treatment (14 to 7 percent), though 56 percent supported ability. A 1991 *News-week*/Gallup poll asked the question in a more meritocratic light: "Do you believe that because of past discrimination against black people, qualified blacks should receive preference over equally qualified whites in such matters as getting into college or getting jobs?" Still, 72 percent of whites said no, and 19 percent yes. Though 48 percent of blacks supported the idea (while 42 percent said no preference should be granted), this is hardly a ringing endorsement from the ostensible policy beneficiary.[9]

A recent analysis of public attitudes toward affirmative action found public opinion goes beyond simply rejecting affirmative action. The very idea of racial preference had a negative effect on the attitudes of white Americans toward blacks, seeming to provoke a generalized antipathy. Using a questionnaire format designed to test the effects of the "mere mention" of affirmative action on respondents' views toward African-Americans, the researchers found that "merely asking whites to respond to the issue of affirmative action increases significantly the likelihood that they will perceive blacks as irresponsible and lazy."[10] Not only do whites tend to dislike affirmative action, but it appears that the policy tends to make whites think less of African-Americans as a group.

If the Left was not responding to public opinion in supporting affirmative action, perhaps the policy has its origins in some complex ideology of civil rights lobbyists, who, through superior organization and resources, diabolically pushed through an unpopular racial/group-rights agenda. After all, civil rights lobbyists were important in pushing Title VII through Congress, setting the terms of the debate in 1964, and legitimating the Left's demands and arguments.[11] Some on the Right have concluded that affirmative action must be an alien creature brought by an out-of-touch civil rights lobby.[12] But we already saw that the mainstream civil rights groups avoided advocating affirmative action. In fact, another irony is that affirmative action became a political possibility *without* the benefit of any organized lobbying for the policy. There was never any march on Washington for affirmative action, never any consistent pressing of politicians to acquiesce in a policy of racial hiring. Though civil rights and African-American groups may have supported affirmative action as a preferred civil rights measure since at least the 1970s, the policy is largely the construction of white male elites who traditionally have dominated government and business. The historical record shows that these elites (who are often assumed by the Left, by definition, to act *against* minority interests) advocated different parts of the affirmative action model before or without the influence of any organized civil rights group that was lobbying for affirmative action. At one point, the White House actually lobbied the civil rights groups to support affirmative action. Assuming the most cynical notions of our government, and power/interest-group frames for understanding, we are left with a puzzle: Why would the white males assumed to be pulling the strings in the commanding positions of government go against the apparent wishes of the white majority and do something to help one of the most marginalized and politically weak groups in society? Why would white males support a model of policy that is designed to confer a positive meaning on all group markers but their own? And why would the Left support such a politically unpopular policy?

There is a flip side to the irony regarding the lack of pro-affirmative action lobbying. Equally ironic is that the Right did virtually nothing to stop affirmative action. Thus affirmative action had almost no organized support *or* opposition. In fact, as we will see, affirmative action briefly had the support of some on the Right at the most crucial juncture in its development. Again the notion of politics as clashes of interest groups seems to fail us. If affirmative action is against the Right's (and, apparently, against the mainstream public's) interests today, why was it not against their interests in the late 1960s? Why let what was outrageous in 1964 slip by without a fight over the next several years? *Someone* was touching that third-rail political issue—why did they survive?

Accounting for these ironies on the Right and Left is the central task of this book. Another contribution to the national conversation on affirmative action is necessary to understand the origins of the battle over this policy, the positions of the Right *and* of the Left, and how and why they came to be in the social, cultural, and political maelstrom that was the late 1960s. Through this analysis, we can refine the analytical tools used by sociologists and political scientists to understand American politics.

What Is Affirmative Action?

Before we continue, we must specify what we mean by *affirmative action*. The term predates the civil rights movement. The basic idea comes from the centuries-old English legal concept of equity, or the administration of justice according to what was fair in a particular situation, as opposed to rigidly following legal rules, which may have a harsh result. The phrase *affirmative action* first appeared as part of the 1935 National Labor Relations Act. Here, it meant that an employer who was found to be discriminating against union members or union organizers would have to stop discriminating, and also take affirmative action to place those victims where they would have been without the discrimination.[13]

In the civil rights context, affirmative action has come to mean much more than this, and has become a very politically loaded term. To understand this political loading, and the distinctiveness of civil rights affirmative action, it is best not to try to identify affirmative action with any specific law or program. In this study, affirmative action will be seen as a model, or to use political scientist Peter Hall's term, as a *policy paradigm,* a way of seeing and constructing the world that specifies what is real and important, and which tools are best for achieving goals.[14] I will use the terms *model, paradigm,* or *approach* synony-mously.

The affirmative action model is best understood if we first recall the taken-for-granted model of civil rights that preceded affirmative action: the color-blind model. I will use the term *color-blind* here because it is so familiar and entrenched in the debates, though it is an unfortunate term, unnecessarily spe-cific. Those who support color blindness almost always justify it on the grounds of a more general difference blindness or abstract individualism, sometimes also called classical liberalism, because of its similarity to the ideals of classical liberals such as John Locke. In this model of justice, employers were supposed to view job applicants and candidates for promotion as abstract individuals, dif-fering only in merit or qualification for the job or promotion. Civil rights law was understood to be a force moving America beyond its odious, racist past into a future of individual freedom and equality where only talent or ambition would matter. Thus, the law was designed to protect individuals, who were constructed as universal abstractions, differing only in merit, from maliciously intended ra-cial discrimination.

In civil rights, the term *affirmative action* first appeared in President John F. Kennedy's Executive Order 10925, wedded to this color-blind view of the world. The term was repeated in President Lyndon Johnson's (primarily organi-zational) revision, Executive Order 11246. Firms under contract with the fed-eral government were to not discriminate, and were also to "take affirmative action to ensure that applicants are employed, and that employees are treated during employment, without regard to their race, creed, color or national ori-gin." Section 706(g) of the Civil Rights Act of 1964 also permitted courts to order "affirmative action" in cases where an employer was "intentionally en-gaged in" an unlawful employment practice (the denial of opportunity on the basis of race).

As it was developed in the civil rights administrative agencies and the courts, however, affirmative action, as well as simple nondiscrimination, came to mean something quite different from any color-blind approach. It came to mean, to continue with the dichotomy of terms in the debate, "race-conscious," rather than color-blind. There are several building blocks, or unit ideas, of race-conscious affirmative action which are counterpoints to unit ideas in the color-blind model, and which are controversial in themselves. In this study, affirma-tive action will be recognized as a model more or less advocated in public or official statements or institutionalized in particular practices or laws, on the basis of the extent to which the following unit ideas are present: (1) a require-ment that employers see in their everyday hiring and promoting practices group difference and specifically race as real (rather than unreal or irrelevant), (2) an emphasis on counting anonymous minorities in the workforce (rather than treating each individual as an individual), (3) a de-emphasis rather than emphasis on discriminatory or racist intent and on finding individual victims of discrimination, (4) de-emphasis or re-evaluation rather than emphasis or acceptance of previously accepted standards of merit (usually with a critique of the traditional concept of merit in employment as "white" or "middle class"), and (5) an overriding concern with representation, utilization, or employment of minorities, rather than stopping harmful, "bigoted" acts of discrimination.

Though the color-blind model and the affirmative action model represent two starkly different ways of constructing the American labor force, there is much subtlety to this story. For example, affirmative action did not simply replace color blindness; the two coexist as possible civil rights models, and both are institutionalized in civil rights enforcement. Also, the affirmative action model did not spring out fully formed. It was legitimated in a piecemeal fashion, with different building blocks, or unit ideas, being propounded in different contexts to different audiences, and over a period of time. To understand the origins of the affirmative action debate, we must be sensitive to the ways that the model was embodied in a wide variety of government and business practices, policies, and discourses in various forms, and to the necessity of a new approach to understanding political/moral controversy. Power-hungry interest groups and the cool, utility-maximizing actors of a rational choice theory seem out of place in understanding a third-rail political/moral issue like affirmative action.

Strategy of Analysis

To understand the ironies of affirmative action, we need a theoretical perspective which can account for them. The one used here, which I would argue is essential to understanding affirmative action, is based on a combination of insights from the "new institutional" theory in both sociology and political science.[15] The perspective as used in this book is based on some simple ideas, though their combination and multiplicity may be a bit confusing to readers unfamiliar with the approach. I will state here only what is necessary to understand the affirmative action story, beginning with a brief introduction.

Everyone knows the difference between playing it safe and taking a risk, whether in action or in the spoken or written advocacy of certain actions or positions. Some actions and arguments of advocacy (discourses) are safe, appropriate, or legitimate, while others skirt the danger zone—they are risky—and still others go beyond risky and well beyond safe—they are illegitimate, having an almost taboolike nature. In politics, when we initiate any public action or discourse, we risk creating rancorous, unified opposition, rousing controversy, and losing our own status as serious players in politics—our own legitimacy. This suggests a familiar analogy: Politics is like a game—play by the rules or don't play at all. These taken-for-granted rules are *institutions*. The institutionalist perspective adds that playing by the rules means remaining legitimate, and thus a legitimacy imperative underlies all political action and discourse.[16] In the 1960s in mainstream political arenas, in centers of power (especially Washington), advocacy of affirmative action was beyond risky. Discourse about racial preference was simply illegitimate or taboo. Advocating affirmative action was certain only to destroy the advocate's legitimacy as a political actor.

These boundaries of safe/legitimate, risky, and illegitimate action and discourse are not so obvious in all cases of political change, because much political debate occurs between competing safe or legitimate views. On the other hand, debates between two legitimate policy options often involve political strategy that attempts to make the opposing side's view appear to be outside the zone of culturally safe politics, to be illegitimate. The boundaries are always present, and they enable, shape, and constrain action and discourse. It must also be stressed therefore that these essentially cultural boundaries direct the logic of political action. The boundaries are usually taken for granted, and to the extent that social action is based on calculations, they are usually factored into the calculation unreflectively. Thus, the interests and rationality, or logic, of political actors are essentially constituted by these boundaries of legitimacy and illegitimacy.[17]

How do we know where these boundaries are? Their location is often easy to detect, because it corresponds with formal, written rules or laws. Stealing is an obvious example; in most cases, it is clearly beyond the boundary of legitimate action, and the law and state stand ready to make one pay the price for violating this boundary. Often, however, a boundary line has little or no relation to the boundaries established in written rules or laws, or even in accepted hierarchies of power. A clear example is the power of national leaders to use nuclear weapons. Completely aside from any cost-benefit analysis of the potential gains of using nuclear weapons weighed against the likely material losses, most leaders, particularly in America, will not even discuss the *possibility* of using the weapons, even if they are legally or potentially legally empowered to use them or encourage their usage. Discourse that advocates the use of nuclear weapons is clearly outside the safe zone of American politics, as was discovered by George Wallace's 1968 running mate, General Curtis LeMay, who said in his first press conference that he would immediately use nuclear weapons in Vietnam.[18] LeMay immediately lost his legitimacy, and became a drag on the Wallace ticket. Most people believed that using nuclear weapons in Vietnam was "unthinkable," and thus did not even consider it, let alone publicly advocate it, and this is the point: The logic of action usually stays unreflectively in the safe zones of legitimacy.

Not necessarily enshrined in concrete formal political or legal structures, the logics of action and their attendant discourses of advocacy are ultimately enabled, shaped, and constrained by taken-for-granted rules of a *cultural* nature. What does this mean? It does *not* mean that legitimacy or illegitimacy is simply rooted in values or public opinion (some political actions may be unpopular but will not risk the sacrifice of legitimacy if undertaken), though in some instances there will be a clear correspondence. Another simple idea is required to understand political change in general and affirmative action in particular, and that is that the boundaries of legitimacy and risk, as well as the logics of action, are shaped by the perceived context, by the perceived audience, of the action and/or discourse and the assumed expectations of that audience. To present an obvious example, if an act of embezzling occurred in a context of widespread embezzling (that is, if the audience was composed of thieves), it clearly would not be illegitimate; it would not sacrifice a new embezzler's legitimacy as a social actor in this unfortunate setting. For a political example, if our audience is perceived to be national, as it often is for many actions in the domestic policy arena (to the extent that these actions are done openly), this will suggest different boundaries and logics of action than in matters of foreign policy, which usually adds or substitutes a different (global) audience and thus different boundaries, rules, and logics of action and legitimate discourses. And of course, local political actors will be enabled and constrained by the assumed expectations of their local audience to the extent that they perceive the local people as their audience. In the early stage of the civil rights struggle, these different boundaries were obvious; when southern political elites practiced repression of civil rights activists, their actions were quite legitimate in the eyes of the perceived audience (white southerners), who were the primary concern of local southern governing elites. On the other hand, the national and especially the international audiences increasingly saw the southern repression as illegitimate.

Another dimension of complexity is necessary: we must remember that contexts and audiences are not necessarily perceived only along geographical lines. Clearly, as the example of the South shows, it is not the expectations of *everyone* in a bounded geographical region that usually constitute the rules of the game, or boundaries. The relevant audience may be limited to different elites: citizens of a certain status (southern whites), media organizations, and/or activist groups. The relevant part of the audience thus comprises players in politics who generally shape the rules of the political game. Most policymakers will unreflectively discount the views of homeless people when considering which political action will be appropriate, even in the area of policy regarding the homeless. The fellow players are often defined not along geographical lines but along professional lines; judges, for example, will articulate logics of action shaped in part, if not primarily, by the likely audience of fellow judges and legal professionals. As we will see, administrators of civil rights agencies followed actions which eventually led to affirmative action advocacy following a logic of action defined by the parochial context of government administrators.

It is essential to emphasize that the placement of these boundaries of legitimacy, the logics of action, and the nature of the actor's interests, as well as the likelihood that particular audiences will be relevant to particular actors, are socially constructed. Thus, the rules of the game are likely to change over time. Students of political change must be aware of taken-for-granted cultural boundaries, the importance of perceived context or audience, *and* the constructedness of boundaries and interests. For example, the world audience was not a relevant part of domestic social policy for most of the nineteenth century; following World War II and the advent of the Cold War, however, a world audience and new rules and boundaries were introduced into American politics, particularly in the area of racial policy. I will argue later that the Cold War world context and the logic of legitimacy maintenance based on the expectations of a new global audience were necessary for the development of the Left's eventual support for affirmative action and for the lack of resistance from the Right.

What more needs to be said about these boundaries and how they affect change in American politics? While the politics-as-game metaphor is helpful, it is too frivolous to capture the high moral stakes of politics. We should be aware that there are some very general *moral* rules to American politics, rules common to all polities of the modern West: Modern politics, ultimately, is about the achievement of justice and progress.[19] Certainly, some notion of order will be the first priority (though exactly what constitutes order will vary from polity to polity and over time—many nations are much more alarmed by the violence Americans have tolerated for years, for example[20]). But the vast majority of laws and policies will be justified ultimately on the basis of what contributions to justice and progress they make, rather than having no justification or having premodern justifications, which were primarily religious in character—for example, policies or laws that celebrated the Glory of God.[21]

Thus, in the context of modern politics, the legitimacy imperative, a part of all political action in the new institutional framework, becomes a *justice* imperative. Policy or legislative initiatives will ultimately be enabled and constrained by cultural rules or boundaries of a moral character. Often, as in the case of affirmative action, this will be quite explicit. In many areas, political actors will expect the significant or active audience to generally agree on what is just and unjust, good and bad, right and wrong, and who is deserving and undeserving. Of course smart and stupid are often salient concerns, but there is generally less heated controversy here, except as these policy questions will ultimately be moral questions (though one can imagine that the advocacy of extremely stupid policies can undermine the advocates' legitimacy and continued effectiveness in the political arena). When there is enough perceived strong agreement among the relevant audience, a third-rail political issue and discourse may be created: racial supremacy, gay rights in the military, socialized medicine, anti-Semitism, and drug legalization are some examples.

Many have sought to understand Americans' distinctions between what is just and unjust by reference to general values or traditions in American political and moral culture. For example, Seymour Martin Lipset has stressed the importance of egalitarian values versus achievement values;[22] Alasdair MacIntyre stresses various religious traditions;[23] Robert Bellah and his colleagues stress the American liberal, republican, and biblical traditions;[24] Rogers Smith adds that traditions of racial, ethnic, and gender superiority historically have also been significant factors in American politics.[25] The relationship of these values or traditions to actual policies, however, is considerably more messy than has been recognized. Politicians and their speechwriters, groping for the right buttons to push, cannot blindly push buttons of the liberal tradition or achievement values. They must know the complex ways in which ideas of justice have come to be taken for granted in specific policy and legal contexts: State paternalism in granting welfare to the poor is *bad;* state paternalism in the form of subsidies for American farmers is *good.* As we will see, affirmative action is good for some groups and bad for others. The great mass of often inconsistent, incoherent ideas of justice and desert taken for granted in myriad policy contexts forms a presumed model of general American justice or morality.[26] This will be explored in more detail for the case of affirmative action in Chapter 3. The point here is that in expressing their views and in assuming boundaries of legitimacy, politicians take for granted a very messy model of American justice, of what is right and wrong in specific contexts and for specific potential recipients of policy benefits, as well as certain causal principles of the outcomes that the just policy is assumed to produce.

A final point on the strategy of analysis in this book: I was careful in the preceding discussion to emphasize legitimate political *discourse* along with legitimate political *action* because what political actors say, which is often ignored by students of policy change who focus on the power of interest groups, provides much of the data for this study. Sociologists and political scientists are increasingly focusing on talk or discourse as a key to understanding cultural or political change.[27] When pursuing change, or a new goal such as a racially based hiring policy, political actors wisely justify their pursuits with the available, legitimate sets of arguments (discourses) related to advocacy. As political scientist John Kingdon explains:

> Study of the world of talk gives us clues about the world around the talker . . . [Politicians] must couch what they want, not in terms of their own advantage, but terms of some larger theme that others will find attractive. They choose some words rather than others because they find those words have some appeal to larger publics, to undecided fellow legislators, to constituents, or to whomever is important to them in that situation. Thus a study of their words indicates something about the context within which the politicians work . . .[28]

These discourses are a central feature of this book. We can understand the emergence of the formerly "unspeakable" affirmative action model (and therefore the origins of the Left's support) by examining the contexts and discourses of advocacy that could be safely used to justify the affirmative action model for blacks. Similarly, we can gain understanding of the Right's position on affirmative action by discerning for which groups the affirmative action model is assumed to be legitimate.

To sum up: Understanding the ironies of affirmative action requires a fundamentally cultural interpretation of politics, policy, and law. The approach is inspired by a simple notion: The most important thing one can know about a people is what they take for granted.[29] An adequate understanding of American politics should begin with a focus on these taken-for-granted boundaries of legitimate action and discourse, the social construction of interests, and with an appreciation of the often very powerful moral expectations in politics, rather than with the assumption that groups rationally pursue their interests in some universal or natural way, and succeed or lose depending on their organization or resources. In 1964, even if civil rights interest groups wanted it (which they did not), no significant resources could be raised for a racial preference lobby, and no amount of money could have pushed racial preference into a national policy without a revolution.

A Preview

Part 1 of the book will make sense of the resistance to affirmative action by showing what the Right and the majority of Americans take for granted. Resistance to something new, or the illegitimacy of affirmative action, is not easily traceable historically, but the historical sources of basic support and institutionalization of the color-blind model can be identified (Chapter 2). The basis of the importance of this abstract individual model in the area of *racial* employment preferences is best shown analytically; in Chapter 3 we will see, by examining the development of policy and law regarding employment preferences for other groups, the contours of a general model of American justice shaping a cultural logic of employment preferences. This logic follows from the historical constructions of certain groups as morally worthy—moral "desert" is key. I will argue that the Right's position is best understood on the basis of the meaning of race in America, rather than simply on the basis of the importance of equal opportunity or the importance of merit. In other words, there is a difference between the fundamental justice or moral model Americans identify with and refer to in the defense of color blindness, and the model that actually sets the boundaries of legitimate policy and law.

In Part 2, to understand the origins of the Left's position, we must be able to see how and in what contexts it became safe to advocate affirmative action when previously only the discourse of color blindness was legitimate. Part 2 contains four different narratives, simplifying the "patterned anarchy"[30] of different institutional contexts where affirmative action advocacy was not illegitimate and where in fact the maintenance of the actors' own legitimacy suggested the affirmative action model as the logical policy choice.

Chapter 4 presents the 1960s race riots as crucial to the affirmative action story. Political and business elites followed a logic of crisis management, seeking to maintain order and control through affirmative action, one of the few means legitimate in the context of the Cold War and the rise of a global audience concerned with human rights. In Chapter 5, we will see administrators of civil rights enforcement agencies seek to maintain their own legitimacy by pursuing demonstrably effective and efficient policy in the context of the apparent failure of the color-blind model, advocating clumsy affirmative-action-building administrative innovations with a discourse of administrative pragmatism. Chapter 6 describes how, for many inspired by the traditional American goals of justice, equality, and equal rights, it became safe (or at least less risky) to advocate affirmative action by linking it to cherished traditions. Again, in the Cold War context it became possible to construct affirmative action, increasingly seen as the pragmatic approach to civil rights, as simply a part of a venerable American tradition of rights and equality, using discourses of tradition which denied that any change was taking place. Here the courts, where a logic of tradition is institutionalized, play a central role. In the Cold War context it also became increasingly risky to criticize any policy that was called *civil rights*. Finally, in Chapter 7, we will see a Republican president elected with an uncertain mandate in a time of transition, who saw in affirmative action a way to confound the Democrats and establish the legitimacy needed for the creative leadership project built into the logic of the American presidency. An audience of fellow Republicans was surprisingly receptive.

Organizing the story of the rise of affirmative action along the lines of the different logics and discourses of often unintended advocacy makes the complex jumble of events easier to understand. Affirmative action was legitimated very quickly, in a matter of a few years, in a very turbulent time, and by a variety of people pursuing very different goals. A straight chronological telling of the story obscures the patterns of action and their defining contexts, which are so crucial to understanding. Pursuing the more analytic strategy here, however, necessitates frequent references to other chapters, and a small amount of repetition. I believe this is a minor inconvenience and well worth it; nevertheless, I ask for the reader's patience.

In separating the analyses of Right and Left into Parts 1 and 2, I do not wish to give the impression that they have no unity or no common ground. Both color blindness and affirmative action are of course models of *justice*. Though the two models are incommensurable, there is a theme running throughout Parts 1 and 2, especially in Chapters 2, 5, and 6. We will see that *the seeds of affirmative action were contained in the color-blind model*. Color blindness in discrimination law is partly derived from a taken-for-granted principle of causality, based on the utopian American colonial belief in "natural society" that prevailed in the early republic, that a fair and equal society will *naturally* occur when people are free.[31] The principle is a familiar one, associated with the old idea of laissez-faire. When the color-blind model was passed into law, it was done with the belief or expectation that freedom from discrimination would bring about black equality—comparable statistical rates of black and white employment and unemployment. Congressional documents reflect this expectation. This proportional racial equality was thus implicitly, as an expected consequence, a part of the color-blind model of justice now supported by the Right, and of course is explicitly a part of the Left's affirmative action, as a part of formal procedure.

Two final caveats before we can continue: First, a theme that runs through the book is the difference between logic, justice, and morality as they are studied by philosophers and logic, justice, and morality as they are actually institutionalized and taken for granted in American society. The two are clearly different, and I do not mean to say that what I will argue to be the American moral model is in fact the Good or the Just in any absolute sense, or that the logic of action in some contexts is in fact the correct or right thing to do.

Second, women and various racial or ethnic groups are a part of affirmative action, but they are not considered in this book, except for women's rights in a few illustrations in Chapter 3. Part of the reason for this—perhaps another irony—is that women and other groups are conspicuously absent in the affirmative action debate. Though much of the law applies equally to women, the arguments in the scholarly articles and mass media almost always center on (black) racial preferences, not on gender preferences. More important, women, other groups, and affirmative action are not explored here because, as we will see, affirmative action developed as a model of justice for African-Americans, in response to a struggle for racial equality and a racial crisis; therefore, this is the focus of the book.

PART ONE

Understanding Resistance to Affirmative Action

2

The Appeal of Color-Blindness

The purpose of Part 1 is to show why the affirmative action model was taboo in 1964, and why so many on the Right (and in the mainstream) continue to resist it today. In other words, the purpose is to show why there were taken-for-granted boundaries of a moral character that limited employment justice for blacks to the color-blind model. This chapter contains the first step: We must first see the historical sources of the color-blind discrimination law and policy model. The logic of modern institutions of organization and American political culture had been to deny the meanings of some, if not most, differences, to see humans as abstracted individual citizens, of equal dignity as a matter of right. A color-blind (or more generally, difference-blind or abstract individual) logic can be seen in social, political, and economic institutions and intellectual currents of modernization. Prior to affirmative action, discrimination law was an extension of these institutions and ideals, supported by the ideals of the American revolution. Those supporting the Right's view believe that the historical sources of the color-blind model also directly gave rise to the boundaries that once made (and presumably again should make) affirmative action illegitimate and taboo.

This chapter first reviews arguments against affirmative action and in support of the abstract individualism and meritocracy that forms the basis of the color-blind model. Next, we examine the institutions and ideas characteristic of modernity in general and the United States in particular that provided sources for color-blind approaches. Last, we look at the historical development of the actual difference/color-blind antidiscrimination law, demonstrating the importance of moral boundaries and assumptions that shaped the civil rights movement's interest in color blindness, and also the grand expectations of those who supported color blindness.

The Case for Resisting Affirmative Action

As previously mentioned, one of the problems of an approach to politics which emphasizes politics as a conflict of interest groups without examining the cultural forces shaping their interests is that one cannot explain the nature of the resistance to affirmative action. Most resistance to affirmative action is centered on its inherent injustice, derived from its incongruity with institutions and ideas considered just. Daniel Bell makes the point forcefully. A color-blind classical liberalism, based on the idea of the freedom and independence of the individual, is at the very foundation of our society, he argues. One of the fundamental tenets of classic liberalism is that "the individual—and not the family, community, or the state—is the singular unit of society, and that the purpose of societal arrangements is to allow the individual the freedom to fulfill his own purposes— by his labor to gain property, by exchange to satisfy his wants, by upward mobility to achieve a place commensurate with his talents."[1] Affirmative action is decried by scholars such as Bell because of its departure from this classic liberal stance. Specifically,

> The liberal and radical attack on discrimination was *based on its denial of a justly earned place to a person on the basis of an unjust group attribute*. That person was not judged as an individual, but was judged—and excluded—because he was a member of particular group. But now it is being demanded that one must have a place primarily because one possesses a particular group attribute. The person himself has disappeared. Only attributes remains (*sic;* italics in the original).[2]

Seymour Martin Lipset argues along similar lines, though he relies on the interpretation of public opinion polls to make his point. For example, in explaining the affirmative action debate,[3] he maintains that the real issue is the war of core American values: individualism (understood as self-reliant achievement), and egalitarianism. While Americans support both principles, they will give support to individualism over egalitarianism when forced to make a choice, as is the case with affirmative action policies. Thus, poll results show Americans supporting "compensatory action" (such as Headstart programs), which, Lipset argues, is in line with egalitarian values and also makes competition more fair without compromising the basis of competition. Americans will be opposed, however, to the "preferential treatment" of affirmative action, "since such treatment precisely violates the notion of open and fair individual competition."[4] A fair competition, or an equality of opportunity, is part of the American creed, argues Lipset, and affirmative action "clearly involves an effort to guarantee equal results to groups."[5] Though not actually claiming that affirmative action is a bad thing, Lipset suggests that it is controversial in America because it is out of place in America; it violates the American value of individualism and the institution of merit allocation.

Morris Abram sees the distinction between the color-blind model and affirmative action as a distinction between "fair shakers" and "social engineers." Though active in the early years of the civil rights movement, Abram was alienated by the apparent switch of policy paradigm. Abram continued to support the color-blind, classically liberal approach, "limited to vigilant concern with equal opportunity, procedural regularity, and fair treatment of the individual." This "fair shake view" is "in keeping with our legal and political traditions"; however, "the social engineers' advocacy of result-oriented and color-coded group rights is inconsistent with these traditions and violative of other democratic ideals and principles."[6]

Sociologist Nathan Glazer has been perhaps the most outspoken critic of affirmative action. His view mirrors the above, but in his numerous writings, his criticisms have gone far beyond the ideas described above, including assertions that affirmative action is not needed, that it does not work anyway, and that it has many internal logical contradictions. He is perhaps best known, however, for emphasizing another line of argument: the effect of the policy on whites. In titling a book *Affirmative Discrimination,* Glazer sought judiciously to highlight the insidious effects of a benign race-based hiring policy (otherwise antagonistically termed *reverse discrimination*), since "the point of setting a [racial hiring] goal is that one will hire more of one group, less of another, simply because individuals are members of one group or another." The term *affirmative discrimination* highlighted the idea that discrimination was still occurring. Also, by using the term *affirmative discrimination,* one could distinguish this policy of making hiring decisions based on race from the original meaning of affirmative action, which involved vigorous promotion of a firm's policy of equality of opportunity, or programs to recruit or train blacks who could then compete in a fair competition for jobs.[7]

The above writings have been selected because of their eloquence and high profile in the affirmative action debate. The ideas in them have been expressed by other intellectuals, by other opinion leaders—and by common Americans, as Jonathan Rieder found in his study of middle-class Italians and Jews in the Canarsie neighborhood of Brooklyn.[8] Similar ideas have also been espoused in the mass media, which has never tired of reporting on the affirmative action controversy. A study of media treatments of the policy from 1969 to 1984 identified changing affirmative action "packages," or the ways in which the issue is framed or presented by the media.[9] Among the negative packages that were identified in television, newsmagazines, political cartoons, and opinion columns are the ideas of *No Preferential Treatment* ("The consideration of race or ethnicity, however benignly motivated, is not the American way"), *Reverse*

Discrimination (affirmative action *excludes* individuals on the grounds of race), *Undeserving Advantage* ("Affirmative action gives minorities something they have not earned and do not deserve"), and *Blacks Hurt* (racial preferences reinforce stereotypes that minorities cannot do it alone, thus stigmatizing them).[10] The reverse discrimination package is shown to be the most dominant, as it

> had well-organized and articulate sponsors who actively promoted it. It met the news needs of working journalists for balance and dramatic form. Finally, it had strong positive resonances with larger cultural themes of self-reliance and individualism, and used antiracist and equality symbolism.[11]

What is important about the above arguments is their similarity. Affirmative action is *bad,* they say, because difference blindness, legally treating individuals as abstractions, rewarding only achievement or merit in the employment arena, is *good.* But why do these ideas seem so natural? What are the sources of these ideas, this discourse of abstract individualism that is so clearly legitimate to the national audience?

Institutional and Ideal Sources of the Color-Blind Model in Modern Political Culture

Pillar organizational institutions of the modern West—a money economy, capitalism, citizenship—have no logical place for group differences such as race in their operation. They are based on and construct people as universal abstractions, anonymously, though each individual may be important and special. For example, Georg Simmel, in his classic *The Philosophy of Money,* argued that money was a "basically democratic levelling social form,"[12] was characterized by "complete indifference to individual qualities,"[13] and, as it allows us to be dependent on a great number of people (who can be total strangers), money "is conducive to the removal of the personal element from human relationships through its indifferent and objective nature."[14] There is nothing inherent in money that suggests a racial particularism, then, and in fact, the concept of money would discourage it. One person's money is as good as any other's.

Like money, another modern organizational institution, bureaucracy, has a democratic leveling effect. This idea was first touched on by Max Weber, but more recently has been developed by sociologist Peter Berger and his colleagues. Their understanding of the "cognitive style" associated with bureaucracy matches a color-blind view of the world. They argue that in modern bureaucracies, a principle of "moralized anonymity" exists as a principle of social relations. This is the case because there is an assumption of equality among all those persons in a particular bureaucratic category.[15] Thus, the typical encounter with a bureaucracy occurs in a mode of "explicit abstraction." A person expects to be treated fairly, that is, as just another case falling within the purview of certain rules.[16] The reality of the person will be apprehended by the bureaucratic officials only as the person is relevant to the rules of operation. Therefore, in the rationalized organization system of modern society, the bureaucracy, persons are abstracted from any particular differences about themselves, including, one may not unreasonably expect, racial differences. To the bureaucracy, we are all just so many numbered cases to be dispensed with. The bureaucratized procedure of job application, one might expect, would also be characterized (in the initial stages) by anonymity and abstraction, as employment officers sort applicants on the basis of qualification.

The logic of capitalism also constructs individuals as universal abstractions, and thus is color-blind. This idea has been explicated many times, but perhaps most clearly (and dramatically) by that famous student of capitalism, Karl Marx. The vanguard of capitalism, argued Marx in *The Communist Manifesto*, had "pitilessly torn asunder the motley feudal ties that bound man to his 'natural superiors,' and has left remaining no other nexus between man and man than naked self-interest, than callous 'cash payment.' "[17] People in a capitalist system are owners or wage laborers. Thinking of people in any other way would get in the way of profit, and hence, "All fixed, fast frozen relations, with their train of ancient and venerable prejudices and opinions are swept away, and all new ones become antiquated before they can ossify."[18] The concept of honor would evaporate, and though Marx had in mind aristocratic honor, there is little reason to think a race-based honor would fit into capitalism any better.[19]

Ernest Gellner emphasizes different points while coming to the same conclusion in his more general assessment of the organization of modern society. An impersonal, anonymous, abstracting quality of modern life is important, he argues, for modern life to work smoothly. Everyone in a modern society must be mobile, must be able to plug into different parts of the economy, must be able to follow anonymous instruction manuals, must be able to communicate impersonally in "to-whom-it-may-concern" type messages.[20] Education becomes a universalizing medium, as the nation becomes a homogenous whole while subgroups erode. Whereas premodern societies may be held together by bonds of loyalty or tradition, modern societies are fluid, relatively disordered, "entropic."[21] In this milieu of constant movement and institutional anonymity, race consciousness has no place.[22]

Modern citizenship is the political institutionalization of this anonymous abstract individual. Citizenship institutionalizes universalism and individualism in the sense that it makes each person an equal member of a community.[23] With membership come legal protections in the form of rights, formally inhering in the individual. In the view of sociologist T. H. Marshall, rights are usually understood to be of three types: civil (rights of speech, assembly, due process, and freedom from cruel punishment, for example), political (access to office and voting), and social (a decent standard of living, protection from illness, education).[24] The oldest, and those of central concern for this study, are civil rights, often described as negative rights. Some have seen capitalism as a force for the institutionalization of civil rights in citizenship, as the bourgeois economic activity of long-distance traders and early manufacturers encouraged rights of movement, free choice of occupational activity, property, and equality before the law. According to John Boli, the right to choose one's religion, the legacy of the Reformation, "became the prototype of inalienable rights inhering in individuals regardless of their social characteristics or citizenship."[25] Formally, the notion of citizenship at the basis of rights is abstract, and racial statuses should fade into irrelevance along with family background or place of birth.

Contract law generally developed with the growth of commerce and civil rights, further reinforcing individualism and the notion of the abstract individual at the basis of the color-blind approach. Philip Selznick writes that contract law was the foundation of larger legal structures, and that "The freely contracting individual, creating relations of his own making, was the paradigm of legal man."[26] There is little in the logic of contracts that would suggest color-consciousness; as A. V. Dicey wrote in 1905, "(T)he substitution of relations founded on contract for relations founded on status was for individualists generally . . . the readiest mode of abolishing a whole body of antiquated institutions, which presented, during the eighteenth century, a serious obstacle to the harmonious development of society."[27] All rights, civil, political, and social, were seen as naturally, universally inhering in the reasoning individual, and were not status dependent.

The concept of the citizen as universalizing and individualizing is usually considered a product of the French Revolution.[28] Though the American notion of citizenship is obviously more relevant to understanding American civil rights law, it is worth noting that America had no monopoly on the model of society that constructed citizens as equal abstractions. In the French Revolution's "Declaration of the Rights of Man and the Citizen," the world received a charter for the institutionalization of an individualist/universalist society, legitimated by the sanction of universal reason.[29] Writing in 1789, Emmanuel Joseph Sieyès neatly described the color-blind reality of the citizenship ideal: "I picture the law as being in the center of a huge globe; all citizens, without exception, stand equidistant from it on the surface and occupy equal positions; all are equally dependent on the law, all present it with their liberty and their property to be protected; and this is what I call the common rights of citizens, the rights in respect of which they are alike."[30] Room was made, however, for one legitimate differentiation between men: "utility." Rather than from wealth or lineage, power or privilege were to be derived from a different basis. Modern society was to be a meritocracy.[31]

Paralleling these institutionalized principles of economic and political organization were cherished teachings of religious leaders and philosophers. In fact, the ideas of universalism and individualism at the basis of the abstract individualist color-blind model have roots much older than modernity as usually understood. As Orlando Patterson points out, the ideas can be traced back to the teachings of Christianity and the Stoics.[32] The Stoics taught that truth is accessible to all human beings; whether or not one will come to know the truth will depend on one's upbringing, rather than status. Stoic universalism is "implied in its strong insistence on the moral autonomy, worth, and existential freedom of the person."[33] Jesus also preached a universalist message, as Patterson describes, in which all of humanity was seen as "perfectible, god-like, god-achievable."[34] Preaching universalism, Jesus necessarily also preached an individualist message, as natural differences are irrelevant when it is the soul that is the locus of meaning and value. According to Patterson, for Jesus "All persons, being the children of God, are obviously equal as brothers and sisters and in worth."[35] Of course, Jesus's crucifixion was understood as the salvation of *all* people, not only some chosen group. Sociologists John Meyer and his colleagues assert that this worldview and the symbols that went with it lent a common frame of reference to the West.[36] The notion of a united Kingdom of God supplied a common authority and guidelines of action, thus uniting otherwise diverse peoples.

The universalism of the Stoics and Jesus received its modern, secular voice from the Enlightenment, an intellectual movement championing the power of universal reason in its attack on traditional authority. Implicit in the faith in reason rather than tradition for knowledge was the idea that everyone had access to the truth. All one had to do was think clearly and logically—which unfortunately was hard to do if one was caught in the archaic and corrupting status institutions of the medieval order. Part of the Enlightenment project was to foster emancipation from status ties. Here again were the ideas of universalism and abstract individualism, with both also suggesting the idea of equality. Reason was key, everyone had it, thus each individual could be self-reliant and go as far as reason would allow. Congruent with this logic is the logic of the color-blind model, which was to free individuals from the chains of racial status differences.

Universalist intellectual currents and abstracting institutions like capitalism, contracts, and citizenship are bound up in a larger, taken-for-granted metaproject of the modern West: the pursuit of justice and progress.[37] New policies and laws must ultimately be justified by their contributions to justice and progress (as opposed to the arbitrary will of a charismatic or holy leader or the glory of God), making equality and fairness central concerns. These basic rules condition modern political discourse in a very general way. To complete our understanding of the sources of the color-blind model in the United States, however, we must focus our investigation. The United States was only one particular setting of the larger modern project, but one with a particularly utopian flavor.

The Abstract Individual Model in America

The United States shared the logically color-blind modern institutions and religious and philosophical ideas described above, but enshrined them with a great reverence, which is important to understanding their extension into the sphere of civil rights law. American traditions gave flesh and meaning to the institutions of modernity, and shaped the thinking of the framers and supporters of color-blind law in important ways. The ideology of the American Revolution drew together strands from numerous sources, including ancient Greece and Rome, Christianity, and British common law.[38] Enlightenment thought also played a role in the American founding beliefs, providing encouragement and supporting analogies (especially the use of "nature" as a model) for the political and judicial institutions of America.[39] English foundations of liberty, constitutional limitation of power, and representative government were thus imbued with natural rights philosophy and an outlook of optimistic humanism—the ideal of active citizenship, with faith in the reason and progress of men.[40]

A common thread in the ideology was the reference to universals; as Richard Hofstadter has said, "The eighteenth century mind had great faith in universals."[41] Universalism in the United States was expressed in the doctrines of natural rights and the equality of men. The idea of natural rights was derived from the idea of natural law; the natural law prescribed moral duties, and the rights were necessary to perform these moral duties.[42] According to Bernard Bailyn, the emphasis on natural rights evolved out of the debates about constitutionalism. Constitutions, after all, existed to protect these universal rights. Pennsylvania lawyer John Dickinson, for instance, wrote of human rights:

> We claim them from a higher source—from the King of kings, and Lord of all the earth. They are not annexed to us by parchments and seals. They are created in us by the decrees of Providence, which establish the laws of our nature. They are born with us; exist with us; and cannot be taken from us by any human power without taking our lives. In short, they are founded on the immutable maxims of reason and justice.[43]

Robert Bellah and his coauthors of *Habits of the Heart* maintain that if we are to look for universalism in American political culture, it will be bound up in the idea of utilitarian individualism, and not equality. The value of self-reliance and the idea of natural society, of the social good emerging *naturally* from the activities of self-interested individuals, have been staples of the American political culture.[44] Bellah and his colleagues argue that the struggle against arbitrary aristocratic authority led to a notion of almost *sacred* individuals in America, using the Reformation-inspired idea of government based on the voluntary participation of individuals.[45] Individualism in America meant self-determination, moral freedom, rule of liberty, and the dignity of men.[46] With Bernard Bailyn, Edwin Dorn, Louis Hartz, and others, they point to the importance of the Lockean tradition in American political discourse.[47] The idea of the ontological individual, prior to society, and the notion that a social contract refereeing self-interest was all that was necessary to produce justice, led in the United States to the celebration of individual rights and individual dignity. The land of opportunity was thus meritocratic: one deserved all that one could attain by talent and industry.

All of the above, what Samuel Huntington has identified as a not necessarily coherent but widely acknowledged "American Creed,"[48] would suggest that when Americans begin to consider how they might protect civil rights in employment (indeed, that it would even *occur* to them to protect "civil rights" in employment), they would think in the terms described above, which rather neatly correspond to the color-blind, abstract individual model. The basic ideas of a color-blind approach are all here: there is a natural order to society which would satisfy personal needs. The government's job was to allow—not force— this to happen. (Thomas Paine, calling government "a necessary evil," said, "Society is produced by our wants and government by our wickedness; the former promotes our happiness *positively* by uniting our affections, the latter *negatively* by restraining our vices [original emphasis]."[49]) Give people the freedom to pursue their ends and make contracts, and justice will result. There was a utopian element in all of this, emphasized in an early nineteenth-century magazine, the *Democratic Review*. "It is true," the *Review* sighed in 1839, "a long time must elapse before the point of ultimate perfection is attained; though, meanwhile, the duty of Democracy is to correct abuses, one after another, until the nature of individual man is thoroughly emancipated."[50] The color-blind model is thus thoroughly American, and it was not only a model of procedural justice, but also substantive justice. Equal opportunity of men would lead to "ultimate perfection."[51] This may seem a "strangely unrealistic attitude," but according to Arieli, this lack of realism is a characteristic of American ideology.[52]

Finally, the Constitution was no impediment to a specifically color-blind dis-crimination law. Because it does not *enforce* color blindness, recognizes slav-ery, and was written by some men who owned black slaves, some have concluded that "it is irrefutable constitutional history that the Constitution of the United States was not color-blind."[53] To be more precise, while the Con-stitution did not (and still does not) make color blindness the law of the land, neither does it enshrine race consciousness with a Constitutional basis. Signifi-cantly, the *language* of the Constitution is color-blind, using the universalist term *people* instead of *whites,* and even managed to describe slavery, as Andrew Kull has pointed out, as "having no necessary racial component, as if America were ancient Rome."[54]

The Color-Blind Model in American Discrimination Law

The abstracting logic of central modern institutions and American ideals was generalized to the first equal employment statutes, from their very beginning in Massachusetts in 1884, in a law designed to protect those seeking employment in the civil service from religious discrimination. Early laws followed a stan-dard format, barring appointments "in any manner affected or influenced" by "religious opinions or affiliations."[55] The essential individual was to be ab-stracted from accidental properties. By 1945, twenty-two states had discrimina-tion laws regulating civil service employment, with eleven of these including race with religion as aspects of a person that were officially to be considered unreal.[56] By this time, antidiscrimination clauses in state contracts with private firms were also common.[57]

This law was seen as necessary, of course, because African-Americans had found that the nation's labor markets had somehow withstood the abstracting logic of modernity. Obviously, only blacks were enslaved. But after emancipa-tion, they found employers both in the South and the North resistant or reluctant to hire them. Jobs were given to immigrants more readily than to African-American citizens.[58] The idea of even color-blind protections from discrimina-tory hiring practices was rejected by a conservative opinion which deemed un-acceptable state involvement in such a private decision as who an employer could hire.[59]

The story of the legitimation of the color-blind antidiscrimination law could be the subject of a separate study. The climate of public opinion, as well as a perception of legal impossibility, resulted in little interest at the federal level in employment civil rights. However, a 1937 Supreme Court case upholding a fed-eral law barring discrimination against employees or job applicants on the basis of anti- or pro-union activities appeared to open up new vistas.[60] With the out-break of World War II, the United States's impending battle with a racist dictator and government concern with a new world audience for American racial practices began to change the boundaries of political possibility, and some black leaders organized to correct the situation (See chapter 6). Thus, in 1941, President Franklin Delano Roosevelt acted to stave off the international embarrassment of a threatened march on Washington, and signed Executive Order 8802, which protected against discrimination in defense industries and government. The order set up the Committee on Fair Employment Practice, designed to "receive and investigate complaints of discrimination in violation of the provisions of this order and [to] take appropriate steps to redress grievances which it finds to be valid." It was also to "recommend to the several departments and agencies of the Government of the United States and to the president all measures which may be deemed by it necessary or proper to effectuate the provisions of the order." It received a budget of $80,000 for its first year.[61] The order was novel in that it marked the first serious federal government involvement in equal employment opportunity regulation, but its color-blind, classically liberal approach was similar to other laws, such as the National Labor Relations Act,[62] as well as the precocious forays into discrimination law at the state level. And of course it was an extension of the logic of the modern institutions and American ideals discussed earlier. Individuals who were not treated as equals, who were instead treated in a way that recognized and gave negative meaning to some trait other than merit, were to bring their complaints of unequal treatment to the government.

The end of World War II ended federal involvement in shielding citizens from discrimination, as Roosevelt's Committee was abolished, but in 1945 New York passed the Ives-Quinn bill, which set up a similar commission-based process in that state, this time regulating *private* hiring and promotions, and other states began to copy this model. State equal opportunity law, according to this model, generally proceeded in the following way: (1) An individual would make a complaint; (2) an investigation would follow; (3) a determination of probable cause would be made; (4) conciliation followed (conferences and persuasion, which ideally would end with the employer making several promises, such as offering a job to the complainant, or offering to stop discriminating in the future, to advertise jobs and claim equal employment opportunity, and to submit to future investigations). If this failed, (5) a public hearing could be held, and (6) a cease and desist order might be issued. This order could be enforced judicially, and failure to obey was punishable as contempt of court.[63] By 1960, seventeen states had Fair Employment Practice Commissions (FEPCs) enforcing this color-blind model of justice, with jurisdiction over both public and private employment.[64]

The color-blind model received considerable support from the groups that it was supposed to help. Not only did it seem to be the logical approach, but it seemed to verify those classically liberal causality principles that were prevalent and taken for granted in American political culture—it seemed to *work*. For example, Leon Mayhew writes

> The equal-treatment movement reached its culmination in the successful demand for Fair Employment Practice Commissions during the forties and fifties. Aided by wartime manpower shortages, the Negro made important advances during the World War II era. It was natural to attribute part of this progress to the success of the FEPC movement, and thus equal treatment under law became the central focus of Negro hopes . . . Negro leaders put considerable faith in the potency of "color-blind" attitudes.[65]

Their faith was not lost in the 1950s, however. Civil rights leaders continued to have faith that the white people of the United States would awake from what seemed—to the civil rights leaders—to be a race-obsessed trance. Whites in America had to open their eyes and their minds, and they would see true classical liberal reality. The most famous of the leaders was Martin Luther King, Jr. As head of the Southern Christian Leadership Conference, King emphasized the universalism of Christianity, but always connected this with the secular, universalist American discourse, too. Reality was not skin pigment, or religion, or nation. Reality was the human soul, all of the human souls on Earth, equal before God. King lamented, "We see men as Jews or Gentiles, Catholics or Protestants, Chinese or Americans, Negroes or whites. We fail to think of them as fellow human beings made from the same divine stuff as we, molded in the same divine image."[66] While King taught that African-Americans should be proud of their heritage, he was always careful to assert that this was not the essential part of their personhood. Most important for King was the "Image of God," which

> is universally shared in equal portions by all men. There is no graded scale of essential worth. Every human being has etched in his personality the indelible stamp of the Creator. Every man must be respected because God loves him. The worth of an individual does not lie in the measure of his intellect, his racial origin or his social position. Human worth lies in relatedness to God. An individual has value because he has value to God. Whenever this is recognized, "whiteness" and "blackness" pass away as determinants in a relationship and "son" and "brother" are substituted.[67]

King also believed that these basic ideas formed the true model of justice of the United States, which he felt had (somehow) strayed from its classical liberal "home" to a race-conscious model:

America has strayed to the far country of racism. The home that all too many Americans left was solidly structured idealistically. Its pillars were soundly grounded in the insights of our Judeo-Christian heritage: all men are made in the image of God; all men are brothers, all men are created equal; every man is the heir to a legacy of dignity and worth; every man has rights that are neither conferred by nor derived from the state, they are God-given. What a marvelous foundation for any home! What a glorious place to inhabit![68]

While King was perhaps the most eloquent exponent of this view, he was joined by others who saw the color-blind model as being in their interest, by those fellow mainstream leaders who had the most clout in Washington. Bayard Rustin, for example, sought coalition building in the effort to effect fundamental restructuring of American political institutions. Near the end of 1963, for instance, he preached this message at the fourth annual Student Nonviolent Coordinating Committee (or SNCC) meeting in Washington, where he announced, "we need a political and social reform program that will not only help the Negroes but one that will help all Americans." Aware of the moral boundaries which had shaped the movement's interest in color-blind abstract individualism, Rustin warned of a disintegration of the movement unless it broadened to include other disadvantaged groups. He claimed to oppose the idea of preferential treatment for Negroes in employment because unemployment affected more whites than Negroes, and declared full employment to be the Negroes' national goal.[69] Rustin, throughout the 1960s, argued for a coalition of Negroes, trade unionists, liberals, and religious groups to use political power within the system.[70]

Similarly, A. Philip Randolph, president of an influential black union (The Brotherhood of Sleeping Car Porters), made a speech at the Negro American Labor Council in May of 1965 urging an "alliance of the Negro and labor and the black poor and white poor" to be used as a "new weapon against the problem of unemployment." He also called for a massive federal investment in public works projects. The coalition was needed, he explained, because the civil rights movement was "wholly inadequate successfully to grapple with the basic economic and social problems of black Americans."[71] For both Randolph and Rustin, class was a more important reality than race in American politics, and they did not see racial preference as in the interest of black Americans.

One leader did test the boundaries of legitimacy and initially pushed for a race-conscious policy, but found little flexibility in the political culture. This was the Urban League's Whitney Young, who had become Executive Director in 1961. The basic foundation for his approach was a call for an American Marshall Plan, conceived in 1962, actually issued in 1963, and published as a book,

To Be Equal, in 1964. An examination of Young's ideas is useful because they show the cultural resistance that race-targeted ideas faced, the power of the boundaries of legitimacy—even within a civil rights group, whose members always remained aware of the national audience. Truly a man before his time, Young, at the League's national meeting in September, 1962, declared that "300 years of deprivation" called for "a decade of discrimination in favor of Negro youth." In February, he complained to League trustees that "Our present concept of equal opportunity is not sufficient," and called for a racial Marshall Plan, comparing the economic problems of America's blacks with the economic problems of post–World War II Europe. Color-blind justice, he claimed, was "unrealistic at this moment in history." "Higher value" must be placed on "human potential when it comes incased in a black skin." Therefore, "Token integration and pilot placement in business, industry, and government is not enough"; "qualified Negroes—because they are Negroes" must be placed in employment at all levels. Young mentioned the civil service preferences for veterans as a precedent.[72]

Much of this (at the time) heretical language was eventually eliminated from Young's plan. His colleagues were uncomfortable with such dangerous discourse. Pittsburgh Urban League president Wendell G. Freeland said, "I have serious reservations about stamping the concept as official League policy" and foresaw "adverse reactions to the pronouncement as such" that "our definition of 'equal opportunity' has changed." Lawrence Lowman, of the Urban League in New York, was also turned off by the idea of "seeking special privileges" and called the claim that Negroes had received a special consideration of exclusion for 300 years "misplaced sarcasm." Lowman was most strongly resistant to "the heart of it," which he saw as the "business of employing Negroes 'because they are Negroes.'"[73]

Nevertheless, Young risked the Urban League's legitimacy, giving the plan public exposure to a potentially national audience in a debate with Christian race relations commentator Kyle Haselden, originally published in the pages of the *New York Times Magazine* on 6 October 1963. Young began by citing precedent for his argument of special effort: The United States gives special help to victims of natural disasters, as well as veterans. He then listed a litany of statistics of Negro inequality: the average Negro family makes $3,233 compared to the white family average of $5,835; 75 per cent of Negro workers in the categories of service workers, semi-skilled workers, and unskilled labor, compared to 39 per cent for whites; unemployment two and a half to three times that of whites.

Eschewing the label of "preferential treatment" for his plan, Young explained that "We prefer that our recommendations be seen as necessary and just corrective measures that must be taken if equal opportunity is to have meaning." The "crash program," or "domestic Marshall Plan," described in this public forum was surprisingly race blind and universalist, given the introduction of the essay. Young called for "the deprived child—Negro as well as white—provision for first-class schools," with the best available facilities. He also abstractly advocated increased aid to "low-income neighborhoods" and "troubled families." However, the plan still had a controversial, though tempered, race-reifying element: "A planned effort to place *qualified* Negroes in all categories of employment" (emphasis in the original). Young explained that there was no desire to establish "a quota system—an idea shunned by responsible Negro organizations and leaders," but that "because we are faced with the hypocrisy of 'tokenism' . . . we are forced, during transitional stages, to discuss numbers and categories." Young thus now presented his program with a lot of safe, classically liberal, universalist language, a denunciation of quotas, and a meek call to temporarily "discuss" hiring numbers of "*qualified* Negroes."

Nevertheless, he was still in the danger zone for the public audience, and predictably, Haselden pounced on the "discussing numbers" suggestion, and declared that Young wanted quotas. He argued that Young's plan would politicize race, and thus "legalize, deepen, and perpetuate the abominable racial cleavage which has ostracized and crippled the American Negro." Furthermore, the plan would penalize the living for a debt owed by the dead, take away Negro initiative by patronizing Negroes, and would be unfair to other minorities.[74]

In 1964's *To Be Equal*, the transformation of Young's plan continued, further shaped by the logic of the color-blind model and by increased sensitivity to the potential loss of the League's legitimacy by advocacy of risky or illegitimate policy. His Marshall Plan in this public document is cleansed of any language that suggests quotas. He calls for special effort, but keeps it vague: employers should use the "same creative zeal and imagination to include Negro workers at all levels that management has used throughout the years in excluding them."[75] The program, in the end, called for a mild affirmative action (a form considered least objectionable to critics[76]) and equal treatment: vocational training, special recruiting, job creation, "fair" hiring standards, and "Enlightened managements that will earnestly and wholeheartedly adopt the principles of advancement on merit and train Negroes for supervisory and executive posts."[77]

King, like Rustin, hardly wavered from a color-blind approach, organizing, shortly before his murder, the Poor People's Campaign. It is true that in the late 1960s, King did lead "Operation Breadbasket," which threatened boycotts of local industries that did not have a proportional representation (based on the local black labor supply) of black employees. It is important to note, however, that race-conscious justice, while "practiced" by King in this later period before local audiences, did not appear in his list of policy recommendations before a national audience in a 1967 book, except as a vague reference to percentage hiring of the "difficult-to-place" (clearly, a more abstract, universalist term). Instead, King's focus was on the development of a human services industry that could give job opportunities to African-Americans.[78]

When the machinery of federal civil rights enforcement was created in 1964, it was safely designed to enforce equal employment opportunity law following the color-blind model. Group differences, in the perspective of the law, did not exist. Ontological primacy was given to something thought in this context more essential, more real—the *real* person, or soul—or, to borrow a few of King's now famous words, the content of character was real, rather than the color of skin. Following this logic were the primary agencies created for civil rights enforcement: the Equal Employment Opportunity Commission (EEOC), created to enforce Title VII (the employment section) of the Civil Rights Act of 1964, and the Office of Federal Contract Compliance (OFCC), created to enforce nondiscrimination by government contractors by Lyndon Johnson's Executive Order 11246. These will be discussed in greater detail in a later chapter. The point here is that originally, their task was to eliminate race, ethnicity, gender, religion, and national origin from the reality perceived by American employers.[79]

It must also be added that this color-blind model was seen as legitimate and in the interests of blacks because at this time it was unreflectively attached to a causal principle: it was believed to *result* in black equality, understood in terms of near equal participation in society. This was apparent in debates and reports for Title VII. In 1963, for example, a House report made a notable connection between unemployment and discrimination. The report stated, "Testimony supporting the fact of discrimination in employment is overwhelming. The following table contained in the Manpower Report of the President, 1963, prepared by the Department of Labor, presents the dramatic contrast." The table showed unemployment rates substantially higher for blacks in every demographic breakdown: gender, age, and selected occupations. Similarly, a Senate report for a bill that was to become Title VII made the discrimination-equals-unemployment connection in 1964: "The precarious position of the Negro American in today's labor market is dramatized further by the nonwhite unemployment rates." Following a very thorough recitation of the statistics, the report continued, "Discrimination in employment thus begins at the top of the economic system and filters down through the lower levels despite educational attainment."[80] If discrimination produced unemployment of blacks, color blindness, then, was understood as a model that would result in gains in employment—gains that could be measured easily with the same statistics.

At first glance, there seems to be no shortage of reasons why the color-blind model was and is supported in civil rights by so many. Color blindness means universalism and abstract individualism, and appears to be a simple extension of the primary institutions of modernity—a money economy, capitalism, and citizenship—as well as of ideas with long Western cultural pedigrees, reaching back to the foundations of Christianity and a major Greek and Roman school of philosophy, and in this country to the founding principles. None of these sources have much room for racial particularism in their internal logics. Primary legal institutions in the United States, contract law and the Constitution, are both color blind (though not necessarily enforcing this view). Other regulatory and enforcement agencies in the United States, such as the National Labor Relations Board, have shared central building blocks of the color-blind model, investigating complaints of union discrimination to ensure that all workers are treated equally. It was also in the interest of civil rights supporters because best of all, in the American natural society model, equality was assumed to arise naturally when individuals were emancipated from corrupt status relationships. Equality of results would naturally follow from equality of opportunity.

But we have only explained part of the resistance to affirmative action. It is true that the abstract individualist color-blind model was generalized and extended from and is congruent with central institutions in the organization of modern life, and it fits in nicely with prominent ideals that are frequently expressed in American political discourse. But this does not explain why the boundaries of legitimate policy options were so narrowly placed around the color-blind model in 1964, and why color blindness is so overwhelmingly preferred by Americans today. In other words, that the logic of color-blind institutions and ideals would be generalized to employment protections is not surprising, but that the advocacy of anything race-conscious would so consistently be politically risky still requires explanation. This explanation is the goal of Chapter 3.

3

American Justice, Acceptable Preference, and the Boundaries of Legitimate Policymaking

In the previous chapter, I described the cultural and institutional sources of support for a color-blind law in employment civil rights. It may appear obvious that what makes affirmative action so objectionable to so many Americans is that it goes against so many of the forces just described; indeed, this is just what many of the most eloquent spokesmen for the color-blind approach have argued. The problem with affirmative action in American political culture, however, is more complex than this. Despite the difference-blind institutions of modernity and America specifically, everywhere around us there are exceptions. American society is replete with preferences and categorical separations of various sorts. The conflict over employment preferences for African-Americans, I will argue, has more to do with African-Americanness than it does with preferences per se. The key idea in the cultural logic of employment preferences is the social construction of desert or worthiness. Some groups, we shall see, have been constructed as being more deserving than others. And exactly who is considered deserving can be shown to be highly contingent—it is based on historically constructed meanings and little else. There is, then, a taken-for-granted moral model which shapes policy boundaries independently of our ubiquitous American universalist and meritocratic discourses, a model of amazing complexity. The real mystery, one may conclude, is our perceived sense of moral consistency when there is so little to justify this perception.

The essence of the color-blind model, as its defenders express it, is merit allocation of employment opportunities. Color should not matter; only merit should. Affirmative action is bad because it is unfair to whites. But is this the entire explanation? This chapter subjects the claims of the abstract individualists to some empirical tests. First, I will test the rigidity of policy boundaries based on rules of merit hiring by examining the history of veterans' preferences. Second, I examine the possible qualification that merit and abstract individualism are the rule when ascribed (biological) traits are at issue by showing similarities between the controversial racial preference and the generally accepted practice of nepotism. After other tests of the ostensibly universal ban on preferential policies, I conclude with a picture of a moral model in America quite at variance with that described by the critics of affirmative action.

What is important and remarkable about arguments against affirmative action is that similar ones are not made more frequently against other policies that embody the affirmative action model, practices and laws which exist in America, nestled much more comfortably within presumed boundaries of legitimacy. A broad-minded survey of employment practices and policies suggests that the American embrace of the abstract individual model is so qualified as to make its impassioned assertion in the area of race rights something of a curiosity, suggesting that the issue here is more the meaning of race and less the importance of meritocracy or equality of opportunity. Precisely the same arguments that have been made to show that affirmative action is bad can be made, and *have* been made, though not nearly to the same extent, or with much forcefulness, in response to other "difference-conscious" preferential practices and policies.

Is Affirmative Action Resisted Because It Is Unmeritocratic? The Case of Veterans

If Americans reject affirmative action because it is a violation of cherished principles of equal opportunity and meritocracy,[1] we might expect the merit system to be guarded zealously, and a difference-blind policy paradigm to shape the discourse in all employment-related policy and law. This, however, is not the case: outright employment preferences for veterans for jobs in the civil service are enshrined in federal and state law. Unlike racial preferences, which have been called "underhanded" by Harvey Mansfield, Jr.,[2] and "covert" by Thomas Sowell,[3] veterans' preferences are naked, particularistic affronts to the meritocratic rules of the American job market—they are simply called veterans' preference, rather than hidden with an ambiguous term like *affirmative action*.[4] At the same time, they are relatively uncontroversial and are protected by the courts. The federal government and forty-seven states give preferences to veterans who take the civil service examination, which, ironically enough, was designed to ensure merit hiring.[5] The federal government and most states, among sundry other measures, simply add ten points to the scores of disabled veterans or their wives, and five points to the scores of nondisabled veterans. After the bonus points are added, veterans are often to be preferred over nonveterans with equal scores. Seven states give absolute preference to all veterans who pass the examination. An attempt to eliminate lifetime veterans' preferences in selection and layoffs in the federal civil service failed in 1978.[6]

It is important to make a comparison of veterans' preference and affirmative action because by doing so, we can begin to map out that complex, socially constructed moral model which shapes legitimate policy boundaries in the employment arena. The comparison shows striking differences and similarities. One difference is that, though initially rebuffed, the veterans groups were able to be much more bold in their demands than blacks have been. The veterans did not lose legitimacy by making bold claims, and the resistance/boundaries were never very strong. But the historical record suggests that events *could* have made the two cases fall into the same boundaries, and a striking similarity among them is the nature of the resistance to veterans' preference and affirmative action—both stressed difference blindness and classical liberalism. However, the moral worthiness of the veteran for preference became institutionalized, the boundaries moved, and veterans' preference was never seriously challenged again.

THE EARLY YEARS: UNCERTAIN BOUNDARIES

Veterans' preference had been customary in the patronage-ridden civil service throughout American history, most notably under President Jackson. It was coded in law under Lincoln, as part of the generous provisions accorded to Civil War veterans.[7] The deserving group at this time, however, was limited to *injured* veterans.

Still, the veteran lobbying organizations, to paraphrase Wallace Evan Davies, soon discovered the welfare state.[8] The demands and the targeted classes quickly snowballed. Disabled veterans were eventually seen to be deserving of civil service employment preferences, bonus payments and pensions, 160- acre homesteads, tax breaks, and peddler's license waivers. The Grand Army of the Republic, an organization of Civil War veterans, led this push for benefits. Trying to expand employment preferences to all veterans, disabled and able-bodied, the argument of the *Grand Army Record* of March 1887 stated that "the man who went to the front should be preferred for public service to those who remained at home to advance their personal interests while the soldiers were undergoing the hardships of war."[9] The Grand Army also advocated the augmentation and enforcement of the preference laws, supplied resources for litigation to establish their constitutionality, and demanded new laws in areas where none existed.

Despite varying levels of success at the state or municipal levels and the persistent demands, the boundaries of worthiness remained largely limited to disabled veterans.[10] There was resistance to this seemingly un-American granting of preference, even for disabled veterans in the crony-ridden and hardly meritocratic pre-reform civil service. To illustrate, a letter in the August 1866 issue of *The Soldier's Friend* tells of a job-hunting ex-soldier's meeting with a government bureaucrat:

> I asked him whether a vacancy could not be made for me. He then said that he could see no reason for making a change. Now, if my empty coat sleeve does not show reason enough for making a change, then I can see no reason either.

Next month, the magazine featured an editorial urging self-help:

> [The veteran] will, in four cases out of five, gain more in the end by self-reliant independence than by a pitiful political subservience to any conscience-keeper, or any superior who can sell his place on thirty days' notice, or less, on demand.[11]

Limited as it was, veterans' preference initially had little impact. For instance, in 1900, only 45 of 7,138 hired applicants to eligible federal positions had been granted a preference on the basis of having veteran status.[12] Little change was made to the preference or the impact until 1919, when preference was finally expanded. Two riders, referred to together as the 1919 Preference Act, gave preference to honorably discharged *able-bodied* veterans and the wives of disabled veterans who could not work.[13] The law gave a five-point bonus to a veteran's test score, and any veteran with a score of sixty-five or better was placed at the top of the eligible list ahead of any nonveterans.[14] The percentage of new employees offered preference on the basis of veteran status quickly jumped from less than 1 percent to around 25 percent.[15]

However, this absolute preference met with resistance that shows parallels with the affirmative action debate. In 1918, the Civil Service Commission had tried to remind the Congress that its new notions of the moral worthiness of veterans were in direct conflict with other notions of fairness:

> The civil-service law is based upon the principle that every citizen should have equal opportunity to compete for appointment in the public service, and that in each case the most efficient should be appointed. The extent of preference depends upon the degree to which this principle should be departed from in recognizing military service.[16]

A report from the Committee on Public Health Relations of the New York Academy of Medicine criticized the appointment of veteran chemists, who sometimes scored in the sixties but received absolute preference over nonveteran chemists who scored in the nineties. The report included the following statement:

> The course of civil service preference legislation and regulations . . . shows that once a special privilege is granted to a favored class, the flood-gates are opened for further and further favors to larger and larger classes, regardless of the disadvantage to the unprivileged majority and of its serious detriment to the efficiency of the public service.[17]

Similar warnings of the expansion of preference have been given with respect to affirmative action. For instance, Nathan Glazer has argued that a statistical racial hiring goal for blacks "encourages other groups to demand the same protection of statistical goals. Many ethnic and racial groups not included in the initial list of 'affected classes' can point to discrimination in their background."[18]

Protests against veterans' preference such as these led President Harding, on 3 March 1923, to issue an executive order repealing the section granting absolute preference, though retaining preference for all veterans by simply giving five points for able veterans and ten points for disabled veterans or their wives. But this did little to settle the moral boundaries in this area.

The American Legion immediately complained that nonveterans would always be chosen over veterans with equal scores because the personnel officer would know that the veteran's score was actually five or ten points lower, and lobbied Congress for stronger measures. In the Legion's view, "Anyone who opposed absolute preference was opposed to giving disabled veterans the recognition which a grateful nation owed them."[19] Again, a comparison with Glazer's writing on affirmative action shows parallels: "[T]he critic of quotas or [racial hiring] goals and timetables is regularly attacked as being opposed to [the original meaning of] affirmative action."[20]

In 1928, President Coolidge vetoed a resolution which would have made the appointment of eligible veterans mandatory.[21] A compromise was eventually worked out under President Hoover which gave disabled veterans, their wives, or widows of veterans a ten-point bonus and absolute preference, while giving able-bodied veterans simply a five-point bonus.

The battle over the fair place of policy boundaries regarding veterans (deserving of preferential treatment versus undeserving) was being fought concurrently, but with a slightly different discourse, on the front lines of a demand by veterans for bonus payments. The debate on this issue was actually much more pronounced and dramatic than the debate on employment preferences, mobilizing three presidents and members of the cabinets. Though the fundamental issue of the meaning of veteran status was the same, opposition to job preference was much weaker than opposition to the bonuses.[22] This was partly because veterans' job preferences did not involve actual transfer of state revenues.[23] Preferences undoubtedly gained some support among state officials as a costless way to show support for the veteran cause.

The bonus demand, however, though made by the American Legion, the Disabled Veterans of America, and the Veterans of Foreign Wars, was met with especially strong resistance, enacted through a discourse emphasizing a universalist conception of citizenship, which also should have precluded employment preferences.[24] Andrew Mellon, the secretary of the treasury under Presidents Harding, Coolidge, and Hoover, was against the bonus demand. Not only would it interfere with "fiscal integrity," costing $4.5 billion, but it was an affront to the notion of a patriotic citizen. In a letter to a senator on 2 July 1921, Mellon said that "[w]ar service should be performed as the highest duty of citizenship and is a sacrifice that can never be measured in terms of money."[25]

Presidents Harding and Coolidge also subscribed to this conception of military service. What the veterans did (fighting for their country) was important but nothing special, and further, according to Harding, "this menacing effort to expend billions in gratuities would imperil the restoration of normalcy." (J. P. Morgan wrote a letter on 15 July 1921 thanking Harding for his "extremely courageous action.") Calvin Coolidge also saw veterans as equal abstract citizens, undeserving of categorical benefits, warning, "[W]e must stop this bill or revise our definition of patriotism."[26]

The Franklin Roosevelt administration continued the struggle to define veterans as undeserving of special treatment on the persistent bonus issue, often using a discourse of difference-blindness that technically precluded employment preferences also. Secretary of the Treasury Henry Morgenthau said that "[t]he veterans had no special claim on the government" and viewed the bonus bill being considered by Congress as "an unsound, unwarranted, *even immoral* subsidy to a special-interest group" (emphasis added). Congress passed the bill anyway, but President Roosevelt vetoed, and read his veto message to Congress in person, the first time a president had done so. On 22 May 1935, Roosevelt said that recovery would be impeded, "debt structure weakened, other interest groups would be enticed to rush to the federal till, and energy would be drained from more permanent and helpful recovery measures if the bonus redemption plan were adopted." Clearly identifying himself with the classical liberal model of justice (though still making age distinctions), he went on to say,

> Able-bodied veterans should be accorded no treatment different from that accorded to other citizens who did not wear a uniform during the World War. . . . There is before this Congress legislation providing old-age benefits and a greater measure of security for all workers

against the hazards of unemployment. We are also meeting the . . . need of immediate relief. In all of this the veteran shares.[27]

This classical liberal perspective had been voiced by Roosevelt before. In a Chicago speech to the American Legion in October 1933 he said that government should aid disabled veterans, but added "[t]hat no person, because he wore a uniform, must thereafter be placed in a special class of beneficiaries over and above all other citizens."[28] In 1936, however, Roosevelt's definition of moral desert—that service to the country was a civic responsibility analogous with paying taxes, and did not earn the individual any special desert—lost. Congress overrode the veto. The moral boundaries were settled: veterans were special after all.[29]

THE VETERANS' PREFERENCE ACT OF 1944

World War II did more to institutionalize able-bodied veterans as a deserving class than the previous several decades of lobbying. The memories of uncertain boundaries quickly faded, especially among policymakers, and the public hardly noticed. In a striking contrast to affirmative action for blacks, meritocratic cultural rules and abstract individualism were now no barrier to veteran worthiness. Though pollsters were routinely asking the public their views about whether or not blacks even deserved a difference-blind model of justice protection, public opinion data on veterans' preference is very difficult to find, underscoring its legitimacy. The data that do exist suggest the perceived justice of the preferences. An opinion poll conducted by Jerome Bruner for the National Planning Association in June 1943 asked respondents the following question: "After the war do you think soldiers should be given first choice of the jobs that are open, or do you think that everybody should have an equal chance to get jobs?" If anything, this question is biased towards the latter response, as giving preference to veterans is not even considered giving them an equal chance (proponents of affirmative action for blacks sometimes claim that it is not preference but an equalization being granted). However, fully 64 percent of respondents sided with the unmeritocratic competition, "Soldiers first," while only 33 percent chose "All equal" (3 percent were "Not sure"). The survey found almost no difference between men and women and rich and poor on this question. Age did seem to be a factor, though, as 51 percent of respondents under the age of thirty were willing to give soldiers first choice, 64 percent of those aged from thirty to forty, and 69 percent of those aged over forty.[30]

In 1944, Congress greeted the principle of preference with a warm embrace. Despite the problems of establishing the legitimacy of preference for uninjured veterans in the past, Congress passed the Veterans' Preference Act of 1944 with startlingly little debate. The bill, which strengthened and gave legislative sanction to the previous twenty-five years of executive orders, amounted to a comprehensive affirmative action package. Disabled veterans, their wives, and widows of veterans were to receive the ten-point bonus, and if the augmented scores were passing scores, they were to be placed at the top of the list. Five points were given to able-bodied veterans, and they were to be preferred over nonveterans with identical scores. In addition, the positions of guards, elevator operators, messengers, and custodians were *restricted* to veterans as long as they were available. This absolute reservation of jobs was to be terminated, however, five years after the end of the war.

Lest there be, in today's language, any systemic discrimination or disparate discriminatory impact against veterans, minimum education requirements, and requirements as to age, height, and weight were to be waived if they would operate to keep a veteran from a job, unless they were absolutely necessary. The Civil Service Commission was required to make a public record of its decisions as to which jobs would have minimum education requirements.

This list of preferences continued on and on. Veterans were also exempt from any antinepotism regulations. Rules allowing relevant work experience were loosened for veteran candidates. As civil service rules dictated that appointing officers were to make selections of hires from the top three eligibles from the examination, "an appointing officer who passes over a veteran eligible and selects a nonveteran shall file with the Civil Service Commission his reasons in writing for so doing, which shall become a part of the record of such veteran eligible, and shall be made available upon request to the veteran or his designated representative." These reasons would be evaluated by the commission. If these reasons are found to be "insufficient," the appointing officer will be asked to submit "more detailed information." In other words, not hiring the veteran eligible would mean paperwork headaches for the hiring officer.

There was more. Veterans were also to be protected from layoffs. The length of time in the military service would be added to the length of time in the civil service job in determining seniority, and "preference employees whose efficiency ratings are 'good' or better shall be retained in preference to all other competing employees and that preference employees whose efficiency ratings are below 'good' shall be retained in preference to nonpreference employees who have equal or lower efficiency ratings."[31]

The wartime hearings for the bill produced a total of one who testified against the principle of preference, a Mr. N. P. Alifas, president of District No. 44 of the International Association of Machinists. Alifas had difficulty being heard and taken seriously by the congressmen, and at least once the room broke out in laughter during his testimony, which was mostly the seemingly unfunny articulation of the thoroughly American discourse of difference-blindness. Fearing a division of working Americans, he advocated a full-employment policy as the only solution consonant with the cultural rules of American justice, quoting the Declaration of Independence and the Constitution, and explaining, "[T]he idea of creating in the United States after this war a preferred class of citizens is repugnant to our entire concept of government. We have been accustomed to believe as Americans in the principle of equality of opportunity, equality before the law, equal rights for all and special privileges to none." But Alifas's impassioned pleas produced no discussion at all, no follow-up questions. On this March afternoon in 1944, Alifas and his moral model, which was virtually identical with that described by today's opponents of affirmative action, were but a curiosity, a diversion.[32]

Similar consensus reigned in the House discussion.[33] Alabama Representative Joe Starnes introduced the bill with an explanation of the now settled cultural logic of veteran desert, echoing that view in the hearings and Senate and House reports:

> Mr. Speaker, from the very inception of our Republic our Government has extended certain special benefits and privileges to the men who have offered their lives in the defense of the country and its institutions. This is a sound principle. Those who are selected from among us to wear the uniform and to serve the country on the firing line are certainly entitled, when peace has been won through their efforts, to be selected and given special consideration and preference in employment by their Government in peacetimes. That is a reward to an American who has willingly and gladly offered his life in an effort to save and to sanctify for us the principles of government under which we live, and which by their sterling efforts is being handed on to posterity.[34]

While ambitious veteran demands were limited by boundaries that excluded regulation of private employment, the morality of veteran preference still crossed the public/private line. Though officially untouched by the bill, private enterprise was also expected to recognize the paramount claims of veteran worthiness, as Starnes declared: "There should be a job ready and waiting in private enterprise or with the Government, Federal, State, and local, for every American fighting man when he comes home when victory has been won."[35] Another representative warned, "If the Government does not protect these servicemen with respect to getting jobs, then we are not in very good shape to ask industry and business to give them preference for jobs."[36]

These themes were mentioned several times throughout the short discussion, particularly the bill's basis in legal tradition and the worthiness of the soldiers, who were consistently defined as benevolent people who had acted for the benefit of the country.[37] The consensus of support for the bill was also mentioned frequently, both in the House and in the Senate. There was only one question as to whether or not the bill was just, only one moment of moral drama. Representative Jessie Sumner from Illinois tentatively ("Perhaps I do not understand this legislation correctly. Is this the way it works?") requested clarification as to whether the bill gave veterans absolute preference, no matter their score on the examination. She was told that this was not the case. But she still seemed incredulous at the antimeritocratic provisions of the bill: "But if he got 70 percent with his preference, he would knock out a man who got 80 percent; is that right? He could do that?" This heresy was promptly rebuffed. These preferences were already on the statute books in many states, she was told, and anyway, "This guarantees the soldier a job after the war is over when the soldier returns who has been willing to fight for this country on the fighting front."[38] The message was clear: Sumner, somehow ignorant of the new moral boundaries of the deserving veteran, had to be educated, and quickly *was* educated.

Debate over justice was over. The bill passed the House with a vote of 312 to 1,[39] and was passed in the Senate without debate. Perhaps even more striking than the consensus was the new position of Roosevelt. Previously an outspoken supporter of a universalist justice based only on need, the president was now leading the veterans' preference parade. In a letter (read to Congress) addressed to Georgia Rep. Robert Ramspeck, Chairman of the Civil Service Committee, President Roosevelt said,

> I believe that the Federal Government, functioning in its capacity as an employer, should take the lead in assuring those who are in the armed services that when they return special consideration will be given to them in their efforts to obtain employment. It is absolutely impossible to take millions of our young men out of their normal pursuits for the purpose of fighting to preserve the Nation, and then expect them to resume their normal activities without having any special consideration shown them. . . . Surely a grateful nation will want to express its gratitude in deeds as well as in words.[40]

It is difficult to gauge accurately the reception of this law and preference laws in general, because so little has been written about them. The near unanimity of support in the government, along with the public opinion data which exist, as well as the lack of discourse on the topic all suggest that the moral worthiness of all veterans had been thoroughly institutionalized. It must be emphasized, however, that the world did not have to be this way; it was not so before, and there were still a *few* wayward voices raised in protest, articulating a discourse of difference-blindness like that used in the affirmative action debate. For example, an editorial in *The Washington Post* for 11 July 1944 begins by asking sarcastically, "We wonder why Congress did not think of extending veterans' preference benefits to former servicemen who might want to run for election to the national legislature." This posture echoes an aspect of the "undeserving advantage" media package identified by social scientists studying media treatments (discussed in chapter 2), which "emphasizes the hypocrisy and arrogance of affirmative action bureaucrats" who do not have to pay the cost of race-conscious justice.[41] Adopting a position analogous to the "blacks hurt" affirmative action media package, the 1944 editorial continues:

> [T]he status of these men can only be debased by treating them as inferiors incapable of securing jobs through free competition with their fellow citizens. And the status of the Government can only be debased if it selects its personnel on the basis of sentiment rather than merit.

Some scholarly literature also attacked the policy. In a staunch 1945 defense of the merit system, Samuel H. Ordway, a Naval Reserve Commander and former U.S. Civil Service Commissioner, foresaw a doomsday scenario of the government overrun by incompetent veterans. Anticipating the reverse discrimination controversies that have marked the history of affirmative action, he pointed out the victimization of those "veterans" who fought the war at home, but were not recognized for their contribution. He predicted that "the number of misfits, failures, and dismissed veterans" would increase their proportion of the civil service.[42] Ordway warned that "to the extent that excessive security founded on preference rather than merit takes incentive from effort, the administration of government in the United States will deteriorate."[43]

In another scholarly 1945 article which anticipated the current debates of pluralists, feminists, and postmodernists on the political salience and meaning of *difference* and *otherness,* political scientist Roy V. Peel makes a case for the "separateness" of the veteran, probing the origins of the "stigmata of identity."[44] Peel's strategy is to justify government action by establishing the fundamental difference between the veteran and the "stay-at-homes"—differences that ultimately require preferential treatment. Presaging Lyndon Johnson's famous metaphor of blacks as formerly shackled runners (see chapter 6), who could not rightly be expected to compete immediately with unshackled runners, Peel describes the evolution of policy towards veterans: "[W]e began to recognize that if the veterans were to compete successfully with others in their old jobs or schools, we had to give them help in the form of cash bonuses to clear up debts, meet insurance payments, pay tuition fees, and so forth."[45]

IRONIES: COURT CHALLENGES TO VETERANS' PREFERENCES

Veterans' preferences in civil service employment have been challenged in court many times since the Civil War. The male nonveteran challengers usually made due process and equal protection arguments, that is, arguments based on the difference-blind, classical liberal model advocated by most affirmative action critics. But the courts routinely upheld the preferences.[46] Why did they do so?

Often the courts simply agreed with legislatures that veterans were especially deserving. For example, one court argued that employment preferences were a proper reward and that they were properly permanent:

> A preference in appointment or promotion in a civil service is in the nature of the payment of a debt of gratitude by the people of the state to persons who loyally served their country in time of war . . . The people of the state may properly feel that passage of time should not dissipate or extinguish the debt of gratitude owing to veterans of wars prior to World War II.[47]

Another possible justification for the preferences mentioned in Congress was instrumental in nature: preferences would make for more patriotic citizens. Some courts agreed. In reviewing a Massachusetts preference statute, for instance, a court pointed out the state's argument that "the recognition of the services of veterans in the way provided for by the [preference] statute would promote that love of country and devotion to the welfare of the state which it concerns the Commonwealth to foster."[48]

An additional recognized justification for the veterans' preferences was based on the veterans' disadvantage of being frozen out of civilian life and having to reenter it suddenly at the end of a war. In *Mitchell v. Cohen,* the Supreme Court determined that veterans' preference was justified as a means of helping soldiers readjust to civilian life. Justice Frank Murphy, in reviewing legislative intent, stated that "[i]t was felt that the problems of these returning veterans were particularly acute and merited special consideration. Their normal employment and mode of life had been seriously disrupted by their service in the armed forces and it was thought that they could not be expected to resume their regular activities without reemployment and rehabilitation aids."[49]

It is apparent, however, that the courts were quite uncomfortable with the new moral boundaries which led to this affirmative action model for veterans. They often took the trouble to point out that the law was "unwise."[50] They also sometimes endeavored to make the preferences fit in with the merit-based model. A common strategy for judges uncomfortable with the moral worthiness of veterans and the apparent conflict with the cultural rules of meritocracy was to equate veteran status with job qualification. In this view, not only were veterans perhaps especially morally worthy, but simply by virtue of being veterans, they were also super-workers, especially for government. Thus, a Pennsylvania court explained that

> As a basis for appointment it is not unreasonable to select war vet-
> erans from candidates for office and to give them a certain credit in
> recognition of the discipline, experience, and service represented by
> their military activity. No one should deny that these advantages are
> conducive to the better performance of public duties, where disci-
> pline, loyalty, and public spirit are likewise essential.[51]

The boundaries marking off the moral worthiness of veterans have withstood the test of time. Heretical male nonveterans no longer cry reverse discrimination. In recent years, however, in an ironic twist that is typical of the entire equal employment opportunity arena, the principle of equal employment opportunity has been used to fight veterans' preferences, but not in support of opportunity for all Americans. The new argument is that they are unfair to women.[52]

The Supreme Court ruled on the issue in *Personnel Administrator of Mass. v. Feeney*.[53] In the case, the plaintiff argued that the exclusionary impact of Massachusetts's absolute veterans' preference (that is, all veterans who passed were to be selected over nonveterans) on women was too severe not to have been intended. Thus, the veterans' preference was said to have been discriminatorily enacted to exclude women from the civil service.

In the Court's opinion, Justice Potter Stewart mentioned that veterans' preference has been challenged enough times that the rationales behind seeing veterans as "particularly deserving" of a "competitive headstart"[54] have been standardized: "to reward veterans for the sacrifice of military service, to ease the transition from military to civilian life, to encourage patriotic service, and to attract loyal and well-disciplined people to civil service occupations."[55]

Though some courts sharply distinguished between the constitutionality or rational basis of the laws and their wisdom,[56] Stewart's discomfort seemed to go further: "Veterans' hiring preferences represent an awkward—and, many argue, unfair—exception to the widely shared view that merit and merit alone should prevail in the employment policies of the government." Though passed without opposition, they "have come to be viewed in many quarters as undemocratic and unwise."[57] However, though the "substantial edge granted to veterans by (the law) may reflect unwise policy," still, the *goal* was a worthy one, and the Fourteenth Amendment "cannot be made a refuge from ill-advised laws."[58] Because the legislatures did not intend to discriminate against women, and because women veterans benefitted and many (nonveteran) *men* were also disadvantaged, the law was upheld and did not constitute gender discrimination.[59] It is difficult to imagine a less enthusiastic endorsement for the concept of veterans' employment preferences—but the absolute preference survived.

Justice Thurgood Marshall, a strong supporter of affirmative action for blacks and women, filed a notable dissenting opinion. The dissent is notable both for its thorough trashing of the logic of veterans' preference and for its ultimate embrace of the principle, an ironic pattern exemplified in the majority opinion. He severely criticized the preferences shown for veterans in Massa-·chusetts as being "overinclusive," since they had no expiration date, and allowed veterans to take advantage of them throughout their postwar working lives.[60] He also questioned their use as a reward or encouragement of patriotism, since the preferences benefitted ex-soldiers who had been drafted, as well as those who volunteered.[61] Though the case at hand dealt only with gender discrimination, it is notable that in his free-wheeling attack Marshall remains culturally blinded to the discriminatory effect of the law on nonveterans. That issue, those boundaries, were settled. Even with a champion of equal opportunity such as Marshall, the nonveterans are ignored, as no mention is made of discriminatory effects on them. Indeed, Marshall mentions that a point preference system would be acceptable.[62]

Perhaps the most ironic development in the political culture of veterans' preference is that the policy is guaranteed invincible by the great protector of equal employment opportunity, the Civil Rights Act of 1964. The act contains a saving clause which protects laws of veterans' preference: "Nothing contained in this subchapter shall be construed to repeal or modify any Federal, State, territorial or local law creating special rights or preferences for veterans (42 U.S.C. § 2000e-11 [1970])." Thus, the "equal opportunity" law protected "special rights or preferences." No one considered the inconsistency of a discrimination law that protected veterans' preferences. According to legal scholar Grace Blumberg, there is virtually no legislative history on the saving clause.[63] The clause put the Equal Employment Opportunity Commission into a position at odds with its illustrious name, and in 1973 the EEOC declared officially (in response to a charge, "I was told that veterans had to be referred before me. I feel that this policy is discriminatory") that Title VII does not apply to nonveterans.[64]

Because of the taken-for-grantedness of moral boundaries, virtually no one in government has seen a connection between the veteran case and the plight of blacks and women and civil service affirmative action for those groups. This is perhaps not so surprising, given the institutionalized cultural logic in the civil service. After all, like the Civil Rights Act, the Pendleton Civil Service Reform Act of 1883, which established the merit system, simultaneously contained a saving clause for veterans' preferences. Yet when the prospect of *racial* preferences became a reality in the late 1960s and 1970s, it produced great consternation. Clumsy efforts were made to show the merit system was still in good standing, though it had been seriously compromised for decades by the veterans' preferences. Affirmative action was seen by many as an audacious affront to the Civil Service Commission's commitment to merit hiring, and the civil service was slow to implement affirmative action programs.[65] When finally defending affirmative action in 1974, however, executive director of the

Commission Bernard Rosen appears to forget about the plight of nonveterans entirely, and states, "The overall goal here [in affirmative action] is to eliminate any practices which in effect are barriers to the employment and advancement of members of *any group"* (emphasis added).[66] Were not veterans' preferences barriers to nonveterans? Forgetting the rigid policy of veterans' preference, he feels it necessary to add in his affirmative action defense that it must be "flexible" and "should never be permitted to become mandatory quotas requiring selection on factors other than merit." In a letter to the National Civil Service League, Commission chairman Robert E. Hampton, concerned to defend the merit system despite over a century of veterans' preference, wrote, "There is no question in our minds that [affirmative action] goals and timetables are in harmony with the merit system."[67] In the case of preferences for African-Americans, it was necessary to continually underscore fidelity to merit rules.

Are Preferences Based on Ascribed Traits Forbidden?
The Case of Nepotism

Believing that the moral model which shapes the boundaries of legitimate employment policy is coherent and consistent, one may object at this point. The issue with affirmative action for blacks (or women), one may argue, is different. It is preference based on an *ascribed* trait. Americans allow for veterans' preferences, because they are rewards for service or patriotism, whereas a racial preference is *unearned,* it is something that someone is simply born into.

This argument, however, is inadequate. It does not follow that by performing some special act for the good of the community, one should be exempt from cherished rules of equal opportunity. In other words, if Americans cared about equal opportunity principles as much as they say they do in critiquing affirmative action, then surely a better reward would be found than the job preference.

One might add that the preference-as-reward principle is sustainable only if one assumes that fighting in a war *is* something special, something above and beyond the call of citizenship—a view that happened to have won out in history but which was argued against at one time and could quite possibly have gone the other way (recall that initially, one must have been injured to be morally worthy). Also, for veteran preference to be consonant with classical liberalism, the opportunity to perform this special duty must be open to all, which, as we saw from the court challenges, is certainly not the case. Women have historically been excluded from the armed forces, to say nothing of the approximately one third of World War II selectees who, through no fault of their own, were rejected from service, usually due to medical problems or illiteracy.[68] Veterans' preference can also be seen to discriminate against those whose religious beliefs do not allow military service.[69] Following the logic of preferences-as-reward, we may also ask why widows of veterans are included in the preference (a true equal opportunity/merit supporter would have to ask, What did the stay-at-home widows do for the U.S.A. to deserve a reward?), and why there is no effort to distinguish between those veterans who actually saw combat duty and those who were stationed far from battle, or between volunteers and those who only went when legally required. But a distinction of desert *was* constructed, and moral boundaries were presumed to exist between veterans, regardless of their desire, effort, sacrifice or contribution, and those who "fought the war at home," who deserved no special consideration. And this construction was not simply behind-the-scenes political chicanery. A national audience supported the construction of veteran employment preferences and the affirmative action model for veterans.

Let us concede the point, however, that blacks are seen as undeserving of affirmative action because this would violate American ideals and institutions that disallow preferences based on ascriptive traits. If this is true, then we would hypothesize that American society tolerates no preferences based on ascriptive traits, and, save for the case of veterans or comparable "reward" cases, the American moral model is meritocratic, based on the idea that all should be judged as equal abstractions, differing only in ability or ambition.

This hypothesis does not get very far, however. The widespread practice of showing favoritism in hiring to family relatives (nepotism) can be considered discriminatory to nonrelatives, unmeritocratic, an illiberal recognition of arbitrary *ascriptive* traits, and the granting of group rights to family members. In short, it could be attacked on the same grounds as affirmative action, with the discourse of difference blindness. Surely one does not *earn* birth in a particular family. But again, if a lack of discourse about an issue indicates its unproblematic acceptance, then we can conclude that Americans are quite comfortable with nepotism in the job market. There is almost no literature on this subject. American laws of equal employment opportunity in the private sector ignore nepotism utterly as an injustice in itself. And while some firms police *themselves* to avoid nepotism, these self-imposed rules, which presumably open up jobs to more people, have been challenged as being unfair, primarily to women. The irony can be stated simply: Hiring by blood is sometimes just or appropriate (family preference) and sometimes not (racial preference).

Philosopher and social theorist Michael Walzer is one of the few to discuss nepotism in the context of meritocracy and equal opportunity. He traces the origin of the term (which is from the latin *nepos,* meaning nephew) from the practice of popes assigning offices to their nephews (believed to have often been their illegitimate sons). Walzer explains that "[s]ince it was one of the purposes of clerical celibacy to cut the church loose from the feudal system and to ensure a succession of qualified individuals, the practice was identified as sinful early on."[70] This negative perception remains, but curiously, it is limited to the government.

Indeed, the federal civil service in the United States has impressively comprehensive regulations prohibiting nepotism. Defining *relative* as "father, mother, son, daughter, brother, sister, uncle, aunt, first cousin, nephew, niece, husband, wife, father-in-law, mother-in-law, son-in-law, daughter-in-law, brother-in-law, sister-in-law, stepfather, stepmother, stepson, stepdaughter, stepbrother, stepsister, half brother, or half sister," the rule states that "[a] public official shall not advocate one of his relatives for appointment, employment, promotion, or advancement to a position in his agency or in an agency over which he exercises jurisdiction or control."[71] Antinepotism laws in the civil service are a legacy of sweeping legislation in the late nineteenth century that sought to ward off corruption and aim for a meritocratic civil service (though making allowances for veterans' preferences).[72] Nepotism has lived on in the upper echelons of government, however, with President John F. Kennedy's appointment of his brother Robert as attorney general being perhaps the most well-known example.

The limitations on nepotism in government suggest that support could be mustered to end the practice elsewhere and that a discourse of abstract individualism, always available to challenge affirmative action, could be available to challenge private nepotism. The zealous preservation of the merit system, which has held off nepotism in the government and a full development of affirmative action law for blacks, however, is absent in the copious legislation now regulating the private sphere. Among private businesses, nepotism has been taken for granted, as the institution of family capitalism implies. Sons of entrepreneurs have simply been expected to succeed fathers.[73] In 1957, for example, six of the nine board members for Oscar Mayer & Company were family.[74] But it is not only sons of entrepreneurs who benefit from nepotism. A 1957 survey of 175 of the largest U.S. companies for *Fortune* magazine found that 55 percent had close relatives or in-laws in management jobs in the same company. Nepotism was apparently assumed by some to be of no concern to outsiders, "since an incompetent relative can hurt only the owners and employees." One psychologist and executive for a Chicago management consulting firm claimed that it was human nature for bosses to want to surround themselves with trusted and enjoyable relatives.[75] In the survey, "[t]he point was repeatedly made by personnel managers that a son will work harder, and be more enthusiastic and more loyal to his father's company, than other executives."[76]

This may seem perfectly just, a matter of property right. Part of owning property, including a company, is being able to do with it what one wills. This also includes passing it down to family as inheritance. Thus, we do not bristle with moral discomfort when encountering a company sign that trumpets nepotism, that shows off what is almost certainly an unmeritocratic allocation of the top positions in a company: "Smith & Sons Chair Company," for example. To continue with this example, we may imagine Smith, a white gentleman, displaying a different sign: "Smith & Fellow White People Chair Company." Seeing this, we would probably do more than look askance. The injustice that such a sign suggests, the denial of equal opportunity, would be an outrage to most modern people. (With a successful affirmative action program, the company might title itself "Smith & A Proportional Representation of Area Minorities Chair Company," which would also sound conspicuously unmeritocratic.) But preferring relatives and preferring racial groups are both violations of the abstract citizen model of just employment policy, though they are not both violations of the taken-for-granted moral rules that shape legitimate policy interests.

Nepotism was actually once considered by the Supreme Court in this light, as an affront to the abstract individual model at the heart of color-blind justice. The opinion is interesting in that it captures the present argument: Nepotistic preferences can be considered unmeritocratic—even equated with racial preference—but they are *not* seen by Americans as unjust. The year was 1947, and the case was *Kotch v. Board of River Port Pilot Commissioners*.[77] Here the Court was to evaluate Louisiana's river pilot certification law, which appellants argued was an unconstitutional violation of the Fourteenth Amendment. A six- month apprenticeship was needed to acquire a boat operator's license, and incumbent pilots were free to choose apprentices. Rather than choosing the most qualified, they almost always chose their friends or family. In deciding the case, the majority opinion distinguished nepotism from racial or religious preferences as potentially acceptable if related to the objective of the law in question.[78] The law's purpose, it was decided, was to ensure the safest and most efficient system. Pointing out that pilotage was a unique occupation (river port pilots must have intimate knowledge of the local waters), the Court argued that "the advantages of early experience under friendly supervision in the locality of the pilot's training, the benefits to morale and *esprit de corps* which family and neighborly tradition might contribute, . . . might have prompted the legislature to permit Louisiana pilot officers to select those with whom they would serve."[79] Thus, nepotism was just, because it furthered the state objectives of efficient and safe waters.

In a sharply worded dissent written by Justice Wiley Rutledge, who was joined by three other justices, the point was made that nepotism was a violation of difference-blind justice. Arguing that "[b]lood is, in effect, made the crux of selection," the dissent claimed that there was no difference between skin color or family, "race or consanguinity": "The discrimination here is not shown to be racial in character. But I am unable to differentiate in effects one founded on blood relationship."[80] These justices thus argued that the nepotism was a violation of the constitutional right to be treated by the laws as an abstract individual.

And yet, this opinion was not a condemnation of nepotism. Conceding that nepotism was perhaps the most effective scheme for training in many occupations, the opinion wistfully recalled a more nepotistic past: "Indeed, something very worth while largely disappeared from our national life when the once prevalent familial system of conducting manufacturing and mercantile enterprises went out and was replaced by the highly impersonal corporate system for doing business." Their point on the case was simply that the *law* should not be repairing our lost nepotism.[81] Presumably, all of the justices agreed that Americans without relatives in positions of ownership or power deserved no equal employment opportunity.

In fact, it was not until a few years later that American businesses in the 1950s began to institute a "highly impersonal corporate system" of hiring—making nepotistic hiring against company rules. It was not, however, citizens or government that demanded equal opportunity for all citizens for the best jobs. Family capitalism dissolved in the wake of a more scientific quest for competitiveness. Capitalists in search of efficiency and a competitive edge began to make rules against nepotism. As one executive said, "We might miss some real good talent that way."[82] Some firms openly cited a "no relatives" policy as the reason for their success. A 1955 American Institute of Management survey found seven percent of 379 companies rated as "excellently managed" had antinepotism rules, but by 1963, 28 percent of 530 companies had antinepotism rules (slightly larger percentages for both years had unwritten antinepotism rules).[83] A 1965 *Harvard Business Review* survey found that 60 percent of 918 executives professed an unfavorable attitude toward nepotism, though, significantly, 51 percent would prefer a relative over another equally qualified candidate.[84] Still, competition-minded corporations commonly made such rules in their own self-interest: "Such rules were, for the most part, directed at the hiring of incompetent male relatives, the abuse that gave rise to the pejorative connotation of nepotism."[85] Curiously, continued discrimination against nonwhites or against women was not seen as a cause of missing "real good talent."

Nepotistic hiring has crossed paths with the law of equal employment opportunity in recent decades, though it has played out in a most peculiar way. Notwithstanding the abstract individual model that formed the rationale and rationality of the 1964 Civil Rights Act's Title VII, nepotism can now be legally seen as a violation of America's most cherished principle of justice, but *only* if it harms certain groups, specifically, groups circumscribed by race, national origin, gender, age, or religious difference.[86] But the situation is more curious than this. A firm's self-imposed antinepotism policy *can also* be seen as a violation of equal employment opportunity. Antinepotism rules, it has been argued, impede the efforts of women to find and keep jobs, as the rules prohibit married couples from working for the same employer, and often even stipulate that one employee must leave his or her job if he or she marries another employee. Title VII has been used to fight antinepotism rules in a great number of court cases across the country (though with mixed success). If rules against nepotism "infringe upon a class of people protected because of its race, religion, age, or sex, a claim of direct discrimination or of disparate impact discrimination may be upheld."[87] Despite the legal development, it remains that the most sweeping equal employment opportunity law in American history made no attempt to protect nonrelatives from discrimination.[88]

For the employer and the employee, the law must be seen to construct a confusing reality. The evil of nepotism is curiously circumscribed by whom it injures; only nonrelatives of color or another protected class are protected from its limitations on equal employment opportunity. For instance, one court decided that a union had violated Title VII by a nepotistic work-referral practice, explaining, "Since the relatives being preferred were disproportionately white, the nepotism discriminated against blacks whether or not appellees (the union) acted with a discriminatory purpose."[89]

In contrast, consider the fate of one Joseph Sogluizzo (an Italian-American). Mr. Sogluizzo was not a union member but worked in a union hiring hall for a number of years that was open to union members and nonmembers, and he wanted to join the union. The union, however, operated on a nepotistic basis, and his efforts were thwarted. Instead, he watched ten men with less seniority than himself jump over him for membership into the union. Feeling discriminated against, he approached the New York Human Rights Commission, but being a white male, he was told the Commission would only accept his case if he claimed discrimination on the basis of age or national origin. For purposes of getting a hearing in court, he claimed discrimination on the basis of national origin. The court objected; 25 percent of the union was Italian-American, and two of the ten who had jumped ahead of him had been Italian-American. Responding to the objection to the case, Mr. Sogluizzo explained he was discriminated against because he "wasn't related [to] or sponsored by anyone who was a member of the union." In its opinion, the court showed no sympathy to the apparent violation of equal employment opportunity, simply explaining, "Nepotism of itself does not violate Title VII. To come within the Civil Rights Act, nepotism must somehow be related to a pattern of discrimination based on national origin or another protected class."[90] Mr. Sogluizzo was judged on the basis of an ascriptive trait, denied opportunity, and also denied protection by the equal employment opportunity law.

There are some interesting parallels and points of comparison between the moral culture of affirmative action and that of nepotism. Much of the discourse is shared. As examples of common rationales for prohibiting nepotism, the Bureau of National Affairs cites the low morale of "those [nonrelatives] who feel that promotions and rewards are given unjustifiably to a relative." Also, "Relatives of supervisors do not know whether they earn rewards or receive them because of who they are,"[91] or, as one executive put it, "The trouble with nepotism is that the nepot has no way of knowing his 'real' worth or what he is capable of."[92] The first rationale would have its analog in minority discontent with racist hiring practices, and white male discontent with "reverse discrimination." The second echoes the "blacks hurt" media package identified previously for affirmative action, which is based on the claim that affirmative action stigmatizes African-Americans.

There are further parallels. Former chairman of the Equal Employment Opportunity Commission Clifford Alexander once complained that discriminating businesses gave the "traditional" excuse for not hiring blacks: they simply could not find them.[93] Similarly, companies in small communities on average practice nepotism more often than those in larger cities, because, they claim, they cannot find nonrelative workers. Some executives, though, have sounded like EEOC representatives on this issue; as one said, "It seems to me that most small firms who 'can't find' good managers among nonrelatives haven't tried very hard!"[94] In the racial context, Alexander also tried to encourage businesses to "treat the utilization and the finding and employment of minorities as a business problem rather than a problem they handled on Brotherhood Week."[95] One might think that it would be only a short step from voluntarily policing one's organization to prevent nepotism to policing it to prevent discrimination against talented blacks or women, but most businesses waited until a law was passed that forced them into this presumably wise business move.

It is worth mentioning that a kind of nepotism has been institutionalized in the nation's most prestigious colleges, involving a favoritism toward children of alumni. In a study sponsored by The College Board, it was found that colleges regularly made exceptions to formal admission requirements. While these exceptions aided racial or ethnic minorities 23 percent of the time, they aided alumni relatives 15 percent (and those with athletic talent, arguably another ascriptive trait unrelated to scholastic merit, 12 percent) of the time.[96] Another study showed that of applicants for the Harvard class of 1975, those students ranked as 2 or 3 (on a 1 to 7 scale, with the lower numbers going to the most qualified, based on test scores, grades, recommendations, interviews or essays) had a 30 percent chance of being admitted, while alumni sons with a 2 or 3 score had 60 percent chance of being admitted (athletes had a 64 percent chance). Blacks had a 73 percent chance of being admitted.[97] At Princeton, alumni children of this approximate ability level had a 100 percent chance of being admitted for the class of 1983, while the figure for the class as a whole was only 21 percent.[98] While Ivy League universities are few, this elite preference is significant in that these elite seats are generally associated with upward mobility. One might expect that in this crucial context, merit would especially be stressed by a resentful public, but this has not happened. The zig-zagging boundaries of moral worthiness leave these alumni preferences safe, legitimate, and unchallenged.

Alternative Explanations?

To recapitulate: Many have resisted affirmative action because it is seen as unjust. True justice is color blind, goes the argument: it sees all citizens as equal, universal abstractions. We may differ, however, in merit, talent, or ambition, and should be rewarded on the basis of those qualities. Talent or ambition make one morally deserving, and thus for employers to choose or promote employees on the basis of something else, to prefer someone because of their race or gender, is patently unjust.

We have seen, however, that employment preferences for veterans have had a long history in America. Unlike affirmative action for African-Americans, veterans' preferences have been blatant, unabashed. They are called *preferences*. Though resisted with a discourse of difference blindness and meritocracy, they have never been stopped, hardly even slowed. This resistance has been slight compared to that which fights racial preferences or color consciousness; indeed, public opinion has supported veterans' preferences. When the issue has been employment preferences for blacks, merit has seemed to be a most sacred principle of job allocation (moral/political boundaries proscribing racial preference were unassailable in 1964; they became blurred, but affirmative action remains highly controversial). When the preferences have been for veterans, merit has meant very little. Vague boundaries which made them disputable vanished in the face of a justification for veterans' preferences which was never entirely clear. They were justified as a reward (though some critics considered military service a duty of citizenship, akin to paying taxes), a way to encourage patriotism (though no distinction was made between volunteers and those who went only when forced), a compensation for sacrifice (while distinctions were made between the injured and uninjured, there were no distinctions between those who saw battle and those who were kept from harm's way), an aid in making the transition to civilian life (though the preference was permanent), and as being in harmony with meritocracy, since soldiers were ipso facto the most qualified (though this was never tested).

One may argue that this was not the result of constructions of deserving groups, that taken-for-granted boundaries of legitimacy were not relevant, but that the crucial difference here is that the veterans' lobbyists were simply stronger than the civil rights lobby. Even if this were true, the point still remains that the mainstream civil rights lobby (NAACP, Urban League, Southern Christian

Leadership Conference) has rarely lobbied in Washington for something as direct as a racial *preference*. And if their demands have in effect required preference, they have in such an obscurantist way as to suggest the effects of some cultural rules—"equal opportunity" is the demand. While veterans had the support of public opinion, African-American demands for racial preference would weaken lobbying power by dividing their coalition with liberal supporters. As we shall see, in fact, when Congress first debated the notion of racial-percentage hiring goals, the civil rights lobby was strangely silent.

Is it simply that the national audience for the veterans' demands was made up mostly of veterans, that a greater number of veteran voters paved the way to moral worthiness? While veterans were identified as being ten percent of the population in the Congressional debates in 1944 (roughly the same as blacks today), they were also one quarter of the voting age population, according to Peel.[99] It is worth noting that the group was actually more advantaged than non-veterans in 1970, averaging 12.5 years of schooling to 12.1, and a higher income ($8660 a year to $5860).[100] African-Americans have made up about 11 percent of the national population throughout the civil rights era, though much larger percentages occur at the state level, for example, in Mississippi, and they even constitute majorities in many cities. This voting strength, however, has never translated into naked racial preference. And of course women, another group seen as undeserving of employment preference, make up around 50 percent of the national population.[101] Moral boundaries of policy legitimacy and a group's "interests" are clearly not a simple function of demographics or voter strength.

One might object that the reason for legitimacy and lack of discourse regarding veterans' preferences was that they were limited to the civil service. This limitation is surprising, and there was little attempt to expand the preferences to the private sector. On the other hand, this probably results more from the illegitimacy of regulating private hiring decisions in 1944 than from the illegitimacy of the model of preference. In other words, as mentioned previously, even the juggernaut of veteran worthiness was hemmed in by taken-for-granted boundaries of just regulation. On the other hand, the Congressional "debate" shows there was every expectation that private employers would also practice preference, as discussed previously. One may even argue that the perceived moral worthiness of veterans is underscored by the legitimacy of preference in the civil service of all places, where merit hiring has been a major issue and the goal of an elaborate testing system. And one need only imagine the public outcry if Congress were to pass a statute granting, for example, a five-point exam preference for all blacks, and a ten-point and absolute preference for blacks who lived under Jim Crow—and called it the African-American Preference Act.

Finally, one may object to the comparison between blacks and veterans, since the preferences for veterans go to those who actually served and who may have actually suffered, whereas the racial preferences of affirmative action go indiscriminately to all African-Americans. However, we have already seen that the veterans' preferences were actually indiscriminate, failing to note any distinctions between those drafted and those who volunteered, those who actually fought and those who may have had a cushy desk job and remained in the United States, and are extended also to widows or wives of the disabled. What is more, the veterans' preferences have gone to those who were simply fulfilling a legal obligation. At any rate, millions of African-Americans who suffered under unjust discriminatory laws are still alive, and could be singled out for preference if that was required, if the preferences were justified by a logic of compensation. For example, legal scholar Boris Bittker has concluded from a dispassionate legal analysis of monetary reparations for African-Americans that

> Far from being a bizarre, outrageous, and unprecedented proposal, [black reparations] turns out to be a concept that invites, and is susceptible to, ordinary legal analysis. More than that, the demand for compensation has fraternal links with familiar legal doctrines and institutions, links that are so numerous and so powerful that the response 'Why not?' might be more appropriate than 'Why?'.[102]

The differences between the plight or desert of African-Americans and veterans begin to melt away when we consider the discourse of veterans' preference in relation to African-Americans. For example, in a "fireside chat" on 28 July 1943 President Roosevelt said, "The members of the armed forces have been compelled to make greater economic sacrifice and every other kind of sacrifice than the rest of us, and they are entitled to definite action to help take care of their special problems."[103] "African-Americans" could easily be inserted into the statement, instead of "members of the armed forces." Certainly, the discrimination that was openly practiced until 1964 also entailed a tremendous economic sacrifice. The best jobs, schools, and housing usually went to whites. One may add that the building of the economy of the South on the backs of forced labor, with no retribution save for the aborted Reconstruction, could be considered an economic sacrifice. The slaves were forced to sacrifice their freedom for the economic well-being of the United States. Or consider aid for "mustering out." In the Supreme Court case cited previously, *Mitchell v. Cohen,* the reasoning for veterans is still sound if it is applied to blacks: "It was felt that the problems of these returning veterans [newly protected African-Americans] were particularly acute and merited special consideration. Their normal employment and mode of life had been seriously disrupted by their service in the armed forces [second-class citizenship] and it was thought that they could not be expected to resume their regular activities without reemployment and rehabilitation aids." Just as the discourse of difference blindness and merit made sense in resistance to veterans' preference, the discourse of compensation for sacrifice or mustering out makes sense in support of affirmative action. It is the meaning of race that keeps the two in seemingly separate universes.

We have also seen that nepotistic hiring—family preference—has existed in the United States without provoking public ire. It has been challenged with the discourse of difference-blind justice, of equal employment opportunity, but has received little sympathy. Dissenting justices of the Supreme Court even equated it with the dreaded racial preference, since, after all, both nepotism and racial preference are limits on opportunity based on blood. But these same justices managed to venerate nepotism in the same opinion.

These justices, along with probably a majority of Americans, most likely felt that the law had no place telling someone (particularly an entrepreneur) that they could not prefer their own sons or daughters in employment. The family is just too intimate. Suddenly, private property, inheritance, seems sacred, and the boundaries or rules of appropriate or just employment practices shift. But this is precisely the point. Support for institutions of abstract universalism, color blindness, or meritocracy is contingent on the meanings of those in competition. *Family member* has a meaning, as does *veteran*. Both have suggested a justified exemption from the merit competition (though it took some time and effort to make "morally deserving" a part of the meaning of *veteran*). *Race* also has a meaning, especially *black*, but the notion of moral desert has little to do with it.

Meritocracy and Meaning

Thus far, we have avoided scrutiny of the meritocratic model itself; does it hold when group differences are held constant, when the issue is only whites hiring the most qualified white? That the best person usually gets the job is an assumption which undergirds much resistance to preferential policies. Evidence suggests, however, that this assumption is faulty. In a study of how Americans gain employment, Mark Granovetter discovered that 37 percent of his sample found employment through formal, ostensibly meritocratic procedures, such as responding to advertisements, using an employment agency, or applying directly, while 57 percent found jobs through personal contacts. Granovetter concludes that "better jobs are found through contacts, and the best jobs, the ones with the highest pay and prestige and affording the greatest satisfaction to those in them, are most apt to be filled in this way."[104] Do those with contacts deserve the jobs they gain through their contacts? Is this ability to make strategic contacts a qualification, a standard of merit, a fair competition? The closer we look at what Americans take for granted as justice in job allocation, the more confused the picture becomes.[105]

There can be no doubt that Americans are attracted to a society based on equality of opportunity and the reward of merit, usually understood as hard work and talent. We may leave aside the question of whether or not this model has any basis in reality; we can be more certain that (except for affirmative action) it is assumed to exist and it is used as an image, a standard of justice with which Americans strongly identify. But a closer look shows that American meritocracy is qualified, confused, unexamined. We have a moral model that actually guides policymaking, to be sure, but it is not the model we celebrate.

In fact, the disjunction between the *celebrated* American abstract individualism and the actual understandings and expectations was apparent from the beginning. The idea that "all men are created equal" meant "only that British colonials had as much natural right to self-government as Britons at home, that the average American was the legal peer of the average Briton."[106] The Founding Fathers were most concerned with the freedom to accumulate and hold property. Preferring, as did Jefferson, the rule of a "natural aristocracy," they feared the masses, were quite aware of tremendous status differences between themselves and the masses, and defined women and blacks as entities outside of the polity (they were dependent or lacked the great Enlightenment equalizer, reason).[107] The list of qualifications for office, for example, was a long one: white, male, propertied, and Protestant.[108] By couching their legitimating documents in universalist language, however, the Founding Fathers supplied a powerful discourse for two centuries of struggles with various marginalized groups.[109]

The distinction between the universalist and abstract individualist discourse and actual policy boundaries which made various exclusions and preferences quite safe and legitimate has not gone unnoticed. Abraham Lincoln, for example, was personally against the granting of citizenship to African-Americans. But he simultaneously understood the reach of the language of the founding charters of the nation. He denied allegiance to the racist doctrines of a group called the Know-nothings, and wrote:

> How can anyone who abhors the oppression of Negroes be in favor of degrading classes of white people? Our progress in degeneracy appears to me to be pretty rapid. As a nation we began by declaring that "all men are created equal." We now practically read it "all men are created equal except negroes." When the Know-nothings get control, it will read "all men are created equal, except negroes and foreigners and Catholics." When it comes to this, I shall prefer emigrating to some country where they make no pretence of loving liberty,—to Russia, for instance, where despotism can be taken pure, and without the base alloy of hypocrisy.[110]

It is tempting but misleading to conclude that the American identification with equal opportunity, meritocracy, and so on, is a hypocritical sham.[111] It is not one or the other—that America is the land of opportunity or a hypocritical racist state. It is both, depending on context. We have seen that the logic of the moral model which shapes policy boundaries is not based on a few premises and then smoothly and syllogistically applied to policy, law, and group interests. American citizens and American policy and lawmakers believe in equal opportunity, but not in every instance, and they also believe in exclusion and preference, but not in every instance.

Observers of American political culture have perceived the disunity in different ways. Seymour Martin Lipset sees conflicting values in American policy-making, specifically values of individual achievement and egalitarianism.[112] The most prevalent view is to see America or the modern West as shaped by a classically liberal or abstract individualist tradition or model, but to acknowledge that there are frequently exceptions or violations to this.[113] More perceptively, Alasdair MacIntyre has argued, "[W]hat many of us are educated into is, not a coherent way of thinking and judging, but one constructed out of an amalgam of social and cultural fragments inherited both from different traditions from which our culture was originally derived (Puritan, Catholic, Jewish) and from different stages in and aspects of the development of modernity (the French Enlightenment, the Scottish Enlightenment, nineteenth-century economic liberalism, twentieth-century political liberalism)."[114] Rogers Smith has argued that "American politics is best seen as expressing the interaction of multiple political traditions, including *liberalism, republicanism,* and *ascriptive forms of Americanism*" (original emphasis).[115]

But to conceptualize this situation in terms of competing values or different traditions does not take the complexity far enough. It is not just a jumble of several different though internally coherent justices, but a model of justice based on sometimes quite specific, historically contingent meanings of moral worth. Put another way, American justice involves different principles of justice which become institutionalized for different groups at different times, forming the safe boundaries of discourse for political action before the national audience and the likely basis of mainstream group interests.

When forced to examine what is usually taken for granted, Americans usually integrate these different group meanings into the equal opportunity model they identify with, as if these are "special cases" built in all along, not quite violations but logical detours of an assumed natural law of amazing complexity. But it is misleading to characterize it as an equal opportunity model with "exceptions"; our justice is socially constructed and changes over time. Race has been special in the model in that it was a legitimate basis of legal exclusion, but it is also special in that preference is expressly not considered just.

The point here is not that veterans' preference is bad, or that affirmative ac-tion is good, or that blacks are actually morally deserving. These are things for American voters and the courts to decide. But it is important for them to decide with a clear notion of the moral culture. In understanding resistance to affirma-tive action, we must realize that the modern and American identification with the abstract individual model, or meritocracy and equality of opportunity, only tells part of the story. It is very important and was crucial in the destruction of *de jure* segregation in the United States. But what is also important in the affirma-tive action debate is the often taken-for-granted meaning given to different groups in society. This is not built into some overarching, self-consistent *natu-ral* law, with a predetermined degree of desert and set of rules for every possible group. Throughout American history some groups have simply been con-structed as morally worthy, and others have not. As sociologist Theda Skocpol argues, "Institutional and cultural oppositions between the morally 'deserving' and the less deserving run like fault lines through the entire history of American social provision."[116] Americans who resist affirmative action are simply articu-lating the American model of justice as it relates to race and employment prefer-ence. Affirmative action is objected to because of its racial beneficiary.

The question remains for the rest of this study: Given the resistance to race-conscious hiring, how did the affirmative action model move beyond its taboo status of the early 1960s? With some understanding of why conservatives and most Americans have resisted the policy, we must now see how and why lib-erals, initially the champions of the color-blind paradigm, came to support it.

PART TWO

Understanding Support for Affirmative Action

4

Crisis Management through
Affirmative Action

The interest of the Right and of mainstream America in resisting affirmative action is largely a moral one: blacks are not seen as deserving of preference, and while affirmative action is not a taboo in the last third of the twentieth century, its advocacy continues to disturb people for this reason. In explaining the Right's resistance, we thus saw as most important the moral boundaries taken for granted by a national audience. To explain the Left's eventual support, we must look for those contexts where people had an interest in affirmative action and those audiences for which the advocacy of affirmative action was not illegitimate.

In one of the ironies that permeate the issue of affirmative action, advocacy of parts of the affirmative action model was to come from the very centers of power in America, and quite soon after color blindness was made the law of the land in the Civil Rights Act of 1964. In this chapter, we will focus on how a crisis is handled in late modern democratic politics, emphasizing the unintended consequences of crisis management. For it was in the handling of a crisis, defined here as a perceived threat to elite control,[1] that moral cultural boundaries limiting civil rights in employment to color blindness were expanded to allow for the building of the affirmative action model. More specifically, a racial crisis, the severe race rioting of the 1960s, made available a discourse of crisis management with which affirmative action or other normally risky, race-targeted measures could be advocated by political and business elites.[2]

Crises have historically been associated with significant relaxations of the taken-for-granted boundaries and models of the organization of politics and life. As Stephen Krasner puts it, "During periods of crisis, politics becomes a struggle over the basic rules of the game rather than allocation within a given set of rules."[3] The crisis that comes with war is the most familiar example. The goal of maintaining control and order (in this context, against the threat posed by the enemy) renders cherished or unquestioned practices, even the basic moral boundaries of justice, negotiable or expendable—it "deinstitutionalizes."[4] Though perceiving the rules of laissez-faire capitalism as the basis of rational management of the economy, government leaders can suddenly, in the context of war, take firm control of the economy.[5] State control over the American economy during World War II, for instance, is well known. The Emergency Price Control Act is but one example.[6] President Truman tested the limits of crisis allowance for new models of action during the Korean War in 1952 when, in a controversial action, he seized control of the steel industry when a strike seemed imminent.[7] But a crisis may also relax boundaries and allow new understandings of life outside of politics. Women, though understood in the 1940s as properly limited to careers as homemakers, could suddenly become a major force in the paid economy. Just as soon as the crisis had passed, however, the old understandings and logics could come back.

Wartime has been crucial in the advance of civil rights. It was no coincidence that the first major equal employment opportunity order was issued by Franklin D. Roosevelt during World War II, and after a threat of a mass demonstration in Washington. The black-owned *Pittsburgh Courier* relished the event: "What an opportunity the crisis has been . . . to persuade, embarrass, compel, and shame our government and our nation . . . into a more enlightened attitude toward a tenth of its people."[8] It is also no coincidence that Roosevelt's Fair Employment Practices Committee had its funding eliminated by Congress when the war was over.

This suggests a discursive strategy for challenge to the status quo. Advocates of change, both within and without the state, will push a new idea, such as affirmative action, with the explicit or implicit explanation that the idea will mitigate the crisis, it will help maintain control and order. The greater the perceived threat of disorder, the greater the interest in crisis management, the more relaxed the boundaries of American justice, and the more acceptable this justification will be.[9]

In this chapter, we will see that some of the liberal (and conservative) support for affirmative action came as a result of the sudden elite interest in crisis management. The 1960s urban riots had several important effects. They challenged the authority of mainstream civil rights leaders, who had been committed to a policy of nonviolence and color blindness. Government and business elites responded with race-conscious policies and programs, understood and now more safely advocated as tools of social control and hedges against further disorder, which served to empower people (promising jobs, training, or education), rather than repress them. These moves blurred the boundaries between ensuring a fair competition for jobs and hiring by race, and embodied unit ideas of the affirmative action model, most obviously the idea of sorting the population by race in order to help the more disadvantaged, but also revising concepts of merit and discrimination. In addition, a high-profile government report gave great publicity to unit ideas that form the basis of the affirmative action model. Taken together, the crisis and the response to it shook the foundations of the culture of equal employment opportunity, and in this context, particularly as government and business elites communicated with each other, affirmative action became a safe, even legitimate policy option.

Setting the Scene: Civil Rights in Post–Civil Rights Act America

After the passage of the Civil Rights Act of 1964, one thing was clear: Race problems and race inequality look very different when discrimination laws *are* on the books than they do when they *are not* on the books. Simple racist exclusion was such an obvious problem that it consumed the energy of the civil rights groups and the attention of the sympathetic public. With the passage of the Civil Rights Act (and later the Voting Rights Act), the movement had achieved its goals. It had emerged victorious.

It immediately seemed to the leaders of the Southern Christian Leadership Conference (SCLC), the National Association for the Advancement of Colored People (NAACP), and the Urban League, however, that this victory was a hollow one. The problem was that the assumed "natural society" causality principle which had guided the movement's interests—that color blindness could bring into being an integrated, equal society—suddenly seemed hopelessly oversimplified and utopian. While state laws and private companies would now no longer legally treat blacks as less than equals, the situation was still quite grim. The unemployment rate for blacks was still twice that of whites, and those blacks who were employed were concentrated in low-paying jobs. Americans have generally avoided coming to terms with an obvious implication of the cherished abstract individual model of equal opportunity justice, so cheerfully advocated in support of civil rights in the early 1960s: It virtually guarantees that large numbers of people (the least qualified or occupationally meritorious) will cluster at the bottom of the social ladder. Civil rights leaders were suddenly forced to face that fact. A greater percentage of blacks were still undereducated and inexperienced in skilled jobs.

It is true that economic goals had been major priorities in the movement for some time. After all, 1963 had seen the historic "March on Washington for Jobs and Freedom." But the emphasis here was on eliminating race as a reality in public life. The goals were passage of Kennedy's civil rights bill, the addition of civil rights protections in employment (still lacking in the Kennedy proposal), desegregation of schools, as well as a minimum wage and a federal public-works jobs program aimed at helping all the poor.[10] Therefore, Lee Rainwater and William Yancey could write, "The year 1965 may be known in history as the time when the civil rights movement discovered, in this sense of becoming explicitly aware, that abolishing legal racism would not produce Negro equality."[11] Bayard Rustin wrote in *Commentary* in 1965 that the civil rights movement had undergone "an evolution calling its very name into question." The movement was "now concerned not merely with removing the barriers to full *opportunity* but with achieving the fact of *equality*" (emphasis in original).[12] Similarly, James Farmer of the Congress on Racial Equality (CORE) said in 1966,

> There have been great gains in job opportunities and educational opportunities for Negroes over the last few years and with organizations like CORE demanding justice, these opportunities will continue to expand. But we can no longer evade the knowledge that most Negroes will not be helped by equal opportunity. These are staggering problems for which the traditional CORE program of anti-discrimination is ill-equipped. We are now seeking new techniques and emphasis that will serve not only today's Negro masses but also tomorrow's teeming millions.[13]

Thus, the civil rights movement, having achieved its primary goals, seemed destined for some kind of transformation, and seemed open to new ideas that could make that American color-blind model reach its promised result of "ultimate perfection," as the *Democratic Review* had put it in 1839.[14]

Burn, Baby, Burn: Riots and the Urban Crisis of the 1960s

Any transformation of the civil rights movement would not occur in a context of cool intellectual deliberation. The urban race rioting of the 1960s, one of the most enigmatic social phenomena in American history, was to threaten not only government and business elites but was to give the movement leadership its own crisis, its own threat to control, which ultimately weakened the movement as a lobbying force in Washington. While black violence such as occurred in Jim Crow Birmingham, Alabama, in 1963 was understandable if not justified in the minds of many Americans, the violence which occurred in the North, and after the Civil Rights Act, where and when race supposedly had no relevance, came as a shock to most and an outrage to many. The wave of violence had its beginning in the North in 1964. While Congress debated the new civil rights bill in the early part of that year, a disturbance occurred at the New York World's Fair which was to be a harbinger of the rest of the decade. CORE National Director James Farmer led nonviolent picketing and protests to dramatize the predicament of New York blacks. Farmer was one of 294 persons arrested. Upon release from prison on 24 April, he warned of a "longer and hotter summer than this country has ever seen," and declared that "Now is the time for anger."[15] He was correct—though "now" was to last several years.

The Civil Rights Act of 1964, the most sweeping civil rights legislation in the country's history, was passed on 2 July. Sixteen days later, black rage erupted in Harlem.

The riot had characteristics which were to become typical. It started with an alleged incident of police brutality, in this case after an African-American was shot by police. Also typical of this violence was the reception given to national civil rights leaders. After the funeral, a restless crowd gathered in the streets. Bayard Rustin climbed on top of a sound truck and urged the crowd to disperse: "We know that there has been an injustice done," he told the crowd. "The thing that we need to do most is to respect this woman whose son was shot." The crowd, reportedly, replied by shouting, "Uncle Tom!" and ignored Rustin's message.[16] Demonstrations followed, which evolved into full-scale rioting, replete with looting, vandalism, and violent attacks on police. Robert Fogelson captures the irony of the new situation: "Having organized a quarter of a million Americans who marched on Washington in 1963, Rustin could not persuade a few hundred blacks to clear the streets of Harlem a year later."[17]

On the second day of the rioting, even CORE National Director James Farmer, who had announced the "time for anger" a few months earlier, was booed when he tried to address a rally. However, positive responses were given to a local leader, in this case Jesse Gray, who called for "black revolutionaries who are ready to die" to use guerrilla warfare tactics to fight the police. After four days, 1 black had been shot to death and 5 others wounded from gunfire, 81 civilians and 35 policemen otherwise injured, 112 businesses damaged, and 185 persons were arrested.[18]

The following week, riots erupted in Brooklyn and Rochester. The Rochester riots required the National Guard to help restore order. One white was killed, and 350 people were injured. Over 400 persons were arrested. Property damage was estimated at over several million dollars. Again, the precipitating event was an alleged instance of police brutality. That summer also saw riots in Philadelphia, Jersey City, Paterson, New Jersey, Elizabeth, New Jersey, and Dixmoor, Illinois. As in the Harlem riot, civil rights leaders failed to keep order. The generally middle-class moderate leaders, the symbols of color-blind civil rights, had lost authority to control their ostensible constituency. An NAACP leader in Rochester said, "Very few of us are considered one of our own in these ghetto communities."[19]

These 1964 disturbances, now mostly absent from any discussion of the 1960s urban rioting, were perceived as threatening enough and serious enough for Democratic President Lyndon B. Johnson to take some action. First, he ordered an FBI investigation which (counter to Johnson's initial suspicions of the riots being the work of "extremist elements") concluded that the riots were spontaneous and "senseless attacks on all constituted authority without purpose or object." In September, President Johnson ordered the FBI to make riot training available to police departments, the National Guard to prepare riot-control techniques, and the Department of Health, Education, and Welfare to study Washington, DC's programs for high school dropouts.[20]

The riots of the summer of 1964, then, were considered serious enough to provoke presidential action, but they were nothing compared to what was to follow. It was the 11 August 1965 riot in the Watts section of southern Los Angeles that was to sound alarms in Washington and across the nation that something had gone terribly wrong. It followed the typical pattern: white police arrested a black man (Marquette Frye, suspected of drunk driving). This time, a crowd gathered *during* the arrest. The crowd grew quickly, and became violent. At least a thousand blacks had gathered within an hour, and they began to throw rocks and bottles at police. With shouts of "Burn, baby, burn" (the slogan of a local radio disc jockey), the six days of rioting began, with attacks on whites in cars, police, and white journalists. Arson and looting on a massive scale began. One black observer wrote,

> It's a wonder anyone with white skin got out of there alive. . . . Every time a car with whites in it entered the area the word spread like lightning down the street: "Here comes Whitey—get him!" The older people would stand in the background egging on the teen-agers and people in their 20s . . . When there were no whites, they started throwing rocks and bottles at Negro cars . . . Everybody got in the looting—children, grownups, old men and women.[21]

After the National Guard arrived on the fourth day, the violence began to subside. The six-day toll of the Watts riot included 34 killed and 1,072 injured (the vast majority black), 977 buildings destroyed or damaged, and over 4,000 persons arrested. Later estimates held that 30,000 engaged in the riot violence, and at least 60,000 more were supportive spectators.[22] President Johnson was shocked at what was transpiring. Domestic policy adviser Joseph Califano said of Johnson, "He refused to look at the cables from Los Angeles . . . He refused to take calls from the generals who were requesting government planes to fly in the National Guard . . . We needed decisions from him. But he simply wouldn't respond."[23]

Again, the leaders of a color-blind civil rights movement had no authority to keep order. In Los Angeles in 1965, Wendell Collins, vice-chairman of the Los Angeles CORE, Reverend Hartford H. Brookins of the United Civil Rights

Committee, John A. Buggs of the L.A. County Human Relations Commission, and congressman Augustus F. Hawkins could not keep order, despite great efforts on television and radio, and direct negotiation with youth leaders, police, and rioters. Civil rights activist Dick Gregory was shot in the leg trying to restore order.[24]

Such was life in mid-1960s urban America. The mysterious black violence continued to explode in hundreds of cities across America, apparently at random. Doug McAdam, in one of the few studies of the civil rights movement to go beyond the legislation passed in 1964 and 1965, counted 290 "hostile outbursts" in the period from 1966 to 1968. One hundred sixty-nine persons were killed in the violence, 7,000 were wounded, and over 40,000 were arrested. And these figures are conservative. The Civil Disorders Clearinghouse at Brandeis University recorded 233 disorders in 1967 alone, and 295 disorders in the first four months of 1968. McAdam states that "It would not seem an overstatement to argue that the level of open defiance of the established economic and political order was as great during this period as during any other in this country's history, save the Civil War."[25]

The Urban Riots, the New Black Audience and the Loss of the Color-Blind Consensus

"IS THE U.S. ABLE TO GOVERN ITSELF?" screamed the cover of *U.S. News and World Report* on 31 July 1967. "Anarchy Growing Threat to Big Cities?" it asked the following week. Racial problems were the cover stories for *Time* for three consecutive weeks in this period. But it was not just in the summer of 1967 that the issue received great amounts of attention and concern. Summer, in fact, was getting a new name in the media: riot season. Police began to purchase armored personnel carriers. Fire departments shopped for armored fire trucks. Sales of guns to white suburbanites soared. Even army officials worried about the country's ability to contain the violence.[26] There was nothing absurd in the title of historian Garry Wills's 1968 book on the situation, *The Second Civil War: Arming for Armageddon*.[27]

The rioting had powerful effects on the civil rights movement, which ultimately affected the movement as a lobbying force. Most directly, the riots encouraged the fragmentation of the movement, already losing coherence in the wake of legislative victories. This occurred because the moderate leaders preached nonviolent means to clear, concrete legislative goals, and the riots were proof that some black Americans were ready to use violence *without* clear goals. New militant leaders increasingly began to position themselves at the forefront of what they called "ghetto revolts," and made vague demands for radical change and "black power."

Militant leaders, black nationalists, and separatists upstaged the moderates during the riots and captured the media's attention. The militant leaders were in a good position to gain attention without responsibility. They were charismatic, free from financial accountability to whites, more newsworthy, not required to produce as much, and from the same generation as ghetto youth.[28] The moderate, "responsible" leaders, on the other hand, were faced with a problem of incredible complexity. The overwhelming task of coming up with a program to combat the causes of ghetto unrest (still unknown), silence the militants, and remain a legitimate player in politics pushed King into depression. Many were looking to him for guidance, but as he explained to his wife, Coretta, "I don't have any answers."[29]

The issue of black power specifically put the participants of the movement at odds with each other, as militant groups, such as the Student Nonviolent Coordinating Committee (SNCC), embraced the slogan, as well as a borderline group, CORE. The expression *black power* was not completely new when it swept across the country in June 1966, but its rise in the civil rights movement is usually dated to this month, when the slogan was used by Stokely Carmichael of SNCC at a march for voting rights in Mississippi. The march had united the more radical SNCC with King of SCLC and Floyd McKissick of CORE. At a protest rally on a summer's evening, Carmichael and his colleagues led a chant: "We want black power!"

The idea of black people demanding power in the name of blackness quickly became a media sensation. King immediately sensed the threat to the legitimacy of the civil rights movement. He disavowed the phrase (calling it "an unfortunate choice of words"), and warned that the slogan would "confuse our allies, isolate the Negro community and give many prejudiced whites, who might otherwise be ashamed of their anti-Negro feeling, a ready excuse for self-justification."[30] However, CORE associate director Lincoln Lynch said on 21 June that King's statement "shows a basic misunderstanding of what the Negro on the farm and on the streets is really asking for," and that "history has shown that if you're really depending on the vast majority of whites to help, you're really leaning on a very broken reed." Not surprisingly, at the 1–4 July national convention, CORE officially endorsed the slogan *black power*. Director Floyd McKissick explained, "As long as the white man has all the power and money, nothing will happen, because we have nothing. The only way to achieve meaningful change is to take power." Nonviolence is passé, he announced. Carmichael, speaking at the convention, declared that integration was "irrelevant." King was scheduled to speak, but did not come; later he stated that he would not speak at any function that would urge racial violence.[31] The civil rights movement, formerly a near consensus force behind or at least deferring to the color-blind model, was clearly in great internal conflict.

The black audience for civil rights group public statements, now dominated by militants, seemed to separate from the national audience and now had different, conflicting boundaries of legitimate action and discourse. The national audience continued to demand fidelity to color blindness from serious civil rights leaders, but it was precisely the advocacy of color blindness which now threatened movement legitimacy for the black audience. Here, radical demands became the safe demands.

Consensus thus proved to be elusive, if not impossible. Moderate, mainstream civil rights leaders, such as King and NAACP executive director Roy Wilkins, would denounce black power, which seemed to resist tenaciously a clear ideological formulation, and would be labeled Uncle Toms for doing so by those such as Alfred Black, of the Newark Commission of Human Rights, who stated starkly, "A black man today is either a radical or an Uncle Tom." McKissick searched for "ways and means of dealing with those Negroes who sell us out—who betray their people."[32]

The movement that could unite and push through the Civil Rights Act of 1964 began to unravel in the wake of violence and the rise of militants. There was no concerted push for any policy, including a systematic development of a model of justice like affirmative action. For example, James Farmer, former leader of CORE, said in 1966 that the movement was "reeling," and that major organizations "didn't know where they were going or what to do at that point," and for the first time there were arguments on goals or objectives.[33] A. Philip Randolph, president of the influential Brotherhood of Sleeping Car Porters, also stated in October 1968, "Well, the civil rights movement is undergoing great frustration and fragmentation at the present time. There is a multiplication of groups espousing various ideas and policies about civil rights, strategy and tactics, and so forth."[34] The title of King's last book, published in 1967, itself was a commentary on the movement's confusion: *Where Do We Go From Here?*[35]

These developments also put the Johnson administration in a difficult situation. There was a cacophony of demands for action, but increasingly there seemed to be no leadership with whom the solutions could be hammered out. Still there were the mainstream leaders, sinking precipitously in influence and authority, paralyzed by the contradictory boundaries of the national audience and the vocal black audience. Burke Marshall, former assistant U.S. attorney general, said in 1968, "Who are the civil rights leaders? I don't know who they are. I don't think there are any civil rights leaders as that term is normally used."[36] Marshall explained that at one time

> You could get in Whitney Young, Roy Wilkens [*sic*], Dorothy Height, Martin Luther King, A. Philip Randolph, and there you had the civil rights leaders and nobody would question that you had the civil rights

leaders . . . But you can't do that now. It's just absolutely meaningless. I don't know whether President Johnson would agree with that,
because sometimes he still does get those people in. But from the
point of view of the black community, they wouldn't pay any more
attention to Roy Wilkens [sic] than to George Wallace, maybe less.[37]

The other possibility was to deal with the radical groups, but this was unreflectively dismissed by the administration. Dealing with radicals would almost certainly sacrifice the administration's legitimacy. Told of the urgency of
developing contacts with the younger black leaders, Attorney General Nicholas
Katzenbach responded, "Younger leaders who now exist are precisely those
who . . . have consistently chosen an 'outside course': that is, Stokely Carmichael."[38] In an interview in 1968, Katzenbach dismissed what he described
as the "nuttier groups," admitted that they may have lost faith in the government, but added, "[Y]ou don't really want their help anyhow."[39] Special Counsel to the President Harry McPherson also dismissed the militants in a memo to
White House Press Secretary George Christian (who passed it on to Johnson),
stating simply, "[I]t is ridiculous for the President even to consider meeting with
the 'Black Power' people."[40] Thus, in the Johnson administration's view, the
decline of the mainstream civil rights movement (Martin Luther King especially fell out of favor for his outspoken views of the war in Vietnam) was not
met with the rise of any legitimate replacements.

Civil Rights Groups and the Discourse of Crisis Management

The moderate civil rights leaders struggled to retain their authority and address
the riot issue in a constructive way. They knew that a need for crisis management offered opportunities for new approaches. To make any points forcefully,
however, the civil rights leaders had to engage in a political struggle over the
very meaning of the riots, over how they would be defined. Were they the long-
time-coming expression of black frustration and revolutionary drive for justice,
or were they, as conservative forces claimed, the work of a few subversive
forces, "riffraff" among the basically law-abiding people? Civil rights leaders,
desirous of change, furthered the former point, and continually warned that
more disorder was in store for the nation unless something drastic was done to
help African-Americans. By emphasizing crisis, the risky issue of moral worthiness was avoided. Potentially risky specific program solutions, however,
were often conspicuously absent.

For example, black leaders used the opportunity of a White House civil rights
conference to emphasize the threat to order in June 1966. In his welcoming
speech, honorary conference chairman A. Philip Randolph likened black anger
to a massive, "volcanic" social force, that expresses itself in riots, such as in

Watts: "Let me warn this conference that the Negro ghettoes in every city throughout the nation are areas of tension and socio-racial dynamite, near the brink of similar racial explosions, of violence."[41] Vice President Hubert Humphrey seemed to need little convincing, offering a similar warning at the conference, and a political (rather than criminal) definition of the riots: "[T]he lesson of the revolution of rising expectations, which is not only in the foreign countries, but is here at home in America, must be writ large. That lesson—20 million Americans will no longer be pacified by slogans or tokens."[42]

The following day, Roy Wilkins continued to hammer this point home. He repeatedly emphasized the urgency of the situation, and declared that "urgency" was the key word of the whole conference. Quoting from a section of the conference report on Economic Security and Welfare, he called black economic insecurity the most "ugly and urgent crisis facing this nation today," and said that "Negro unemployment is of disaster proportions. Creative and large scale action must be taken to achieve full and fair employment for the Negro working age population."[43] After a reference to Watts, Wilkins called for "a discarding of the past routines, a welcome to daring, to innovation, to unorthodoxy."[44]

While here emphasizing the threat to order and the need for freedom from cultural constraints on responses, moderate and militant civil rights leaders also used the threat of black violence and crisis discourse to carry some suggestions for action, though almost never explicitly for preferential hiring (as the veterans had done before them). In the aftermath of the Detroit rioting, King and Wilkins made a call for $30 billion dollars in federal aid. Dick Gregory called the riot a turning point in history, and added that adequate funds for urban blacks would only be equal to the moon program or Vietnam expenditures.[45] Floyd McKissick, chairman of CORE, spelled out his riot sociology in the pages of the New York Times, saying, "Bad conditions make for violence" and "You will have violence as long as you have black people suppressed."[46] A. Philip Randolph added, "Teenagers with jobs don't throw Molotov cocktails."[47] In a booklet called Lessons of the Long Hot Summer, Bayard Rustin argued for a full employment policy. Against right-leaning economists, who claimed that this policy would "overheat" the economy, Rustin answered, "A non-economist may, however, be permitted to observe that if the long hot summer of 1967 proves anything, it is that the 'danger of "overheating" the economy' may turn out to be as nothing compared with the dangers of our present employment policies."[48]

A typical position was expressed by young black leaders at testimony for a House anti-riot bill on 30 August 1967. The bill reflected the conservative view of the riots—that they were caused by outside agitators—and made it illegal to cross state lines to incite violence. The leaders said that the riots were not the work of outside agitators, but resulted from unfulfilled promises and a lack of jobs. They explained that the black person "these days is tired of promises. He's been promised things for 400 years. He wants to see something concrete."[49]

These efforts, however, were hardly an effective lobbying force. They encouraged the perception of crisis, but gave little guidance for government officials. Randolph explained that, "The implementation of the legislation will be increasingly difficult because of the fragmentation of the civil rights movement. You don't have a unified force striking at any essential or particular and difficult objective."[50] Legal scholar and former EEOC counsel Alfred Blumrosen lamented the lack of lobbying influence on government agencies such as the EEOC, maintaining in 1971 that the civil rights movement "is virtually without theory" and "lacks staying power."[51] Funding for all civil rights groups except for the NAACP went down beginning in the middle 1960s.[52] The riots, the loss of consensus in the civil rights community on the goal of color blindness, and the new vocal (and newsworthy) black audience severely limited the role of civil rights groups to lobby successfully for any major policy initiative, let alone something still as risky as affirmative action.

The Affirmative Action Taboo and the Federal Response to the Rioting

The rigid boundaries which had made race-targeted policy and affirmative action employment approaches taboo can be seen in the efforts of government officials to manage the crisis. While the logic of crisis management and its attendant discourse led them to articulate such approaches, they did so with extreme trepidation and almost always with a mask of universalism and color blindness. Business elites also reluctantly moved to race-based hiring practices, though as private firms (rather than public policymakers), they were less encumbered by the limits of legitimacy. While an affirmative action model was not likely to result in lost revenue for business leaders, even in the crisis it promised to result in a weakened electoral coalition for the Democratic leadership in the White House and Congress.

EARLY CRISIS MANAGEMENT AND POLITICAL RISK

Though rioting provoked a sense of crisis when it began, the threat of widespread rioting actually *preceded* the widespread rioting. That is, some perspicacious government officials saw it coming. President John F. Kennedy's aid Harris Wofford, who had close ties with the civil rights movement, had been warning Kennedy even before he was sworn into office that conditions in northern cities were "explosive," and that "rising tensions can lead to serious race riots."[53] The situation was not seen to improve. On 13 May 1963, White House aid Louis Martin told Attorney General Robert Kennedy that a race riot in Birmingham "seemed to electrify Negro concern over civil rights all across the country," and Martin anticipated "the most critical state of race relations since the Civil War."[54] Many in the administration were now warning the president of the impending crisis. It was in this climate that President Kennedy, on 19 June, introduced a relatively modest civil rights bill to Congress. This bill was to become the Civil Rights Act of 1964.[55]

Kennedy proposed a bill which he believed fit into the limits of political possibility, sharply defined by the intolerance of the southern Democrats, and lacking any employment protections, but he did not believe that this bill was enough to manage the coming nationwide racial crisis. Kennedy therefore arranged unpublicized meetings of high-ranking officials from his administration with various groups, including conferences of mayors, religious leaders, lawyers, civil rights leaders, labor, and women. "The basic purpose," explained Attorney General Robert Kennedy later, was to show White House and presidential leadership, and "to try to focus people's attention on their own responsibility—what they needed to do, what could be done, and why it was in their interest to do something rather than to wait until violence occurred."[56] The list also included two meetings with business leaders, where the effort was to encourage businesses to desegregate and hire more black workers.[57] The president's message was expressly justified as a response to incipient racial unrest, not just in the South but throughout the country. In other words, affirmative action was urged to these limited audiences to mitigate disorder and maintain control.

On 11 July 1963, there was a meeting with the Business Council, an organization of large-scale business leaders often considered by some scholars to have tremendous power in its relationship with the government.[58] Notes from this meeting give an extremely valuable inside view of how the government manages crisis, and shows how and why the nation's top leadership, including the president, the vice president, the attorney general and the secretary of state— white males all—advocated an affirmative action approach to about seventy business leaders behind closed doors. A memorandum, written by the Business Council's F. R. Kappel, gave details of the meeting and was submitted to Business Council members (as well as White House aid Lee White, whose copy contained a cover note saying that the memo "has not been published and should be handled very securely").

How does a president sell affirmative action to an audience limited to the elite business community? According to the memo, as the meeting began, "The President pointed out that the [racial] problem had become critical and must be dealt with directly if the situation is to be kept within bounds. This requires attention, cooperation, and action by every responsible citizen." In addition, the high black unemployment rate was pointed out, and "The speakers commented favorably on the role the businessman had been pursuing in this critical situation and cited instances where there was increased utilization of Negroes and where considerable effort and expense had been made by business to train them." So "utilization" was urged, not just the termination of discrimination. Vice President Lyndon Johnson "urged that special emphasis be given to the school drop-outs, to out-of-hour training and the advancement of any program which would make them more capable of self-support through employment."

In discussing the coming civil rights legislation, Robert Kennedy also exhibited a clear concern with maintaining control, and not fidelity to any ideas of justice. Injustice, in fact, was reduced at this meeting to the Negroes' "claim." The attorney general, according to the memo, was careful to reassure the business leaders that the current situation was not mainly the result of the leaders' employment practices, and accordingly the new laws would not focus on this. He explained that "the key to the demonstrations, the riots and other serious situations" was based mainly on discriminatory access to public facilities and business establishments, an insulting situation which keeps the "pot boiling." The legislation that had been proposed "was the minimum that would be required to overcome the obstacles to getting people off the streets and the situation under control."

Having absolved the council from any blame, the president then hit on the council members' hiring practices. They should "take a hard, personal look at the employment situation in their respective companies." Despite progress that had been made, "more was necessary because the situation had become so critical." Trying to avoid discussing the dreaded racial preference, President Kennedy stressed that "it was equal opportunity that was involved, and he did not want action that would discriminate against the employment of whites, but he felt that in some circumstances business would be justified in going out and finding qualified Negroes in order to get programs started and established."[59]

Following an hour of general discussion, the president made a final plea to Kappel, as chairman of the Business Council, to keep the council focused on the problem. Kappel reports that "I stated that there was no question about the seriousness of the problem and need for a constructive solution." As a part of Kappel's compliance with the president's request, Kappel sent copies of the memo to all members of the Business Council, with a cover letter explaining that the "racial problem is a serious one. It does or can involve every business and community as well as the country, and its resolution is urgent."[60] Thus, the president's message of race-targeted hiring and *utilization* (a key affirmative action term), advocated on the basis of crisis management, was taken seriously and spread to business leaders across the country.

When Lyndon Johnson assumed power following the assassination of President Kennedy, he continued Kennedy's *publicly* color-blind course. His tenure began with two major initiatives, both designed to protect Americans regardless of race, but which he hoped would have the effect of ameliorating the precarious poverty of black Americans. The first of these was the Civil Rights Act, which was passed with a title protecting against discrimination in employment. The other was the War on Poverty.

The origins of the War on Poverty, like those of the Civil Rights Act, are in the Kennedy Administration. In 1962 Kennedy asked the chairman of his Council of Economic Advisers (CEA) to gather statistics about the "poverty problem in the United States." This initiative arose in something of a political vacuum. There was no special-interest push for a federal poverty program, and no attempt to make it a black program and to secure black loyalty to the Democratic party. Instead, social scientist Margaret Weir concludes, "the president's vague request to the CEA appears to have been motivated by a more general desire to devise some policies that would give his administration a stamp of originality and energy."[61] Two years later, on 8 January 1964, President Lyndon Johnson announced, in his first state of the union address, "This administration today, here and now, declares unconditional war on poverty."[62] Thus, the War on Poverty predated the beginning of the wave of urban riots by a few months.

The idea became reality in August 1964 when the Economic Opportunity Act was enacted. The Act created the Office of Economic Opportunity (OEO) and gave it the responsibility of administration of the Community Action Program and the Job Corps. The former was designed to administer services to the poor, coordinate poverty functions of the federal, state, and local governments, and to give the poor some responsibility and power in these policy programs. The Job Corps was a job training program aimed at America's disadvantaged youth.[63] Though both were color blind, the Civil Rights Act and War on Poverty seemed likely to help many black Americans.

Despite these initiatives, the threatening racial situation only worsened. Though the crisis was making affirmative action less risky, both the Democrats and the moderate civil rights leaders knew the scrupulous honoring of the affirmative action taboo was the key to maintaining the Democrats' increasingly shaky coalition. The Johnson administration followed a course of color blindness as long as possible.

If color blindness was to be the official justice model of the Johnson administration, however, it would have to be finessed in a way to seriously address the impending racial crisis. This at least was the conclusion of one of the initial architects of the War on Poverty, Assistant Secretary of Labor Daniel Patrick Moynihan. Moynihan sought in early 1965 to convince his fellows in government that there was a threatening racial problem, manifested in the crumbling black family structure. In March, his report, "The Negro Family: The Case of National Action," circulated through the administration.

The report was not designed to advocate any specific policies, but only to focus the upper levels of the government on the problem. The thesis of the report was that racism and three hundred years of deprivation had created a "tangle of pathology," mostly visible in the condition of the African-American family. High rates of divorce, illegitimate births, and drug use kept poor black families poor, and ensured that "in terms of ability to win out in the competitions of American life, they are not equal to most of those groups with which they will be competing." Therefore, "A national effort is required that will give a unity of purpose to the many activities of the Federal government in this area, directed to a new kind of national goal: the establishment of a stable Negro family structure."

Moynihan quite explicitly justified his case with the discourse of crisis management. The report began ominously, with a one-sentence paragraph: "The United States is approaching a new crisis in race relations." Policy directed toward establishing a stable black family structure offered "the only possibility of resolving in our time what is, after all, the nation's oldest, and most intransigent, and now its most dangerous social problem."[64] Writing before Watts or any of the major ghetto uprisings, Moynihan said,

> The principal challenge of the next phase of the Negro revolution is to make certain that equality of results will now follow. If we do not, there will be no social peace in the United States for generations.[65]

Both the Moynihan Report and a major civil rights speech by President Johnson at the Howard University commencement (which was based partly on the report; see chapter 6) said very little about policy, and instead dramatized the special problems of African-Americans. The speech received favorable support from the civil rights community. Not so with the report, which began to leak to the press in the spring and was soon made public, but reported in a distorted way which emphasized its secret nature and its focus on Negro family problems but not the complex causes identified by Moynihan. After Watts, interest and press coverage of the document grew. In this context, Moynihan's emphasis on the family structure of the blacks seemed to trivialize the entire situation, angering black leaders and making race a hypersensitive subject.[66]

Even more precarious, however, was the possibility of offending whites. The riot in Watts established black unrest as a major issue. The taboo on race-targeted justice was then exacerbated by the perceived moral bankruptcy of any government actions which would "reward the rioters" with benevolent social programs. *Any* nonrepressive crisis management strategies carried some risk.

Thus, while there was a controversy on how to define the riots (political uprising/ghetto revolt versus criminal conspiracy of riffraff), there was also a corresponding dualism in what was seen as the proper response to the riots. The most popular response, and the response dominating public discourse, was to repress the unrest, and avoid the appearance of giving of any rewards to the rioters. According to most scholarly accounts, the riots were viewed negatively, and contributed to a backlash against civil rights and the black movement.[67] In public opinion polls, there indeed seemed to be a slight edge to the backlash position. For example, asked whether the policy of shooting on sight anyone found looting stores during riots is "the best way to deal with this problem," 54 percent of respondents felt this was the best way, while 41 percent felt there was a better way. Asked who was more to blame for the present situation of Negroes, 54 percent said the Negroes themselves were to blame, while only 24 percent thought whites were at fault (22 percent had no opinion). When Californians were asked what were the most important causes of the Watts riot, 36 percent chose "lack of respect for law and order," 28 percent chose "outside agitators," while only 22 percent felt "widespread unemployment" was a cause.[68] Many in government responded to this point of view. The House of Representatives refused to debate a bill from President Johnson to fight rat infestations in slums, but passed with little trouble the antiriot bill mentioned earlier.[69] The presidential campaign in 1968 had law and order as an issue at center stage, with the eventual victor, Richard Nixon, advocating a strong position on the issue. Also, an extreme law and order candidate, former governor of Alabama George Wallace, while losing the election, did surprisingly well, attracting more than 13 percent of the vote.[70] Nixon, in his memoirs, states the "backlash" position clearly:

> I had watched the sixties from outside the arena of leadership, but I had strong feelings about what I had seen happen. I saw the mass demonstrations grow remote from the wellsprings of sensitivity and feeling that had originally prompted them, and become a cultural fad. . . . I had no patience with the mindless rioters and professional malcontents, and I was appalled by the response of most of the nation's political and academic leaders to them. The political leadership seemed unable to make the distinction between a wrong that needed to be set right and the use of such a wrong as a justification for violating the privileges of democracy. . . . By proving themselves vulnerable to mob rule, the political and academic leaders encouraged its spread.[71]

Mindful of this view, and the political gains that the Republicans could win by identifying with it, the Johnson administration was very careful to avoid the appearance of coddling rioters. In other words, there was concern as to whether or not using the discourse of crisis management would be a safe way to advocate and to legitimate race-targeted policies of empowerment to the American public.

Some of the earliest discussions of riot management came in the aftermath of the debacle in Watts. A temporary body, headed by ex-CIA Director John A. McCone, was appointed by California governor Edmund Brown to study the problem. There had been much finger-pointing as to the cause of the Watts riot. For example, Los Angeles mayor Samuel W. Yorty identified the federal government as culpable for cutting off poverty funds to the city, while Office of Economic Opportunity Director Sargent Shriver admonished the confrontational L.A. police department. The McCone commission singled out the repeal of the California Fair Housing Act, the inadequate federal poverty programs, and the "angry exhortations" of civil rights leaders.[72] Meanwhile, Vice President Hubert Humphrey called on business to find work for Watts residents. Aerojet-General, a West Coast subsidiary of General Tire, sprang into action, setting up a factory (tents were the chosen product, since no special skills were required) and hired only blacks with unattractive work records.[73] Soon, five thousand jobs were created by ninety employers targeting the black and unemployed.[74]

To be sure, though business had been quietly encouraged by the government to stave off crises by hiring more blacks as early as 1963, some firms were led to affirmative action by local civil rights demonstrators.[75] But even here, there was an element of threat and disorder. In the summer of 1965, some firms, such as Campbell Soup Company, were engaged in on-the-job training of blacks. Campbell also offered after-hours educational programs. *BusinessWeek* reported numerous corporate attempts at achieving a "balanced" workforce— often in response to threats of picketing, boycotts, and demonstrations. Still, Archie Williams, employment director for the NAACP in Boston, warned, "It will be a long, messy summer in Boston, with a great deal of picketing, selective buying, and litigation."[76]

THE CRISIS WORSENS AND BOUNDARIES BLUR

While business managed the crisis on the front lines, the Johnson administration began to move ahead cautiously and quietly. A surreptitious social policy showing hints of the affirmative action model had supporters in the executive branch at least as early as 13 December 1965, when a memo to Califano from Attorney General Nicholas Katzenbach discussing potential new civil legislation stated,

> Secretary [of Labor Willard] Wirtz is in charge of a task force on employment which is concentrating on affirmative action programs. He believes, and I concur, that the requisite educational, training and related programs which are required should not be devised for Negroes, as such, but for all disadvantaged persons. *Obviously, however, this would permit, and should permit, the concentration of these pro-*

grams in areas in which the beneficiaries would be predominately Ne-gro [emphasis added].[77]

Though he offered no explanation, Katzenbach also cautioned that "it would be wiser as a political matter if the affirmative action programs were not labeled civil rights proposals, as such, although the aims and objectives of this type of legislation could be referred to in a civil rights message."[78] Race-targeting was clearly becoming a legitimate option, if not yet publicly, at least inside the Johnson administration.

As the rioting worsened, Democrats and some members of Johnson's team began to call for stepped-up federal crisis management, seeing in the War on Poverty and the Great Society (the name given to Johnson's overall package of social programs) potential solutions to racial unrest. Senator Stephen M. Young from Cleveland, following rioting in his city's Hough area, demanded "federal action on a large scale . . . The housing program is too small. The poverty program is too small. The program for slum schools is too small. . . . It is clear that the elimination of slum misery will require new programs and much money." Also in 1966, Housing and Urban Development Secretary Robert Weaver said, "Society has to act effectively to redress the deprivations of the environment that occasion despair. We must diagnose the ills of our ghettoes and move to heal their sickness before they explode."[79] OEO director Shriver likewise seemed to share the riot sociology of the civil rights leaders. He told Congress that

> This social dynamite comes from discontent with joblessness, dis-content with inhuman housing, discontent with money-hungry land-lords and merchants, discontent with the raw differences between justice, health, and convenience for the poor and the rest of America. These are the combustibles that fire up a riot.[80]

The Johnson administration was acutely aware of a crisis and seemed desper-ate for insight as to what was going on and what could be done. By the summer of 1967, Johnson was receiving detailed reports on every instance of racial vio-lence for each week. Johnson had appointed a behind-the-scenes working group in the cabinet, chaired by Vice President Hubert Humphrey, to focus on the crisis in the cities.[81] The administration was so concerned and confused (and cut off) that even the most impressionistic accounts of the most casual encounters with young black Americans seemed worth communicating to the President. When George Reedy, former press secretary and member of Johnson's National Advisory Commission on Selective Service, went to Yale University to give a speech on selective service, Reedy reported to Johnson in some detail of his unofficial conversations with black Yale students, from which he believed he received insight into "one of the factors behind the city riots" (this was a pervasive distrust of whites).[82] Similarly, McPherson assumed Johnson would be interested in what insights McPherson could glean from conversations with some local African-American teen-agers whom he knew and invited to dinner.[83] A memo to Califano from a witness at some of the hearings for Johnson's appointed National Advisory Commission on Civil Disorders (to be discussed in more detail shortly) which took place in riot-torn Newark told of how the hearings highlighted the magnitude of Newark's "problems and needs" and the "temperament of the Negro community." The testimony of Newark Negroes was described as being of "electric intensity"; young blacks "alleged to be *fearless*" (original emphasis) and "willing to risk their lives wantonly because they had lost faith in progress by any other route."[84]

The problems of Johnson's reticent leadership and the fundamental tension of perceiving a need for race-targeted approaches, but still finding such approaches too risky politically, had been exacerbated when Newark exploded in July 1967. The apparent necessity of both some kind of empowering action *and* a political smokescreen for the national audience can be seen in a 15 July 1967 memorandum to the president during the riot:

> [Attorney General] Ramsey Clark and [Deputy Attorney General] Warren Christopher are now firmly in the center of the Newark problem. Pursuant to your earlier approval, they are the focal point on Newark programs within the Federal Government and are now quietly inventorying the programs we have in Newark.

The memo went on to add that New Jersey government officials realize "the approach must be 'real slow' because we do not want to pour in new programs to reward the rioters."[85]

Many administration officials began to worry that being less than open about the administration's efforts at crisis management was giving the impression of not doing anything. The crisis led to a most basic legitimacy imperative: a legitimate President had to *lead* (somehow). Certainly Johnson offered no publicly announced repression measures, a fact that was seized on by the Republicans. GOP leaders, including Senator Everett Dirksen and former President Eisenhower, began making wild, unsubstantiated charges about the riots being organized by a nationwide organization and that police had uncovered Molotov cocktail factories. House Speaker John W. McCormack defended the Democrats' color-blind riot responses, including the model cities program, rent supplements, aid to education, and the rat control bill. He argued that the Republicans were attacking these very riot-control measures, and that the riots

must not become "an excuse to turn our backs on the evils of poverty and illiteracy, unemployment and despair."[86]

Under increasing pressure from both Republicans and members of his administration,[87] Johnson felt compelled to make an important statement on how
he was managing the crisis. His conflicting political stance was apparent in a 27
July television address during the Detroit riots. After beginning with a strong
condemnation of the criminal acts which occurred during the rioting and vow-
ing strong support for law and order, he continued by tying government action
not to sympathy for the rioters but to moral traditions:

> The only genuine, long-range solution for what has happened lies in
> an attack mounted at every level upon the conditions that breed de-
> spair and violence. All of us know what those conditions are: igno-
> rance, discrimination, slums, poverty, disease, joblessness. We
> should attack these conditions—not because we are frightened by
> conflict, but because we are fired by conscience—we should attack
> them because there is simply no other way to achieve a decent and
> orderly society in America.

That the rioters were criminals, Johnson agreed. But, he added, "It is responsible Negro citizens who hope most fervently—and need most urgently—to
share in America's growth and prosperity."[88]

Johnson was more specific, but still careful to avoid race labels, at a press
conference on 31 July. Asked what preventive measures could be taken on the
rioting, Johnson mentioned a $75 million dollar fund for summer employment
for (not blacks but) "unemployed young people." Johnson explained, "I think
that work with the various Mayors and appealing through private employers,
and to public officials to show deep concern for the needs of the unemployed in
these areas is absolutely essential." He added, "We must never let up on that."[89]
When speaking to the public, Johnson couched politically risky, nonrepressive,
empowering measures in a safely legitimate color-blind discourse.

A LIMITED AFFIRMATIVE ACTION SOLUTION

There were overt, though limited, race-targeted employment ideas circulating
through the government, seen as logical responses to racial crisis. The threat of
a particular riot situation, as it was occurring, can be seen to make safe advocacy
of an emergency move to the affirmative action model. The legitimacy of race
consciousness to a limited audience of White House officials is apparent in a
memorandum to the Vice President from White House Fellow Wally Baer during the Newark riots, dated 14 July 1967. Police brutality was, as usual, an issue
in the Newark riots:

> The mayor had chances yesterday to head off further trouble, after hearing complaints from Negro leaders, by: . . . Dispatching all available Negro policemen to the trouble area . . . [and] accepting some Negro demands to hire more Negro Police Officers and patrolmen (Negroes comprise over 50% of the population in Newark but only 10% of the police force).[90]

Baer added disapprovingly that Newark Mayor Addonizio instead said he would ask for "money to promote one Negro police lieutenant to captain." A clearer demonstration of this crisis-legitimation effect is a memorandum from Attorney General Ramsey Clark to the president, dated 21 July 1967:

> The deployment of military forces composed almost entirely of whites heightened the tension and anger in the Newark riot area. Undoubtedly, a visible Negro presence would have made it easier for peaceably inclined persons to support the Guard's efforts and would have had a general moderating effect on the residents of the area. The Army states that the Guard has a 30% annual turnover, and determined steps should be taken immediately to correct the racial imbalance.[91]

Affirmative action in the National Guard and police was also taken very seriously by the National Advisory Commission on Civil Disorders, appointed to study the causes of the riots. A 10 August 1967 letter to Johnson from the commission stated that "[o]n the basis of testimony to date," immediate action should be taken to "increase substantially the recruitment of Negroes in the Army National Guard and Air National Guard." Statistics were supplied, showing blacks making up 1.15 percent and 0.6 percent of these organizations, respectively. "The Commission believes strongly that this deficiency must be corrected as soon as possible," the letter added.[92] The letter was immediately passed from Johnson to Defense Secretary Robert S. McNamara, with Johnson explaining, "As you are well aware, this is a matter of highest urgency and I know you will give it your immediate attention."[93] These calls for race consciousness, and the affirmative action unit ideas of focus on racial imbalances or deficiencies in employment, would have been unthinkable in the government in an orderly, noncrisis context. In the effort to manage a racial crisis, however, the ideas were legitimate.[94]

THE REWARDS OF RIOTING

Thus, despite the public appearance of no rewarding of rioters, evidence shows that late twentieth-century crisis managers will empower and not repress. While there is some disagreement as to whether or not the Economic Opportunity Act was originally targeted at African-Americans,[95] the evidence clearly shows that the programs became more black-oriented as the rioting worsened, thus showing government attraction to the most basic unit idea of affirmative action: managing the polity on the basis of race. A disproportionate amount of funding for community action programs began to go to urban areas with large black populations, so that by 1966 racial minorities constituted over half the persons involved in poverty programs taken together (black Americans constituted about 30 percent of the poor at this time). Black participation in institutional manpower training jumped from 21.4 percent in 1963 to 45.4 percent in 1968. Black participation in Neighborhood Youth Corps Projects also was near 45 percent. Another job program, color-blind on its face, the Concentrated Employment Program, had an 81 percent black participation rate in 1968, the year it began. Blacks comprised 54 percent of the Job Corps in 1966 and 60.8 percent in 1970. It was this evolution that led Frances Fox Piven and Richard Cloward to state that "the hallmark of the Great Society programs was the direct relationship between the national government and the ghettoes."[96]

Margaret Weir and James Button see part of the increased black targeting as a response to rioting.[97] In a comparative study of 40 U.S. cities, Button found that OEO program increases were directly related to the riots—specifically, the number of riots a city had experienced from 1963 to 1968. This variable had more explanatory power than either the percentage of poor in a city or the percentage voting. Controlling for numerous variables, such as Congressional power and local government characteristics, Button concluded that the "black riots had a greater direct, positive impact than any other independent variable upon total OEO expenditure increases in the latter 1960s," with the number of riots alone accounting for over half (30 per cent) of the total variation explained by the model (50 per cent).[98]

BUSINESS MANAGES CRISIS WITH AFFIRMATIVE ACTION

By 1967 and 1968, business elites were increasingly advocating racial hiring, usually articulated in the available discourse of crisis management. Alfonso J. Cervantes, in a *Harvard Business Review* article entitled "To Prevent a Chain of Super-Watts," painted a grim picture, with the threat to business's control coming from both rioting *and* potential government response to rioting: "If the businessman does not accept his rightful role as leader in the push for the goals of the 'Great Society' (or whatever tag he wants to give it), we will be increasingly smothered by a growing welfare state ridden with riots and arson and spreading slums largely unchecked by the proliferating programs for the unemployed poor."[99] He went on to advocate special attempts at recruitment, eliminating traditional job testing and qualifications, and special treatments and training programs.[100] Similarly, the Ad Council, a group of advertising executives and businessmen originally formed during World War II in aid of the war, but which continued as a major producer of public service announcements, swung into action in 1968 with a "Crisis Series" of advertising promotions.[101] The council and the National Alliance of Businessmen produced a campaign which implored business, according to one observer, "to give jobs to ghetto blacks before their businesses burned down." The campaign received the largest amount of support of the council's endeavors, with the business press contributing 306 full advertising pages.[102]

This logic, that black violence was to be controlled by hiring black Americans, became widespread. Describing a series of business moves, such as Jersey Bell in Newark hiring black high school dropouts who failed the normal application tests, or Standard Oil of California hiring black employees with arrest records for work at service stations, *U.S. News & World Report* explained, "The aim would be to ease discontent that has brought violence and destruction to many of America's big cities in recent summers."[103] Prudential Insurance began to aid ghetto businesses and hire more blacks after a riot in its home city of Newark. Paul Gorman, president of Bell Systems' Western Electric Company, told the *Wall Street Journal* matter of factly, "If the cities continue to deteriorate, our investment will inevitably deteriorate with them."[104] The Life Insurance Association of America became involved in a $1 billion project to create job and housing opportunities in over two hundred cities.[105]

Any sort of move to get black Americans into the system was increasingly advocated as logical crisis management. Thomas H. Burress of the Greater Philadelphia Enterprises Development Corporation, which was developing a shopping plaza in a black neighborhood and sought to incorporate African-Americans in another way (making residents small stockholders), explained, "If people in the neighborhood own a share of the business, when someone with a Molotov cocktail approaches the place, windows will fly open and residents will say, 'Don't you dare burn my dollar's worth.' We need to build in a vested interest."[106] Black employment specialist and Wharton School professor Herbert Northrup maintained, "The more educated, the more experienced, and more integrated the Negro labor force becomes, the less tension and the fewer problems we'll have in this country." He advocated lowering hiring standards to increase minority employment, warning, "Industry in this country cannot survive with an unintegrated, angry minority."[107]

In the post-riot Detroit climate, affirmative action seemed relatively uncontroversial. White people began to question the universality of their "rational" practices; specifically, "merit" began to change shape and meaning. One utility company official explained,

We believe that we have been unconsciously screening out Negroes by using standards which we once thought appropriate but are really discriminatory. We believe some of these standards should be relaxed and that some people we have rejected were capable of doing the jobs they sought.

Another official explained, "This is discrimination in reverse, but such steps are required to convince the Negroes that we are serious and want them to apply for work with us."[108] Ford Motor Company and 17 other firms promised several thousand jobs to hard-to-employ ghetto residents, and actually hired 55,000 persons. Ford also established two employment offices in the ghettoes of Detroit.[109]

Leading the way, government continued, following the Kennedy precedent and the urging of those studying the riots, to encourage business to hire blacks.[110] And business also worked *with* government in reaching out, race-consciously, to the poor in an effort to secure employment for them. In early 1968, a new program, called Job Opportunities in the Business Sector, was implemented. The program focused on partially government subsidized on-the-job training in the private sector. This program worked with the National Alliance of Business, organized to secure promises of job openings from private businesses. After a year and a half, 150,000 persons had been placed in jobs. The two-year racial breakdown of the program showed 75 per cent of those placed were black.[111] This cooperation also worked on a local level. The Detroit jobs mentioned earlier were a part of program organized by the New Detroit Committee, which represented area industrialists, state and local government officials, as well as black militants. In Tucson, public and private organizations working together produced 125 private and 75 city jobs.[112]

In personally organizing the National Alliance of Business, Johnson relied on the discourse of crisis management at the first meeting to persuade this voluntary organization to reach out to the "hard core unemployed," and to "wake them up in the morning," "scrub them," "teach them real basics: reading, writing, arithmetic," and put them to work. According to Califano, Johnson explained that this was "no bullshit meeting," and that

> You can put these people to work and you won't have a revolution because they've been left out. If they're working, they won't be throwing bombs in your homes and plants. Keep them busy and they won't have time to burn your cars.[113]

The Kerner Commission and the Limits of Color-Blindness

While the above represent concrete benefits that were initiated through fears of violence or demonstrations, there was also a less concrete, though equally important victory. This came as a result of the efforts of a high-profile commission appointed by Johnson to study the riots. The riots focused attention on problems of the black community to an unprecedented degree. Focusing on these special problems with color-blind laws *already in effect* and, as suggested by the violence and the perceived need for a commission, very likely to be seen as inadequate, the commission came to publicize building blocks of the affirmative action model as solutions to the crisis.

The president of the United States appointed the commission during his nationally televised speech on the riots during the Detroit debacle. The commission, christened the National Advisory Commission on Civil Disorders (henceforth the Kerner Commission), was regarded as moderate in political character. It was chaired by the governor of Illinois, Otto Kerner; the vice-chairman was New York City Mayor John Lindsay. It featured I. W. Abel, president of the United Steelworkers of America; Herbert Jenkins, chief of police in Atlanta; Charles B. Thornton, chairman of the board of Litton Industries; Roy Wilkins, executive director of the NAACP; Katherine G. Peden, commissioner of commerce in Kentucky, and four Congressmen: Senator Edward Brooke, Republican, of Massachusetts; Senator Fred Harris, Oklahoma Democrat, and Representatives William M. McCullock, Ohio Republican, and James C. Corman, Democrat, of California. The Kerner Commission lacked spokesmen for highly conservative positions, and was criticized for this. It also lacked radical, militant spokesmen, and was criticized for this also.[114] Johnson explained that leaders were not chosen according to political label; rather, men and women were selected on the basis of "experience, ability, and judgment" who were thought to be able to weigh all the evidence "and make a judicious finding."[115] Openness and rising above politics were constantly stressed.

The hearing of 7 October 1967, on employment policy, was of special interest to the commission since, as Kerner stated at the beginning of the hearing, employment was mentioned by witnesses as the most urgent need of the inner-city black community. Based on the premise that there was a crisis and that the status quo was not working, this was a friendly forum for new and controversial ideas. Thus, when University of California-Berkeley economist Arthur M. Ross cited black unemployment statistics as evidence of discrimination, the meaning was different from when similar statistics were recited in hearings for the Civil Rights Act of 1964, when the issue was whether or not there was a need for a color-blind law. Now, with a color-blind law in effect, the imbalanced numbers still suggested discrimination to those present, but also suggested that a different conception of discrimination was needed to manage the crisis. Ross thus cryptically introduced his recitation of black employment statistics: "Of course, it cannot be expected that any population group would ever have strictly proportional representation in all occupations, but if the principle of equal opportunity is translated to results, then Negroes will gradually obtain a more equal share of the better jobs."[116]

The words *equal opportunity* and *discrimination* thus showed some fluidity in meaning in the discussion, and emphasis tended to center on *unintentional* discriminatory acts—acts not then thought to be covered by Title VII. That is, the meaning of *discrimination* was used to cover unintentional hiring practices that have a differential impact against blacks, an important component of the affirmative action model and a bone of fierce contention in the twenty-five years hence (often called the adverse or disparate impact theory; see chapter 6). So while some witnesses at the hearings expressed classical liberal ideals, such as industrialist H. C. McClellan (training programs were best since blacks want an equal chance and not a "cheap" job; hiring by numbers and not competence was contrary to the "whole concept of the American system"[117]), most witnesses expressed doubts about the utility of training programs for overcoming the problems of the "hardcore unemployed." This was the universalist euphemism of dubious sensitivity for inner-city blacks, chronically unemployed due to inadequate education, work experience, and/or police record—"discrimination."

The affirmative action concept of discrimination was advocated with a sense of urgency. Some critics of race-conscious hiring have questioned the need for immediate results that affirmative action has come to represent.[118] One can see the source of this impatience in the riot-torn political climate of the middle 1960s. The testimony of chairman of the National Manpower Advisory Committee and Columbia University economics professor Eli Ginzberg is revealing. Mentioning an EEOC report on white-collar labor which found that over 25 per cent of firms in New York City did not have any black white-collar employees, Ginzberg asked rhetorically, "So how much evidence do you need of the continuing fundamental nature of the discriminatory pattern?"[119] He also, quite ominously, warned how easy it would be for riots to paralyze New York, explaining that urban blacks could not be hidden, as blacks had been in the South for 350 years.[120]

Ginzberg argued against training, which he characterized as just "nibbles" at the problem, to address the present crisis. His attitude toward traditional approaches bordered on contempt as he argued, albeit with a peculiar twist, for employment quotas:

> I think training in many instances is only a second-best approach to employment. I think a lot of people need the jobs . . . the thing that people need most and want most is to get locked into a normal part of the economy, to begin to earn some money, to be fitted into a real work environment. You have to coach him, support him, give him a little training. But the important thing is to lock him into a job. The other thing is too distant, too far away from them.

> I think your Commission should give consideration to taking a
> much more strenuous position of saying, "Look, the Negroes in the
> numbers that need to be fitted into the economy are not going to be
> fitted in easily, and let's stop fooling around, and let's move to a quota
> system." *You obviously include poor whites also.* But to simply stipu-
> late that larger employers—employers from fifty or a hundred
> workers up—will have to take one or two workers designated by the
> employment Service as needing jobs. [emphasis added][121]

It is interesting that Ginzberg felt it was necessary to include whites in his quota system, an idea that was hardly "obvious" to later affirmative action supporters on the Left. But the liberal economist Ginzberg still saw the problem of unemployment in a color-blind way. Though nothing else in his testimony—or indeed, in the entire undertaking of the commission—gives any indication that there was interest in poor whites, he saw black unemployment as part of a larger unemployment problem.[122] A *racial* quota would not solve the employment problem in its totality, so it was (in this soon to be strangely anachronistic view) obvious to include whites. Still, Ginzberg warned that unless there were thirty-five years of major special efforts, riots would only get worse.

The Kerner Commission hearings were also an occasion to pay special attention to the culture and rationality of the "hardcore unemployed." Their characteristics were often discussed in relation to the qualifications that employers usually deemed indicators of merit but which were now being seen as discriminatory. Particularly targeted were testing practices. Ginzberg attacked the civil service exam, maintaining that good workers flunk the exam, and that the Civil Service Commission "is a disgrace."[123] Frank Cassell, Assistant Vice President at Inland Steel and former director of the U. S. Employment Service, called for the end of any "discriminatory practices which may exist." He meant discrimination as conceived in the affirmative action model. He argued that it was not always best to select the "most qualified" job applicants as revealed by standard evaluation techniques. "I would like to say that the object of testing is to screen people into the system instead of screening them out of the system."[124] Truman Jacque, representing an Employment Service Center in Watts, shared this point of view, urging people to get past

> the screening and measuring devices to what the devices are attempt-
> ing to measure. Since the measuring devices were not standardized in
> ghetto communities, it stands to reason that they are faulty in measur-
> ing traits of character acquired in or colored by the ghetto. When we
> do this, we find many concepts, crucial to the issue, in need of re-
> definition.[125]

Associate research economist at UCLA Paul Bullock also stressed a culture clash between the ghetto blacks and white employers. The government commission was told that ghetto language, demeanor, appearance, ability to adhere to traditional time and work schedules, and tendency toward short-run thinking would all work together to give impressions of unambitiousness.[126]

Thus, traits that may have been thought of as indicators of an unmeritorious or unqualified worker were being redefined as not the worker's problem, but the *employer's* problem. Conventional notions of a "poor work record" were also criticized in the hearings as being inappropriately "middle class." For example, the stigma attached to a record of arrests was seen as hopelessly inappropriate for life in the ghetto, and would have to be eliminated. Failure to overcome these cultural differences, warned Bullock (clearly no stranger to melodrama), "will lead to an intensified conflict in urban America which ultimately—and I mean this quite literally—may tear asunder the very fabric of society itself."[127]

This discussion is important because it showed how much the culture had changed in the three years since 1964. While a Kerner Commission hearing is not the same as a Congressional hearing or debate, it is significant that it was precisely these parts of the affirmative action model, the fragmentation of the merit concept and the movement away from discriminatory intent, which were resisted by the framers of Title VII. Attention was brought to the issue in the spring of 1964 by a case before the Illinois Fair Employment Practices Commission (FEPC), involving a young black man who was denied employment at Motorola Corporation in Chicago. The man, Leon Myart, was denied employment allegedly because of his performance on a multiple-choice general ability test. Myart complained to the FEPC, which held a hearing on 27 January 1964. The hearing examiner eventually ruled against Motorola on 5 March, since the ability test was unfair to "culturally deprived and disadvantaged groups" for failing to take into consideration "inequalities and differences in environment," and Motorola was ordered to eliminate the testing. Motorola was outraged, and appealed to the FEPC, joined by the Employers Association of Chicago (1,400 firms strong), the Illinois Manufacturing Association, and the *Chicago Tribune*. The decision was also blasted by *New York Times* columnist Arthur Krock. Texas Republican Senator John Tower, already suspicious of the powers of the pending Title VII enforcement agency, had the Motorola decision printed in the *Congressional Record* as an argument against a strong enforcement agency. Tower successfully added an amendment to Title VII that stressed that employment tests were to be allowed, unless they were "designed, intended, or used to discriminate" (this language became Section 703 (h) of Title VII).[128]

The opportunity of the crisis thus allowed for an elaborate public exposition of the concept of "systemic," non-intent-based, discrimination. It is notable, however, that these progressive thinkers in 1967 shared a view with civil rights conservatives of the 1970s, 1980s, and 1990s: that the Civil Rights Act proscribed *only* intentional discrimination, outlawed only hiring practices which intentionally used an individual's race against him or her. As Bullock explained it, "So what we must overcome is not merely the factor of discrimination in an identifiable and overt sense, but the results of past discrimination and the results of translating this kind of overt, legally actionable kind of discrimination into other forms of 'discrimination' which get the same results, but without bringing anybody within the purview of the existing legislation."[129] In 1971, the Supreme Court would express a very different view. In *Griggs v. Duke Power,* the Court ruled that in fact Title VII *did* make illegal those acts which may have been instituted for reasons irrelevant to race, but which had the result of harming protected classes (see chapter 6).

Finally, especially notable was the testimony of Martin Luther King, who came about as close as possible to advocating affirmative action without actually doing so. *Twice* King discussed the idea of racial preferences in employment, and twice he avoided calling for their implementation. First announcing that he was going "to be as candid and truthful" as he knew how,[130] King defended the idea of "compensatory or preferential treatment," though he acknowledged it was an idea which makes "some of our friends recoil in horror." King mentioned a meeting he had with Prime Minister Nehru of India in which they discussed preferential policies for bottom caste Untouchables there. King said that Nehru explained that these policies were their "way of atoning for the centuries of injustice [they] have inflicted upon [their] brothers and sisters." Yet King did not specifically advocate the Indian approach, saying instead that "America must seek its own way of atoning for the injustices she has inflicted upon her Negro citizens" and that "[n]ew ways are needed to handle the issue before we have come to a new stage in the development of our nation, and the one intent of its people."[131]

Later in the testimony, King mentioned the veterans' Bill of Rights, and the civil service and employment preferences for veterans, saying that the Negro and the veterans have been deprived in similar ways. Remarkably, King did not suggest a Bill of Rights for Black Americans, or black employment preferences: "I am proposing, therefore, that just as we granted a GI Bill of Rights to war veterans, America launch a broad based and gigantic bill of rights for *the disadvantaged,* our veterans of the long siege of denial" (emphasis added). King went on to emphasize the plight of the white poor, whose labor, he said, was also hurt by slavery.[132]

The Kerner Report: An Affirmative Action Publicity Blitz for the National Audience

In a sense, the entire undertaking of the Kerner Commission was race-conscious, despite the color-blind name "National Advisory Commission on

Civil Disorders." It was blacks who rioted. This fact was basic to the whole project. All training, welfare, education, and housing programs discussed, whatever the color-blind label, were discussed in the context of how they would change the situation of blacks in the cities of America.

Despite the obviously racial character of the disorder, the great majority of the recommendations of the Kerner Commission's *Report of the National Commission On Civil Disorders* (or *Report*) struggle to retain a color-blind, need-based orientation. For example, in the area of government hiring practices, the *Report* states: "We strongly recommend that local government undertake a concerted effort to provide substantial employment opportunities for *ghetto residents*" (emphasis added).[133] Similarly, in the area of private employment, the commission urged "[o]pening up existing public and private job structures to provide greater upward mobility for the *underemployed,* without displacing anyone already employed at more advanced levels" (emphasis added).[134]

While the above are clearly intended to focus specifically on the disadvantaged, the *Report* did go to some lengths to advocate the new idea of discrimination, redefining it in terms of whether or not blacks get jobs and not in terms of the color-blind approach, which hinges on the malicious intent of employers. In its recommendations for employment policy, the *Report* asserted that "[a]rtificial barriers to employment and promotion must be removed by both public agencies and private employers." It then went on to explain that "[r]acial discrimination and unrealistic and unnecessarily high minimum qualifications for employment or promotion often have the same prejudicial effect."[135] Similarly, in the area of the civil service, the *Report* stated,

> [W]e recommend that municipal authorities review applicable civil service policies and job standards and take prompt action to remove arbitrary barriers to employment of ghetto residents. Re-evaluation is particularly necessary with respect to requirements relating to employment qualification tests and police records.[136]

It is notable that, despite the long tradition of simply adding points to the scores of a group seen as disadvantaged (the veterans), no one ever suggested this model for blacks. Instead, elaborate ruminations of what qualifications were really necessary for a job were spelled out. The fidelity to color blindness in the term *ghetto resident* also is notable in this context: one wonders how it would be determined which applicants lived in "the ghetto," unless elaborate official ghetto boundaries were determined (bringing up the ironic possibility of people moving into ghettoes to take advantage of relaxed standards of qualification). Still, the *Report* was a strong defense of what became known as the disparate impact approach to theorizing discrimination, and significantly, the Kerner report is cited twice in the petitioner's brief in the landmark *Griggs v. Duke Power*

Supreme Court case, in which several parts of the affirmative action model received ultimate approval in 1971 (see chapter 6).

While the *Report* helped to broaden the definition of discrimination, it did the same for racism, removing any notion of evil intent. The introductory summary was especially controversial for its sweeping indictment of white society, which was seen as racist and *guilty* in a general way that today is familiar but which, at the time, was new and radical. The *Report* claimed that not lawless blacks but "[w]hite racism is essentially responsible for the explosive mixture which has been accumulating in our cities since the end of World War II."[137] Trouble stemmed from the "racial attitude and behavior of white Americans toward black Americans." Not necessarily consciously racist, the *Report* explained that "[w]hat white Americans have never fully understood—but what the Negro can never forget—is that white society is deeply implicated in the ghetto. White institutions created it, white institutions maintain it, and white society condones it."[138] Here, then, was a publication, authorized by no less of an authority than the president of the United States, telling the rest of government and the American people that racism was not just segregated lunch counters or epithets shouted in hatred. Racism was apathy, lack of empathy, and insensitivity towards the plight of African-Americans, and *all* white Americans were guilty.[139] A point underscoring the radical nature of the *Report* is that the basic conclusion, "Our nation is moving toward two societies, one black, one white—separate and unequal," was surprisingly similar to the view expressed by that great Cassandra of the Cold War, *Pravda*: "two Americas which are at war with each other—that of the rich and strong and that of the poor and humiliated, of whom the majority are Negroes."[140] *Newsweek* observed, "Here was the formal ethic for action missing conspicuously from recent proclamations of the Congress and the President himself: an indictment of the System, by a top-level organ of the System, that might ring louder and clearer than all the thunder of the ghettos themselves."[141]

The *Report* did make two recommendations for affirmative action, in two specific areas. One of these, not surprisingly, was in the area of law enforcement, where it was urged that recruitment and promotion policies be reviewed to result in more black hiring.[142] A similar plea for race-conscious hiring was urged in news organizations, which lacked "an effective link to Negro actions and ideas."[143] Neither of these examples, however, actually represent "pure" race-based hiring. Like the strategies of some courts in a different context, where veterans' preference was equated with merit hiring, in both of these examples race is understood as a qualification. This is particularly true in the case of the police force, as tense relations with the white police forces almost always initiated the rioting. However, the *Report* statement that "[i]f the media are to report with understanding, wisdom, and sympathy on the problems of the cities and the problems of the black man . . . they must employ, promote, and listen to Negro journalists"[144] was especially significant, as it flies in the face of modern notions of truth accessible by reason alone, by suggesting a racial epistemology, and anticipates later academic debates over who can rightly teach in college ethnic studies courses.

The work of the Kerner Commission directly produced very little in the way of concrete policy initiatives. Its basic recommendation was for the creation of one million jobs each in the public and private sectors. To the surprise and disappointment of many, the Johnson Administration, increasingly involved in the war in Vietnam, said very little about this or the *Report*. Johnson wrote later that the primary problem was funding the recommendations, which the Bureau of the Budget estimated would have cost an additional $30 billion on top of the $30 billion worth of programs already planned. He explained,

> That was the problem—money. At the moment I received the report I was having one of the toughest fights of my life, trying to persuade Congress to pass the 10 per cent tax surcharge without imposing deep cuts in our most critical Great Society programs. I will never understand how the commission expected me to get this same Congress to turn 180 degrees overnight and appropriate an additional $30 billion for the same programs that it was demanding I cut by $6 billion. This would have required a miracle.[145]

However, the lack of an authoritative statement from the administration had some insiders nervous. On 1 March, the release date of the *Report* summary (the full text was released on 3 March), McPherson expressed his doubts about the policy of silence in a memo to Califano. McPherson felt that ordinary moderate people were disturbed and wanted answers, though he was hopeful that "the same moderate people who are concerned about answers to our dilemma will understand the budgetary and other strictures that prevent the complete implementation of the report."[146]

Moderate civil rights leaders, apparently, did not understand. For example, a letter to McPherson from Roy Wilkins, dated 4 April 1968, approximately a month after the Kerner Report was released, shows Wilkins sensed the closing of the policy window, to use political scientist John Kingdon's term.[147] Wilkins wrote, "I would be deeply distressed if this significant opportunity for developing the commitment to the big programs were to be lost."[148]

While the *Report* amounted to little in the way of policy, it was a smash hit in terms of publicity. Here was its true role in the legitimation of affirmative action: bringing heretofore obscure and controversial affirmative action ideas to a wide audience, sanctioned with the escutcheon of a (reluctant) president. Bantam Books's first edition of 30,000 copies was sold out in three days, and 1.6

million more were sold between March and June, 1968. After four years, the paperback edition had gone through twenty printings. The *Boston Globe* devoted twenty full pages to the summary on 1 March, and fourteen more pages for the full text on 3 March. Members of the commission were interviewed on television. Marlon Brando read aloud from the *Report* on the Joey Bishop television show on 25 April.[149] And of course the *Report* had its political uses:

> The Kerner *Report* clearly served to punctuate dialogues in domestic political affairs. Political figures tended to use it to confirm or restate their previous positions or commitments, or to launch more vigorous efforts to pursue policies they sought anyway. Thus, the *Report* became a legitimating instrument for diverse public-policy proposals. It was also used symbolically. A black politician such as Representative Adam Clayton Powell, in addressing his supporters, could rhetorically document the view that whites are guilty of oppressing blacks by holding up a copy of the *Report* as he talked.[150]

Its most powerful role was as a legitimating instrument. While it was not surprising that the Kerner report would receive endorsements from Martin Luther King, Floyd McKissick of CORE, Whitney Young of the Urban League (and even black power advocate H. Rap Brown), it is more significant for this study that the *Report,* with its clear support of the affirmative action concept of systemic discrimination, the notion of a justice which requires treating "differences" differently, its indictment of white society writ large, and also some recommendations for racial hiring, received considerable support from white groups at the center of power. Tom Wicker of the *New York Times* wrote the following on the Kerner report: "Reading it is an ugly experience, but one that brings, finally, something like the relief of beginning. What had to be said has been said at last, and by representatives of that white, moderate, responsible America that, alone, needed to say it." Mayors Carl Stokes of Cleveland, Jerome P. Cavanagh of Detroit, Hugh J. Addonizio of Newark, and Samuel W. Yorty of Los Angeles supported it. "Many Protestant, Catholic, and Jewish organizations endorsed the report, too; and so did thirty-six liberal congressmen from New York City and a few other urban areas."[151]

Racial Crisis After the Kerner Report

The threat of racial violence continued to affect policy into the Nixon administration. Though rioting had peaked in 1967, as measured by number of deaths, it had flared up again with King's murder and after in 1968, when the number of racial incidents and the amount of property damage exceeded any of the previous years,[152] and it was unclear whether the lower level of violence in 1969 was a part of a simmering-down trend or just a temporary cooling. Even in June 1970 one report held that black upheavals were occurring at the same rate as in 1969, and warned that the potential for urban riots continued to be great.[153] Despite Nixon's basic "law and order" campaign theme, his administration followed a similar logic of crisis management.

In fact, his campaign suggested an explicitly race-conscious crisis management strategy. Nixon advocated the development of "black capitalism," pushing the importance of private property, explaining, "People who own their own homes don't burn their neighborhood."[154] The campaign also aired television commercials which promised that black capitalism would end racial strife.[155]

In a speech to the Industrial Relations Research Association on 30 December 1968, Republican Secretary of Labor designate George P. Shultz gave a high priority to racial inequality in employment, calling black teen-age unemployment "appalling," and stating that under the "explosive" circumstances of huge black unemployment, "supervisors cannot conduct business as usual." According to Shultz, "special measures" would be needed in a new approach to employment.[156] Historian Hugh Graham argues that in 1969 rioting was not just spontaneous and chaotic, but that demands were becoming increasingly organized for specific objectives, with violence used as a bargaining chip.[157]

It was in this context that Shultz and Nixon advocated the Philadelphia Plan, an affirmative action program for government construction contractors which required contractors to show manning tables (promising proportional representation of blacks in the workforce) in order to win government contracts. There is more to the story of the plan, as will be described in chapter 7, but part of the reason for its safe advocacy was crisis management. For example, at a meeting in Philadelphia on 29 April of government leaders and Philadelphia civil rights leaders, Clarence Farmer, from the Philadelphia Human Relations Commission, predicted a race riot if the government did not implement the controversial Philadelphia Plan.[158] Farmer also wrote a letter to Comptroller Elmer Staats, a staunch critic of the plan, warning that its cancellation would "cause tensions which may erupt into demonstrations or civil disorders."[159]

On Chicago's South Side, job protests forced the suspension of twenty-three construction projects in 1969. Also in that year, demonstrations in Pittsburgh turned into a melee, injuring fifty black protestors and twelve policemen. Seattle also saw violence over job opportunities, and job protests occurred in New York, Cleveland, Detroit, Milwaukee, and Boston. In Boston, the chairman of the Massachusetts advisory committee to the U.S. Commission on Civil Rights and dean of Boston College Law School, Father Robert F. Drinan urged a Philadelphia Plan for Boston. He asserted to the Department of Labor, "If serious disorders break out in the near future, the Department of Labor can be cited as the proximate cause of such disorders," and also wrote to Shultz, "I cannot predict what might happen when the black community of Boston learns that you have broken your promises."[160]

In Congressional debates on the Philadelphia Plan, the threat of loss of government control was also cited in efforts to gain support for the affirmative action plan. For example, Republican Senator John Pastore of Rhode Island stated the logic of crisis management:

> What we are confronted with is the fact that this Nation suffers with a difficult situation, a very distressing one, which erupted in Philadelphia not too long ago. Because the administration has the responsibility of doing something about it before it erupts all over the country, it initiated a plan it thought would solve the problem for the time being . . .
>
> [W]e are disrupting that program, which I think is essential for the stabilization of the situation, which has become a quite irritable one and serious one in the Nation.[161]

While no federal court cases (to this author's knowledge) made reference to the riots in the opinion, there was one important case which came down in favor of race-conscious hiring and which seemed clearly influenced by the rioting, if not the Kerner report also. The case, *Porcelli v. Titus*,[162] involved the school system in the city of Newark, New Jersey, which had been the site of some of 1967's worst rioting. It was one of the first reverse discrimination cases. Titus, the Superintendent of Schools, had urged the school board to suspend the normal procedure of promoting teachers to administrative-level jobs, which had involved promotion lists based on an examination procedure. The move, which was accepted by the school board, would allow more blacks to move to these administrative positions. In Titus's testimony, cited in the opinion, he explained that in the more than two decades since the old promotion procedure was developed, "the conditions in the City had changed, educational philosophy had changed. There was a high [*sic*] premium on sensitivity than had existed hitherto." Titus continued,

> Sensitivity, as I see it, is that element of a person's personality which makes him aware of the problems of the ghetto, unique to the circumstances surrounding being a member of a minority group, sensitive to the educational needs that go [*sic*] out of the deprived conditions in many of our—most of our neighborhoods. * * * As I see it, and I see it very clearly in my own mind, anybody who is in a position of leadership today in a city like Newark has to be able to identify, has to be able to understand.

Titus also explained, with support from other witnesses, that suspension of the promotion lists was the right move because the lists "didn't represent the kinds of racial mix that I feel is most important in accomplishing an educational program in the City of Newark."[163]

Various educational experts also testified in the case, arguing that an "educational crisis" existed in Newark. This was supported with evidence of reading levels in Newark's schools, consistently below the national median at all levels. Incredibly, while the nation was beginning its agony over the issue of forced *integration* of schools, the low-achievement evidence was used in the Porcelli case to support the right of blacks to have black school leaders. Dr. Robert Trent, an urban education professor at Brooklyn College, testified that "if you want significant change in the school performance of the ghetto population, it is highly advisable to involve as much as you can competent black professionals." Trent argued that blacks could serve as inspiring role models, blacks would be better at disciplining black children, and blacks would be better at bringing black parents into the educational process—though in some circumstances a white person could also do the job.[164]

The opinion, noting the similarity between Trent's testimony and that of Titus and school board members, concluded that discrimination did not occur in the case, since, "despite a desire to provide an avenue for the appointment of more Negro administrators, the ultimate objective of the Board was to promote those persons most qualified to suit the needs of the Newark school system."[165] The plaintiffs appealed and lost.[166] Racial hiring was thus successfully equated with merit hiring in a case that almost certainly would never have happened had Newark not been rocked by rioting in the summer before Titus began to reevaluate the promotion procedure. The rioting and the need to maintain order had made room for a discourse of affirmative action which avoided the tricky issue of African-American moral worthiness. To maintain order and control, justice could now institutionalize the "reality" of race.

Why Did the Discourse of Crisis Management Justify Racial Hiring?

In this chapter, I have argued that race-conscious employment measures became legitimate in part as a way for elites to maintain control, to manage a crisis. But the logic of crisis management, which put affirmative action in the interest of (mostly white) elites, is still not explained. There are potentially many ways to manage a crisis. The more obvious method is brute force, domination, or repression. Put another way, if someone breaks the law, why give that person a job? White society, as the Kerner Commission told us, was thoroughly racist, and one may expect such a society at least to stick to the backlash position: Manage the crisis with police, not programs. Thus the question remains, Why was not repression the method of federal crisis management?[167] Why was the discourse of crisis management available to justify these controversial policies?

The answer can be approached on many different levels. We can focus on President Johnson, the man who had the power to order repression, or simply to let the states repress, if he so desired. On a personal level, it would seem unlikely that this often compassionate, sensitive man would ever order repression of black rioters. He was personally concerned about minority welfare. Teaching Mexican-American children in Cotulla, Texas, as a young man in the 1930s seemed to have had a significant effect on his ability and tendency to empathize with the marginalized, and he reportedly kept a picture of the students in his Oval Office desk.[168] He chose aid to minorities to be one of his enduring legacies, explaining to visitors to his Texas ranch, "This is the tree I expect to be buried under, and when my grandchildren see this tree I want them to think of me as the man who saved Asia and . . . who did something for the Negroes in this country."[169]

Johnson's hopes for his place in history suggest another level of explanation, focusing on the institution of the presidency. Presidential scholar Stephen Skowronek suggests that one of the taken-for-granted rules of the presidency is that each president will strive for some creative leadership project—that presidents seek unreflectively to go down in history in some distinctive way.[170] Though Johnson identified strongly with Franklin Delano Roosevelt, the architect of twentieth-century American liberalism, Johnson's goal was not simply to emulate Roosevelt but to surpass him. He explained that his goal since youth had been "improving life for more people and in more ways than any other political leader, including FDR."[171] This was a president who saw as his mission government- aided empowerment of the people, who preached a liberalism determined to use government to maintain and strengthen rights and protect the people from almost any potential harm.[172] Johnson seemed to think unreflectively of government empowerment and assumption of responsibility as panaceas.

Choosing the aid of African-Americans along with Vietnam's protection as historical achievements seemed to limit options. The riots came as a terrible shock to this president. At first, he simply could not understand it and denied it was happening. Recall his reluctance to act during the Watts riot, and his unavailability to Califano. "How is it possible after all we've accomplished? How could it be? Is the world topsy-turvy?" he asked.[173] After some reflection, Johnson concluded that the problem was "We're not getting our story over" to blacks, and challenged his cabinet, "When members [of Congress] complain about riots, ask them what they're doing to build programs like Model Cities and rent supplements."[174] To begin shooting blacks would be to admit to the failure of not only his civil rights laws but the Great Society—and even implicate his foreign policy project: "I'm concerned about the charge that we cannot kill enough people in Vietnam so we go out and shoot civilians in Detroit."[175] Ultimately, Johnson, despondent, seemed to empathize with the rioting black: "He's still nowhere. He knows it. And that's why he's out on the streets. Hell, I'd be there, too."[176] For Johnson, repression was an option only of last resort, for though affirmative action measures were risky, shooting black Americans undermined his entire leadership project and threatened his legitimacy as a president.

While Johnson saw himself as completing FDR's New Deal and committed to empowering approaches to crisis management, this may be a comment less on this man than on 1960s liberalism. No one in the administration thought repression was the answer. Johnson's aids and advisors were all guided by a logic that led them unreflectively to a race-targeted solution of aid and augmentation of Great Society programs already in existence. Repressive measures were attractive only as smoke screens and stopgap measures.

While this thinking may have been guided by liberal ideology, it may also have been shaped by lessons of history. There was a pervasive sense that repression alone would not work. Robert Kennedy argued that repression would mean greater problems for future generations; Minnesota Democratic Senator Walter Mondale agreed that repression was "a clear invitation to greater trouble."[177] This may have been the lesson learned from the government's experience with organized labor, which remained bloody and violent for decades until suppression was supplemented with legislation recognizing labor unions and empowering them in the 1930s.[178]

It must also be noted that while some public opinion polls showed Americans tilting toward repression, this view was by no means unanimous. One Gallup poll in August 1967, which asked what could be done to prevent riots in black areas, showed 41 percent of the sample chose various repressive options, such as "institute stronger repressive measures" (19 percent) and "find and punish groups that are responsible" (14 percent). However, another 41 percent of respondents chose various empowering measures, such as "make more job opportunities available" (10 percent) and "provide education for Negroes, vocational training" (9 percent).[179] Not given a chance to choose repression, many seemed to concede that the Great Society strategy of crisis management had merit. Some of Johnson's own poll reports showed 66 percent of whites agreeing that "setting up large-scale work projects to give jobs to the unemployed" would be "effective" at preventing future riots.[180]

Yet the race-targeted empowerment and affirmative action logic of crisis management cannot properly be considered opinion-poll driven, President

Johnson crisis management, or even liberal crisis management. It is true that Republicans and conservatives in Congress stressed law and order, as did Nixon in his 1968 campaign, but on this, they were not united. Kentucky Senator and ex-GOP National Chairman Thurston Morton called reliance on repressive measures "irresponsible," and asked for a $1-billion anti-riot chest.[181] Though it is not surprising that liberal Republican Senator Jacob Javits would advocate nonrepressive crisis management measures, he did so with the unpublicized approval of Everett Dirksen, who was then spouting law-and-order rhetoric.[182] Eight Republican governors (including Spiro T. Agnew of Maryland, Nixon's conservative vice president) met in August of 1967 and released a report which advocated both better police training and programs to get at the causes of the riots, maintaining that both would be needed to avoid the "unacceptable ultimate result of a society based on repression."[183] And with the stench of burning ghettos still lingering in the air, and the threat of more carnage, the Nixon administration showed many signs that it was quietly following the same logic of crisis management that guided Johnson.

There were, in fact, constraints perceived or taken for granted which trumped all of the concerns in domestic politics. Considerations of liberalism or domestic politics aside, the reason the discourse of crisis management worked to legitimate affirmative action was that the global cultural rules of crisis management in the 1960s, a global moral model, granted legitimacy only to nonrepressive measures. In other words, there was a global audience for the federal government's crisis management, and this led to a limited range of possible legitimate actions. The global audience of American domestic race policy became important in the World War II battle with a racist dictator in Europe and a nonwhite imperial power in Asia. The ensuing rise of worldwide human rights discourse and newly independent states in Africa and Asia, the importance of both intensified by Cold War moral competition with the Soviet Union, would shape the logic of crisis management for American leaders of any ideological stripe, and within the government and private meetings, race-conscious approaches were legitimate. (For the national public audience, Johnson officials tried to remain faithful to color blindness.)

Indications that America's stature in the world system would render some domestic practices in the area of race relations illegitimate can be dated to the rise of the Nazis. President Franklin Delano Roosevelt's promotion of America as a force of democracy in a battle with a racist dictator and against Japanese expansion in the developing world transformed domestic racial repression and discrimination into foreign policy disasters (and thus made American traditions of equality and universalism much more powerful discursive resources, a point developed in chapter 6). The world context thus affected domestic policy boundaries. Typical was a Public Affairs pamphlet which urged Americans to see racial equality as a war issue, pointing out that the Japanese were publicizing American mistreatment of blacks to developing nations. The authors explained, "In effect they said: 'Why should you believe what any American white man says? Look what happens to the colored American citizens; do you think that anything better will happen to you?'"[184]

The Cold War only intensified the importance of the world audience. The United States was then competing with the Soviet Union for dominance in the ultimate struggle of modernity: attainment of the most just and advanced society possible. This moral struggle was not simply a clash of incommensurable ideals of justice, though there were obvious and considerable differences between the two countries' ideals. Following World War II, the world saw the institutionalization of the doctrine of human rights, most clearly articulated in the 1948 Universal Declaration of Human Rights. While part of the competition of the Cold War was the demonstration of the superior justice of political and economic systems, the discourse of human rights set up a global model of this justice, and thus some boundaries or rules for the competition.[185] Violent repression, not uncommon in dealing with labor unrest in the nineteenth century, was now out of the question. America, as leader of the free world, was especially scrutinized by both Communist countries and newly independent "third world" states.

In the first civil rights crisis of the Cold War era, President Dwight Eisenhower invoked the world context in justifying his use of troops for enforcement of school desegregation. Using troops embarrassed the United States, but the resistance of whites in Arkansas was even worse, and the immorality of it threatened the legitimacy of the United States as a leader in the Cold War. President Eisenhower told a national television audience,

> At a time when we face grave situations abroad because of the hatred that Communism bears toward a system of government based on human rights, it would be difficult to exaggerate the harm that is being done to the prestige, and influence . . . of our nation . . .
>
> Our enemies are gloating over this incident, and using it everywhere to misrepresent our whole nation.[186]

Domestic policy and foreign policy had thus become linked. The liberation of Western colonies in the developing world only reinforced the new global boundaries of legitimate action and made race a particularly salient issue. The rise of the civil rights movement was proof to the increasingly curious world that America's domestic situation was immoral. Secretary of State Dean Rusk explained in August 1961,

> The biggest single burden that we carry on our backs in our foreign relations in the 1960s is the problem of racial discrimination here at home. There is no question about it.
>
> We are dealing with forty or fifty new countries that have become independent since 1945, and we are living through a decade of read- justment of the relationships between Western Europe and the rest of the world—a decade when the white race and the nonwhite races have got to re-examine and readjust their traditional relationships.
>
> Our attitude on a question of this sort is of fundamental importance to the success of the foreign policy of the United States.[187]

The world press gave the Civil Rights Act of 1964 rave reviews, as the ad- ministration knew,[188] heightening the tension surrounding the federal response to the riots. The race riots, which affected the entire country, threatened Ameri- can legitimacy before the world audience. They were signals to the world that racial injustice in the United States was not simply confined to a few states in the South. Every riot was a Communist victory in the Cold War—which at this time was actually raging hot, as American troops battled a nonwhite people in Vietnam.

Predictably, the world press gave extensive coverage to the riots. While some papers emphasized the irony of race riots in the wake of important civil rights gains, it was difficult for even the most sympathetic observer to put a positive spin on the events. The conservative *London Telegraph* urged more efforts at treating the underlying causes. Papers in the developing world tended to treat the riots sensationally, as rebellions or as part of a civil war. Radio Moscow, Johnson was told, "highlighted news reports on the riots and has editorialized extensively on the economic weaknesses and the class distinction which have resulted in a breakdown of law and order." Despite Johnson's careful efforts to avoid repressive measures, and even before he sent troops into Detroit, Peking radio announced, "racist authorities, under Johnson's instructions, brought in more than 4,000 National Guardsmen and state police, armed with rifles, pis- tols, and machine guns" to help Newark police "in the wholesale arrest and slaughter of Afro-Americans."[189]

Stopping the riots was thus essential, but the logic of crisis management re- quired that techniques must be quiet or congruent with the new moral bound- aries of human rights. In dealing with the riot situation, Johnson explained later,

> I knew what I had to do, but I could not erase from my mind the awful prospect of American soldiers possibly having to shoot American cit- izens. The thought of blood being spilled in the streets of Detroit was like a nightmare. I could imagine the inflammatory photographs ap- pearing within hours on television and on the front pages of news- papers around the world.[190]

The "inflammatory photographs" would probably have been published around the world, with the ensuing erosion of American legitimacy in Vietnam and the world arena in general, whether the President who ordered the repression was a Democrat or Republican, liberal or conservative.

The black urban rioting coincided with major United Nations human rights initiatives, including the International Convention on the Elimination of All Forms of Racial Discrimination (1965), the International Covenant on Economic, Social, and Cultural Rights (1966), and the International Covenant on Civil and Political Rights (1966). In this context, it is understandable that a U.S. delegate at a human rights conference in Tehran would gush with relief in a telegram to Washington detailing the successful appearance of African-American civil rights leader Roy Wilkins at the conference, which took place after King was assassinated and black violence swept across America in response. Wilkins received great amounts of attention from the world press and foreign diplomats, and he defended U. S. interests and foreign policy against what were described as "Soviet-initiated attacks":

> Delegation believes Wilkins visit major success from U.S. standpoint. It undercut any tendency to use King assassination and aftermath as springboard for criticism of U.S.; highlighted broad American unity in facing up to admitted U.S. race problems; and projected calm conviction that U.S. would work through its problems, by democratic means, to successful solutions. We have been immensely helped by his presence.[191]

Thus, the discourse of crisis management in the 1960s was available to legitimate government race-conscious policies for elite audiences since there were constraints on government response to the violence, and it was these constraints that were seen as ultimately more binding than domestic policy taboos. In a sense, a world model of human rights (which the United States ostensibly shared, albeit with its own peculiar qualifications of the taken-for-granted meanings of certain groups) limited responses in much the same way that the color-blind model limited the ways that civil rights would be conceived in the early 1960s. The goal of maintaining order and control superseded the goal of maintaining color-blind orthodoxy, though it is notable that Johnson stretched the discourse of color blindness as far as he could in justifying his administration's furtively race-conscious actions, and it was primarily a temporary body, the Kerner Commission, which made the clearest government moves to affirmative action in response to crisis. It is also worth noting that the Johnson administration hardly gave the Kerner *Report* a ringing endorsement.

The liberal identification of affirmative action and race-targeted policies of empowerment thus results partially from the simple fact that the riots occurred on the watch of a liberal leader. Nixon and the Republicans were mostly playing politics with the rhetoric of repression or law and order, hoping to de-legitimate the Johnson administration in the eyes of the national audience, many of whom said they wanted repression. There is little reason to suspect that they would have responded differently than the Johnson administration, however, and in the early years of the Nixon team, Republicans quietly hedged against additional disorder with its own affirmative action programs.

For crisis-managing business leaders, different boundaries of legitimate action applied. As private companies, they did not clearly have an audience for their employment policy actions. They promoted *their own* racial hiring (as opposed to general policy advocacy) in local contexts, almost always in cities that saw bloody rioting, and in these contexts their action produced little if any public outcry. The fact that overall unemployment was very low—averaging 3.8 percent in the riot years—also made it easier for companies and the public to accept private affirmative action crisis management.[192] Cold War capitalists as well as Cold War government with global aspirations had an interest in taking responsibility for urban rioting.

In summary, the legacies of the urban riots and the cultural logic of crisis management were, first, a fragmented civil rights movement, a radicalized black audience, and an ensuing decline in the authority of the spokesmen for a color-blind, nonviolent approach. Second, business elites were forced to institutionalize building blocks of the affirmative action model in order to maintain order and control. Energetic recruitment and training, the original meaning of affirmative action, blended into overtly racial hiring decisions, the erosion of traditional ideas of merit, and the fading importance of discriminatory intent. Third, while not advocating racial quotas, the federal government began to advocate policy on the basis of its ability to reach out to black Americans and get them to work, to be a part of the system. Fourth, the report of a high-profile government commission spread the word of a race-conscious theory of discrimination, the disparate impact approach, and widespread white responsibility for black unemployment.

The urgency of the crisis would also be burning in the background of actions by all civil rights officials, including those of the bureaucrats who were to enforce the law. As we will see, however, their eventual advocacy of the affirmative action model was addressed to a very different audience, and rooted in a very different logic.

5

Administrative Pragmatism and the Affirmative Action Solution

We have seen how the Cold War context shaped a jobs-for-black-Americans logic of crisis management when a racial crisis was perceived. Affirmative action was legitimated with a discourse that justified advocacy with the belief or promise that the policy would bring about control or order in a climate short on both. But there is much more to the story. There is another story which shows the rise of affirmative action following a very different logic and carried by a very different discourse. In one of the ironies of affirmative action, the government administrators who were to enforce the color-blind law were also led to affirmative action. They were guided by the logic of what will be called administrative pragmatism,[1] something largely taken for granted in administrative government. Following the logic of administrative pragmatism, and for a parochial audience of fellow administrators, concerned citizens and civil rights groups, affirmative action was justified—affirmative action, it was said time and again, was effective, it was technically necessary, it *worked*.

The focus of this chapter is on the government agencies that were created to enforce both Title VII and the Lyndon Johnson executive order that was directed at preventing discriminatory practices among government contractors. The behavior of these and other agencies tends to follow the logic of administrative pragmatism, that is, the pursuit of cost-effective ways to achieve the agency's goal or purpose.[2] "Success" comes through demonstrably effective and efficient strategies for attaining the agency goal; it is a technician's logic that gives priority to substantive goals rather than legal proprieties.[3]

To a considerable extent, this logic is *built into* administrative agencies, which were created to solve problems, and to do so fairly but more efficiently than the courts could.[4] Though the pursuit of justice is built into or taken for granted in the Western project of modernity (as discussed earlier), and the use of state power to achieve substantive goals of justice is apparent throughout American history,[5] it was not until the turn of the century, the Progressive Era, that problem-solving administrative agencies began to be created on the state level in significant numbers. America was industrializing rapidly, with new complexities and new dangers. Like good modern people, the Americans applauded the progress but demanded justice, and many saw the courts, wed to conservative legal formalism, as a frustrating obstacle.[6] Enter the administrative agencies.

Given a problem to solve, the value of any agency can be determined by how effectively and efficiently it solves the problem. On a more personal level, the careers of administrators may often be judged by this measure. Consequently, they strive hard for success and perhaps even harder to avoid some embarrassing failure. For example, "In regulating pesticides, EPA [Environmental Protection Agency] is keenly aware that if a product it has registered is later shown to produce cancer on a large scale, the agency will be crucified and the careers of all concerned blighted, if not destroyed."[7] Administrative agencies will thus often tend toward a logic of administrative pragmatism, which in this parochial context may supersede other cultural rules—even the moral boundaries of the color-blind model. In other words, it would be less risky to advocate affirmative action than to preside over a demonstrably failing agency.

This is, as we will see, roughly the story of civil rights administration. Some scholars have argued that the civil rights enforcement agencies were the sites of a group-rights, affirmative action ideological takeover.[8] But as we saw in the preceding chapter, civil rights groups were not pushing any ideology and were in no position for any sustained takeover activities, and in fact we do not need an ideological takeover theory to explain what happened. Nor will it do to simply say that the administrators were being rational—rationality and interests are shaped by contexts and assumptions that are fundamentally cultural. The EEOC and the OFCC were created to solve a problem, but it was not just to stop discrimination. The tragic black unemployment picture was mentioned again and again in congressional reports and hearings for the Civil Rights Act. Following the American causal model of natural society and abstract individualism in the racial context, the agencies were created to *bring about black economic equality* by preventing discrimination. The legitimacy of this goal of substantive justice (racial equality) formed a precondition that made a largely technical discourse of administrative pragmatism a safe vehicle for affirmative action advocacy. The goal was taken for granted as part of American tradition (the focus of the next chapter).

The organization of the chapter is as follows. First, I give some historical background on discrimination law, and highlight the inherent pragmatic difficulties in administration. Then I examine the development of affirmative action building blocks in administration in the EEOC and OFCC. Finally, I illustrate parallel pragmatic practices in the courts, which have also tended toward goals of substantive justice.[9]

Failures of the Classical Liberal Model and the Recurring Affirmative Action Solution

The history of the administration of equal employment opportunity is the history of the dominance of the color-blind model and its continual subversion by the logic of administrative pragmatism. Put another way, the practical difficulties of the color-blind, classical liberal antidiscrimination program became apparent many times to government officials even before the Civil Rights Act of 1964 became law. As described in chapter 2, the classical liberal enforcement model of equal employment law before the Civil Rights Act of 1964 fit what has been called the responsive role of government, that is, a low-visibility posture, responding to individual complaints rather than undertaking systematic regulation and surveillance.[10] The approach is color-blind. The state sees no racial differences, only abstract, freely contracting individuals, and assumes that society also sees no racial differences. If a person can show that racial difference has gotten in the way of his or her employment aspirations, that is, this person was discriminated against, the state was to intervene to protect this person's civil rights.

Civil rights groups embraced this model and saw it as in their interest to stamp out any institutionalized racial recognition, either in government or in private industry, which had for so long held African-Americans subordinate. Despite the faith that civil rights leaders may once have had in this model, Roosevelt's first wartime Fair Employment Practice Committee (FEPC), the limited federal agencies of the 1940s, the 1950s, and 1960s, and the state FEPCs showed a clear pattern of pragmatic difficulties enforcing it, and again and again sought to go beyond it—usually tending toward the affirmative action model.

As mentioned earlier, President Franklin D. Roosevelt began the tradition with the 1941 Executive Order 8802, which prohibited discrimination in defense industries and in government. This order established the five-person FEPC, setting the federal precedent for the agency approach, which relied on color blindness and moral persuasion and conciliation but lacked real enforcement power. In 1943, Executive Order 9346 expanded coverage to all government procurement contractors, and re-created the FEPC with seven persons, but similar impotence. At the end of the war, Congress dissolved the FEPC.

President Harry S. Truman got into the act in 1948 with Executive Order 9980, which created the Fair Employment Board within the Civil Service Commission, to ensure equal opportunity in government, and then again in 1951 with Executive Order 10308, creating an eleven-person Committee on Government Contract Compliance, which studied the problem of discrimination by government contractors. It accomplished little, but it did issue a report on discrimination that provided impetus for President Dwight D. Eisenhower's 1953 contribution, Executive Order 10749. This order created the fifteen-person President's Committee on Government Contracts, headed by Vice President Richard M. Nixon. The committee broke no new ground, other than the expansion of the number of persons in the organization; its roles included advising, investigating, and making compliance reviews.

The first order to give real power to a watchdog agency was President John F. Kennedy's 1961 Executive Order 10925, which created the President's Committee on Equal Employment Opportunity (PCEEO), chaired by Vice President Lyndon Johnson. The PCEEO was to supervise government contracting agencies to ensure that the contractors did not discriminate, and also was to take some undefined "affirmative action" to ensure that considerations of race, creed, color, or national origin did not enter into the hiring process. A special effort at color blindness was appropriate, Kennedy ordered, apparently unaware that being more neutral than neutral was a confusing demand to say the least. The PCEEO had power to enforce penalties if it found discrimination by government contractors. The PCEEO, however, never issued any penalties.[11]

From the very beginning, the 1941 FEPC was an inhospitable environment for any kind of justice administration. Several of the problems which were to plague the EEOC and exacerbate pragmatic difficulties also had uncanny precursors in the first FEPC. Many of these exacerbating problems stemmed from a lack of commitment. One of these, which cursed both the first FEPC and the EEOC, was an unjustified delay in getting started. Though the executive order which created it was signed on 18 July 1941, the first FEPC investigator was not hired until 25 September, and while the EEOC was not to be given sufficient funds to start regional offices, the same was true for the FEPC, which was given only $80,000 for its first year of operation. The FEPC's six-person leadership committee (Mark Ethridge, a newspaper publisher from Kentucky as chairman, David Sarnoff, a Jewish industrialist, Milton Webster and Earl B. Dickerson, two black leaders, and William Green and Philip Murray, representatives of the AFL and CIO, respectively) had chronic problems of staff turnover, a problem which was also to plague the EEOC. For example, the patriotic leaders of labor appeared to have their minds on things other than the government's new commitment to color blindness. Murray, due to illness, did not attend any of the first four meetings (though he did send a proxy once), and Green attended the first but then disappeared.[12]

Most importantly, though, the FEPC was hindered by a pragmatic problem inherent in color-blind employment justice—the difficulty in proving discrimination. Finding discriminatory intent, crucial in this approach, to be elusive, the FEPC very soon was establishing rationalized guidelines for finding discrimination which would stray from a focus on intent, but promised more effective administration. This project led to hallmarks of affirmative action: a focus on group differences and numbers of blacks employed. Taking account of zero or few minorities in employment would "lend support to the conviction" that discrimination was occurring.[13]

The obsession of the EEOC (and of the OFCC, as I will discuss later) with finding something that *works,* that gets *results,* even if that included race consciousness, can also be seen to a lesser degree in the FEPC hearings, which often ran up against apathetic employers. The FEPC appeared in public as most concerned not necessarily with stopping discriminatory intent, but with getting "results." For example, in a hearing with a shipbuilding executive, Sarnoff chided the executive, who claimed that discrimination was a problem that workers would have to sort out for themselves. Sarnoff argued that the situation required the efforts of government, management, and labor, all of whom

> must cooperate toward the results. I think management has a very serious responsibility, and the first thing I would suggest is that you get yourself in a frame of mind such as that you would feel you have to comply with that Executive Order 8802, that you have got to use your ingenuity to see how to meet the problems as they arise.[14]

It was to be a familiar pattern: A civil rights administrator demanding a demonstrable, result-oriented implementation, though hedging the issue of how this could legally be done.

Throughout the 1950s and 1960s, agencies in search of a useful tool for fighting discrimination were continually led to the affirmative action approach, monitoring numbers and percentages of African-Americans hired as a measure of discrimination. What is interesting is that this "discovery" had to be made time and time again in the years before the EEOC was established, attesting to the extent to which the color-blind model was taken for granted. As early as 6 June 1951, a letter from James L. Houghteling, Chairman of the Fair Employment Board in the Truman administration, to President Truman's administrative assistant Donald S. Dawson was using the discourse of administrative pragmatism to push a racial numbers approach for solving a social problem ("full utilization" being the problem):

> During our telephone conversation this morning, I spoke of the difficulty encountered by the Fair Employment Board in determining what progress may currently be attributed to its efforts and those of

the Fair Employment system set up by Executive Order 9980; and also of the plan of the Board to ask departmental Fair Employment Officers for detailed information as to the employment of Negroes in various categories of the Federal Service.

One of the greatest obstacles at present confronting the Board and the Fair Employment Officers of the various departments is lack of factual knowledge concerning the extent to which minority groups of citizens, and particularly Negroes, are being employed in the Federal Service. The absence of such information stultifies the Board and the Fair Employment Officers in their efforts to carry out the purpose and intent of the Executive Order. Information concerning the spread of Negro employment in the Federal Service would enable the Board and the departments to confine their limited resources and energies to those areas, job categories, and grades needing particular attention. The full utilization of all qualified citizens is especially desirable today because of existing manpower shortages.

This is the logic of administrative pragmatism identifying a goal and sacrificing color blindness in order to attain it—though the letter emphasized the universalist terms (*citizen* and *all qualified*). The letter added, "The securing of information which would pinpoint the departmental areas requiring detailed study and attention would be another step toward economy and efficiency in promoting the objective of the Executive Order."[15]

Similarly, an undated report from Houghteling's Fair Employment Board to the Civil Service Commission, detailing operation for its first year (1 October 1950 to 30 September 1951), reached some "emphatic conclusions," one of which was "that the number of formal complaints and appeals is no measure of the prevalence of such discrimination" and "that the core of any constructive program under the Executive Order must be a systematic, persistent assembly and analysis of the facts, statistical and other, which will determine with some exactness whether, where, and to what extent discrimination is practiced, and how, and by whom." The board suggested as a "logical step" the focused monitoring of the hiring of blacks by the government. This "survey" approach could help reveal "patterns of [black] employment"; in addition, there would be a pragmatic benefit: "One practical result will be to permit the Board and the Fair Employment Officers to concentrate on the areas which require special attention and thus carry out more effectively and realistically the provisions of the Executive Order." Houghteling closed his report with a pragmatically grounded dismissal of the color-blind model:

There is an alternative course—which, however, this Board regards with complete lack of enthusiasm. It is to confine all actions under the Executive Order to the maintenance in good working condition of the machinery for handling complaints of discrimination . . . with this Board merely sitting as a review body for appeals from departmental decisions and abstaining from all efforts to explore the Fair Employment problem beyond the scope of complaints actually filed. If this more limited program is to prevail, this Board is of the opinion that it will be tantamount to nullification of the most important and progressive steps contemplated by the Executive Order.[16]

Houghteling's documents are valuable evidence that it is the logic of administrative pragmatism which led to affirmative action principles and building blocks, *before* the development of the civil rights movement, *before* the racial crisis in the cities, *before* the rise of militant black groups and theories of compensatory preferences. There was no ideology here, no attempt to challenge moral boundaries. In the early 1950s, this technical logic of administrative pragmatism led to a simple conclusion: Choose race consciousness and effectiveness, or choose color blindness and failure.

But the color-blind model was tenacious; it remained as the assumed approach. A decade later, the Kennedy administration made the same pragmatic search for demonstrable effectiveness. However, with the rise of the civil rights movement's crusade of color blindness, Kennedy seemed ambivalent about documents recording the racial breakdown of the government workers, and relied instead on on-the-spot head-counts. A never-issued press release from 20 July 1961 touts a "survey" of minority employment conducted by the President's Committee on Equal Employment Opportunity. Kennedy, using the familiar pragmatic discourse, explained, "The census points up where work is particularly needed to assure equal employment opportunity, and I trust that next year's survey will show great improvement." The release weakly deferred to color blindness, adding, "Since personnel records properly do not include racial information, the survey was made on a 'head-count' basis, and the figures consequently are not necessarily exact."[17]

Part of Kennedy's PCEEO effort with private government contractors was the Plans for Progress program. This was a government-coordinated, voluntary association of large companies who, in return for their special voluntary efforts, were exempted from potential sanctions for violations, which the PCEEO had the authority to wield. The program, directed by Kennedy friend Robert Troutman, Jr., was criticized by civil rights groups who had little faith in the voluntary approach (though Kennedy considered the approach "successful"[18]), and Troutman resigned after a year.[19]

Though criticized for ineffectiveness, Plans for Progress was another early example of an affirmative action approach, an effort directed at getting the right numbers of blacks hired, and not at stopping intentional discrimination. Troutman's focus was on group difference, not evil intent. According to a 23 August

1962 press release of Troutman's official resignation letter, Kennedy's response, and a Plans for Progress report, Troutman had organized a massive statistical analysis of racial hiring patterns of Plans for Progress companies, in pursuit of results measured not by fewer complaints of discrimination but by successful minority hires. The report explained that he wanted to study the big picture of racial discrimination, and requested details from companies of over 500,000 employees. Troutman argued that from experience with "prior approaches to major employers regarding this problem" which were "limited mainly to policy statements of nondiscrimination, . . . it was clear that results based on such efforts alone would require many generations, if ever, for Negroes to enjoy a respectable proportion of the nation's better jobs." Troutman added, "As I saw it, an active effort by these firms, directed by their presidents, was badly needed."[20] Troutman established a series of one-year goals, including asking one hundred firms to design some plan for "progress"; Troutman's subcommittee would then measure the "results" of these plans. Like some of the ventures the EEOC was to undertake some years later, the project had a rationalized, social science approach: "[W]e devised a gauge of 52 jobs and compensation categories so that measurement from time to time would be possible."[21] Troutman's report was filled with statistical data of ratios of blacks hired in various jobs. Kennedy expressed great satisfaction at this, and defended his friend in his official letter accepting Troutman's resignation, saying, "We are indebted to you for the creativity and ingenuity you have shown in attacking a great national problem, for your remarkable contribution of time and energy, and for the leadership you have provided."[22] Troutman's affirmative action goal of a "respectable proportion" of jobs to be filled by blacks escaped comment.

State commissions modeled after the first Roosevelt FEPC also seemed to have pragmatic difficulties with the color-blind model, and sought (meekly) to move beyond it.[23] These state FEPCs, more long-lived than the early federal efforts, were the subjects of criticism and studies which focused on their machinery of justice, the reliance on the complaints of individuals. For example, Leon Mayhew, in his doctoral study of the Massachusetts FEPC carried out in 1961–62 (published as a book in 1968), found that there was a marked tendency for African-Americans to make complaints against the specific firms that did *not* discriminate. This was because they tended to apply for jobs where there were already other blacks hired, usually friends or family. Firms with no blacks, which may have been guilty of discriminating in the past, were not receiving black applicants and thus were not the subject of complaints.[24] Thus, the enforcement mechanism could not touch those firms which were the most egregious discriminators. In addition, relying on individual complaints was often criticized as being too slow and laborious, thus putting great strain on the

FEPCs and the individuals who had filed the complaints of discrimination and who, one would assume, were in need of a job. Also, some critics charged that the complaints made did not reflect the actual experiences of discrimination, because those who did not believe in the system would not file complaints.[25] Difficulties with the FEPCs even had the character of a game of logic. The anti-discrimination statutes considered a purposely concealed job notice an act of discrimination, an act of evil intent aimed at persons of color. However, since the enforcement mechanism was only activated when an individual made a complaint of discrimination, the FEPCs *could not know about an effectively concealed job notice,* simply because by definition those whom it harmed could not know about it. They could only know if an inquisitive person somehow discovered that job notices at a firm were being concealed, and made a complaint.[26]

One of the primary pragmatic complaints against the FEPCs and the classical liberal conception of discrimination has long been that it places an unreasonable burden on the complainant. The records of FEPCs in finding probable cause in investigations of *sworn* complaints of discrimination are surprising. For example, in New York, 8,973 complaints were received in the first twenty years (1945–65), with finding of probable cause to verify discrimination in 1,753 of them—only 20 per cent.[27] In New Jersey, probable cause was found in 14 per cent of cases.[28]

Instructive in this regard is a document from the EEOC, intended as a guideline for minorities, entitled "How to File a Complaint Against Unlawful Job Discrimination." A clear picture emerges from this document as to why these cases were so hard to verify. The document includes the following statements:

You have a right to complain if: Employer refuses to hire you when you are qualified for a job opening.
Employer refuses to let you file application but accepts others.
Union or employment agency refuses to refer you to job opening.
Union refuses to accept you into membership.
You are fired or laid off without cause.
You are passed over for promotion for which you are qualified.
You are paid less than others for comparable work.
You are placed in segregated seniority line.
You are left out of training or apprenticeship programs.
    AND . . .
The reason for any of these acts is your race, color, religion, sex, or national origin.[29]

This was a rather big "AND." Significantly, there are no guidelines provided for *how* people could know if these opportunity denials were the result of their race, sex, religion, or national origin. This was precisely the problem the administrators themselves faced in attempting to verify complaints.

Not surprisingly, then, many argued even before the EEOC experience that discrimination was an injustice that was simply too difficult to prove. Mayhew suggested that the difficulty is inherent in the job system: "The mechanisms for allocating persons to occupational and residential roles or niches are so constituted and structured as to regularly produce situations which give the appearance of discrimination, or which are easy to interpret as discrimination, but which do not involve any discrimination in the legal sense of the word."[30] Communication failures (for example, a memo that was never sent), common in any complex organization, may give an appearance of discrimination, or qualified complainants may not realize that their competition is even better qualified, and so are left with a feeling of being discriminated against. There are, in fact, *many* potential excuses for discrimination, and many benign business actions which could lead one to feel discriminated against. The point here is that the classical liberal conception of discrimination seemed to have demonstrable practical inadequacies in protecting individuals from having some status trait inhibit their free pursuit of ends, their equality of opportunity. Discriminatory intent is difficult to prove *and* discern. State agencies were thus seen by critics as "floundering" in the "bog of individual case handling."[31]

The logic of administrative pragmatism tended to point to affirmative action in myriad minor agencies well before the passage of the Civil Rights Act of 1964, though the color-blind model never lost its hold on the policymakers who created the agencies. Still, these past forays into the classical liberal concept of discrimination foreshadowed what was to come for the EEOC of the 1960s. Based on the previous twenty-five years, it seems remarkable that the EEOC clung as mightily to classically liberal color blindness as it did.

The EEOC and Its Inauspicious Beginnings

The Equal Employment Opportunity Commission was created to enforce Title VII of the Civil Rights Act of 1964. This section of the law declares, "It shall be an unlawful employment practice for an employer . . . to fail or refuse to hire or to discharge any individual . . . because of such individual's race, color, religion, sex, or national origin."[32] Thus, "The mission of the Equal Employment Opportunity Commission is to obtain the highest possible degree of compliance with Title VII of the Civil Rights Act of 1964, which eliminates all employment discrimination based on race, color, religion, sex, or national origin in all industries affecting interstate commerce."[33] Nothing in the law orders the EEOC to be concerned with racial proportions in employment and, in fact, one section, 703 (j), specifically prohibits such a concern:

> Nothing contained in this title shall be interpreted to require any employer . . . to grant preferential treatment to any individual or group on account of an imbalance which may exist with respect to the total number or percentage of persons of any race . . . employed by any employer . . . in comparison with the total number or percentage of persons of such race . . . in any community . . . or in the available workforce in any community.[34]

Title VII thus embodies the classical liberal, color-blind model of justice in that it is designed to protect abstract individuals from having legally unreal status traits get in the way of their economic activities. Economic equality was assumed to result from this model.

The jurisdiction of the EEOC was initially discrimination by private employers with at least one hundred employees, labor organizations, and employment agencies. Each year, the minimum number of employees dropped by twenty-five until it reached firms with only twenty-five employees. This included, by 1971, 328,000 employers, or about 75 percent of the nation's labor force, excluding the self-employed and smaller employers.[35]

The central office of the EEOC included five commissioners who were to serve terms of five years, including a presidentially appointed chairman and vice chairman, as well as a supporting staff. As mentioned previously, the EEOC was to enforce justice in a way similar to the World War II FEPC and the state FEPCs. A sworn charge (or complaint) would be filed by an individual within ninety days of the alleged discrimination. An investigation would be carried out to determine probable cause. Following such determination, the EEOC was to initiate confidential conferences, conciliations, and persuasions with employers. The law placed a sixty-day limit on this processing time. Failing this, however, there would be no public hearings held, as with many state FEPCs. Instead, the Commission was to merely notify the complainant that it had failed. The complainant could then attempt enforcement on his or her own. The statute would allow thirty days from receipt of the Commission's notice to begin suit in the courts if the complainant desired to do so.[36] At this point, the attorney general could intervene if the action was seen as a matter of public importance, and then the Justice Department would carry the burden of pressing the lawsuit.[37]

While the Civil Rights Act of 1964 was widely hailed as the most important civil rights legislation in American history, it was also severely criticized. In terms of its antidiscrimination law, it was susceptible to all criticisms made of the color-blind model of justice as utilized by the FEPCs in the preceding two decades. In addition, the EEOC was even weaker than the FEPCs. It was described as enfeebled, even powerless. Michael Sovern wrote in 1966 that

Title VII's enforcement machinery has no precise precedent any-where in the history of fair employment practices legislation. Prede-cessors can be found, however, for each of its major elements. The commission with power to conciliate but not to compel has been tried and regularly found wanting. Letting the complainant sue was one of the original modes of anti-discrimination law enforcement (criminal prosecution was the other), and it has never worked.[38]

Head of the NAACP Legal Defense and Education Fund Jack Greenberg called the EEOC "weak, cumbersome, probably unworkable"; James Farmer of CORE declared that "before an aggrieved person can get a remedy, he may have found another job or starved to death."[39] Thus, the EEOC seemed to have a mechanism that would be even more ineffective than the state FEPCs, which already had demonstrable inadequacies.

Compounding the EEOC's problems, however, were the circumstances of its beginnings, which could fairly be described as a fiasco. For example, following the passage of the Civil Rights Act of 1964, there was a one-year moratorium set before Title VII was to go into effect, to give firms time to cease their discrimi-natory practices. However, during the first eleven months of this period, no move was made to get the fledgling agency off the ground. Thirty days before enforcement day, the EEOC had no leadership, no staff, and no office. The U.S. Commission on Civil Rights has stated that "[o]n the date Title VII became ef-fective, EEOC had only a skeletal organization and staff and no operational pro-cedures." Communication and supervision problems made it even more difficult to get started.[40]

The first years of the EEOC were characterized by disorganization. Professor Alfred Blumrosen, on leave from Rutgers Law School to assist the new agency, wrote, "When I arrived in Washington to deal with the federal-state regulations of EEOC, I found total confusion."[41] While the EEOC was in such an organiza-tional shambles, Franklin Delano Roosevelt, Jr., the EEOC's first chairman, seemed to have his mind on other things. Sworn in on 2 June 1965, and with one month to start the historic civil rights enforcement agency from scratch, Roose-velt excused himself for a week of yachting. Two months later, "when Congress was considering the next fiscal year's budget for the EEOC, Roosevelt, aston-ishingly, was off sailing again," and was thus conspicuously unavailable for testimony.[42] Blumrosen describes the fearless leader as a competent bureaucrat, but "forever chasing the will-o'-the-wisp of political office"; he adds that the "office songwriter took the tune of the Navy 'Fight Song' and wrote a parody beginning, 'Franklin's away, my boys, ...' "[43]

As with the first FEPCs, staffing the EEOC with both commissioners and per-sonnel proved to be quite difficult. In its first five years, the EEOC had four different chairmen, with none retaining office as long as two years. Staff turn-over was equally rapid across upper levels. Roosevelt, Jr. abandoned ship after less than one year at the helm, to attempt what was to be an unsuccessful bid at the office of governor of New York. In addition, between Roosevelt's May 1966 departure and the swearing in of Stephen Shulman in September 1966, were three crucial months where the EEOC was *without any chairman at all*. Other commissioner posts remained vacant for more than a year on three different occasions.[44] Significantly, one of the results of the tumult at the top was, in Blumrosen's words, "de facto staff power" to be creative, to chart a new course through the "open water" of discrimination law.[45]

In this atmosphere of discontinuity and disarray, the EEOC struggled to set up its civil rights shop with what most observers considered to be a grossly in-adequate budget, putting strong cost pressures on all policy decisions. The EEOC budget for fiscal year 1966, negotiated while the chairman of the EEOC was delighting in his yacht, was $2.75 million, considerably less than the $3.2 million requested (thus putting the EEOC below the Office of Coal Research and the Federal Crop Insurance Program in terms of budget and staff[46]). It was enough of a decrease, in fact, to prevent the struggling EEOC from open-ing its planned regional offices,[47] a problem which had also affected the first FEPC.

Each year, while the coverage of Title VII was increasing, the EEOC re-quested a budget increase, and was denied its full request.[48] For example, for fiscal year 1967, the EEOC asked for $6.6 million, an increase of $3.85 million from the previous year, partly to cover costs of a staff increase of 196 positions. The staff increase was disallowed, $5.87 million was requested instead, and $5.2 million was granted. Fiscal year 1968 brought the EEOC's jurisdiction to its maximum, and the request of $7.15 million was downsized to $6.5 million.[49]

The drama of these budget debates, which were at times quite hostile,[50] can-not be properly understood without some knowledge of the predicament that the EEOC was in at the time: The agency was being "deluged" with complaints of discrimination.[51] The backlog of complaints, which was there from the first day that the agency was open, overwhelmed the tiny, hastily organized agent of jus-tice. Apparently, no one had anticipated the massive number of cases that the EEOC would receive.[52] During its first few months of operation, it was receiv-ing about two hundred complaints a week—far more than the inexperienced, meager staff could handle.[53] None of its first 8,854 complaints were processed within the statutory limit of sixty days, and a backlog of 3,000 cases accumu-lated in only one year.[54] Of the first 15,000 complaints received, 6,040 were earmarked for investigation, and 3,319 investigations were completed. At the level of conciliation, only 110 were actually completed. One of the reasons for the absurdly low rate of conciliations was the fact that for the entire United States of America, there were only five conciliators employed by the EEOC.[55]

The case backlog seemed to dominate the consciousness and culture, almost as legend, of the newborn EEOC. One observer characterized the early years of the EEOC as "the birth pangs and infancy of a new agency struggling for life under what have to be regarded as difficult conditions."[56] A staff member from the early days said, "The agency was new, there was so much work to be done. We needed more people, more positions, more money." Comments from the early staff suggest the image of a ship under siege:

> "Very hectic. Very hectic. Loads and loads of work. We worked all the time. I had worked overtime so much until I had gotten to the point I didn't know what my normal salary was . . . After the opening up of the EEOC, [charges] just poured in."
>
> "The stacks of files mounted up and mounted up and mounted up . . . You'd write your decisions and they would sit in your supervisor's office for months sometimes."
>
> "Well, EEOC was just a big hustle and bustle and it was unorganized. They just had pounds and pounds of paper stacked here and there."
>
> "[W]e were initially programmed for something like about 2,500 charges. We received 6,000. We've been dying ever since."
>
> "Someone once told me that 4,000 charges were waiting the day they opened the door. So we were always overwhelmed by the numbers, even in the early days."[57]

With the massive number of cases to be investigated (the backlog was over 125,000 cases by 1976[58]) came delays in the time of processing. As noted above, the law stated that complaints would be processed in sixty days. By August 1968 the average case was taking sixteen months to complete;[59] other estimates were as long as *two years*.[60]

Civil rights leaders were, predictably, unhappy with this state of affairs. One leader stated, "After the first flurry of hope among Negroes in small town or rural areas, where complaints were filed, there came a feeling of complete hopelessness, when the complainants never heard from the EEOC." In May 1967, Whitney Young said before a Senate committee that

> The actual agency experience, which has demonstrated that the Commission cannot enforce compliance, has given rise to disillusionment and lack of confidence. These conditions have led the American Negro to suspect that legislation, supposedly guaranteed to provide equality of opportunity, is full of loopholes and political terminology.

He is rapidly losing faith in the democratic process to achieve his goal of equality of opportunity.[61]

In short, the EEOC was perceived by many as a failure.

Non-Race-Conscious Pragmatic Innovations

As described earlier, the logic of administrative pragmatism will direct agencies toward the means believed necessary for effective implementation and amelioration of whatever social problem the agency was designed to address. The perception of failure is precisely what administrators want to avoid. For the EEOC, this aversion was undoubtedly heightened by the fact that unemployed blacks were burning down cities.

The search for a more efficient way to process the EEOC's caseload within the constraints of its budget and staff was a major focus of activity. There was a clumsy, pragmatic search for a solution which would reduce costs and maintain the color-blind approach. Various "remedies" tried by the EEOC in the 1965-68 period included " 'outstationing' of personnel, written interrogatories, investigation by telephone where possible. . . . Major emphasis was placed on the decentralization of the investigation and conciliation functions as the way to solve the problem of the great number of cases."[62] Other efforts included a production point system which would give three points to an investigator for completing a job; each investigator was expected to earn twelve per month. Special task forces for specific geographic areas were also tried.[63] An effort was made to computerize the whole process.[64] While some in the agency were already seeing affirmative action as a more effective approach, the agency could not simply ignore sworn complaints of discrimination from real people across America. In other words, "[T]he need to respond to the tremendous caseload made academic (temporarily, at least) the debate going on both inside and outside the Commission on the most desirable approach for eliminating employment discrimination."[65]

But it was increasingly clear that responding only to the complaints of properly abstract citizens was a blueprint for failure. The panacea for the EEOC's ills, however, was seen by most as the granting of cease and desist powers to the beleaguered commission. In other words, more enforcement power, and not affirmative action, was seen by most civil rights activists and EEOC staff members as the best solution. In 1969, when EEOC Chairman Alexander was asked in a senate hearing on equal opportunity procedures by Edward Kennedy what suggestions he had "to make equal opportunity less cumbersome and more adequate," Alexander answered by stressing continuing attempts at efficiency but also sanctioning proposals for more enforcement power for EEOC (that is, cease and desist powers, and not greater freedom to pursue racial quotas).[66]

The view of the Johnson administration seemed to be similar. A 1966 memo to Johnson's domestic policy adviser Joseph Califano from Attorney General Ramsey Clark, subtitled "Summary of Proposals of the Task Force on Civil Rights and Recommendations of the Attorney General," contains the results of a task force whose job it was to dream up "proposals for possible legislative and executive action in 1967."[67] Fully fifteen proposals are included under the heading "Nondiscrimination in Employment." Incredibly, *none* of them suggest racial quota hiring or hiring to reach racial "goals"; the affirmative action model is hardly hinted at. The number one proposal, predictably, was to give the EEOC "powers similar to those of the NLRB to hear cases and issue cease and desist orders enforceable in the courts."[68] Two proposals (numbers Nine and Ten, buried amongst the others which focus on technicalities of agency authority) are race-conscious, though they are in the tradition of early calls for affirmative action, relying on talk and training. For example, number Nine proposes "Legislation to provide technical assistance for metropolitan job councils to be established in urban areas to provide local leadership and plans for creating job opportunities for minority groups,"[69] while number Ten proposes (vaguely), "To step up commitment of personnel and funds to development by the federal government of a comprehensive human resources plan for improving employment and training opportunities for minority groups."[70]

As late as 1972, Vicente T. Ximenes, former EEOC commissioner, said,

> That Commission has to be a first-class Commission, if it ever is to function properly. At the moment, it is a second-class Commission. It needs Cease and Desist powers. Unless we get those enforcement powers into that Commission, the name of the game for those people who complain of the companies and the unions is delay. Delay, delay, delay. We had complaints there from people who would have to wait two and three years to finally sit down and negotiate—not receive justice, just negotiate and conciliate.[71]

In the early years of the commission, increased enforcement powers for the EEOC would have had to come from efforts of Johnson's Task Force and the cooperation of Congress. Efforts there, however, were thwarted. Several years later, the Equal Employment Act of 1972 did give the EEOC the power to bring lawsuits against employers, but it stopped short of giving cease and desist authority, as wielded by the National Labor Relations Board.

Affirmative Action as Pragmatic Solution

In retrospect, the move from the color-blind model of justice to the race-conscious model can be seen less as an ideological move and more as one dictated by pragmatic logic. The model of justice which viewed all individuals as universal abstractions appeared not to work, either towards the ends of social problem-solving effectiveness or cost effectiveness. To the EEOC bureaucrats, whose agency was showing few signs of success, and who were under political pressure from civil rights groups to do *something* and also perhaps stressed by a siege mentality, a new approach appeared to be necessary to attack the mountains of paper in the EEOC offices. The EEOC had a limited audience for its performance, and that audience was already booing loudly.

There was a crucial event in the administrative history of the development of affirmative action. An analogy with architecture captures the significance: design critic Charles Jencks claims that modernism ended its reign on 15 July 1972, at 3:32 P.M., when the Pruitt-Igoe Housing projects in St. Louis were dynamited.[72] Similarly, a symbolic moment occurred which marked the decline of the modernist, color-blind model of justice and the official arrival of a racial view of reality from the federal government. This moment came on the day in March 1966 that the EEOC sent out its racial reporting (EEO-1) forms to every employer in its jurisdiction, requiring employers to keep track of the race of every employee—marking the benign institutionalization and reification of blackness in America. Instead of protecting abstract Americans from the harm of discrimination, the form explicitly created *whites* and *blacks,* who were hired in each firm in varying proportions.

Legal scholar and EEOC adviser Alfred Blumrosen instigated the development of what was to become the EEO-1 form, though as we saw, he was one of many in the history of government equal employment opportunity efforts who were guided by the logic of administrative pragmatism to see race reporting as necessary. The EEOC happened to share a building with the PCEEO, the small, short-lived agency whose Kennedy-era job was to oversee equal employment opportunity in companies under contract with the government. Blumrosen went to PCEEO offices one day in the summer of 1965 to ask a question, and found boxes of the PCEEO's Form 40s—or, as he puts it, "There I discovered a goldmine." Form 40 contained race counts ("zero lists" of employers with no black workers, "underutilization lists" of employers with very low percentages of black workers) of the workforces of government contractors, though they were not used in any program by the PCEEO. Blumrosen likened the potential of this kind of reporting to a "sociological radar" which the government could use to find the most serious discrimination without having to sit and wait for complaints to bubble up. He explains:

> I saw this as perhaps the most important tool in any program to elimi-
> nate employment discrimination. Here were lists of major employers
> excluding minorities in a massive way which outraged any reader of
> the statistics . . . Here at last was a basis for government-initiated pro-
> grams which were not based on complaints and which could focus on
> possible potential discriminators effectively . . . There was a peren-
> nial shortage of manpower and money in antidiscrimination pro-
> grams. If government could focus, through the reporting system, on
> those employers where underutilization was sharpest, there was a
> possibility of successfully combatting discrimination.[73]

The importance of racial reporting, among other topics, was then discussed in late August 1965, the EEOC's second month in operation, at the White House Conference on Equal Employment Opportunity. The racial reporting proposal was vigorously debated at the conference. EEOC staffers, joined by state anti-discrimination commission officials and some civil rights activists, argued in favor. Protests came from other liberals and blacks who had fought for years to rid American society of discriminatory racial categories and identifications, and had, with the passage of the Civil Rights Act of 1964, apparently succeeded. For example, Clarence Mitchell of the NAACP in Washington, DC, said at the conference, "The history of the reason why we do not include this [racial identifica-tion] is sadly and surely proven, that the minute you put race on a civil service form, the minute you put a picture on an application form, you have opened the door to discrimination and, if you say that isn't true, I regret to say I feel you haven't been exposed to all of the problems that exist in this country." Mitchell called racial reporting the "crevasse which has no bottom" and said that it would "put us back fifty years."[74] Those against the reporting (a coalition which also included business groups, thus forming the unlikely alliance of civil rights *and* business groups against the EEOC), according to a summary report from the conference, claimed with Mitchell that it undermined past efforts to "eradicate racial designations and to encourage employment according to ability and merit." It was also feared that the reports would give tools to those who wanted to discriminate, and that they would be hard to keep away from personnel staffs. Finally, it was argued that voluntary compliance should be emphasized, since reporting "added a suggestion of police action to the activities of the Commis-sion."[75] But the conclusion of the conference summary was that "[r]ecord-keeping requirements would provide employers with a more efficient and accu-rate means of submitting annual reports" and that "[a] well-developed reporting system and similar means of observation of industry and labor practices should help to disclose the existence of unlawful labor patterns."[76]

A letter to President Johnson from yachting enthusiast and part-time Chair-man Roosevelt is revealing of the nonideological, pragmatic discourse used by the EEOC in this early period. As had been the case with agency administrators in general, Roosevelt expressed little concern for legality, issues of justice, or ideology, and one might add that (like many other civil rights administrators) he showed little interest in whether it was sociologically correct to deduce discrimination from black employment rates.[77] In his letter, he wrote,

> Estimates for Fiscal Year 1967 have been submitted to the Bureau of the Budget, designed to meet the pressing complaint load and other needs which far exceed the estimates made last year. Preliminary work has been done on a supplemental budget request for FY 1966, based on the heavy complaint load and the *need* to move forward with affirmative action programs . . . [emphasis added]. The Commission's immediate and pressing effort has been to devise external reporting instructions and forms that will reflect meaningfully the employment patterns in industry without imposing undue burden on employers . . . The objective will be to identify the principle sources of complaints and improve investigation and conciliation procedures.[78]

On the issue of affirmative action programs, "designed for affirmative results," Roosevelt, as if looking for permission, wrote, "The Commission welcomes this responsibility."[79] It is clear that Roosevelt very much wanted to move from the color-blind model, if only to keep his agency alive and prospering, and perhaps aid his gubernatorial aspirations.

On 16 December 1965, the EEOC held its own hearings on the racial reporting system. Support for the system was strong. The discourse of pragmatism was prevalent, exemplified by Dwight Zook, commissioner of the California Fair Employment Practices Commission, who stated, "I think it is absolutely necessary, in measure, to determine not only the current status of equal opportunity, industry by industry, and area by area, but it is very necessary to determine progress, which we all are very interested in." Dismissing dogmatic classical liberals, Zook continued,

> I am a little amazed at the interest of some people in the Civil Rights movement wanting to take the color-blind approach but I think it is very idealistic and unrealistic . . . [S]taff members don't need racial information to practice discrimination but top management needs information to eliminate the practice of discrimination.[80]

William Higgs, of SNCC, reading the statement of Marion S. Barry, Jr., Director of the SNCC Washington office, made similar pragmatic arguments, but added a compensatory argument, missing from the administrators' discourse: "Companies have to make a conscious effort to make up for the past injustices."[81]

At these hearings, there was little voice of protest against this profound change in the construction of identity in the workplace. Only Bernard Frechtman, General Counsel for the National Employment Association, offered any moral/political resistance. Frechtman was baited in a manner similar to the way civil rights representatives had been earlier, when suspicious Congressmen tried to tease out elements of race consciousness in Civil Rights Act proposals. Already, the tables were turning. Frechtman was defensive about his negative position on racial reporting, sheepishly explaining, "I think it [the reporting system] would do nothing more than to initiate and condone a type of discrimination that we are trying to prevent. . . . I would say that this is just not a good idea."[82] Besides the valorous Mr. Frechtman, no one defended the tradition of classically liberal color blindness. The character of the EEOC's audience seemed to mystify even those present at the hearing. They expressed surprise, and even spent time discussing and theorizing about it, suggesting that it was the result of genuine good will on the part of companies, or the recognition of the usefulness of Troutman's Plans for Progress program. The EEOC had then met its audience, and the audience wanted effective enforcement. Sharp boundaries proscribing race consciousness began to blur.

Still lacking confidence, the financially strapped EEOC funded a study, conducted by the Wayne State-University of Michigan Institute of Labor and Industrial Relations, to examine the usefulness of this race-focused approach. The report, made available in September 1966, gives a ringing endorsement to unit ideas of the affirmative action model. The study was, essentially, a trial for color blindness. The report cited a "growing consensus" among intergroup relations professionals on the ineffectiveness of individual complaint processing "on overall patterns and practices of manpower utilization and employment discrimination." A loss of confidence in the model by the black community was attributed to the slowness of the process and the "slight probability that the claimant will obtain the job he originally sought."[83] Following two hundred pages of detailed study, the report concluded, under the heading "Lesson," with advice for agencies like the EEOC. The lesson came down squarely with advice on the pragmatic virtues of the affirmative action model, and specifically the categorization of employees with regard to racial difference:

> Within their legislative mandates and limitations, they might exhibit a great deal more aggressiveness than they have done in the past to collect information with a view to changing existing employment patterns. Systematic data collection can help an agency to assess its effectiveness over a period of time and also to determine existing "soft spots"; both can indicate types of affirmative action which can realistically be undertaken.[84]

A concluding statement, written by Project Director Frances R. Cousens, argued that "pressure" is key in equal employment opportunity, and urged, using a provocative metaphor, a new approach for the EEOC:

> Perhaps it would be more productive for the commissions to study ways of preventing fires whether due to arson or inadvertent causes than to limit themselves to putting out fires. The objective of enlarging employment opportunities for minority group individuals can be served better by various types of affirmative action than by processing any number of complaints.[85]

The statement is important, since Cousens clearly disregards, in the name of administrative pragmatism, one of the cornerstones of the color-blind approach—the intent of the discriminator. In the classical liberal concept of discrimination, evil intent is necessary to make an act discriminatory (arson, following Cousens's metaphor). In Cousens's message to the EEOC, whether or not a fire is arson or accidental is irrelevant. It is still causing damage, part of the problem to be solved.

It was now safe for the EEOC to proceed. With the race-reporting EEO-1 form, the administrators could sit back and look at entire industries or geographic areas, and see racial differences and not just freely contracting, abstract individuals. Thus, in early 1966, the EEOC began to consider investigating employment practices in various industries (and not individual complaints in those industries). The idea was to hold hearings in areas or industries showing few black employees. This new strategy for justice followed from the logic of administrative pragmatism: "[G]iven EEOC's limited budget and restricted enforcement powers, such hearings would be the best available technique for focusing attention on the problem of employment discrimination."[86] It was felt that "The massiveness of the Commission's task tailors its use of EEO-1 data to what has been characterized as a 'wholesale approach,' where the reports are used in grouped efforts in geographic areas."[87]

There was also a more positive attraction to the racial approach. The logic of pragmatism stressed the need to operationalize discrimination in terms of numbers. Since the 1940s, government officials had been speaking of the need for an accurate and consistent measure of discrimination, and this seemed to lead ineluctably to notions of numerical representation. Even in the debates on the Civil Rights Act of 1964 this tendency was apparent. Advocates for Title VII continually used statistics showing that blacks were concentrated in low-paying and low-skilled jobs to legitimate the need for new law (as discussed in chapter 2).

Attempts by the EEOC to justify the use of its controversial race-based numerical reporting system are fraught with pragmatic logic and social science language concerning the need to operationalize the behavior that was supposed to be regulated. For example, EEOC staffers at the White House Conference on Equal Employment Opportunity had argued that the EEO-1 would "*[m]easure* an employer's compliance with the law" and "*[m]easure* the effectiveness of the equal employment opportunity program in the long run" (emphasis added).[88] Rather than the massive institutionalization of the EEO-1, dissenters at the Conference preferred on-the-spot head-counts. Supporters of the EEO-1, according to the EEOC's *Administrative History,* claimed that head-counts would be "unreliable."[89]

The EEOC then held hearings (called "forums") targeted at specific industries in specific areas. These hearings were not based on findings of discrimination, but on findings of statistical underrepresentation—though the distinction was increasingly blurred. Forty witnesses representing management, labor, government, and private citizens contributed testimony in January of 1967 for a forum for the textile industry in the Carolinas. At times, discrimination even began to drop out of the picture as another (more easily measurable) problem took its place. EEOC Chairman Stephen Shulman later wrote that "[t]hrough the forum technique, the Commission was able to focus public attention on employment patterns of a major American industry, and to enlist the interest of a broad cross-section of the community *in a continuing program to develop the human resources of the area*" (emphasis added).[90]

Later targets of the EEOC forums included New York City white-collar employment and the pharmaceutical industry in Washington, DC. Taken out of the context of development, the context which suggests that the EEOC was struggling for a pragmatic approach to demonstrably effective enforcement, the efforts may seem bold, confident, and, in one observer's words, "ideologically militant."[91] For example, the invitational letter to the white-collar hearings did not make reference to the goal of stopping discrimination but stated, "The Commission's principal objective in holding these hearings can be simply stated: to facilitate greater utilization of minorities in white collar jobs."[92] Of course, by looking at America through the numerical racial data of the EEO-1, greater utilization simply meant less discrimination.

On 6 October 1967, new Chairman Clifford L. Alexander, Jr., explained the purpose of the forum more clearly, with more emphasis on pragmatism, neatly laying out the two ends of the EEOC, effective enforcement (a wholesale approach, through education of employers) and efficient enforcement:

> First, we want to show each of you, who is undoubtedly aware of minority employment patterns in your own company, the picture for the industry as a whole. We do not believe it is a picture of which you will be proud.

Second, we want to describe the kind of effort that could help change that picture. We want to attempt to avoid, in both your interest and ours, the time-consuming complaint process which could well be the inevitable alternative to the kind of voluntary action we seek to initiate today.[93]

Alexander stressed the necessity for swift voluntary actions, what another speaker called "preventive medicine."

A similar approach, reflecting frustration with impractical color blindness, can be seen in a July 1968 project outline by the EEOC Office of State and Community Affairs, entitled "Elimination of Discrimination by Affirmative Government Action." The report has an air of confidence and stiff-upper-lip determination that belies the shambles that the commission was in at the time, beginning by stating "These are not survey projects. They are action projects." Citing the high unemployment of blacks, the outline states boldly, "The objective of this project is to increase the proportion of the minority group individuals participating in the labor force as well as numbers of minorities actually hired and to do so by eliminating the discriminatory practices and patterns which have excluded them."[94] The outline also used pragmatic discourse, defending its effrontery: "The project is designed to obtain a maximum return for the investment of limited government effort; the return will be measured in the form of new hiring of numbers of minority employees."[95] The "action projects" were essentially the same as the industry-wide forums already taking place, but more focused. Hearings were to be held with "target firms," identified as discriminatory not by investigated complaints of discrimination, but by EEO-1 data of minority representation or utilization: "Particularly appropriate targets would be firms located in an SMSA [standard metropolitan statistical area] having more than 10% Negro or Spanish-Surnamed population, where the establishment employs 3% or fewer Negroes or Spanish-Surnamed Americans." The agency seemed to relish this thoroughly rationalized approach, offering a mathematical formula for converting percentages of minorities hired to an "index" of utilization.[96]

Administrative Pragmatism in the OFCC

A pragmatic, trial-and-error process can also be seen in the other major civil rights enforcement agency, the Office of Federal Contract Compliance, or OFCC. Created by a 24 September 1965 executive order by Lyndon Johnson and not bound by the prescriptions of the Civil Rights Act (see chapter 3), the OFCC had a different structure than the EEOC and targeted not all firms of a certain size but only government contractors. On the other hand, it was at first similarly clumsy and ineffective.

Johnson's order followed on the heels of similar executive orders, as mentioned earlier, written by Roosevelt, Truman, Eisenhower, and Kennedy, but was different from the previous orders in that it located the enforcement agency, the OFCC, in the Department of Labor, rather than in some free-floating presidential committee, like the earlier PCEEO. The secretary of labor, through the OFCC, was to submit regulations, investigate complaints, review compliance, hold hearings, and penalize noncompliers. The OFCC was also to work with the contracting agencies of each branch of government. Executive Order 11246 obligates government contractors not to discriminate on the basis of race, color, creed, or national origin. Like the earlier Kennedy order, it also requires that affirmative action be taken to promote equal employment opportunity:

> The contractor will take affirmative action to ensure that applicants are employed, and that employees are treated during employment, without regard to their race, creed, color, or national origin. Such action shall include, but not be limited to the following: employment, upgrading, demotion, or transfer; recruitment or recruitment advertising; layoff or termination; rates of pay or other forms of compensation; and selection for training, including apprenticeship.

In other words, the contractor was to make a special effort to ignore race, and to affirmatively ensure that specific individuals were not harmed by their race. At the time, most who paid attention to this uncontroversial part of the order assumed it meant a willingness to recruit and train minorities.[97] Failing these obligations, the OFCC could cancel the contract. Though the OFCC wielded considerable power, by 1969 it had never canceled a contract. Richard Nathan wrote in his report for the U.S. Commission on Civil Rights that "[t]he fact that the sanctions and penalties provided in Executive Order 11246 have been used so infrequently tends to undermine the credibility of the contract compliance program and thus reduce its effectiveness."[98]

What was the OFCC doing, if it was not canceling contracts? It was fumbling around, searching for an administrative strategy that "worked," that could be demonstrably effective. Like the EEOC, the OFCC was not exactly enjoying state profligacy in terms of budget or staffing. Leonard Bierman, senior compliance officer of the OFCC, said in 1969 that the lack of an adequate staff was a major reason that no strong contract compliance actions were taken. The meager staff encountered much resistance from the various agencies within government whose responsibility it was to give contracts, and who did not want to disrupt friendly relations with preferred contractors.[99] For example, when OFCC issued proposed regulations which would require contractors to demonstrate compliance before the contract was awarded, Deputy Secretary of Defense Paul Nitze wrote Labor Secretary Willard Wirtz, explaining that the

OFCC's request "could not be accommodated by this Department" as it was "totally impracticable" for a department "which handled over 15.1 million contract actions in the last fiscal year."[100]

Both government contracting agencies and the contracting companies resented the pressure from the government, and stressed a voluntary compliance approach, like that of the Plans for Progress program. Plans for Progress and its voluntary approach, however, were publicly discredited in 1967 when EEOC Chairman Stephen N. Shulman showed with the EEO-1 forms that Plans for Progress firms in New York City actually employed *fewer* minorities than thirty randomly selected non–Plans for Progress companies (though both groups had minority workforces in the 1 per cent range).[101] Shulman thus gave Plans for Progress the EEOC's and OFCC's worst nightmare: obvious, demonstrated failure, and a resulting loss of legitimacy.

"Affirmative action" was a rather vague thing to require, and the OFCC kept it that way. The OFCC simply did not know how exactly to clarify it, as it was an area of law and policy only then developing.[102] One can sense the frustration of the office, and also its pragmatic, effectiveness-directed rationality, in a statement issued by Edward C. Sylvester, Jr, in January 1967. Sylvester, then director of OFCC, said,

> I don't pretend to have a definition of affirmative action that is going to satisfy everybody here, particularly when viewed in light of your special situation. Affirmative action is going to vary from time to time, from day to day, from place to place, from escalation to escalation. It depends upon the nature of the area in which you are located, it depends on the kind of people who are there, it depends upon the kind of business that you have. There is no fixed and firm definition of affirmative action. I would say in a general way, affirmative action is anything that you have to do to get results. But this does not necessarily include preferential treatment. The key word here is "results."
>
> Affirmative action is really designed to get employers to apply the same kind of imagination and ingenuity that they apply to any other phase of their operation. When there is a breakdown, or when something goes wrong in production, it is known fairly quickly and something is done about it in fairly short order. We expect the same kind of attention and the same kind of focus of interest at all levels on the matter of equal employment opportunity as an integral and important part of a government contract.[103]

Put another way, Sylvester was telling prospective contractors, "Look, we don't know what affirmative action is—*you* figure it out. But whatever you come up with had better *work*."

This loose definition, which put the burden of realization on the employers, was soon to evolve pragmatically into a numbers-oriented affirmative action approach. The transition can be most clearly seen in the OFCC regulation of the construction industry. Construction was a particularly knotty problem for equal opportunity compliance because of the structure of the industry. As the work is of a temporary nature, crews must be assembled for each job, with workers supplied by union hiring halls. Unions select candidates for jobs based on union membership and seniority. The unique character of the construction industry and the lack of experience in enforcing its compliance led to an explicitly experimental, trial-and-error search for a new way of promoting equal opportunity.[104]

Thus, the OFCC began a new project of "special area plans" to enforce compliance on construction contracts in four cities: St. Louis in January 1966, San Francisco in December 1966, Cleveland in February 1967, and Philadelphia in November of 1967. These plans, according to OFCC Senior Compliance Officer Robert Hobson, were especially intended to be developing grounds for an equal opportunity approach that could be used in other metropolitan areas.[105]

The St. Louis Plan was initiated after minority pressures for opportunity to work on a particularly symbolic construction project—the St. Louis Commemorative Arch. OFCC involvement in this project quickly ended in an imbroglio in the courts. Construction firms were told, as a part of a pre-award requirement, to "actively recruit minority group employees for work in the trades where they are not now frequently represented." One firm responded by hiring three minority non-AFL-CIO plumbers, and the unions, who were actually importing white workers to the area, promptly responded to this by walking out. On 6 February 1966, the Department of Justice filed a Title VII pattern or practice discrimination suit against the Building and Construction Trades Council of St. Louis and local unions of the pipefitters, sheet metal workers, electricians, plumbers, and laborers. In these unions, combined workers numbered over five thousand. Three of these five thousand workers, or 0.06 per cent, were black. Because of the walkout and ensuing legal fiasco, the OFCC did not learn much about the utility of its St. Louis Plan.[106] The trial, eventually won by the Justice Department, went on for three years.[107]

In the San Francisco or Bay Area Plan, a similar vague affirmative action pre-award plan was enforced for the Bay Area Rapid Transit contract. Each contractor was required, in the words of an Edward Sylvester memorandum, to first "cooperate with the unions with which it has agreements in the development of programs to assure qualified members of minority groups of equal employment opportunity in employment in the construction trades"; second, to "actively participate individually or through an association in joint apprenticeship committees to achieve equality of opportunity for minority group applicants to participate in the apprenticeship programs"; third, to "seek minority group referrals or applicants for journeyman positions"; and last, to "encourage minority group subcontractors." Contractors did indeed issue detailed statements of plans to "cooperate" and "participate" and "seek" and "encourage." And the OFCC collected, in the view of former OFCC associate solicitor and legal scholar James E. Jones Jr., "beautiful affirmative action programs which resulted in few minority placements on the job."[108]

Again, the seemingly ineluctable tendency to interpret nondiscrimination in terms of numbers of African-Americans hired led the OFCC to feel that it was accomplishing nothing. The programs of (in Jones's words) "paper compliance" were pragmatic failures.

The Cleveland Plan would show the OFCC's narrowing of its pragmatic focus in pursuit of demonstrably effective compliance. The OFCC wanted a plan that *worked*, but they did not yet know what worked. A plan that worked, simply enough, would get "results," and would thus have an effect that the OFCC could see, could measure, and could demonstrate. Therefore, they required that the low bidder in the pre-award negotiations offer an affirmative action plan that was specified to "have the result of assuring that there was minority group representation in all trades on the job in all phases of the work." It was in response to this requirement that a contractor, as a means of meeting the affirmative action requirement, offered to put into the contractor's manning tables (a normal part of the process, usually specifying how many men of a particular skill will be utilized at each point in a project) a specification of the number of minorities to be hired for each trade.[109] The government thought that the manning tables concept was a good idea, and required similar tables for all contractors in the Cleveland area.[110] (This plan was recommended to the Kerner Commission during hearings in 1967 as a way to combat the unemployment which presumably contributed to the summer rioting.[111])

The Cleveland Plan formed the basis of the Philadelphia Plan, which was to refine the race-focused model for justice even further. A group called the Federal Executive Board, or FEB, made up of regional federal officials of each contracting agency in the area, was to help put the Philadelphia Plan together. Jones points out that the FEB could take advantage of the "significant experience" which had been accumulated in the previous efforts. The Philadelphia Plan thus was "the first of the plans to get underway with a rather carefully thought out, written program." There was now a system to review affirmative action programs before contracts were to be awarded and guidelines of affirmative action programs were suggested to all contractors and contracting agencies. In addition, a numbers-based model was to be implemented, by compiling basic information on the construction workforce, sources of minority recruitment, and racial population ratios, as well as the expected amount of construction to be going on in an area.[112]

This meant that the FEB did not set firm compliance numbers, but instead suggested ranges. The affirmative action requirement became, essentially, "Come to us with a promise and details of what you will do to hire about x amount of racial minorities." In practice, then, the pre-award program meant that low bidders would first have their detailed, self-constructed affirmative action programs reviewed by the FEB before the contract could be signed. This vagueness on the part of the government contracting compliance organization was considered a strength. An FEB leader stated, "Although affirmative action is criticized as ambiguous, the very lack of specific detail and rigid guideline requirements permits the utmost creativity, ingenuity, and imagination."[113]

This vagueness, however, was to be the undoing of the Philadelphia and Cleveland Plans. The General Accounting Office, specifically the office of the Comptroller General, set up the next obstacle that was to focus even more clearly the Philadelphia Plan's numbers-based, race-conscious justice. The criticism was that though discriminating against blacks was unfair to blacks, it was also unfair of the government to require affirmative action programs without actually explaining exactly what affirmative action required. The assistant comptroller general stated on 22 May 1968, with regard to the Cleveland Plan, that "[b]asic principles of competitive bidding require that standards and requirements be clearly set forth prior to the submission of bids" and that "[t]he proposed order was defective because it did not contain definite minimum standards on which approval or disapproval of an affirmative action program would be based."[114] The Philadelphia Plan was declared illegal for the identical reason on 18 November 1968. With this roadblock and potentially under increased scrutiny during the presidential election year (and hence with a potentially wider audience), the OFCC's pragmatic search stalled.

The Philadelphia Plan was to be revived during the Nixon administration the following year. The shape of things to come, however, could be seen in a Senate report on the Federal Highway Act of 1968, which was to include Ohio contracts that were a part of the Cleveland Plan. The act was to contain authorizations for work to be done in 1970 and 1971. The report stated that the Cleveland Plan had "the great disability of adding grave uncertainty about the exact nature of the legal obligation and requirements which may be imposed upon the low bidder on Federal-aid highway projects."[115] The Senate report quoted the comptroller's May 22 ruling in recommending that "before the proposed order is made effective, the requirements thereof should be implemented by regulations which should include a statement of definite minimum requirements to be met by the bidder's program, and any other standards or criteria by which the acceptability of such program would be judged."[116] In the summer of 1968, then, the pragmatic sharpening of the tools of justice led to the Senate report unreflectively recommending the dreaded racial quota.

The Nixon administration's revival of the plan eventually involved a different logic, to be explored in chapter 7, but the pragmatic logic that led to the concept of racial hiring goals and timetables in the first place also played a role in the Nixon revival. Assistant Labor Secretary Arthur Fletcher pushed for the plan (and received support from Secretary George Shultz) in late spring, and later explained his reasons for doing so:

> I decided to go ahead with the Philadelphia Plan of putting specifications of minority employment goals in all contracts. I did this because my study and experience had convinced me that such targets were essential if we are to measure results in terms of increased minority employment. Without such targets, the paper compliance, and the interminable ineffectiveness of the government programs would go on. I had not come to Washington to preside over a continuation of the ineffective programs of the past.[117]

Pragmatism and the Affirmative Action Model in the Courts

While the logic of administrative pragmatism shaped administrators' interests to conform to the goal of efficient and demonstrable effectiveness (and eventually affirmative action), to some extent this was shared by the courts, which were ultimately to rule on violations of civil rights law. The same emphasis on problem-solving, substantive justice over procedural justice which had produced the proliferation of administrative agencies earlier in the century was also to shape the logic of the judges' resort to race-conscious, affirmative action models, often employing the same discourse of pragmatism used so frequently in administrative agencies.[118]

The courts were similarly strapped to find realistic modes of proving discrimination. Committed to making the law work but seemingly lacking adequate alternatives, the courts were led to a numbers-based, race-conscious approach. For example, one court stated that "[i]n many cases the only available avenue of proof is the use of racial statistics to uncover clandestine and covert discrimination by the employer or union involved."[119] In fashioning remedies for discrimination, where Title VII allowed "affirmative action" to make race irrelevant, the courts were also led to race-conscious approaches through pragmatic reasoning. The Seventh Circuit United States Court of Appeals stated, "[W]e believe that 'numerical' objectives may be the only feasible mechanism for defining with any clarity the obligation of . . . [employers] to move employment practices in the direction of true neutrality."[120]

The EEOC problem of a crushing caseload would have had its counterpart in the courts, in the midst of a "caseload explosion,"[121] but for practical measures adopted there. One measure was the use of the class action suit, which groups together all members of an aggrieved class. Class actions embody parts of the affirmative action model, in that an individual does not have to have been harmed to benefit, and what is real is not the universal individual but the basis of the difference (race). To illustrate, legal scholar Cornelius Peck has written that

> By virtue of the numbers involved, class actions offer opportunities for departure from the individualized determinations associated with the judicial process in litigation between two parties. In providing such mass justice, courts have found it necessary to devise remedies which have a simplicity in application . . . Courts, like administrative agencies, are utilizing class actions as a practical solution to handling claims which would produce an overwhelming caseload if treated on an individual basis.[122]

One court explained, "It would be wasteful, if not vain, for numerous employees, all with the same grievances, to have to process many identical complaints with the EEOC."[123] Not surprisingly, there was an increasing percentage of class action civil rights suits at the appellate level throughout the late 1960s, and also an increasing likelihood of plaintiff victory in class actions.[124]

A pragmatic logic also dictated the focus of civil rights groups on class actions. Class actions meant expedience in private discrimination suits. For example, legal scholar and civil rights lawyer Robert Belton maintained that the Legal Defense and Education Fund, also struggling with an inadequate staff, made the class action the fund's primary litigation strategy; its members argued that "class actions allowed class members who had filed no charges with the EEOC to circumvent this requirement."[125] Courts also cited the value of the class action as lessening the burden on plaintiffs' resources.[126]

In the pursuit of a legal strategy that could avoid the pragmatic pitfalls of the classical liberal law, civil rights lawyers attempted to redefine discrimination in a way that emphasized objective results (and thus also group difference) and not harmful intent. The classical law left large loopholes for a discriminator to maintain an all-white or segregated workforce, since it was necessary to find the smoking gun of discriminatory intent—a difficult task, as discussed earlier. The feeling of civil rights lawyers at the time was that covert discrimination was occurring, and new tools were needed to bring crafty discriminators to justice.[127] The typical employer defense was to simply say that when the statute became effective, they stopped discriminating.[128] A result-oriented definition of discrimination was therefore an "integral part of the litigation efforts of the NAACP and the Legal Defense and Education Fund, Inc."[129] For civil rights lawyers, results became the only way to stop post-1964 discrimination, which was color-blind on its face, but devised with a discriminatory intent.[130]

The point is that a race-conscious society and a reification of difference were not the ideological goals of the mainstream civil rights movement. Race-conscious justice was a tool that emerged when the classical liberal litigation tools failed to achieve the classical liberal goal of nondiscrimination. Whatever the later arguments of philosophers and legal scholars stressing the justice of race-conscious compensatory hiring, the groups which fought for civil rights, and often the courts which ruled, were following merely a pragmatic logic. Legal Defense Fund lawyer Jack Greenberg explained his groups' support for affirmative action:

> [W]e favored affirmative action because it was frequently the best way to get blacks into schools or jobs from which they had long been unfairly excluded. In many cases it would have been impossible to admit or promote minorities and women if in each instance we had had to mount a full-scale case. Moreover, in many cases, individual discrimination that actually existed might be impossible to prove.[131]

Why Was Affirmative Action the Pragmatic Solution?

I have argued that it was the logic of administrative pragmatism that led civil rights enforcement agencies to the affirmative action model, but there were, conceivably, other potential responses to the pragmatic pursuit of effectiveness. Did the color-blind model really have to be jettisoned so quickly? And why did the discourse of pragmatism justify such a radical departure from the color-blind model?

The EEOC had the problem of overwhelming caseload; the OFCC and the EEOC both had the problems of proving discriminatory intent. One potential solution to the latter problem that was not tried would have been more personnel, to have agency workers on the scene in the nation's workplaces, to police them, to enforce them to see true, color-blind reality. But this was not a possibility. The EEOC, for one, was trying to avoid the impression of a police presence, and support given to programs such as Plans for Progress suggested business preference for a voluntary approach. The affirmative action model, and especially the EEO-1 forms, did suggest a meddlesome policing, but as we have seen, businesses have lobbied little against affirmative action, and certainly, in the riot-torn crisis climate, sometimes had an affinity for an approach that would plug people directly into jobs. Businesses, if left alone, do not seem to mind hiring by numbers,[132] or at least giving the appearance of compliance. In this more parochial world of agencies and their regulated firms, the more important boundaries shaping legitimate agency action preserved the firms' liberty rather than color-blind justice.

In addition, one unfortunate consequence of the color-blind model was that in putting administrators in the position of finding those employers with discrimi-natory intent, they were singling out people with what was basically a moral defect. This law constructed a world of good, law-abiding American citizens—and criminal racists. EEOC conciliators found it difficult to work out solutions with those they were essentially calling racists. A more close policing strategy would only have exacerbated this problem. It was easier to negotiate on a level of business practices.[133] In other words, it was easier to say, "You are under-utilizing minority manpower," than to say, "Your evil views are hurting these citizens."

But perhaps most important, increased color-blind model policing power was simply too expensive. The logic of administrative pragmatism constructed ra-tional action as the cost-effective, efficient pursuit of agency purpose. The agen-cies were already floundering with a massive workload. Various color-blind innovations were tried, but found lacking, given the resources. More funding was requested, but not received in adequate amounts. Affirmative action was a last, affordable resort to avoid the desperately feared exposure of being an agency which failed at its task.

The question remains why a technical discourse emphasizing efficacy and efficiency would be persuasive in the advocacy of a controversial if not illegiti-mate model of justice. The answer requires attention be paid to the broader his-torical context of the civil rights enforcement agencies. As mentioned at the beginning of this chapter, administrative agencies themselves were created as part of an increasing emphasis on the efficient realization of a just society, on solving social problems. The raison d'être of the agencies was problem solu-tion, not the institutionalization of a model of procedural justice.

The results-based shift and the radical departure from the abstract individual paradigm were not without precedent. Though the civil rights administrators did not appear to be consciously following any models, there were arguably more radical departures to serve as guides for the affirmative action model. There was, of course, the policy of preferences for veterans described in chapter 3. Another would be the moral revolution which took place in the area of tort law and workmen's compensation. Originally, the law for industrial accidents was something like the color-blind, classical liberal paradigm. Workers and em-ployers were to be treated basically as abstractions, as self-reliant strangers who happened to be joined in employment. If the worker was injured, the law sought to determine who was at fault. Any negligence on the part of the worker ab-solved the employer from any blame. Or workers were thought to have taken risk into account when choosing a dangerous job. They knew the job was dan-gerous, and accepted it anyway—why should the employer be at fault if some-one got injured?

In the early part of the twentieth century, all of this was changed, a quiet moral revolution in which "fault" was "completely eliminated as a principle in work accidents."[134] With changes in tort law and workmen's compensation, employees were entitled to recovery regardless of fault. To go back to Cousens's metaphor, the government's desire was to prevent and not just put out the fires, to solve the social problem (in this case, of worker poverty resulting from injury), and to disregard how the fire was started. New agencies administered this law and tended to be concerned with results, broadly construed as preventing poverty. Legal issues of rights, responsibilities, and liabilities fell into the distant background.[135]

This is not significantly different from the affirmative action story. Minority employment is to be improved through the elimination of discrimination. Actual minority employment becomes the measure of discrimination—or the problem is redefined as one of underutilization or human resources. Fault and intent disappear in the larger view of the social problem. Little thought is given to the issue of who has enough African ancestry to be "black," or that African-Americans may not naturally distribute themselves proportionally in every occupation. Black unemployment—indeed, poverty—is to be attacked. A technical discourse advocating these typically substantive goals was persuasive to anyone close to the civil rights agencies.

The affirmative action model was also justified because it so easily lends itself to measurement. Though the EEOC could have put all its energy into processing the complaints it received and adjudicating the charges, the EEOC was frustrated with the color-blind model. They had no way of knowing how big a dent their efforts had made in the problem of discrimination (as early as the 1950s, the number of complaints was rejected as an adequate measure of discrimination). Why was ease of measurement a safe justification for the affirmative action model?

First, agencies in general are expected to gather information relevant to their goals. For example, one agency in a different area of regulation was told by a disapproving court that the agency was not "an umpire blandly calling balls and strikes."[136] Second, it should be recalled that arguments made for the creation of the EEOC stressed black unemployment rates. It was reasonable to expect this same standard would be used uncontroversially in assessing the agency's effectiveness. Political scientist John Kingdon cites systematic indicators as being a primary basis for the call for new legislation. This is because Washington is awash in various statistics, rates, and figures. Both the ample supply of statistics and their continued use reinforces the culture of quantification. "Policy makers consider a change in an indicator to be a change in the state of a system; this they define as a problem."[137] Thus, the limited audience for much of the agencies' discourse was likely to take for granted this use of numbers, and would use similar numbers to judge the agencies' legitimacy.

This culture of quantification in Washington is itself derived from the more general project of Western modernity, which seeks *rationalized* means to basic goals of justice and progress. As Max Weber observed, "The peculiarity of modern culture, and specifically of its technical and economic basis, demands this very 'calculability' of results."[138] In this context, administrators will unreflectively think in terms of finding systematic indicators which will demonstrate effectiveness at alleviating the social problem. Accordingly, it does not seem revolutionary for Assistant Secretary of Labor Arthur Fletcher to say, as he did on 20 September 1969, that

> Affirmative action means that Government contractors must pledge themselves to establish goals and timetables for employing minority personnel. They must make an honest and good faith effort to hire a percentage or number of qualified workers. Percentages or numbers are used because industrial progress itself is measured in numerical standards.[139]

This leaves a final question: Why now? As we saw, earlier equal employment enforcement agencies were drawn to the affirmative action model, but they never quite institutionalized it; they never went as far as the EEOC or the OFCC. This was partly because these early bodies had even fewer resources. They also lacked the congressional sanction of a powerful Civil Rights Act, and the outspoken leadership efforts of a Lyndon Johnson. Put simply, the nation had shown some resolve, and civil rights were increasingly supported by the American public.[140] Also, there was a national race crisis perceived in America's cities, which almost certainly affected agency effort.[141] But my focus on the state to explain the origins of affirmative action should not take credit (or blame) from the civil rights groups, which were applying pressure all along. Though fragmented and without coherent philosophy, their moral voice was strong and loud, and it substantially contributed to the agencies' primary interest in demonstrable results. Without a watchful audience, a failing agency's legitimacy may not be in question.

But there is more to the dynamics of affirmative action advocacy in the courts and the administrative agencies. One reason for the availability of the discourse of administrative pragmatism in this context was the legitimacy of the traditionally established goal of equal employment opportunity and black economic equality. A variety of cultural traditions and precedents played an essential role in the legitimation of affirmative action, and were articulated following a different logic, a story told in the next chapter.

6

Affirmative Action as Tradition

In previous chapters, we saw that affirmative action was resisted because of moral policy boundaries which allowed preferences for some groups but defined African-Americans as undeserving of preference. We also saw that parts of the affirmative action model were safely advocated using discourses of crisis management and administrative pragmatism. In their bare bones, the former said, "This change to affirmative action is advocated because it will maintain or restore order and control"; the latter declared, "This change to affirmative action is advocated because it works toward administrative goals." In their respective contexts, these justifications were logical and proved highly effective at moving boundaries, at making some space in the American political culture for a new kind of racial justice.

As these logics provided the dynamism of innovation, another discourse became available for the advocacy of affirmative action. This was the discourse of tradition, which was persuasive precisely because it denied that anything truly new was being advocated. Most basically, it said, "No change is occurring; affirmative action is in keeping with our traditions." The logic of tradition is what gives meaning to the phrase, "a dangerous precedent." The new can be justified with links to the old. In the case of affirmative action, advocates began to say that no new precedent was being set; affirmative action fit with existing precedents.

No one is more familiar with the logic and discourse of tradition than common law judges, whose work involves basing new decisions on old, showing that what appears new actually fits with existing tradition. The courts were major players in the affirmative action story, as they found precedents (traditions) on which to safely build a legal basis and legitimation for affirmative action.

Other political actors are related to tradition in more complex ways. A president, for example, must present a personal leadership project (such as the New

Deal or Great Society) as both original and safely traditional. Lyndon Johnson's speechwriter, Richard Goodwin, wrote that no one could "impose on a living nation some utopian construct, an ideal state framed in philosophic isolation"; a president's goals "must emanate from distinctively American values, look toward a future that was also an invocation of the past."[1]

So, too, with the goals of a policymaker or administrator. It was not some syllogistic logic of compensatory justice, worked out on an EEOC chalkboard, which pointed policy and lawmakers to race-conscious hiring. They constructed affirmative action pragmatically, but they did so assuming the legitimacy of their traditional goal of civil rights and American ideals of equality. The logic of tradition suggested that the tools used and promoted by civil rights protectors in the name of civil rights and equal opportunity were indeed "invocations of the past," and as such inherited all the traditional reverence of civil rights. Put simply, any attack on the affirmative action model could be rebutted by claiming that what was being attacked was civil rights, American ideals and laws, and the American commitment to justice. Affirmative action was continually asserted to be congruent with traditional American values and ideals, the original goals of the civil rights movement, and legal precedents—just as color-blindness was. Nevertheless, traditions available for affirmative action advocacy for both judges and other political actors were strangely limited.

The American moral model which made job preferences for black Americans illegitimate also shaped the traditions that could be safely linked to affirmative action. Neither advocates of affirmative action in the courts nor in other political arenas linked the controversial policy to other traditions of preference, which would have nicely shown that affirmative action was not radical. Naked preference remaining too risky, affirmative action was usually linked in the courts to other racial civil rights traditions, invoking schooling and voting rights, and outside the courts tradition linkages were established to the color-blind traditions embodied in founding documents like the Declaration of Independence (for example, "all men are created equal"), which Americans revere and identify with (but which do not define the boundaries of legitimate policy and law). In the case of affirmative action, therefore, not only was it being denied that there was anything new in affirmative action, but it was necessary also to deny that any preferences were taking place.[2] In both court opinions and other political discourse, affirmative action's radical status was thus mitigated. In fact, with the discourse of tradition, those in resistance looked radical, outside of tradition, and risked appearing illegitimate.[3]

In this chapter, we will see that the civil rights struggle has always been linked to American traditions (especially the moral traditions Americans identify with) and also how these links affected the rise of affirmative action. Then I will show why the traditions linked to civil rights were so difficult to challenge.

But I shall concentrate on how *stare decisis,* the institutional tradition logic of the American courts, allowed for a smooth, precedent-founded construction of affirmative action.

The Tradition of the Struggle for Equality in Employment

Federal protection for black Americans' employment civil rights had been advocated with the discourse of tradition for decades. The color-blind approach was so thoroughly American that it easily lent itself to this characterization. The decades-long struggle continually was articulated in the language of the creed of American ideals, such as equality and natural society (vague to be sure, but this was part of their strength), language from American founding documents, references to vague traditional goals such as justice and fairness,[4] and references to precedent. Even before the glowing words of Martin Luther King, moral traditions were used to define the equal opportunity struggle, imparting to civil rights a moral, almost sacred quality. Those opposing policies advocated in the name of civil rights increasingly risked appearing outside of American moral traditions.

The discourse of tradition was often overt, but sometimes subtle and implicit, especially in the beginning. Following A. Philip Randolph's threatened march on Washington (discussed previously), Franklin Delano Roosevelt's 1941 Executive Order 8802, the first antidiscrimination measure, was justified in the following way:

> I do hereby reaffirm the policy of the United States that there shall be no discrimination in the employment of workers in defense industries or government because of race, creed, color, or national origin, and I do hereby declare that it is the duty of employers and of labor organizations, in furtherance of said policy and of this order, to provide for the full and equitable participation of all workers in defense industries, without discrimination because of race, creed, color, or national origin.[5]

By stressing that he was *re*-affirming something which was the longstanding tradition, Roosevelt denied that his new proposal was anything new. (His administration had, some years earlier, overseen a few unpromoted and inconsequential nondiscrimination measures in federal employment.[6]) How could this new law be resisted if it was already a part of American policy?

In appealing to the traditional value of equality, Roosevelt's statement also expresses the ill-fated classical liberal connection between color blindness and "equality." An employer, by not discriminating, is to "provide for the full and equitable participation of all workers." This is a noble goal, passed down by tradition, that is assumed to be appealing on its face. It suggests the old American belief in natural society, that with the removal of artificial barriers, equal participation will naturally result. The normative links also receive expression in the very name of the enforcement agency created by the order: the Committee on *Fair* Employment Practice.

Though the mainstream white press largely ignored the order, the black papers gave rave reviews. Randolph himself tied the order to American tradition, comparing it to the Emancipation Proclamation. Typical of the positive response from blacks was an editorial in the *Amsterdam News,* which said the order was "epochal to say the least. . . . If President Lincoln's proclamation was designed to end physical slavery, it would seem that the recent order of President Roosevelt is designed to end, or at least, curb, economic slavery."[7] Civil rights in employment laws could be understood to be as American as Abraham Lincoln.

President Truman was not as subtle as Roosevelt in invoking the traditions of the American creed in his renewal of the federal effort to help the fight for equal opportunity, rarely missing an opportunity to invoke them, along with the traditional authority of the founding documents, such as the Constitution. For example, Truman had made some public statements in support of permanent FEPC legislation, and at a 1 March 1946 press conference, he met with the Executive Committee of the Negro Newspaper Publishers' Association and reiterated his support, hitting several traditional themes. After the group commended the president and made other civil rights requests, Truman explained,

> There are things that are necessary today, of course—it's a pity that they have to be done—but there are certain things that are necessary to be done to give us the Bill of Rights as it is written in the Constitution of the United States. We want to see equal opportunity for everybody, regardless of race, creed or color. . . . We want to see an implementation, through this FEPC legislation, of what is in the Constitution. We all have the same feeling inside of us here, that we should have that, that men are created equal—with equal rights. We have to have special legislation to enforce it—to implement the thing that God Almighty intended us to have automatically.[8]

Not needing to paraphrase, a 1958 report from the President's Committee on Government Contracts, *Five Years of Progress,* simply quotes the Declaration of Independence in its opening pages: "We hold these truths to be self-evident, that all men are created equal, that they are endowed by their Creator with certain unalienable Rights, that among these are Life, Liberty and the pursuit of Happiness. That to secure these rights, Governments are instituted among Men, deriving their just powers from the consent of the governed." The report reminds us of the symbolic date of these words: 4 July 1776.[9] Also included is a quote from Eisenhower reaffirming these consensus principles of America, and then slipped in is a quote from Vice President Nixon, that ostensibly is connected to the same American traditions: "Encouragement and incentive for higher training is needed by all youth, and it is particularly needed among the youth of minority groups . . . for the increasing number of skilled and technical jobs now available." This was an early call for the classical version of affirmative action, though couched in universalist terms, and careful to stress job growth, indicating that minority training would be a part of universal youth training and recruitment would not crowd out whites from scarce jobs (Nixon would show no such concern eleven years later, as the first president to advocate minority hiring goals).

Samuel Huntington argues that the American creed is so closely identified with being an American that failure to embrace the creed puts one's very Americanness in question.[10] Never mind that the creed is not what actually shapes policy boundaries in the United States. Americans consciously identify with the creed. The struggle for civil rights and its close affinity with creedal ideals also meant that those against civil rights could be considered un-American in the discourse and that, conversely, pro–civil rights people were "true" Americans. Typical is a 14 June 1952 telegram from Thurgood Marshall to Truman commending a Truman speech on civil rights. Marshall stated, "Your reaffirmation of need for adequate civil rights legislation is most encouraging. All true Americans must be still applauding. During periods when civil rights are being shamelessly kicked around we need and appreciate your fearless stand as a real president in the true American tradition."[11]

The support of presidents themselves became a discursive resource for the struggle for equal employment opportunity, as advocates, sometimes uncertain as to whether the policy could be passed off as tradition, were able to employ the traditional cultural authority of the president to support their cause.[12] Invoking this traditional authority mitigated the radical nature of the policy, since resistance, now defined as insolence, was close to an illegitimate radicalism. Presidents, such as Truman, Eisenhower, and Kennedy, would lend their title to the names of administration agencies that were created to oversee still controversial color-blind equal employment opportunity in government and government contractors. The agencies themselves could use this in their efforts at spreading the word of nondiscrimination. For example, in a report to President Eisenhower and his cabinet on 25 March 1960, Chairman of the President's Committee on Government Employment Policy Archibald J. Carey, Jr., explained, "In the matter of persuasion the members of the Committee and the staff have engaged their fullest resources to win a sympathetic understanding of the purposes and objectives of the President's policy and Executive Order. Needless to say, the most effective instrument at our disposal is the prestige of the Presidential Order and the knowledge of the President's deep, personal concern."[13] In this view, civil rights was as routine as following the president's wishes. Resisting was the radical action.

Americans' unreflective identification with these hallowed moral traditions associated with the nation's founding, the sources of the color-blind model, were again thrust onto the national scene by the civil rights movement, with the tireless efforts of Reverend Martin Luther King, Jr. a major focal point, as discussed previously (see chapter 2). The nature of the legislation sought, as well as King's unforgettable speeches, augmented the movement's atmosphere of moral struggle and historic emancipation. An identifiably American ideal of justice and especially its religious foundations were clearly on their side, a card that was played again and again in their discourse, adding momentum and force to the kinds of traditional appeals already being made.

As the fight moved into the 1960s, it became increasingly risky to resist the civil rights movement. Put another way, the persuasiveness of the American traditions on the side of the civil rights movement crescendoed. There was, of course, King's famous "I have a dream" speech at the 1963 march, which stressed the religious traditions in American ideology. But the president also dramatically used this discourse of tradition to justify a new civil rights law. On 11 June 1963, President John F. Kennedy announced to a national television audience his intention to involve the government, with a new Civil Rights Act, in the problem of ending discrimination: "We are confronted primarily with a moral issue as old as the scripture and . . . as clear as the American Constitution."[14] Similarly, Vice President Lyndon Johnson was allegedly less concerned at this time with the substance of the newly proposed civil rights bill than he was with its legitimation, with strategies to pass the bill, explaining to White House staff that the South must be appealed to in moral, patriotic, and religious terms. Johnson also argued (again stressing tradition) that the administration should seek public support for the measure from the ex-presidents who were still alive.[15] The moral purpose of the bill was also stressed by Attorney General Robert Kennedy, along with several religious leaders, in hearings for Title VII in the Senate Judiciary Committee chaired by civil rights skeptic, Senator Sam Ervin of North Carolina.[16] Appeals to traditionally revered morality or ideals were ubiquitous at this time.

It is very clear from reading the government discourse that the elimination of the meaning of race was closely linked with the elimination of African-American economic inequality, reflecting the utopian ideals of natural society described in chapter 2. The problem to be solved was understood not only as discriminatory acts themselves, but the consequences of those intentional acts. This is most apparent by the recitation of black unemployment statistics (here the value of equality is implicit) in the arguments for Title VII, as we saw in chapter 2, and for earlier civil rights measures. In fact, the goal of reducing racial inequality in unemployment has a long history in arguments in favor of antidiscrimination legislation. It could be seen in President Roosevelt's groundbreaking executive order. President Truman's Committee on Civil Rights produced a report in 1947 which contained a table comparing white unemployment rates with the rates of blacks in selected cities.[17] The framers of Title VII, like their counterparts in the 1940s and 1950s, were trying to enact discrimination law to eliminate racial meaning *and* to bring about economic equality. This was, of course, the standard that civil rights enforcement agencies used to gauge their progress, as discussed in the previous chapter. They knew it was the standard that *others* would use to gauge their progress.

My point here is to stress that while civil rights legislation was being called for in the name of equality, morality, and Americanism, equality was consistently being understood as both an equality of treatment and an equality of economic results. It appears that though this economic equality was to follow naturally from the equality of opportunity (nondiscrimination), it established the elimination of black inequality as the traditional goal of civil rights, giving affirmative action supporters high moral ground when the political boundaries began to blur and shift and opponents allowed for the advocacy of race-conscious principles, since economic equality did not immediately flow from nondiscrimination. That rock-steady, nonwhite unemployment rate, the original problem to be solved, continued to be twice that of whites. Those resisting affirmative action could easily be cast as extremist conservatives, resisting the traditional moral goal of civil rights.

Traditions and the Legitimation of the Affirmative Action Model

The morning after the passage of the Civil Rights Act of 1964, the world suddenly looked different to those concerned with civil rights. Legal equality had finally been attained. The political cultural struggle to legitimate and convince the government of the need for these color-blind laws had been won; the government role in protecting equal employment opportunity was now solidly legitimate. What remained was the struggle to make the law effective, to make it work—largely a pragmatic struggle explored in chapter 5. Still, the link to specific traditional goals and ideals continued to play a part. The equation or causal connection of equal employment opportunity and the equality of economic results, always implicit in the discourse, now came to be explicit, in the new pragmatic drive to be effective. Those who stood in the way of effectiveness, like those who stood in the way of the original passage of the act, could be cast as enemies of civil rights, enemies of the Declaration of Independence, and enemies of the Constitution.

The failure to immediately attain true nondiscrimination/equal opportunity/ equality of economic results proved to be a very uncomfortable if not intolerable situation to many justice defenders. They were conscious of the centuries of subjugation and the current climate of rioting, urgency, and disorder; thus they saw racial justice as being in their interest, the idea "whose time had come," as Illinois Senator Everett Dirksen had called it in 1964, paraphrasing Victor Hugo. Not surprisingly, a moral devotion characterized much of the work that went on in the Equal Employment Opportunity Commission. Of course, the very name of the agency contained a moral message and commitment. Many workers were motivated by the traditions of the American ideals and took for granted the Western project of justice and progress. The commission attracted many workers who already were active in civil rights, and who wanted to contribute to the cause of equality. An EEOC newsletter was called, quite appropriately, *Mission*. Dorothy Howze, an EEOC employee from the early days, remembered, "I was probably one of the few people who came there because it was a job. But once I got into it, you just got kind of caught up in the spirit, and it all became very exciting and very—I hate the word 'meaningful'—but that's really what it was, that you were doing some good."[18]

President Johnson tended to leave the new agency alone.[19] Still, his strong support for civil rights and an important commencement speech at Howard University gave tremendous traditional cultural authority to the administrators who were making the largely pragmatic shift to a race-conscious approach. The speech actually contained no policy ideas, and it is difficult to find any evidence that Lyndon Johnson ever supported a policy of race-based hiring. The speech was meant primarily to "leapfrog" the civil rights movement, to put the administration in the driver's seat, as opposed to merely responding and reacting to the movement's demands. Its most radical element, according to the author of the speech, Richard Goodwin, was Johnson's desire to make whites feel "a little guilty" about the condition of blacks.[20] But the words used in the speech (much of it based on Moynihan's controversial report on the black family) were open to a wide range of interpretation. Indeed, the strong language and vagueness of the Howard Speech operated as carte blanche to any egalitarian initiative. It could therefore be used as a precedent or a tradition to justify the affirmative action model pragmatically developing in the EEOC.

Not surprisingly, the EEOC rarely missed an opportunity to drag President Johnson's name into the discourse. Chairman Clifford Alexander began the November 1968 *EEOC Administrative History* by stating, "An extremely important chapter in the history of the realization of human rights in the United States was written during the Johnson Administration." He quotes selectively from the famous Howard Speech, suggesting that Johnson had racial hiring in mind all along:

> We seek not just freedom but opportunity; we seek not just legal equality but human ability; not just equality as a right and a theory but equality as a fact and equality as a result.
>
> For the task is to give 20 million Negroes the same chance as every other American to learn and grow, to work and share in society, to develop their ability; physical, mental and spiritual, and to pursue their individual happiness.[21]

Alexander, the most committed of the early EEOC chairmen, used the traditional cultural authority of the president with great skill in promoting the EEOC's affirmative action approach during hearings with executives of various industries, in which the government began a policy of asking business to focus on the racial makeup of the workforce. In Alexander's opening statement to the pharmaceutical industry, which was essentially the same statement that he used in similar hearings, he explained that a

> call by the President best describes the reason we exist and the reason we are here today. When I was sworn in the President said—and I quote: "This Commission, like the Civil Rights Act that created it, exists for one reason—that millions of Americans are still barred from full participation in the American dream. We are all equal before God. We are equal in the eyes of the law. If I have anything to do with it in the country we are all going to be equal in seeking a job."[22]

After asserting that racial inequality exists in the drug industry, Alexander went on to cite the standard African-American unemployment rates and income inequality in the larger society, implying that discrimination was the cause. Clearly aware that he was asking the executives to take race into account in their hiring decisions, Alexander was careful to distinguish this from what the Civil Rights Act was designed to prohibit: "It is not preferential treatment to help a convalescent through the door instead of simply telling him it is open." Asserting again that this was not "reverse discrimination," he laid the ultimate trump card of traditional authority, a quote from Johnson's Howard University speech: "You do not take a person hobbled by chains and liberate him, bring him up to the starting line of a race and then say, 'you are free to compete with all the others,' and still justly believe that you have been completely fair."[23] Johnson most likely had in mind color-blind Great Society programs, but in this context, his words gave the authority of tradition to affirmative action.

Because of the legitimacy of the moral traditions that stood behind the name *civil rights,* both American founding principles and the continual reiteration of these principles in the 1940s, 1950s, and 1960s civil rights struggle, the simplest, safest and most frequently used tradition discourse for advocates of race consciousness was to merely articulate that race consciousness and affirmative action *were* civil rights. Little else needed to be said anymore. Many civil rights supporters, both black and white, fired with the goal of the modern and American project of justice and progress, let the color-blind model slip away on the iterative, pragmatic road to race consciousness, and hardly cared. Their commitment to the traditional goal of civil rights was rock-steady. It was still civil rights to them. And though affirmative action, originally a special effort at hiring without regard to race, was now explicitly racial hiring, the traditional name could be used to label the new model. As Nathan Glazer lamented in 1987, "Thus the critic of quotas or [racial hiring] goals and timetables is regularly attacked as being opposed to affirmative action, even though he may well be a supporter of the clear intentions of Title VII in 1964 and of the Executive Order of 1965. But there is no point arguing with what the meaning of words has become: whatever the term meant in the 1960s, since the 1970s affirmative action means quotas and goals and timetables."[24]

As with the debates on the Civil Rights Act of 1964, when there was very little lobbying against the act, few wanted to appear to be standing in the way of justice, even if that justice seemed to be specifically targeting a group seen as undeserving.[25] Thus, once the window of opportunity opened for race consciousness, as when the window opened for the original color-blind law, boundary-maintaining resistance wilted. Alexander and the EEOC rarely received a fight from businessmen in the public forums on race consciousness. Resistance narrowed to a handful of prominent senators, mostly from the South but also including the irascible Everett Dirksen of Illinois, who eventually drove Alexander to resign. The real showdown for affirmative action occurred in the debate over the Philadelphia Plan, to be explored in the next chapter, where the discourse of tradition for the national audience was very prominent, and resistance to the controversial policy surprisingly weak.

Why Was the Discourse of Tradition So Effective?

We have only seen part of this story. We know that African-Americans, being constructed in America's taken-for-granted model of justice as not deserving of preference, could not simply link affirmative action to other traditions of preference, but we also know that, ironically enough, the traditions linked to color blindness could also be linked to affirmative action. Advocates of affirmative action, like advocates of color blindness before them, propounded their policy or law idea by denying that there was anything really new or radical about it, that it was congruent with tradition. They had, it seemed, the higher moral ground—the boundaries of legitimate action blurred and moved. Those upholding the old boundary of legitimate policy action yielded to the discourse of tradition. But why was this so?

Discrimination, it must be remembered, used to have its own legitimating traditions, and was taken for granted in the American model of justice. One important idea which made the legitimation of color-blind equal employment opportunity law so difficult was the principle of small government. This was coupled with the principle of the rights of states to do as they pleased in as many areas as possible, and the rights of property owners to do as they pleased. What right did the northern states have to enforce their beliefs on the southern states? And what right did the government have to tell the owner of a firm who the owner could or could not hire? After all, the owner was the *owner.* Even the veterans' preference statutes stopped short of forcing firms to hire veterans, though this was strongly encouraged. These were the deeply rooted, more purely Lockean boundaries in American justice that had to be moved for the passage and legitimacy of color-blind antidiscrimination legislation.

We are again led to the importance of historical context in understanding the logics and discourses available to those who would advocate affirmative action. Like the discourse of crisis management, the discourse of tradition was available for advocates of affirmative action largely because of world events.

Again, Adolph Hitler, half a world away, loomed large on the domestic politics scene. It was the rise of Nazism that influenced the federal courts to begin to see themselves as the protector of oppressed minorities.[26] Gunnar Myrdal's famous book on American traditions and race relations, *An American Dilemma,*[27] written during the early part of World War II, was clearly influenced by the specter of Hitler, even containing a section entitled, "Is the South Fascist?" (he concludes in the negative). Myrdal argued that the evil of Hitler, and the fact that America was at war with him and what he represented, severely exacerbated the tensions of the American dilemma, or the tension between American traditions and the plight of blacks. He cites Republican leader Wendell Willkie, telling an NAACP conference in July of 1942:

> Today it is becoming increasingly apparent to thoughtful Americans that we cannot fight the forces and ideas of imperialism abroad and maintain a form of imperialism at home. The war has done this to our thinking. . . . So we are finding under the pressures of this present conflict that long-standing barriers and prejudices are breaking down. The defense of our democracy against the forces that threaten it from without has made some of its failures to function at home glaringly apparent. Our very proclamations of what we are for have rendered our own inequities self-evident. When we talk of freedom and oppor-

tunity for all nations the mocking paradoxes in our own society become so clear they can no longer be ignored.[28]

Though the actual moral model which shapes policy boundaries is different
from the professed American creed, these egalitarian creedal traditions are he-
gemonic in the discourse; they are what Americans identify with, and most
would avoid being caught outside of them in the post–World War II era. In the
crisis climate during the war years of Roosevelt's FEPC, when color-blind policy was not illegitimate, supporters and opponents of the FEPC tried to link their
position to American traditions, and used the world context to do so. It was
property rights (and the right to discriminate) versus equal, abstract citizenship,
and Hitler was relevant to both. When boundaries are unclear, there are often
attempts to make the other side appear illegitimate. For example, in a House
debate over an FEPC appropriations bill in 1944, Mississippi Representative
John Rankin bellowed,

> Oh! This is the beginning of a communistic dictatorship, the like of
> which America never dreamed. They want to dictate to you who shall
> work in your factory, who shall work on your farm, who shall work in
> your office, who shall go to your schools, and who shall eat at your
> table, or intermarry with your children.
>
> It is sponsored by the C.I.O. Political Action Committee, headed
> by Sidney Hillman, a Russian-born racketeer whom the anticommu-
> nist Americans of his own race literally despise, and who is raising
> money by the shake-down method with which he is now trying to
> control our elections. He wants to be the Hitler of America.

A pro-FEPC force (New York Representative Vito Marcantonio) countered,

> The real reason (for resisting FEPC appropriations) is because you
> want to perpetuate a Hitlerite concept of race supremacy in this coun-
> try. . . . The fundamental issue involved here is the principle of the
> equality of man, the very foundation of our Nation. You oppose FEPC
> for one reason and one reason alone, the very same reason that the
> Emancipation Proclamation was opposed in these United States.
> FEPC is a continuation of the Emancipation Proclamation; it is de-
> mocracy in action, the democracy for which men are fighting and
> dying everywhere in the world.[29]

Since Americans fought Hitler, not the communists, and since Hitler was a
racist, not an enemy of property rights, this gave primacy to civil rights traditions. This was underscored to President Truman when Charles H. Houston, a
member of the FEPC, wrote a 3 December 1945 letter of resignation, chastising

Truman for inadequate commitment to equal opportunity. Houston wrote, "The failure of the Government to enforce democratic practices and to protect minorities in its own capital makes its expressed concern for national minorities abroad somewhat specious, and its interference in the domestic affairs of other countries very premature."[30] Truman seemed to get the message, and in a 12 September 1946 letter to Lester B. Granger, executive secretary of the National Urban League, he stated, "Since its founding, the American government has been guided by the sacred guarantees of the Bill of Rights . . . To give the Bill of Rights its full meaning, we must work to preserve the same rights at home that we fought for so successfully abroad."[31] American egalitarian traditions took on new persuasiveness when juxtaposed with the unenlightened world and when the American audience was reminded of the now-relevant world audience.

The rise of human rights discourse and a massive and uncommitted developing world audience in Asia, Africa, and Latin America, discussed in chapter 4, ensured that these traditions would retain the higher ground in civil rights struggles, even though the enemy (the Communists) was now a violator of the property rights tradition. In these early years, American traditions were also defined against negative traditions of other countries, showing the influence of the Cold War. Hubert Humphrey, then a Senate candidate in Minnesota, quite consciously used traditions linked to the world context to push back boundaries proscribing civil rights endorsement at the 1948 Democratic convention. In describing his speech years later, he wrote,

> Then I set [the speech] in the international scene. It was the practice in those postwar, early cold-war years to make these international comparisons.
> "Our demands for democratic practices in other countries will be no more effective than the guarantees of those practices in our own country. There are those who say to you: We are rushing this issue of civil rights. I say we are a hundred and seventy-two years late."[32]

Similarly, in the 1953 report of the President's Committee on Government Contract Compliance, under the grandiloquent heading "A Philosophy Is Born," we find the following:

> The United States has assumed leadership of the world in a crusade to extend the blessings of liberty and freedom to all men. This Nation was founded on the fundamental principle that all men are created equal. It is the duty of men of good will to combat undermining prejudices which would deny the fruits of freedom to fellow citizens because of race, religion, color, national origin, or ancestry. . . . [O]ut

of these principles springs our national policy of equal treatment and opportunity. Our government, being a government "of the people, by the people, and for the people," can accept no less.[33]

Notably, Kennedy's 28 February 1963 civil rights message to Congress linked American traditions and world context, arguing that race discrimination "hampers our world leadership by contradicting at home the message we preach abroad. It mars the atmosphere of a united and classless society in which this Nation rose to greatness." Though these egalitarian traditions were dominant due to the world context, Kennedy sought to disentangle them: "[I]t is not merely because of the Cold War . . . that we are committed to achieving true equality of opportunity. The basic reason is because it is right."[34]

The other contextual event that made American traditions linked to discrimination illegitimate was the experience of the civil rights movement itself. This great story has been touched on here and is told in great detail elsewhere. What is important is that it created strong images of good versus evil. It was the anti–civil rights forces that beat and murdered people. It was the anti–civil rights forces which attacked American citizens with dogs and sprayed water cannons at women and children. American television screens were filled with these images of abuse and oppression. What more negative image is there than the image of anti–civil rights individuals bombing a *church* and killing four young, innocent girls, who were attending Sunday school?[35] In no part of American morality is this justified. Adolph Hitler and Bull Connor, the authoritarian, dog-and-club wielding Alabama sheriff, became powerful symbols of violation of tradition and thus illegitimacy. Kennedy recognized this when he quipped, "The civil rights movement should thank God for Bull Connor. He's helped it as much as Abraham Lincoln."[36] Indeed, the very term *civil rights* came to be synonymous with the noble struggle of Nobel Peace Prize winner King and his compatriots.[37]

In struggling to legitimate and pass color-blind antidiscrimination law, the victory was total: it quickly became, in this post–World War II, post–Western colonies, Cold War time, illegitimate to *oppose* civil rights, and the traditions associated with the color-blind model. While the presumed boundaries of American justice do not allow for African-American job preferences and links to preference traditions, the tradition of civil rights was available to deny the significance of the change to affirmative action. Since the original model of color blindness always promised the equal results of affirmative action, many fighting the civil rights cause themselves saw no significant change.

The Logic of Tradition and the Federal Courts

While the EEOC and OFCC were tentatively moving forward with their pragmatically constructed, race-conscious measures (and keeping within tradition by calling it "civil rights" and "equal employment opportunity"), and officials in the executive branch were increasingly talking of the policy without serious resistance as "crisis management" (though with a different logic in the Nixon White House, as we will see in the next chapter), the courts were crucial in establishing the legitimacy of the policy—indeed, even as *the* approach to civil rights in employment. The nation's courts were central in the legitimation of the new model of discrimination and justice, not so much because they broke new ground, as was occurring in the enforcement agencies, but because they underscored these innovations and gave them the force of law.[38] The development of the affirmative action model was thus very much a legal development.

In the courts, the affirmative action approach was called the "adverse impact" or "disparate impact" theory of discrimination, which we saw was increasingly discussed outside of the courts with the discourse of crisis management. It is usually contrasted with the classically liberal disparate *treatment* theory, which simply proscribes, following the color-blind model, treating groups differently because of their race. In disparate impact, an act or practice is discriminatory if it can be shown (usually through numbers of blacks hired) to "disparately impact," or unreasonably limit, the hiring of African-Americans—regardless of the equality of treatment of racial groups or the intent of the hiring organization. A practice could still be legal if it could be shown to be a business necessity, but this was often extremely difficult to prove and thus quite expensive. Once disparate impact was established in the courts, employers and unions knew that they could be subject to (and lose) an expensive court battle if they had a disproportionately small number of minority employees. Thus, some argued that "voluntary" racial quotas could be the best insurance against such an event, as well as against a bothersome EEOC investigation. At any rate, the theory was a building block of affirmative action because racist intent was irrelevant, and firms had to at least be aware of their minority hires qua minority hires; they had to "see" race, and not abstract individuals.

The logic of tradition is the signature institutional logic of American courts. Sometimes a judge will use a pragmatic reasoning and use the discourse of pragmatism to justify a decision, as we saw in the previous chapter, where practicality and efficacy could be paramount. Rarely, if ever, will a judge ground a decision only on the need to maintain control or order because of some immediate threat. Most often, judicial opinions will be presented with the discourse of tradition, grounded on precedents.

A common law judge examines a case by comparing it with past cases that apparently fall under the same principle or rule. The common law thus grows incrementally, by building on itself—the doctrine of precedent, or *stare decisis*.[39] Political scientist John Brigham equates precedent to words in a language; precedent is so central that it is the "language" of the common law.[40] The role of the precedent, of *stare decisis*, is the appeal to tradition to legitimate a decision. A decision is to be accepted because it has already been accepted.

One of the results of the centrality of precedent in the grounding of legal reasoning is that a new principle can become a tradition itself rather quickly. This was the case in race-conscious antidiscrimination law. Once a few decisions were made which furthered this model, future decisions could cite these core cases as precedent again and again. Precedent thus allows for the growth of law (and culture), as "Previous decisions can be stretched to cover new situations and to provide a justification for creation of law and policy."[41] Put perhaps more cynically, precedent can serve as a "cloaking device";[42] it is "often used to disguise change as continuity."[43] Similarly, British legal historian S. F. C. Milsom has commented that legal change in the common law "has the appearance of a conjuring trick: out of the old hat there comes a new rabbit."[44] This is the heart of the logic and discourse of tradition—the linking of the new with the old. It is especially important in the courts, where stability is an important legal value.[45] As sociologist Philip Selznick wrote, "By drawing upon already-legitimated concepts or principles to deal with new situations, the integrity of law can be protected while social transition is eased."[46]

To ground a legal decision on the text or implicit premises of the Constitution, or the intent of the framers, or, analogously, on the text, premises, or intent of Title VII, also entails asserting that what is new (the controversial case at hand) is *not* new. Instead, it fits in with the old, is covered by the old, and thus is part of tradition—tradition which is taken for granted, which is axiomatically good and legitimate. To say that affirmative action is in line with the text of Title VII of the Civil Rights Act of 1964 and the intentions of Congress is to assert that it already fits with what is possessed as legitimate tradition. Affirmative action is thus legitimate because it does not involve any change.

Judges are in an especially good position to move boundaries and legitimate new ideas with the discourse of tradition, since they have considerable control over the use of precedent.[47] This is partly because the facts of a case are often unclear, and the law vague.[48] In addition, the public often knows little of the law. Writing on the Constitution, Karl Llewellyn said in 1934, "There is an unreasoned, unreasoning, tradition-founded loyalty to a symbol of national unity and permanence. Along with this is a pervasive ignorance and indifference as to almost all detail."[49]

Since justification by tradition is what courts do all the time, the discourse of tradition was a safe vehicle for affirmative action advocacy, especially given the usually limited audience of judicial opinions. Appointed for life, a federal judge's own legitimacy is based more on whether or not his or her decisions are frequently overruled than whether or not they are faithful to moral boundaries (though there usually is a connection). Like administrators, judges inhabit a parochial institutional space.

Tradition and the Legal Construction of Affirmative Action

A year after Title VII went into effect, cases began to reach the appellate courts, and civil rights employment law began to emerge. As in the administrative agencies, development was slow and incremental, with no clear direction. It was, however, apparent that it was moving away from the color-blind model. Different building blocks of the affirmative action model began to fall into place, based on traditions and precedents: discrimination occurring without discriminatory intent, statistics as proof of discrimination, and the legality of explicitly race-conscious hiring. (The decline of the abstract individual, to be replaced by race-defined "class actions," was largely a pragmatic move, discussed in chapter 5.)

A bedrock case for the move away from discriminatory intent was *Quarles v. Philip Morris, Inc.*,[50] which argued that plant seniority is discriminatory where it adversely impacts black workers. The court stated boldly, "The plain language of the [Civil Rights Act] condemns as an unfair practice all racial discrimination affecting employment without excluding present discrimination that originated in seniority systems devised before the effective date of the act." This declaration was supported with numerous statements of Congressmen, which, though expressing a desire to leave seniority systems alone, did not preserve *departmental* seniority systems, or systems which counted seniority only in a particular department. This was of course a problem if blacks had been previously held in segregated, low-paying departments, and this was indeed the case at Philip Morris. The legislative history showed that Congress sought to preserve "bona fide" seniority systems, and "Obviously, one characteristic of a *bona fide* seniority system must be a lack of discrimination" (original italics).[51] Philip Morris, Inc., though not actively and intentionally discriminating, was nonetheless against "the plain language of the act," against the intent of Congress, and against tradition.

The *Quarles* opinion also subtly invoked moral traditions through metaphor, as in the following passage:

> The [legislative] history leads the court to conclude that Congress did not intend to require "reverse discrimination," that is, the act does not require that Negroes be preferred over white employees who possess employment seniority. It is also apparent that Congress did not intend

> to freeze an entire generation of Negro employees into discriminatory patterns that existed before the act.[52]

The imagery of the "freeze" metaphor here is powerful, an affront to American ideals of liberty and equal opportunity. Clearly, anyone frozen into place is subject to an injustice, and not in the American class system at all, but a caste system.[53]

One important case helped legitimate the idea that the Civil Rights Act and executive order allowed racial hiring with language that linked the decision to traditionally identified American values or ideals of justice. While this language may be dismissed by a lawyer or legal scholar as mere dicta, these statements had an uncanny way of appearing in later decisions, of becoming the language of the new principle of antidiscrimination law. In *Weiner v. Cuyahoga Community College,*[54] a contractor, Reliance Mechanical Contractors, though the lowest bidder for a federal construction contract, was rejected due to an inadequate affirmative action plan, as judged by the standard of the Cleveland Plan. Reliance had submitted a manning table for a construction job, showing numbers of blacks that would be hired "subject to availability and referral." In other words, Reliance would rely on natural society, on freely contracting individuals to come to them and take advantage of opportunity. Reliance argued that anything more was preferential treatment, and challenged the constitutionality of the Civil Rights Act. The court decided that Reliance's position "deliberately flout[ed] the clear purpose of the law," and though dismissing the idea that preferential treatment was required (citing *Quarles*—already itself an important tradition), defended the constitutionality of this race-conscious interpretation of the Act, stating:

> The Act provides a remedy for a long-continued denial of vital rights of minorities and of every American—the right to equality before the law—the right in every walk of life in a land whose philosophy is that "all men are created equal," to an equal chance of employment in keeping with his ability. To assure obedience to the law is a duty inherent in the government. It may reasonably instruct its agencies how to proceed toward enforcement. There has, as the evidence here shows, come a time when firmness must be used against *all* who do not feel able or inclined to cooperate in the equal employment effort. The statute and the Executive Order [11246] implementing it are in full keeping with the constitutional guarantee of the rights of all citizens [original emphasis].[55]

Such glowing language clearly defined Reliance's position as the illegitimate one.

Another important building block for affirmative action and the disparate impact theory was the use of statistics of racial disparities in employment. Some early cases used statistics as evidence of discrimination in addition to traditional evidence of discriminatory intent. Thus, in a decision such as *U.S. v. Local 73, United Association of Plumbing and Pipefitting*,[56] a union's color-blind but nepotistic recruiting policy could be struck down as discriminatory, but traditional evidence, such as a union giving specific black applicants the "runaround," was presented along with racial statistics showing few black hires. Nepotism, neutral on its face with regard to racial differences, is seen as a mask for classic discrimination—discrimination based on evil intent. Groundbreaking cases which established the use of black employment statistics, such as *Parham v. Southwestern Bell Telephone Co.*,[57] *U.S. v. Sheet Metal Workers International Association, Local 36*,[58] *Local 189, United Papermakers and Paperworkers v. U. S.*,[59] and *Dobbins v. Local 212, International Brotherhood of Electrical Workers*,[60] also used traditional evidence of discrimination in arriving at decisions.

Being in the common law, by far the most prevalent mode of tradition discourse used by the courts, however, was the use of some precedent as a legitimate anchor for the "new" approach. Since this was a relatively new area of law, the precedents were not perfect analogies, but employment law certainly seemed relevant. Curiously, however, use of employment law precedent was rare. The greatest source of relevant precedent and analogy was not the employment tradition (though relevant precedent was there for some more radical affirmative action ideas, such as the departure from intent[61]), but other civil rights cases, in areas of life governed by what may be considered completely different institutional rules, such as school desegregation, voting rights, and jury discrimination. This was crucial for the legitimation of the affirmative action model in employment, since these other spheres are much more amenable to the logic of statistical representation. Specifically, these spheres are based more squarely on the institution of citizenship, the relationship between the individual and his or her government, where rights and duties come by virtue of citizenship; they do not have to be earned, nor are they subject to taste. These citizenship spheres do not follow the rules of the labor market, where meritocracy and employer and employee discretion play a large part. As Nathan Glazer put it, "[O]ne can, on the face of it, discern a very important distinction: Everyone, with minor exceptions, is expected to have the right to vote and is required to go to school, but jobs are based on qualifications and it is well-known that qualifications (such as education) will vary with race and ethnicity."[62] Thomas Sowell adds that, even if we disregard group difference, it is unrealistic, statistically speaking, for proportions to play themselves out exactly in every firm or industry.[63] Rarely, however, did judges make this distinction between citizenship rights and duties on the one hand and jobs on the other, or show awareness of the effect of statistical variance. Judges unreflectively made the presumably safer link of employment affirmative action for blacks to school desegregation or voting rights for blacks, rather than employment affirmative action for blacks with other employment preferences, such as those for veterans.

For example, several early cases which sought to use statistical disparities in African-American employment as proof of discrimination did so by quoting dicta from a voting rights case, *State of Alabama v. U.S.*[64] This case contained the piquant line, "In the problem of racial discrimination, statistics often tell much and Courts listen." This quote from the voting rights tradition was used to justify statistical evidence in four important employment cases (important in the sense that they then served as precedent for statistical evidence in later cases): *Parham v. Southwestern Bell Telephone Co.*,[65] *U.S. v. Ironworkers Local 86*,[66] *EEOC v. United Association of Journeymen*,[67] *Lea v. Cone Mill Corp.*[68]

A clear example of this tradition-building-on-tradition, as well as other institutional practices, is exemplified in *U. S. v. Ironworkers Local 86*. Here, beside relying on the "statistics tell much" voting rights dictum, the court specifically refuted the appellant's argument that equal employment cases were not supposed to rely on racial imbalances: "We believe this argument is without support as the use of statistics is *well established* in *recent* Title VII cases" (emphasis added). In a footnote, the opinion buttressed its use of statistical disparity as evidence of discrimination by citing several Supreme Court cases of jury discrimination (*Patton v. Mississippi*,[69] *Hill v. Texas*,[70] *Norris v. Alabama*[71]). Typical of these cases is *Patton*, where a black was indicted for murder, and the jury was shown to not have had an African-American juror for thirty years. Again, the analogy is imperfect, since the labor market is a matter of employer discretion, worker taste, and merit, while jury duty is part and parcel of American citizenship.

The high-profile school desegregation tradition was also used in the development of the affirmative action model. *Carter v. Gallagher*[72] was an important early case which ordered the Minneapolis Fire Department to hire twenty blacks. The opinion referred to the *Louisiana v. United States*[73] voting rights case, which had involved Louisiana's imposition of a "citizenship test" to earn voting rights (whites, for the most part, did not have to take the test, since most were already registered), to justify in *Carter* "the legitimacy of erasing the effects of past racially discriminatory practices."[74] The *Carter* opinion went on to rest on a school desegregation case in establishing its race-conscious remedy. The opinion stated, "It has now been established by the Supreme Court that the use of mathematical ratios as 'a starting point in the process of shaping a remedy' is not unconstitutional and is 'within the equitable remedial discretion of the District Court.'"[75] The schooling decision was *Swann v. Charlotte-*

Mecklenburg Board of Education.[76] The *Swann* opinion concerned the elimination of a segregated school system, and though it touched on employment, it was not an employment civil rights case.[77]

In the story of affirmative action, few cases were as important as *Contractors Association of Eastern Pennsylvania v. Secretary of Labor,*[78] which upheld the controversial racial percentage hiring goals of the affirmative action Philadelphia Plan. In the crucial passage, the court identified color blindness as extremist, and justified affirmative action with some powerful language and references to tradition:

> To read § 703 (a) [of Title VII, the antidiscrimination clause] in the manner suggested by the plaintiffs we would have to attribute to Congress the intention to freeze the status quo and to foreclose remedial action under authority designed to overcome existing evils. We discern no such intention either from the language of the statute or its legislative history. Clearly the Philadelphia Plan is color-conscious. Indeed the only meaning which can be attributed to the "affirmative action" language which since March of 1961 has been included in successive Executive Orders is that Government contractors must be color-conscious. Since 1941 the Executive Order program has recognized that discriminatory practices exclude available minority manpower from the labor pool. *In other contexts* color-consciousness has been deemed to be an appropriate remedial posture [emphasis added].[79]

Here the court cited *Porcelli v. Titus,*[80] an early reverse discrimination case which helped establish benign racial preferences in employment, though its thrust was school integration. This case was brought (under the Fourteenth Amendment—not the Civil Rights Act of 1964) by white teachers, who were in line for promotion in the Newark school system, but who were passed over as the superintendent of schools sought to promote teachers with adequate "sensitivity," which meant in practice that many whites were bypassed for blacks (see chapter 4). The race-conscious holding in this case was based on the famous school desegregation case, *Brown v. Board of Education.*[81] The *Contractors* opinion also cited *Norwalk CORE v. Norwalk Redevelopment Agency,*[82] a case dealing with a redevelopment project which accidentally relocated minorities in a way that was seen as inferior to the geographical relocation of whites. Last, the opinion cited *Offerman v. Nitkowski,*[83] a school integration case where the city of Buffalo was taken to court for trying to fix its de facto segregated school system by adjusting school district lines.[84] Thus the affirmative action holding in *Contractors* rested on school and residential integration traditions. The search for precedent in "other contexts" always meant other race contexts, not other employment preference contexts.

The lines of tradition (and similarity) thus extended from schooling, voting, and so on, to employment. But were employment, schooling, voting, and so on really the same? Interestingly, these employment opinions made little or no attempt to justify the use of the basic citizenship traditions, to explain why these "other contexts" were relevant to employment. This is especially curious in the *Carter* opinion, since this decision was overturning a previous decision which had specifically disallowed the use of the school desegregation tradition to justify minority preference in the remedy. The earlier opinion stated that "[s]chool integration cases such as *Swann* . . . are clearly distinguishable. Whites have no constitutional right to insist on segregated schools."[85] In *Dobbins v. Local 212,* the opinion also disallowed these other traditions as legitimation for employment civil rights. There the opinion stated, "It is one thing to presume or assume, prima facie or otherwise, that a significant number of a group have the qualifications for schooling or voting, or jury service. It is another thing to assume, prima facie or otherwise, that because a certain number of people exist, be they W. or N. [white or black], that any significant number of them are lawyers or doctors, or merchants, or chiefs—or to be concrete, are competent plumbers or electricians or carpenters. . . . [T]he word 'craft' is necessarily entwined with the word 'skill'. That is true even in the dictionary."[86]

Griggs, the Supreme Court, and Affirmative Action

Perhaps the most important court decision in the legitimation of the affirmative action model came when the Supreme Court weighed in on the issue. In *Griggs v. Duke Power Co.,*[87] the ultimate legal authority in the land came down with its approval of a central building block of affirmative action. Critic Herman Belz has commented, "*Griggs* shifted civil rights policy to a group-rights, equality-of-result rationale that made the social consequences of employment practices, rather than their purposes, intent, or motivation, the decisive consideration in determining their lawfulness. The decision supplied a theoretical basis for preferential treatment as well as a practical incentive for extending race-conscious preference: employers' desire to avoid charges, based on racial imbalance, of discrimination."[88] Due to its importance, it is necessary to examine the case in some detail.

Griggs was not the first race-consciousness case to reach the Supreme Court, as several others had been turned down. The *Griggs* decision was actually a reversal of a decision made in the Fourth Circuit. The case centered on worker qualifications that Duke insisted were not meant to discriminate, and were necessary for the operation of the business. Duke required workers to have a high school diploma, or to pass an intelligence test as a condition of employment or transfer to plant jobs. Black employees brought a suit charging that the requirements were discriminatory. At the time of the suit, fourteen of Duke's ninety-five employees were black, though this statistic is misleading, as black employees had been discriminatorily limited to only one of the plant's five divisions—the Labor Department—which was essentially custodial. As in the *Quarles* case discussed earlier, seniority was by department, and therefore transferring departments meant starting over, with no seniority, in a new department. The high school requirement was instituted in 1955 for all initial job assignments except to Labor. When the company began compliance with the Civil Rights Act in 1965, a high school diploma was required to transfer from Labor to other departments. On 2 July 1965, the day that Title VII went into effect, the company began to require also that new employees to departments other than Labor pass the Wonderlic general intelligence test and the Bennett Mechanical Comprehension Test.

The Supreme Court ruling came on appeal from the Fourth Circuit's decision. Basing its opinion partly on *Quarles* and a few related appellate court decisions, the circuit court determined that "only those six Negro employees without a high school education or its equivalent who were hired prior to the adoption of the educational requirement are entitled to relief."[89] The opinion found the high school and test requirements legal, and that each of the other black employees who "accepted a position in the Labor Department with his eyes wide open"[90] to the educational requirements, was not a victim of discrimination and not deserving of relief. The opinion argued that Duke *did* have a business purpose in making the requirements, as Duke had a long history of training its own employees for supervisory positions. Also, the education requirement was instituted in 1955, nine years before the 1964 civil rights law was passed, and thus could not have been designed to discriminate. The circuit court also argued that Duke had made a good faith effort to end discrimination in employment, transfers, and promotions. Though the requirements adversely affected blacks, they also adversely affected white employees, and, the court argued, Duke offered to pay most of the expenses for an employee to get a high school education or its equivalent, including 75 percent of the costs of one of the plaintiffs. In a footnote, the opinion explained, "It would be illogical to conclude that Duke established the educational requirement for purposes of discrimination when it was willing to pay for the education of incumbent Negro employees who could thus become eligible for advancement."[91] Finally, the court argued that "At no place in the Act or in its legislative history does there appear a requirement that employers may utilize only those tests which measure the ability and skill required by a specific job or group of jobs."[92]

The Legal Defense Fund decided to appeal, and the Supreme Court agreed to review the case. The petitioner's brief, written by Jack Greenberg, articulated the discourses of tradition and pragmatism. The brief argued that "five years of experience" under the Civil Rights Act shows that the "enlightened and perceptive . . . lower courts have generally sought to give it a broad and flexible interpretation." This tradition of broad interpretation had pragmatic value, for "[i]t has given Title VII the potential for becoming an effective force for fair employment in contrast to the many state fair employment laws which languished under restrictive applications."[93]

The brief attaches itself to the safely legitimate, classical definition of discrimination, suggesting that Duke had malicious intent. An upsurge in IQ tests used by employers since Title VII became law (cited, notably, in the establishment *Wall Street Journal*[94]) is mentioned, and then the brief explains that

> While outright and open exclusion of Negroes is passé, the use of neutral, objective criteria which systematically reduce Negro job opportunity are producing the same result. As this Court has long recognized in other contexts of racial discrimination, those rules which are objective and neutral in form may well be racially discriminatory in substance and effect.

The brief reminded the court of the nefarious practices used in voting and school integration cases.[95]

Traditional, classical liberalism is also at the heart of the petitioner's brief, in the insistence that employers' tests must be job-related. Merit is specifically being preserved, and testimony is offered from psychologists and other experts as to the irrelevance of IQ tests and high school diplomas as predictors of ability in industrial jobs. After this safe link to the classical liberal tradition, however, the brief later changes course, and hits on the disparate impact theme, pragmatism, and the equality tradition, arguing that if discriminatory intent must be shown in the use of employment tests, "then Title VII will be rendered largely ineffective in pursuing the goal of full fair employment."[96]

Finally, this important brief even has a hint of the discourse of crisis management, as the Kerner Report is cited twice. Though other citations were available, the report of a national riot commission is cited to show that "[r]acial discrimination and unrealistic and unnecessarily high minimum qualifications for employment or promotion have the same prejudicial effect." The riot report is also the chosen source to remind the Court of the ubiquitous statistic that the black unemployment rate is about double that of whites.[97]

Four *amicus curiae* briefs were supplied in this landmark case to support the petitioner's position.[98] Two of the briefs were from the United States, one including Erwin N. Griswold, solicitor general, representing the Department of Justice, and the other including Griswold and other Justice personnel, plus EEOC lawyers. Both of these briefs articulated the discourse of tradition in equally strong language. Both briefs continue the familiar causal connection of color blindness and economic equality, suggesting both the traditional values and the pragmatic logic of a race-conscious means of attaining these values. The first brief explains that Title VII's goal is equal employment opportunity, "[b]ut the goal of equal employment opportunity remains unrealized; unemployment among Negroes and other minority groups continues to be substantially higher than it is among the population at large, and such unemployment continues to be a national problem" (footnotes excluded). The other brief also invoked the traditional goal of civil rights as it dismissed intent:

> This focus on the employer's motive, rather than its need, is, we submit, what apparently misled the court. For the congressional purpose in enacting Title VII was—as its heading "Employment Opportunities" suggests—to accomplish economic results, not merely to influence motives or feelings. Discriminatory "employment practices"—not attitudes—are declared unlawful.

This second amicus quotes Mr. Justice Black in a thirty-year-old jury discrimination case (*Smith v. Texas*[99]): "What the [Act] . . . prohibits is racial discrimination . . . whether accomplished ingeniously or ingenuously."

The other *Griggs* amicus briefs came from the attorney general of the state of New York, who argued that New York wanted to preserve its state laws and saw the Griggs case as potentially threatening to its tradition, and from the United Steelworkers of America. The union, in an implicitly classical liberal appeal, called the Duke tests "ludicrous" and their use "vicious." The steelworkers' brief provided examples taken from the Wonderlic test, which included the following:

> Answer by printing YES or NO. Does B.C. mean "before Christ"?
> Are the meanings of the following sentences: 1 similar, 2 contradictory, 3 neither similar or contradictory? "All good things are cheap, all bad things very dear. Goodness is simple; badness is manifold."

The union's clear point was that Duke's tests were unmeritocratic, clearly unrelated to industrial jobs, out of the American tradition, and therefore illegitimate and illegal.

In its opinion, the Supreme Court came down solidly in favor of the plaintiffs, and the adverse impact theory of discrimination. Mr. Chief Justice Burger, for a unanimous court (though Justice Brennan did not take part in the decision) defined adverse impact as being a part of tradition, since eliminating barriers, and not racist intent, was what Congress had in mind all along:

> The objective of Congress in the enactment of Title VII is plain from the language of the statute. It was to achieve equality of employment opportunities and remove barriers that have operated in the past

to favor an identifiable group of white employees over other employees.[100]

The Court continued, invoking the tradition-laden negative image of the "freeze" metaphor: "Under the Act, practices, procedures, or tests neutral on their face, and even neutral in terms of intent, cannot be maintained if they operate to 'freeze' the status quo of prior discriminatory employment practices."[101] "Freezing" the status quo was un-American as well as unmodern, suggesting Duke had abandoned the basic project of justice and progress. Similarly, the Court also stated in a frequently quoted dictum, "[G]ood intent or absence of discriminatory intent does not redeem employment procedures or testing mechanisms that operate as 'built-in headwinds' for minority groups that are unrelated to measuring job capability."[102]

The Court also pointed out that the plaintiffs had received poor-quality education in this part of North Carolina, and that the Court had dealt with that in an earlier opinion barring literacy tests for voter registration (*Gaston County v. United States*[103]), thus bringing that tradition into the picture. While brushing aside classical liberal intent, the Court was careful to link itself with the meritocratic tradition—this was not a real change at all; it was only clarifying our meritocratic tradition ("The touchstone is business necessity. If an employment practice which operates to exclude Negroes cannot be shown to be related to job performance, the practice is prohibited"[104]). Many critics, however, such as Michael Evan Gold, have argued that this has amounted to a quota hiring mandate, since valid job-related criteria for all jobs "do not presently exist, and the cost of developing them may often exceed the gain of using them." Consequently, he argues, employers look for loopholes, such as simply hiring minorities proportionally to prevent any appearance of an "adverse impact" on African-Americans.[105]

Whether or not the loophole of quota hiring was in fact seized by American employers is not important here. What is important is that the logic and discourse of tradition moved boundaries, further reinforcing the legitimation of hiring that takes race into account, that constructs race as a positive reality. Legal scholar Alfred Blumrosen, sympathetic to the ruling in *Griggs,* denies that this ruling led to quota hiring but explains, "The most probable consequence of the broad interpretation of the antidiscrimination law is that employers take a 'hard look' at their practices and their candidates."[106] In other words, employers must take "hard looks" and see race. The disparate impact theory in *Griggs* legitimated, by the highest authority in the land, the idea that race was a reality in American life that must be recognized in everyday practice. Employers were not to purge themselves of racist, discriminatory intent. They were to scrutinize their labor practices, the Court ordered, perceiving their employees' race as paramount reality. "Blackness" was real, and for the first time in the nation's history, blackness was *good*. This simple but profound idea, so strangely taboo just seven years earlier, was now enshrined in law.

The Courts and the Protection of Minorities

That the courts would use the discourse of tradition in their advocacy of the affirmative action model is hardly remarkable, since precedent is the language of the courts. But why these mostly white males would abandon the color-blind model and fashion a legal tradition which reifies and politicizes "blackness," and why the Court's audience would allow for the safe advocacy of affirmative action, *are* questions that require a closer look.

One may argue that this was the natural course of a liberal judiciary, that these judges were following the liberal position on affirmative action. Many of the judges ruling in the cases that supplied the legal foundation for affirmative action were in fact Lyndon Johnson appointees, and many have been characterized as liberal.[107] However, linking judges to Johnson's appointment or liberalism in general is not necessarily very informative, since liberalism was not decidedly for the affirmative action model, and one can look hard at the historical record and not find Johnson ever speaking on the topic of racial hiring or adverse impact theories of discrimination. At any rate, Chief Justice Burger, who wrote the *Griggs* opinion for a unanimous Supreme Court, was a Nixon appointee (and as such he was expected to turn the Court around). Along with the civil rights enforcement agencies and the crisis managers, the courts were blazing a new trail.

More promising is a closer look at historical context. A broader view shows the progressivism of the courts to be more institutional than ideological, a part of the court's taken-for-granted rules of operation. The dedication to progress and substantive justice that led Congress to create problem-solving administrative agencies also brought a problem-solving logic to the courts.[108] In other words, we must not see the affirmative action issue as unique, or even the civil rights issue as unique. The growth of the welfare state in general has led to the leading role of the courts on many controversial issues; the role of the courts has simply grown with the state.

The courts have had to take a definitive leading role because, as Donald Horowitz argues, many of these legislative ventures into unknown waters (especially in the 1960s and 1970s) have been "so broad, so vague, so indeterminate, as to pass the problem to the courts."[109] This seems to have been true of Title VII. For example, little is said in Title VII as to what sorts of remedies the courts are to grant. Sorting out the meanings of Congress's laws has also encouraged the courts to define themselves more and more as problem solvers, rather than grievance answerers. "The individual litigant," Horowitz continues, "though still necessary, has tended to fade a bit into the background."[110] This was certainly true in many civil rights cases, particularly in the area of school integration, as the NAACP was often actively looking for someone—anyone— willing to take a case to court. This problem-solving role has led some legislators to assume that courts are willing to "take the heat."[111] This general role of the courts quickly became a tradition itself, and built on itself, much as affirmative action law itself did. More and more frontiers were opened up as the court set more and more precedents and traditions. The courts' limited audience of judges and legal specialists took for granted boundary-blurring behavior.

The leading role in the protection of minorities had its own peculiar origin within this larger expansion of the role of the courts, what Hugh Davis Graham has called "revolution by judicial footnote" and political scientist Richard Pacelle has likened to a "paradigm shift."[112] Again, the world context and a racist dictator loomed large. The year was 1938, and the case was *United States v. Carolene Products Co.,*[113] where the issue was court deference to majoritarian rule in the area of regulation of interstate commerce. Specifically, the Supreme Court upheld a problem-solving federal law which outlawed shipping "filled" milk, or milk that had the butterfat removed and replaced with coconut oil. At first look, this hardly seems an important part of the affirmative action story. But in the now famous Footnote Four of the opinion, Justice Harlan Stone wrote that judicial review may be of a different scope in different areas. One area which Stone declared called for a "more searching judicial inquiry" was legislation dealing with minorities. Stone's reasoning was that one cannot trust "the operation of those political processes ordinarily to be relied upon to protect minorities" because of the "discrete and insular" nature of minorities.

What led to this bold new doctrine? According to Robert M. Cover, Stone was concerned about oppressive prejudice in a world that was then witnessing the rise of the Nazis.[114] In a letter to Judge Irving Lehman, written on the day after the *Carolene Products* decision came down, Stone wrote, "I have been deeply concerned about the increasing racial and religious intolerance which seems to bedevil the world, and which I greatly fear may be augmented in this country," and expressed fear of the breakdown of "the guarantees of individual liberty."[115] Stone thus sought to rescue the "lost opportunity" of the Thirteenth and Fourteenth Amendments, which should have protected minorities. Since "discrete and insular" minorities cannot be expected to be helped by majoritarian politics, and since prejudice and racism can be used to manipulate the masses in democratic politics, the Court had to appoint itself as the guardian of these groups, or else they would forever be steamrolled by the will of the less-than-benevolent majority.[116]

Of course, the Court did not immediately become the great protector of minorities. This is because the Court's role, according to Pacelle, is to stabilize exigent policy areas, and at this time, economic issues were paramount. Footnote Four's meteoric rise came in the 1960s because economic issues were not of pressing importance, national security issues were fading, and the Court had a large number of liberal justices more willing to embrace the protector role.[117]

Footnote Four and the notion of federal courts as institutionalized risk-takers, or last resort, willing-to-take-the-heat minority protectors sheds some light on why affirmative action decisions continually looked to extant traditions of black protection—in whatever context—rather than squarely focusing on the unique cultural rules of employment. The American moral model set policy boundaries which allowed for various minorities to be oppressed in various ways. Seeing the similarities between this and illegitimate Nazism, the courts created the notion of suspect classes, keeping these minorities "special" though worthy of special protection. By focusing on the tradition of suspect classes, rather than employment, the Court did not see labor relations law, veterans' statutes, or nepotism as relevant traditions in the area of employment law which could have been used to legitimate racial preferences. Thus, the courts could have said, "We have long recognized the hiring of veterans as filling an important national interest; the same is true for the hiring of black Americans, who also gave to their country and experienced considerable hardship since; while the Civil Rights Act proscribes preferences 'on account of' racial imbalances, it does not proscribe preferences granted in the national interest"; or, "Preferential hiring of blacks cannot be seen as a violation of white rights in employment, since this nation has always allowed employers to hire nepotistically; the labor market is not a meritocracy, and to pretend that it is for the benefit of one group would be inconsistent with our national traditions." But they did not make such analogies. The courts reasoned in minority terms, not in employment terms.

The minority-based traditions gathered momentum and mass as a snowball does when rolling down a hill. Footnote Four was the rather unimposing beginning, at the summit of the hill. Pacelle traces the growth of the courts' tradition in terms of Supreme Court agenda space granted to different protected classes: first immigrants, then racial minorities, then women, and then minorities based on age, disability, or illegitimacy were granted protection. More significant here, Pacelle notes that the race cases can be seen to expand from elections to education to employment.[118] Though much of this work was done during the liberal Warren Court, the snowball was simply too big for the Burger Court to stop. By this time, it would have been risky, possibly illegitimate, to try to stop it. Thus, the Burger Court continued the race work on to the last step—employment and *Griggs*—and even continued the tradition of Court unanimity on these controversial cases, with Burger showing his leadership by writing the opinion. Of course, Burger's leadership also led to some resistance on the busing issue, but the real meltdown did not occur until the late 1980s.[119]

We can thus see that while Congress may have de facto appointed the courts as interpreters of problem-solving substantive justice statutes, the Court appointed *itself* as the protector of racial and religious minorities. Justice Stone and his colleagues were aware of the proposition asserted in chapter 3: In the American moral/justice model, African-Americans are not constructed as a deserving group. Voters and legislatures could thus continually trample their group interests and rights. Since the democratic masses had often seen blacks as a special class, deserving of nothing but negative treatment, the Court would have to see them as a special class, deserving of special, positive treatment, lest America resemble those other countries that so troubled Justice Stone.[120] After the defeat of Hitler, the Cold War was an influence keeping the rights of minorities paramount. For example, the solicitor general's amicus brief in *Brown* stated, "It is in the context of the present world struggle between freedom and tyranny that the problem of racial discrimination must be viewed," quoting Secretary of State Dean Acheson for testimony of the harmful effects of race discrimination by allowing effective Soviet propaganda.[121] The point is that this understanding of the courts' role set up boundaries of legitimate actions, and for a judge to challenge them would mean risking legitimacy as a judge.

The tradition of Footnote Four is certainly relevant to the explanation of the readiness of judges to support race-conscious approaches and to use precedent from a variety of civil rights cases rather than employment cases to legitimate affirmative action, but it does not completely explain this readiness. It is problematic to treat the courts as necessarily hemmed in by one tradition while they were simultaneously moving beyond the boundaries of others. More insight is gained if we focus again on Horowitz's point that judges have increasingly seen their courts as arenas of problem-solving. Horowitz also observes that courts, lacking manpower,[122] will have little patience for long, drawn-out cases; "Cases requiring repeated intervention quickly wear out their welcome in court."[123] This self-understanding would lend itself to a logic of administrative pragmatism, as we saw in chapter 5. In other words, courts will tend to look for efficient solutions.

In the later 1960s, the courts *had* been through a long, drawn-out series of cases in the civil rights area, and through a pragmatic logic the courts seemed to have arrived at a solution. Superficially very similar to employment, the schooling desegregation problem seemed to be a relevant analogy and tradition. Alfred Blumrosen, a Rutgers law professor working for the EEOC in the middle 1960s, suggests that the model for federal judges in equal employment opportunity was derived from the knowledge gained in the struggle for nondiscrimination in education, where the 1955 *Brown* decision called for school desegregation with "all deliberate speed." Blumrosen suggests that this unspecific, nonaffirmative directive was seen by federal judges as dragging on social unrest for a decade, and they wanted to avoid a similar situation in employment law.[124]

Certainly, much of the school desegregation effort had close parallels which would make for an easy comparison. This story cannot be told here, but a few points will suffice.[125] The development of this law also had to overcome a cultural prohibition against race consciousness and racial percentages. Classical liberalism, the color-blind paradigm in employment, had its analog in school desegregation in the "freedom-of-choice" school integration idea, where students would have the legally protected choice of which school to attend—though little in the way of federal endorsement or protection. In the same way that color blindness was assumed to naturally integrate the nation's workforce, it was assumed to integrate the schools. But freedom of choice produced little progress (demonstrable results) in school integration. An affirmative, race-conscious approach was pragmatically developed to tackle the problem. For example, in *United States v. Jefferson County Board of Education,* the Court stated, anticipating the ambiguity of affirmative action administrators, "The only school desegregation plan that meets constitutional standards is one that works."[126] The court mentioned that the Department of Health, Education, and Welfare (HEW) had drawn up guidelines which contained racial percentages, to be used as "a general rule of thumb or objective administrative guide for measuring progress in desegregation rather than a firm requirement that must be met. Good faith in compliance should be measured by performance, not promises."[127] This opinion also cited a 9 April 1966 letter to members of Congress and state governors, from HEW Secretary John W. Gardner, which explained that the percentages were not to impose racial balance, but to have objective criteria. Sounding like an EEOC official, Gardner explained, "With more than 2,000 separate districts to consider, such percentages are thus an administrative guide which helps us to determine those districts requiring further review. Such review in turn will determine whether or not the freedom of choice plan is in fact working fairly."[128] The Court agreed, stating that "In reviewing the effectiveness of an approved plan it seems reasonable to use some sort of yardstick or objective percentage guide."[129]

The language here is almost identical with that used by the EEOC and in employment discrimination cases generally. It is thus not surprising that a flurry of cases being brought to court under the same act at almost the same time would be linked together and used as precedent by judges looking for efficient solutions. As Horowitz points out, the broad scope of court dockets leads judges to avoid excessive time spent in learning more than necessary about a case, and to

have little patience with drawn- out proceedings.[130] These school desegregation tools, the product of the logic of administrative pragmatism, became the
ostensibly legitimate tradition with which racial hiring practices could be advocated in the courts.

Thus far we have only focused on the development of the building blocks of
the affirmative action model. When the government was managing the racial
crisis, race-conscious measures were propounded but rarely linked explicitly to
any civil rights policy. In the administrative agencies and the courts, important,
fumbling developments were articulated with discourses of pragmatism and
tradition, but before the *Griggs* case, the audiences were still quite limited, and
the effort lacked coherence. There was no recognizable public initiative for affirmative action. For this, affirmative action would have to wait for a most unlikely hero.

7

Creative Destruction in
the Nixon Administration

Perhaps the greatest irony of all in the story of affirmative action is that this controversial model of justice owes its most advanced and explicit race-based formulation to a Republican president who based much of his campaign on appealing to the racially conservative South. This was, of course, the enigmatic Richard Nixon. Whereas President Johnson and his fellow Democrats had struggled mightily both to help blacks and to avoid giving this help a racial label, Nixon, for a time, rather proudly marched under a race-conscious banner. As we will see, for a Republican president in 1969, this was a perfectly sensible thing to do.

By 1969, a few years of crisis management, administrative pragmatism, and the continued advocacy of American traditions and precedents of justice and civil rights had done much to make different unit ideas of the affirmative action model legitimate parts of policy and legal discourse. Moral policy boundaries were blurring, and following the Kerner *Report* the risk of race-consciousness advocacy had declined somewhat. Even to the national audience, it lost its third-rail quality.

But the Left was not yet solidly behind any policy called affirmative action. While suggested in various parts and practices of civil rights enforcement and crisis management, affirmative action was not completely institutionalized in any specific policy. This was finally to occur on 27 June 1969 (and then again on 23 September, after surviving a legal challenge—and then *again,* on 22 December, after surviving a Congressional challenge), when the Nixon administration revived and shepherded past critics the Philadelphia Plan (henceforth, the Plan), the old race-conscious, affirmative action program for the construction industry. The Plan, as discussed in chapter 5, was pragmatically constructed by the OFCC during the Johnson administration and soon struck down by the comptroller general for being too ambiguous. In the Nixon version, designed to meet contracting requirements which state that guidelines for bids must be explicit, the affirmative action guidelines took the form of government-determined, numerically explicit *percentages* of minorities to be hired. Put simply, in the view of many observers, a Republican national government ordered racial quotas. Soon, however, Nixon repudiated them, but not until *after* civil rights groups and their Democratic supporters embraced this new tool, and paid the political costs for doing so. Legitimacy does not necessarily mean popularity.

Making Sense of Nixon's Civil Rights Policy

Understanding the Nixon civil rights agenda has been an exercise in futility for scholars of the American presidency—as well as for insiders in the Nixon White House. The tendency, especially on the Left, was to see Nixon as a villain and enemy of civil rights. After all, in some areas, most notably school desegregation, the Nixon administration *did* try to reverse the prevailing national policy. Even the moderate Roy Wilkins of the NAACP maintained that Nixon sought to "turn the clock back on everything," and was on the side of "enemies of little black children."[1] In a 1973 collection of indignant indictments of "Tricky Dick," *What Nixon Is Doing to Us,* political scientist Charles Hamilton opens his essay by calling Nixon a liar and cataloging Nixon betrayals: weakening the Voting Rights Act, abdicating urban aid, declining civil rights enforcement across the board. The bleak, negative image is easier to maintain when, as in Hamilton's essay, the Philadelphia Plan is completely ignored.[2] Political scientist A. James Reichley made his task of showing the effects of conservative ideology on Nixon civil rights policy easier by also ignoring the Philadelphia Plan.[3] Historian Stephen Ambrose's biography of Nixon mentions the Philadelphia Plan only in passing, and characterizes the civil rights stance as doing only what the law required, put forth in the administration with a "meanness of spirit."[4] Fellow Nixon biographer Herbert Parmet recognizes the Plan explicitly, calling it a "complete contradiction" to Nixon's ideology.[5] Eleanor Holmes Norton, formerly chair of the New York City Commission on Human Rights (and future EEOC head under President Carter), refused to reconcile the Plan and Nixon's other conservative civil rights policies, and concluded there were two Nixons: one benevolent, one not so benevolent.[6] Michael Genovese agreed, but locates them in time—the benevolent Nixon came first (and left early).[7] Steering a middle course is Hugh Davis Graham, who characterizes the civil rights policy as "incoherent," "confused and quite contradictory" with "no one in charge." This was due, according to Graham, to poor organization as well as the inattention of the President.[8] Tom Wicker, looking at the same record, calls Nixon a "centrist."[9]

In Nixon's own administration, there was confusion. Leon Panetta, former

Director of the Office for Civil Rights in the Department of Health, Education, and Welfare and resident liberal, called the Plan "the Administration's chief claim to being rights-conscious at all." Why the effort was made he cannot explain, but emphasizes that "[e]verything seemed short-range, even the political gains to be made by selling out Federal programs."[10] On the Right was an even more confused Patrick Buchanan, who found the entire domestic policy to be a muddle. The speechwriter wrote in January 1971,

> We suffer from the widely held belief that the President has no Grand Vision that inspires him, no deeply held political philosophy that girds, guides, and explains his words, decisions, and deeds. The President is viewed as the quintessential political pragmatist, standing before an ideological buffet, picking some from this tray and some from that. On both sides he is seen as the text book political transient, here today, gone tomorrow, shuttling back and forth, as weather permits, between liberal programs and conservative rhetoric. As someone put it, "the bubble in the carpenter's level."
>
> Left and right, both now argue aloud that the President, and his Administration, do not make decisions on the basis of political principle—but on the basis of expediency; that ours is "ad hoc government," which responds only as pressures mount from left or right. Neither liberal nor conservative, neither fish nor fowl, the Nixon Administration, they argue, is a hybrid, whose zigging and zagging has succeeded in winning the enthusiasm and loyalty of neither left nor right, but the suspicion and distrust of both.[11]

How are we to make sense of such a confusing record? The key, I will argue, is not to focus on Nixon the man but the Presidency as an institution, its logic and turbulent context in the Nixon years. As in each previous chapter, we will focus on what political actors take for granted, and how their interests are socially constructed, shaped by the perceived audiences' boundaries of legitimacy. Combining this framework with Stephen Skowronek's work on the institutional logic of presidential politics, the two Nixons meld into one beleaguered president with a daunting task.

First, presidents take for granted that they must take political risks, they must challenge policy boundaries. Since the founding of the Republic, presidents have been expected to embark on grand tasks, or as it was put in the Federalist papers, "great and arduous enterprises" in pursuit of "fame."[12] Like the agency administrators we encountered in chapter 5, presidents are concerned about their reputations, and seek to make an impact. While for agency administrators this will tend to be defined by some specific policy goal, effectiveness for presidents means carving out a distinctive place in history. Presidents have a national audience for much of their action, and in a very real sense, they also perceive as part of their audience the historians who will scrutinize their administrations and write the books teaching the national memory. Presidents do not want to merit just a footnote in the history books.

The logic of presidential leadership, then, is inherently disruptive, since presidents are expected to articulate a personal vision to form the basis of leadership and policymaking. This was apparent early in the Nixon administration, in a 13 March 1969 memo from Nixon to trusted domestic policy adviser John Ehrlichman. Nixon was seeking good ideas for his administration, which he defined as "ideas that had imagination and emotion," "ingenuity," and were not "routine."[13] For Skowronek, this builds into the presidency a paradox, since the president is simultaneously charged by the Constitution with the executive task of affirming political order, affirming routine.

We may also add that it is a precarious situation, since grand tasks often involve grand risks, and guessing wrong can cause soaring dreams to crash and burn. Presidents must be creative but within the boundaries of the American moral model. They will often try to lessen the risk, as Johnson speechwriter Richard Goodwin said in the previous chapter, by invoking tradition as they present original ideas.

The delicacy of presidential leadership is underscored by the nature of the legitimacy that presidents strive for, which is different from that of other political actors. A legitimate political actor is considered a serious player in the political arena. This is maintained usually by playing by the rules. For example, policymakers avoid third-rail political issues, and agency administrators avoid demonstrable failure. But a president is not just a player but a *leader.* A president must therefore have the legitimacy *to lead,* what Skowronek calls "authority."[14] A struggle for this special leadership legitimacy, for warrants for action, is necessary to create the imaginative leadership project.

The legitimacy imperative is different for each president because each president assumes office in a different context. Skowronek's work on this point suggests the importance of a more transient and more purely political set of boundaries of legitimate action, rather than the relatively stable though complex boundaries based on a moral model. Each new president enters a moving political stream; the country is moving in a general political or ideological direction, dominated by a prevailing political establishment. The basis of a president's leadership legitimacy, the warrants or discourse available for leadership action, will vary depending on the health of the ideological supports for the existing establishment and political direction, as well as whether or not the new president is opposed to or affiliated with this establishment. Thus, not only is it risky to challenge the relatively stable boundaries of morality in American politics, but to the extent that the prevailing general ideological direction of politics is taken for granted, it is also risky to challenge this direction and the establishment empowered by it.

For example, Nixon was opposed to the prevailing establishment and direction, which was welfare state Democratic liberalism at its zenith. While many Americans were disillusioned with this project, and with Lyndon Johnson personally, liberalism still provided the starting points for national politics. Major parts of the Democratic project, including principles of civil rights, still boasted great support both among the public and especially in Washington. It had actually become risky to *challenge* the civil rights tradition in any form. Though Republican Nixon won the 1968 popular election, he did so by a slim margin, and some political observers such as Arthur Schlesinger, Jr. and Louis Harris saw a consolidation of liberal power.[15] To embark on a wholesale undoing of the liberal project, even staying within moral boundaries, was more than just politically risky. It would be almost certain disaster.

A president in this situation, opposed to the assumed establishment, will have great difficulty establishing and maintaining leadership legitimacy. This president follows the logic of what Skowronek calls "the politics of preemption." In this context, "[t]he exercise of creative political leadership hinges on expanding and altering the base of opposition support, and here the leader is naturally drawn toward latent interest cleavages and factional discontent within the ranks of the [establishment's] traditional supporters."[16] Because they are American presidents and want to establish history-making, creative leadership, and because they need special legitimacy to succeed at this, their immediate goal is to "preempt" the existing political agenda "by playing upon the political divisions within the establishment."[17] While honoring opposition supporters, these presidents must still avoid directly attacking the prevailing political direction, and "offer disaffected interests normally affiliated with the dominant coalition" a more attractive modification of the establishment's agenda.[18] Preemption politics is thus premised on the idea of dividing the national audience.

The logic of the politics of preemption clicks into focus the blurry Nixon civil rights agenda. In seeking a broadened political base for the authority for creative leadership, Nixon pursued what was called the "southern strategy," making the Republicans the home for southern whites disillusioned with Democratic liberalism, especially on racial issues.[19] Nixon would supply an alternative— but Nixon could not completely ignore African-Americans, either. Confronting a liberal audience used to having their way and a now institutionalized civil rights tradition, Nixon believed he had to quietly offer *something* in the name of civil rights. In the process, Nixon hoped to empower his leadership by picking up some support from blacks, who had been promised so much by the liberals but were made a secondary priority after Vietnam. In choosing the Philadelphia

Plan, Nixon could focus his coalition-dividing attack on a group that did not vote for him and was a thorn in his side in the first year—organized labor. Nixon thus placed on the table something to help African-Americans at the expense of unions, producing discontent and factional rivalry in two of the liberal establishment's major supporters. The Democratic leadership, formerly committed to a color-blind approach, would thus have to put one group over the other on a controversial issue. In Nixon's other race-reifying effort, black capitalism, Nixon also sought to preempt the liberals, and drive a class wedge into the politically monolithic African-American community. One might say it was more than a politics of preemption; it was a politics of creative destruction.

A final point before we can begin. What about the moral boundaries that had made affirmative action a taboo? By 1969, when Nixon took office, five years of race rioting and crisis management, administrative pragmatism, and spirited tradition discourse had lowered the risk of affirmative action advocacy. This was no longer political suicide. In addition, another controversial issue, busing children to integrate schools, had distracted the national audience from the employment issue. As discussed in the preceding chapter, the civil rights tradition had become a juggernaut in the turbulent, Cold War climate, and it was risky to appear resistant to this progressive march toward justice. Yet while boundaries were blurring, it was still risky to take the affirmative action route. In the Nixon administration, one finds officials articulating all of the discourses of affirmative action advocacy already mentioned: those of crisis management, administrative pragmatism, and tradition. Especially in selling the Plan to an audience of conservatives, however, one finds a new discourse, a discourse of preemption: affirmative action was advocated because it confounded the liberals.

Setting the Scene: An Uncertain Mandate in the 1968 Election

Nixon won the 1968 presidential election with only 43.4 percent of the vote. His margin of victory over his Democratic challenger, former Vice President Hubert Humphrey, was exceedingly small—Humphrey tallied 42.7 percent of the vote. Far behind in votes but not influence was a third party challenger, racist/populist George Wallace, who gained 13.5 percent of the vote, mostly in the Deep South. Whereas in 1964, 61 percent of the electorate had voted for Johnson, now an almost equal percentage (57 percent) repudiated the Democratic candidate.[20]

But a solid repudiation of the Democratic presidential candidate did not necessarily mean the end of liberalism, or a solid affirmation of Nixon. First, obviously, Nixon split that opposition vote with Wallace; this was no landslide of support for Richard M. Nixon. Second, the Democrats still did well in Congress, and controlled both the House and the Senate. The Democrats lost 5 Senate seats, though their majority was still 58–42, and only 4 GOP seats were gained in the House, despite expectations of a gain of at least 35.[21] Third, while the South seemed to have bolted the Democrats for good, with Wallace winning Mississippi, Alabama, Georgia, Arkansas, and Louisiana, and the border states going to Nixon, the core of the New Deal coalition came together for the Democrats again—big cities, Catholics, union members, blacks, and Jews. Indeed, by some measures, the Democratic party was solidifying its support in the working-class white community. John R. Petrocik, for example, found that Polish and Irish Catholics were increasingly identifying themselves as Democrats from the 1950s to the 1970s, and union members continued to identify as Democrats.[22] It was clear that Nixon would have to broaden his base if he wanted to establish solid leadership legitimacy and avoid the historically less significant (almost stigmatizing) one-term presidency.

One clue as to how this could be done came from the Wallace campaign. For part of the campaign, polls showed Wallace making large inroads into the traditionally Democratic blue-collar/union vote. This lasted until the AFL-CIO waged a massive campaign to defeat him, partly based on a desire to defeat Nixon, too.[23] Wallace seemed to fill a void that opened when what influential political observers Richard Scammon and Ben Wattenberg called "the social issue" became prominent in American politics. Scammon and Wattenberg, whose ideas were to become widely known in Washington and especially in the Nixon White House, highlighted as part of the social issue concerns such as women's roles, the boundaries of free expression, sexual norms, and race, the latter being of particular importance to Americans, with polls placing "racial problems" and "civil rights" at or near the top of the list of "most important problems" for 1963–1970.[24] The Democrats were liberal on both the economic and the social issues. The Republicans, following the Goldwater movement, were conservative on both the economic and social issues. This left a dilemma for the working-class voter, who was likely to be liberal on economic issues and conservative on social issues. Wallace added a choice for voters of economic liberalism combined with social-issue conservatism, especially on race.[25]

The Republicans, to be sure, already had evidence that race was an issue with which they could win some votes. While race was a crucial issue for Wallace, it was also crucial for Nixon. Nixon was following in the footsteps of the previous Republican candidate, Arizona senator Barry Goldwater, who was thoroughly trounced by Lyndon Johnson in 1964. Goldwater's laissez-faire conservatism did not win him any states, but an offshoot of his ideology, racial conservatism, did pay off, as Goldwater at least won Deep South states in that election, in addition to his narrow victory in his home state of Arizona. Despite this debacle, Republicans came to embrace certain parts of the Goldwater platform, and thus for some analysts of American politics, the 1964 election marks the end of Republican racial liberalism.[26] Notwithstanding the Goldwater movement's lack of *direct* attention to African-American issues, its antistatist conservatism had a profound influence on the party in this area. The GOP became to the electorate the antiblack party. For example, polls conducted by the National Election Studies show that in 1962 the question of which party "is more likely to see to it that Negroes get fair treatment in jobs and housing," revealed essentially no difference in the public's perceptions of the Republicans and the Democrats. Specifically, 22.7 percent of respondents identified the Democrats, 21.3 percent identified Republicans, and 55.9 percent said that there was no difference. Response to the question radically changed by late 1964, however. In response to a similar question on party support for fair treatment for blacks in job opportunities, only 7 percent identified the Republicans as offering more support, while 60 percent said it would be the Democrats, and 33 percent said no difference. In a separate question on party support for blacks and whites attending the same schools, the figures were 7 percent, 56 percent, and 37 percent, respectively.[27] The civil rights positions of the 1964 candidates got through to the voters: 96 percent knew that Johnson supported the Civil Rights Act of 1964, and 84 percent knew that Goldwater opposed it.[28] Though the Wallace campaign suggested new vulnerabilities of the Democrats, Nixon seemed unaware, and other than in the South, showed no preference as to which usually Democratic group to target.

In the 1968 Presidential election, Richard Nixon skillfully steered his campaign through the middle ground between liberal Hubert Humphrey and reactionary George Wallace. While a relatively unsupportive civil rights image was a Republican given, Nixon's basic position was not established by a coherent middle-ground ideology. Like a good preemptive politician, he established it by mixing surgical strikes into liberal areas with conservative policies which, on the balance, would stake out a middle ground of sorts. In a series of 1968 spring radio talks, Nixon appeared to dance all over the political map. For potential liberal voters, he offered this state-of-the-art liberal gem: Franklin Roosevelt, he said, "promulgated the old, negative freedoms *from*. Our uncompleted task is to make real the new, positive freedoms *to*" (original emphasis). A new coalition was proposed by Nixon, made up of some strange bedfellows: traditional Republicans, the "new South," "black militants," the "silent center," and "thoughtful critics like Daniel Patrick Moynihan and Richard Goodwin—both liberals." As A. James Reichley commented, Nixon's talk showed he was "groping toward new coalitions, examining unusual options."[29]

In terms of civil rights policy, the Republicans continued the promising course charted by Barry Goldwater four years earlier. Nixon, who in 1960 and 1964 had been a strong supporter of civil rights, was now playing the role of a moderate Wallace. This was to work to Nixon's advantage, particularly as Wallace crossed boundaries of legitimacy, such as when Wallace's running mate General Curtis LeMay said that he would immediately use nuclear weapons in Vietnam.[30]

Nixon's position on civil rights during his 1968 campaign brilliantly negotiated the ambiguous moral and political boundaries on the issue, distinguishing between support for civil rights in principle and for civil rights in practice. The political trick in the campaign was to avoid appearing as a racist, to make the necessary obeisances to the civil rights tradition, but also to hedge on implementation, and avoid appearing to support black gains at the expense of whites.[31]

Crucial for the emergence of affirmative action, the more salient implementation issue for the national audience was in the area of education and not jobs. Like Goldwater before him, Nixon came down unequivocally against forced integration, or the practice of busing children in order to desegregate the school system. Nixon stated his strong support for the landmark Supreme Court decision which made maintaining segregated schools illegal, but also showed his conviction that little should be done about positively *integrating* the nation's schools:

> But, on the other hand, while that decision [*Brown*] dealt with segregation and said that we would not have segregation, when you go beyond that and say it is the responsibility of the federal government, and the federal courts, to, in effect, act as local school districts in determining how we carry that out, and then to use the power of the federal treasury to withhold funds or give funds in order to carry it out, then I think we are going too far. In my view, that kind of activity should be scrupulously examined and in many cases, I think, should be rescinded. . . . I think that to use that power on the part of the federal government to force a local community to carry out what a federal administrator or bureaucrat may think is best for that local community—I think that is a doctrine that is a very dangerous one.[32]

Nixon knew that supporting segregation was now a political third rail, but he also knew at the very least the southern audience would applaud some resistance on this issue.

Though Nixon tried to stay in the middle, the taken-for-grantedness of a progressive civil rights tradition was apparent. Moderates and the remaining liberals in Nixon's own party were uncomfortable with Nixon's racial stance. After a Nixon campaign aid, working in the South, reportedly said, "Perhaps we can get George Wallace on our side. That's where he belongs," GOP primary opponent and New York Governor Nelson Rockefeller charged that Nixon was running a campaign with racist overtones, and that there was in fact almost no difference between Nixon and Wallace. Nixon claimed that in twenty-two years of politics he had never had a racist in his organizations, and that the appeal of George Wallace was "in the direction of the racist element . . . [and] such an appeal wouldn't be made by either of the two national parties. We will be able to present the American people a choice, but we will not divide the country on a race basis."[33]

If Nixon was not going to do the dividing, he would recruit a running mate who would. A campaign with two voices could simultaneously appeal to sub-groups in the national audience. Spiro T. Agnew, the eventual vice president, was deliberately used as a strong, conservative force on the social issues. Agnew had come to national attention for his reactionary style when dealing with black leaders. Following the outbreak of riots in Baltimore, Agnew called together about one hundred African-American leaders for a meeting. Instead of offering proposals on how to work together to deal with the discontent, how-ever, Agnew chastised the leaders for allowing the riots. He labeled them the "circuit-riding, Hanoi-visiting . . . caterwauling, riot-inciting, burn-America-down type of leader[s]." He also claimed that instead of trying to stop the riots, the leaders simply ran away. These prominent blacks were reportedly shocked, and eighty of them walked out on the governor. When Nixon heard the story, he remarked, "That guy Agnew is really an impressive fellow. He's got guts. He's got a good attitude."[34]

It was in the area of jobs that Nixon would stake his claim of harmony with the civil rights tradition. A candidate could not completely repudiate civil rights and still be taken seriously, and employment, to Nixon, was an area in which a civil rights liberalism could be advocated to a national audience without offend-ing his conservative, opposition base. For much of his political past, Nixon had been progressive on the issue of discrimination in employment. For example, as discussed in the previous chapter, Nixon served as chairman for the President's Committee on Government Contracts, a group which promoted an affirmative action principle (industry-wide analysis of equal employment opportunity for African-Americans).[35] During the 1968 campaign, while expressing his disap-proval of federally enforced school integration measures and the need for stron-ger law-and-order measures to stop ghetto rioting, Nixon also was stressing the importance of jobs and economic opportunity for blacks. His position in the riot-filled summer of 1967 was that "[j]obs is the gut issue" in racial unrest and that "[i]f you don't have jobs, you don't have housing and you don't get off of welfare."[36]

In April of 1968, Nixon ventured where the Democrats feared to go—an ex-plicit race-targeted program. One of Nixon's risky preemptive strikes was what could be considered a distinctively Republican approach to race-conscious jus-tice. It showed no sensitivity to the New Deal project of universalist social pol-icy, openly advertising a *racial* beneficiary. It would not cost taxpayers anything; it would only nudge the private sector to make an impact. It would split that monolithic black presence in the American electorate, creating a new (presumably Republican) middle class to counter the Democratic lower class, and it would be a tool to manage the racial crisis in the cities (see chapter 4). Thus, it would honor a liberal tradition, by helping blacks, but it would not offend the conservative opposition. This was Nixon's promise to develop "black capitalism."

The idea was laid out in a 25 April 1968 radio campaign speech in which he planned to build

> The bridge of black success—a bridge that can only be achieved by those [blacks] who themselves have overcome, and who by their help or their example can show the way to the American dream.
> The bridge of black capitalism—by providing technical assistance and loan guarantees, by opening new capital sources, we can help blacks to start new businesses . . . and to expand existing ones . . .
> What we need is imaginative enlistment of private funds, private energies, and private talents, in order to develop the opportunities that lie untapped in our own underdeveloped urban heartland. . . . It costs little or no government money to set in motion many of the programs that would in fact do the most, in a practical sense, to start building a firm structure of [black] economic opportunity. . . . Government's primary role [should be] not to do the job by itself, but to assist in getting it done.[37]

Nixon's campaign advisers were against black capitalism, fearing it would upset the appeal to the South,[38] but they lacked the institutionalized interest of American presidents for creativity, originality, and a place in history. The logic of the politics of preemption led directly to risky policies such as black capitalism.

Nixon in Office: The Search for Leadership Legitimacy

Nixon began his term with a shaky warrant for leadership, as his low support in the election attested. He therefore needed to reward his supporters carefully, while managing the delicate task of gaining new support. To reward his southern supporters, Nixon would have to slow down the implementation of civil rights, especially busing. He soon discovered, however, that a civil rights slowdown in any area would come with great pain, as his opposition voice would have to contend with the chorus of liberal voices in Congress, in the media, and in special-interest organizations. Thus, the historical record shows that Nixon ran his campaign and presidency with the hopes of turning down the volume of the liberal audience, actually *appealing* to black voters or at the *very* least, finessing his southern strategy in such a way as not to offend them. His hopes were misplaced.

Despite his relatively liberal racial views in the early part of his career, Nixon was conspicuously lacking in support from African-Americans. He had never done notably well among black voters in any of his previous elections, and 90 percent of black voters avoided him in 1968. He *owed* them little, but he needed to broaden his base to make a historical mark. Before his inauguration he thought it necessary to meet with civil rights leaders, where he reportedly promised "to do more for the underprivileged and more for the Negro than any President has ever done."[39] In his inauguration speech, he took a conservative but supportive stand on civil rights: "The laws have caught up with our conscience. What remains is to give life to what is in the law."[40]

But this early pandering was clearly not enough. Black suspicion remained high enough that it became an issue. At a 6 February 1969 news conference, a journalist asked Nixon about the "distrust among the blacks" toward the new president. Nixon insisted that he would be a "friend to all citizens."[41]

In early May of 1969, Nixon again met black political leaders, including Ralph Abernathy, Martin Luther King's former lieutenant and successor as head of the Southern Christian Leadership Conference. Nixon thought the meeting went well, but afterwards, Abernathy declared the meeting "disappointing and fruitless" to reporters, infuriating Nixon. He scrawled on the bottom of a report, "This shows that my judgment about *not* seeing such people is right. *No More of This!*" (original emphasis).[42] This experience seemed to leave him bitter. Nixon recalls complaining to his staff,

> I could deliver the Sermon on the Mount and the NAACP would criticize the rhetoric. And the diehard segregationists would criticize it on the grounds that I was being motivated solely by public pressure rather than by conscience. So let's just tackle the problems instead of talking about them. We will be judged by whatever we do rather than what we say on this issue.

Nixon, according to his memoirs, interpreted his lack of debt to the civil rights community not as an excuse to do nothing on the issue, but as an opportunity to approach the issues in the way that he saw fit; Nixon felt he could do what he "thought was the right thing." To White House consultant Daniel Patrick Moynihan, he explained, "The problem, as I see it, is that they don't think that I care. We must demonstrate to them that we *do* care by our actions and not just by our words."[43]

This became a familiar refrain in Nixon's discourse of preemption. It was necessary, as he had to cultivate leadership legitimacy by delicately managing subaudiences of the national electorate. Nixon explained he would be quiet about his concrete civil rights gains in office as a counterpoint to Johnson, whom he accused of making a lot of promises, raising a lot of hopes and creating a lot of frustration (the riots) by not delivering. But there was another purpose to a whispered "We shall overcome." He would *quietly,* in his action or deeds, honor the liberal establishment and civil rights tradition, with the hope that the liberal and black audience would notice and appreciate it, but his supportive South just would not notice or remember. And he would help them forget with actions (and words) that expressed indifference or hostility for civil rights. A contradictory policy, if Nixon could make both audiences see what they supported, promised to deliver the wide backing desperately needed to establish legitimacy.

Winning the South (While Appealing to Blacks)

Thus, in office, Nixon generally soft-pedaled the civil rights issue. Domestic policy adviser John Ehrlichman recalled, "[Nixon] insisted that the Government's civil rights enforcers moderate their zeal. Nixon was constantly vigilant for news of some appointee's undue enthusiasm."[44] The crucial topic to shut up about was school integration. Adviser Harry Dent reminded Nixon in a memo on 23 January 1969 that "so far as Southern politics is concerned, the Nixon administration will be judged from the beginning on the manner in which the school desegregation guidelines problem is handled. Other issues are important in the South but are dwarfed somewhat by comparison."[45] By 2 March 1970, Nixon was telling his closest advisers (Chief of Staff H. R. "Bob" Haldeman, John Ehrlichman, and National Security adviser Henry Kissinger) in a private memo that school integration was one of the top three priorities in domestic affairs (along with recession/inflation and crime), explaining, "I must assume the responsibility here because it will be the major issue of controversy for the foreseeable future," and asked for a trusted assistant on the issue who was not biased toward either Left or Right.[46] Outspoken administration supporters of civil rights in the schools, such as Commissioner of Education James Allen, were dismissed. Anyone not opposing busing in public speaking was fired. "Always remember, on this subject a low profile is the key," Nixon allegedly said.[47] He did not send a civil rights message to Congress, and in a meeting on 15 December 1969, with Ehrlichman, press secretary Ronald Ziegler, and chief of staff Bob Haldeman discussing the upcoming state of the union address, it was consciously decided that civil rights would be "very low key."[48]

Still, the priority was to reward the Border South and win the Deep South and something besides being low-key was necessary. A statement was issued on 3 July 1969, declaring that enforcement would now be emphasized in the courts, and suggesting that deadlines for desegregation would be delayed. Civil rights groups reacted strongly. Roy Wilkins said the administration was "breaking the law," and said, "It's almost enough to make you vomit. This is not a matter of too little too late; rather, this is nothing at all."[49] Two times the administration asked for delays in implementing school desegregation in the South, but both times the Supreme Court denied the requests. The delays produced more dismay among civil rights groups, and in the civil rights division of the Justice Department, many lawyers resigned. The administration got into further hot water with civil rights groups by a proposed amendment to the 1965 Voting Rights Act, which would have increased jurisdiction of the act to all fifty states, eliminated the necessity for covered sections of the country to receive federal approval of voting law changes, and set a minimum residency requirement for national election voting. Civil rights groups saw this amendment as a clever attempt to substantially weaken the old law, since it would weaken the law in the areas most in need of it—in the South. GOP Representative Gerald Ford defended the bill by arguing that in specifying the South, the Voting Rights Act was punishing it unfairly (absolving the South from the government's opprobrium was a prominent feature of the southern strategy). The bill was accepted in the House in a close vote (208–203), but shelved in the Senate. Civil rights groups called the House vote the most severe civil rights defeat in ten years.

In the area of employment, the administration was embroiled in controversy just weeks after assuming office. The Department of Defense agreed to contracts with certain textile firms (located in the South) that had previously been ruled as not in compliance with equal employment opportunity standards by the OFCC; in fact, the contracts agreed to were even less adequate than those rejected previously, in terms of equal opportunity. Immediately, voices were raised in protest. The Department of Transportation then contributed to the deteriorating situation by announcing that highway contractors did not have to meet OFCC standards before bidding on jobs. At EEOC, Chairman Clifford L. Alexander resigned on 9 April 1969, citing a "crippling lack of Administration support" as a reason for his departure. The administration was also at odds with many EEOC officials over its resistance to giving cease and desist authority to the agency, instead calling for the ability of the agency to take noncomplying employers to court (the administration position eventually became law in the Equal Employment Opportunity Act of 1972).[50]

These actions and controversies dominated the civil rights image of the Nixon administration. The appearance of a backward slide in the civil rights arena was too much for those most concerned to bear, and the cries of protest were swift and shrill. After just three months in office, the White House was responding to angry inquiries from black congressmen with long, explanatory letters which denied any infidelity to the civil rights tradition.[51]

Actions not directly related to civil rights added to the "backward slide" image, further compromising leadership legitimacy. Nixon's first two attempts at making Supreme Court appointments produced storms of controversy, partly because of the civil rights issue. On 18 August 1969, Nixon nominated Clement F. Haynsworth, Jr., to the Supreme Court. Haynsworth had been chief justice of the Fourth Circuit Court of Appeals, a southern circuit which civil rights advocates argued had been especially slow in desegregating schools. Notably, Haynsworth dissented when his court ruled against resistance to desegregation in Prince Edward County, Virginia, and also dissented in a case in which the court decided that hospitals accepting federal funds could not segregate their facilities.

Organized labor, despite being notorious for discrimination at the level of union locals, was an old civil rights ally in Washington, especially in helping push through Title VII of the Civil Rights Act of 1964, and had joined civil rights groups in opposing Haynsworth, as the southern justice also had a record seen as unfavorable to labor concerns. The Haynsworth nomination was an overtly hostile act to George Meany, head of the AFL-CIO. Meany saw Haynsworth's record as unacceptably antilabor, arguing that the South Carolina justice had an opportunity to decide on seven labor cases, chose the antilabor side every time, and had his decision overturned by the Supreme Court every time. In Meany's view, the Haynsworth nomination "was a declaration of war."

Together, labor and civil rights won the Haynsworth battle, and Haynsworth was rejected 55 to 45 in the Senate. Liberal Republican Senator Jacob Javits called him "insensitive" and "out of date." Democrat Lee Metcalf, in referring to the Nixon campaign's attempt to appeal to voters in the South, said sardonically, "In the light of Judge Haynsworth's record, it is plain that . . . the highest qualification for a seat on the Supreme Court is complete ideological identification with the reactionary tenets of the administration's southern strategy." Much of the negative lobbying of Senators came from the civil rights and labor groups.[52] The defeat infuriated Nixon.

In the spring of 1970, the next choice was G. Harrold Carswell. While not notably antilabor, Carswell was seen as antiblack. To Meany, however, this was the same thing: "[A] judge who is anti-Negro is also anti-labor."[53] Again, civil rights and labor joined forces, and the Nixon appointee, who was also severely attacked on his merits as a judge (one anonymous Senator said that the nomination of the inept Carswell was an attempt to "downgrade" the Court's prestige[54]), was rejected, 51–45.[55] Clarence Mitchell, director of the Washington bureau of the NAACP and legislative chairman of the Leadership Conference on Civil Rights, said, "None of the legislative fights we have made in the field of civil rights could have been won without the trade-union movement. We couldn't have beaten Haynsworth without labor, and the struggle against Carswell would not have been a contest."[56]

While many of these efforts were designed to solidify the South's future sup-port, Nixon could not attack or impede civil rights across the board and maintain legitimacy, and though black voters seemed as hostile as they had been on elec-tion day, incredibly, in his 1969 search for authority, Nixon refused to rule out potential new support from blacks. One simple strategy of quietly honoring the civil rights tradition was to increase funding of the existing civil rights agencies. This was urged on Nixon in July of 1969 specifically to aid his civil rights im-age.[57] Another simple strategy of honoring civil rights as well as appealing to African-Americans and other voter blocks was to make them a part of the Nixon team. In his own administration, the president appeared to be obsessed with the idea of diversity. He kept track of the ethnicity and gender of *all* of his political appointments, to a degree of specificity that made many in government uncom-fortable. A memo to Nixon from aid Harry S. Flemming, dated 19 September 1969, contained exceedingly detailed information in this area. Stating that "[t]he following is an analysis of the ethnic background of persons appointed to non-career positions in the Executive Branch since January 20, 1969," the memo reported that there were now 86 blacks working for Nixon, 74 Jews, 36 Italians, 9 Mexican-Americans, 4 Puerto Ricans, 8 Greeks, 10 Poles, 7 "Orien-tals," 2 American Indians, 601 "Other," and 764 "Unknown." There were 1,360 males and 241 females.[58] It was unclear to Administration officials just what the Nixon administration was hoping to accomplish with this obsession with other-ness, as there seemed to be some recognition that it was too risky. A memo from White House consultant Peter M. Flanigan to Ken Cole on 17 October said, "In our September research effort, we met with considerable hesitation from some Departments and Agencies when we asked them to report all minority and eth-nic appointments made by this administration. . . . A newspaper report on our efforts might well have ballooned into very unfavorable publicity."[59]

Another initiative was following up on his promise of working (without spending money) to develop black capitalism. This was accomplished through an executive order issued on 5 March 1969, which created the Office of Minor-ity Business Enterprise. Though substituting a euphemism for the race label, Nixon still targeted race in a way the Democrats had scrupulously avoided. Ac-cording to Commerce Secretary Maurice H. Stans, the new office was to serve "as a catalyst to draw together resources of government and the private sector to provide the opportunities, funds, know-how, and business orders for promising minority businesses to begin and grow."[60]

Besides the "minority" label, black capitalism/minority enterprise was also notable in that there was no developed pretext of discrimination supposedly be-ing combatted. To hear Nixon tell it in pubic, black capitalism was not an anti-discrimination measure, which affirmative action ostensibly was, but a simple subsidy: "I have often made the point that to foster the economic status and the pride of members of our minority groups we must seek to involve them more fully in our private enterprise system."[61] For wary conservatives, he added, "The first need is to replace dependence with independence."[62] Thus, this race-reifying policy, originally propounded as a crisis management tool, could serve as an instrument for two ends otherwise unrelated to civil rights justice: making a class of black businessmen, and lessening the welfare drag on the economy. The "Bridge of Black Capitalism" was a bridge over an ideological gulf that traditionally separated African-American Democrats from the Republicans. The *Wall Street Journal* gave the program its approval, while also pointing out that the new Office of Minority Business Enterprise would turn rioters into Republicans.[63] Organized labor denounced the idea, calling it "apartheid, antidemocratic nonsense," and self-destructive "attempts to build separate economic enclaves."[64] Black capitalism or minority enterprise, however it was called, looked to labor like a lure to steal away a key political ally.

The "Revised" Philadelphia Plan

The logic of the politics of preemption directed Nixon's energies to another initiative regarding the African-American community that moved beyond established Democratic models. Forces began to come together early in 1969 that would lead to the historic Nixon role in strengthening and refining affirmative action through the contract compliance program. As mentioned in chapter 4, the threatening, potentially violent racial climate led to interest from Nixon's Secretary of Labor George Shultz in strengthening equal opportunity in contract compliance before he took office. Perhaps Shultz's attention was further directed to this area by John A. Hannah, chair of the U. S. Commission on Civil Rights, who sent Shultz, immediately after his 4 February 1969 arrival, a letter of 4 pages, 41 pages of staff material, and a 318-page study of the federal role in equal employment opportunity, all with a strong emphasis on the need to strengthen the contract program.[65] In addition, the early fiascos with the Defense and Transportation Departments' disregard of equal employment opportunity standards in awarding contracts led to March senate subcommittee hearings on the matter. Notes circulated through a nervous White House that subcommittee chair Senator Edward Kennedy was researching all Nixon statements on minority affairs.[66] Shultz was spared the grilling that Transportation Secretary John Volpe endured from Kennedy only because the hearings were suspended when former President Eisenhower died. Shultz's written testimony, however, did promise better efforts from the OFCC.[67]

In the late spring, Assistant Secretary of Labor Arthur Fletcher decided, with Secretary Shultz's backing, to revive the Philadelphia Plan. Labor Department lawyers had been preparing themselves for just such an eventuality since the first Plan was declared illegal during the Johnson administration by Comptroller General Elmer Staats. The illegal version, as discussed in chapter 5, was faulted for not having definite minimum standards for the required affirmative action programs; it was therefore seen as an unfair bidding practice. No move was made to revive the Plan during Johnson's tenure, however. Rumors circulated that Edward Sylvester, Director of the OFCC, was shelving the program so as not to disrupt Hubert Humphrey's presidential campaign.[68] But for the new Republican administration, there were no coalition-sustaining commitments to the color-blind model, which had its taken-for-granted moral status shaken by the events of the previous five years. There was no longer any obvious reason to keep the Plan on the shelf. On the contrary, the Democrats' discomfort provided a good reason to take it off.

While Shultz initially seemed interested in affirmative action as crisis management, Fletcher apparently arrived at the Plan the same way that the OFCC staff did—pragmatically (see chapter 5). Shultz and Fletcher sold the Plan to the White House audience not only as potentially very effective and as good preemption politics but, incredibly, as also in line with the Republican ideology—in 1969, affirmative action was thought to be a safe, conservative move. According to Nixon speechwriter and public relations man William Safire, Shultz wanted "to show blacks that the Administration would help them gain the opportunity for economic advancement, now far more important than new laws or more welfare, the thrust of which was consistent with a spirit of self-reliance." Safire also maintains that this seemingly out-of- place discourse of tradition (affirmative action as traditional individualism and self-help) could be seen at a Cabinet meeting, where Fletcher "transfixed" his audience "when he pleaded his case for black economic achievement," arguing that the Plan could be seen as "the keystone of the Administration's commitment to 'helping people help themselves.' "[69]

The version of the Philadelphia Plan presented by the Nixon administration differed from the illegal one, which lacked definite minimum standards for contract bidding. The way around this problem, obviously, was to supply minimum standards of minority hiring for a contracting company's affirmative action program. This is to say that a quota would have to be filled—a definite minimum standard.

But not exactly. The OFCC proposed a solution to the illegality of the Philadelphia Plan by playing what was to amount to an elaborate semantic game with the discourse of tradition, insisting that there was nothing out-of-tradition about the Plan. Though undeniably race-conscious, the Philadelphia Plan still could be made to fit with tradition because it was not technically a taboo—it was not the unspeakably naughty racial quota. No matter that the text of the Civil Rights Act and Executive Order 11246 also made hiring by race just as illegal as racial quotas. The color-blind model in 1969 was yielding to race consciousness, and the new line in the sand, the new racial boundary, was the racial quota. The OFCC staff, according to Fletcher, proposed that

> specific percentage *targets* for minority employees in several trades, be set forth in Philadelphia and incorporated into the bid specifications in all government contracts issued in that area. OFCC wished to be specific with respect to numbers, and then impose a "good faith" obligation to achieve the numerical results. This was designed to avoid the argument that the numbers constituted "quotas" and hence violated the so-called "no quota" provision of Title VII of the 1964 Civil Rights Act [emphasis added].[70]

This meant that a contractor would have to aim for a target of, for example, 10 to 15 percent minority electricians. The contractor did not *have* to have this percentage, but if the contractor failed, it would have to demonstrate "good faith," that it had tried the best that it could. It would have to prove its innocence to the charge of discrimination/underutilization. If the contractor was not convincing, contracts could be canceled or denied. Fletcher announced the new, Revised Philadelphia Plan on 27 June 1969, adding that it would "be put into effect in all the major cities across the Nation as soon as possible." Aware that he was dancing on the boundaries of American justice, Fletcher diplomatically added that "It might be better, admittedly, if specific goals were not required—certainly the black people of America understand taboos." The history of discrimination, however, affirmed that "[v]isible, measurable goals to correct obvious imbalances [were] essential."[71]

Thus, in Fletcher's view, there was nothing radical here, nothing to get flustered about. The revised version of the Philadelphia Plan did not require a quota, but instead a target or range—which inexplicably had an upper bound as well as a lower bound—and in specifying a "good faith" effort, it did not technically *require* racial hiring. This was buttressed by a legal memorandum by the Solicitor of Labor, Lawrence H. Silberman, who emphasized legal precedent, including the familiar school integration tradition (this time *US v. Jefferson County Board of Education*), which had also used numerical goals.[72]

The comptroller general did not accept it and ruled the *new* Plan illegal, stating on 5 August that while it was specific and fair to bidders, and thus improved on the old Plan, it now made race a determinative factor in employment, required quotas, and thus violated the Civil Rights Act of 1964. Republican Senator Everett Dirksen did not accept it either, and sent letters on 7 August to Nixon, Shultz, and Attorney General John Mitchell, as well as some other congressmen, explaining that Dirksen felt appropriation bills in which the Plan was a condition of contracts were in violation of the Civil Rights Act.[73]

On 26 August, Nixon was told by Ehrlichman that special civil rights consultant Len Garment was "of the conviction that contract compliance [was] probably the most effective federal tool for bringing about equal opportunity,"[74] and the White House continued its support of the Labor Department officials. The powerful Dirksen stepped up the pressure, warning Nixon of the party-splitting potential of the Plan, and Dirksen's own opposition.[75] Dirksen, who had brokered the compromise that led to the Civil Rights Act of 1964, had since February 1969 begun a crusade to blow the whistle on the pragmatic affirmative action developments in the EEOC and OFCC, which he saw as punitive harassment of American businessmen. In Senate judiciary hearings on equal employment procedures in March, he showed just how determined he was. "I had a little something to do with writing the Civil Rights Act in 1964, and particularly Title VII," he bitterly told wayward EEOC Chair Clifford Alexander. "As a matter of fact," he continued, "it was written in my office." He warned Alexander of a growing belief in the Senate as well as in the media and the courts that enforcement had gone off track. Dirksen explained he had a personal stake in the matter:

> I am just as interested in this law and in solving this problem in the country as you, for if I were not I would not have devoted all that attention to the 1964 law and got to my knees to beg those on my side in order to kill the filibuster, so we could get a vote to it. And when you do that, of course, you take your political skin in your hands. But I did not mind that. I wanted to get it done. And I got it. . . . But we did not intend for one minute that the people of this country, and of course particularly the work givers, industry and business, should be harassed. . . . And if there is harassment, maybe we are going to have some new person in [Alexander's position].[76]

Eleven days later, Alexander did resign. But this was to be Dirksen's last crusade: he died suddenly in September, of cancer.

The now emboldened Nixon administration, following the institutional interest in creative leadership and the context-bound logic of preempting the liberal agenda, marched onward. An administration letter of 13 August to four more Democratic congressmen, outraged over the "breakdown in civil rights enforcement," touted the Philadelphia Plan, among other moves, as proof of fidelity to the civil rights tradition.[77] Then, on 23 September, Attorney General John Mitchell, a primary supporter of the southern strategy, originally against black capitalism,[78] and originally against the Plan,[79] declared the Plan legal. Shultz immediately announced that the Plan was ordered into effect. Shultz also explained why it was legal, putting his powerful voice over the semantic squabble. The Plan did not require quotas but goals: "[A] quota is a system which keeps people out. . . . What we are seeking are objectives to get people in." Unconvinced, C. J. Haggerty, president of the AFL-CIO Building and Construction Trades Department, told an AFL-CIO convention, "We are 100 percent opposed to a quota system, whether it be called the Philadelphia Plan or whatever." James Naughton, reporting for The New York Times, sensed the strangeness of the Nixon position, writing that Mitchell's and Shultz's announcements "underscored the apparent decision by the Nixon Administration to concentrate its civil rights activity in the field of equal job opportunities," and adding, ambiguously, "a decision that could have important political overtones."[80]

In fact the civil rights activity was more limited than "equal job opportunities." In a press conference in late September, Nixon was conspicuously careful to limit his civil rights vision to construction unions, stating,

> [I]t is essential that black Americans, all Americans, have an equal opportunity to get into the construction unions. . . . We intend to continue through the Department of Labor to attempt to make progress in this field, because in the long run, we cannot have construction unions which deny the right of all Americans to have those positions.
>
> America needs more construction workers, and, of course, all Americans are entitled to an equal right to be a member of a union.[81]

In his memoirs, Nixon also placed this unjustified restriction on his civil rights policy:

> A good job is as basic and important a civil right as a good education, and many blacks and members of other minorities were being prevented from getting good jobs because of the policies of the major labor unions which excluded them from membership or discriminated against them in hiring and promotion. Therefore the first problem we addressed was unemployment. I asked Secretary of Labor George Shultz to see what could be done. He proposed [the Philadelphia Plan].[82]

The day after the announcements of the Plan's legality, George Meany echoed Haggerty's sentiments while speaking to a convention of the AFL-CIO Building and Construction Trades Department, and let it be known that he felt that Nixon was continuing, following the Haynsworth nomination, a war against the unions. Despite efforts to open membership to minorities,

> Still we find the Building Trades being singled out as being "lily-white" as they say, and some fellow the other day said it was "the last bastion of discrimination."
>
> Now, this is an amazing statement, when you figure how small par-

ticipation of Negroes and other minorities is in, for instance, the banks in this country, the press, on the payroll for newspapers and communications media, and I think there is one Negro in the United States Senate. That is just 1%, 1 out of 100.

I don't think that when President Nixon looks around his cabinet, I don't think he sees any black faces in there either. But we in the Building Trades are singled out as "the last bastion of discrimination."

I want to tell you I resent it just as much as anyone in this room, or anyone here on the platform. I resent the action of government officials—no matter what department they come from—who are trying to make a whipping boy out of the Building Trades.[83]

The convention recorded a statement opposing the Plan as "part of a pattern of conduct formulated by political strategists in the Nixon administration to divide the labor movement while slowing down the process of implementing the civil rights program on voting and education in the South."[84] In other words, labor objected to Nixon's politics of preemption.[85]

A Violation of Color-Blindness . . . or the Separation of Powers?

The struggle of the attorney general versus the comptroller general complicated the issue of the legitimation of the most radical civil rights employment measure in American history. To support the Philadelphia Plan, it was argued, was also to support the power of the Executive to be above the law. To be against the Philadelphia Plan was argued to be in support of an appointee of Congress to supervise the Executive. The debate over the Philadelphia Plan thus came to involve obscure legislation about the heretofore obscure office of the comptroller general, involving the otherwise unrelated issue of the separation of powers. That the issue would come up in this way is part of Skowronek's model of the politics of preemption: "Out to reset national politics and government on their own terms, these presidents [opposition presidents facing a strong establishment] provoked major constitutional crises over the legitimate exercise of presidential power, crises that temporarily warded off the portents of a political reconstruction with a convulsive campaign against executive usurpation."[86] Though executive orders in civil rights had been in effect for decades, it was only when Nixon flexed his executive muscles that Congress seemed to notice. Though this was at least partly because of the race-conscious nature of the Plan, the fact that opponents would emphasize separation of powers over the obvious breach of color blindness underscored the newfound legitimacy of the affirmative action approach—and the new illegitimacy of resisting civil rights however defined.

Thus, opponents did *not* attack affirmative action directly. They attacked the power of the attorney general to overrule the comptroller. The attack was even less direct than this: a surprise rider was attached to an appropriations bill by the Senate Appropriations Committee.

This move occurred after preliminary hearings of a bill, S. 931, sponsored by Republican Paul Fannin of Arizona, that would have suspended outright the legal warrant for the Plan (President Johnson's Executive Order 11246) and made Title VII the nation's only employment civil rights tool. Hearings were held on 27 and 28 October in North Carolina Senator Sam Ervin's Separation of Powers subcommittee of the Senate Judiciary Committee to discuss this bill, producing the potentially interminable debate about the meaning of quotas. The struggle to define the Philadelphia Plan as part of or alien to tradition centered on the very meaning of words in the English language.

Was it outrageous racial quotas or ostensibly traditional racial hiring ranges being demanded? Critics claimed the idea of "ranges" of acceptable hiring was disingenuous. For instance, Harry P. Taylor, executive director of the General Building Contractors Association in Philadelphia, asked, "Except for camouflage, what purpose is served by establishing a range with a maximum figure? If an employer's efforts to recruit minority workers should bear such fruit as to exceed the maximum figure in the range, will the employer be declared in noncompliance for recruiting too many minority workers?"[87]

Unfortunately, no one ever answered Taylor's provocative question. Witnesses, such as GOP Senator Jacob Javits or Assistant Attorney General Jerris Leonard, spent most of their testimony denying to a persistent Democratic Senator Ervin that the Plan violated Title VII, insisting that it did not require quotas, and that it did not also violate Executive Order 11246. This was accomplished by emphasizing that the Plan did not require proportional minority hiring, but only a "good faith" effort at proportional hiring, and that the percentages were not quotas, anyway—they were goals, targets, ranges.[88] The issue of color blindness, central to both Title VII and the executive order, was avoided by Plan advocates. Ervin could not believe what he was hearing, and went so far as to read aloud from the dictionary the definition of *quota*. Ervin also read the definition of *range* to Leonard, and emphasized the apparent breach of color blindness: "I think you have made it as clear as the noonday sun in a cloudless sky that the Philadelphia Plan requires contractors actively to take the race of people into consideration when they employ them, despite the conflicting language of the Executive Order."[89] But the incredulous Ervin was met with a parade of witnesses who continued to assert the contrary, or to deny that it mattered. The Philadelphia Plan fit with all relevant traditions of American justice, he was told. It was Ervin who was outside of tradition.

Typical was the exchange with Secretary Shultz himself, who had been coached by Mitchell on how to handle the questioning. After Ervin again stated that Executive Order 11246 established race-conscious hiring as illegal, but that the Plan called for proportional minority hiring, the following exchange took place:

SENATOR ERVIN: In other words, there is a flat inconsistency between the Philadelphia Plan and that provision in the Executive order.

SECRETARY SHULTZ: I think the difference of view here is that what we are saying is we feel the way the system is working in a particular craft and place is such that you do not have equal employment opportunity there. Now, in order to get it, you have to take some affirmative steps.

SENATOR ERVIN: Yes.

SECRETARY SHULTZ: And bring that about.

SENATOR ERVIN: And your affirmative step is to do exactly opposite of what the Executive order says, and that is not to hire people without regard to race, but to hire them on the basis of race.

SECRETARY SHULTZ: Not to hire them on the basis of race but to take affirmative steps to see to it that you expose yourself to people of various races, and you give them an equal chance at employment, and if you have a system that does not provide you with that kind of choice, and it is possible through recruiting and other methods in the community to give yourself a wider range, you must take affirmative steps to do so, and as I said earlier, I quite agree with you that this means that you pay attention to race.[90]

SENATOR ERVIN: In other words, an affirmative action program within the purview of the Philadelphia Plan is that in order to achieve hiring without regard to matters of race, a contractor must take into consideration matters of race in hiring.

SECRETARY SHULTZ: You take them into consideration in that you must provide yourself with a reasonable range of choice in the hiring process. However, that is not the same thing as saying that when it comes to hiring people, you have to decide between A and B on the basis of race. That is a different kind of decision entirely.[91]

On the issue of quotas, the Ervin-Shultz exchange was also typical:

SENATOR ERVIN: I put a definition of a range and a quota and a goal into the record a while ago. I personally am subject to being educated, but I do not see, in the context in which those words are used to describe this plan, that there is any difference between those three things.

SECRETARY SHULTZ: Well, I certainly respect that opinion. A quota to me, words have a background and a meaning. Quota to me has always meant a limitation. It says that you have an organization here and you have a quota, you can only have such and such a percentage of this particular type of person. It is a limitation, or when we talk about a field like imports of various kinds of things, we will have a quota, which says you can only import so much. It is a limitation. It is a concept that essentially is holding something down. . . . What we are trying to get at here is the opening of opportunity by getting people to aspire to get out and give a greater crack at these jobs to people in minority groups.[92]

Shultz's definition of quotas as limitations left him vulnerable to more criticisms of the strange upper bound of the minority hiring ranges, though he was not pressed on this. Star witness Shultz also argued (pragmatically) that ineffective classical liberal mechanisms were unsatisfactory, always countered by 1964 opponent of Title VII Sam Ervin demanding strict adherence to Title VII. Another star witness, Elmer Staats himself, suggested that the dispute be resolved through congressional debate with a provision in an appropriation bill.

Thus, on the evening of 17 December, the issue of race-conscious, numbers-based justice, which America was to debate for decades, was not explicitly fought with the combined, raw might of the color-blind advocates and their new southern allies in Congress, but with an uncourageous, sniper attack: a rider to a supplemental appropriation bill to aid the areas damaged by Hurricane Camille. The rider asserted the power of the comptroller general by making appropriations unavailable to any Federal aid, grant, contract, or agreement that the comptroller general found to be illegal. That the forces of color-blind justice (and, by 1969, conservative southerners were now counted among their ranks) were reduced to such an indirect attack on quotas itself says much about the changing political culture of civil rights in 1969, the moral/political riskiness of any anti–civil rights position, and the rapid legitimation of race-conscious justice. The discourse of tradition had successfully defined anti–affirmative action forces as antitradition, as extremist or radical.

Though this night attack in the Senate Appropriations Committee was so carefully camouflaged, the White House saw it coming. The following morning (18 December), Nixon had a meeting with Shultz; Donald Rumsfeld, the director of the Administration's antipoverty program; Robert H. Finch, the Secretary of Health, Education, and Welfare; and Moynihan. They decided to concentrate their lobbying efforts on the House, as they were certain the Senate would approve the rider, and to emphasize civil rights instead of the constitutional problems, allegedly to give the civil rights issue "White House visibility."[93]

On the day of the Senate debate, a press conference was held by Shultz and Fletcher, where they publicly defended affirmative action and ridiculed the color-blind model. The defense articulated the discourse of administrative pragmatism. Shultz explained, "[The Philadelphia Plan] is an extremely important matter and it has been, I think, quite helpful in stimulating attention and in actually producing some results, as we are gradually able to implement it, in getting equal employment opportunity in this [the construction] industry. . . . And we think this is preferable to vague statements about, 'You have got to hire more people.'" Asked to explain Staats's position, Shultz offered the following:

> As I understand it, he feels that any affirmative steps for equal employment opportunity automatically take notice of the fact that somebody, who you are trying to hire, might be black, or some color. And if you notice anything like that, then, you are taking account of race. And the Civil Rights Act says you shouldn't take account of race.
>
> That is about the way it goes. I am not really doing it complete justice. But you can see what a sweeping thing this is. I think also what a ridiculous thing this is.

Suspicions continued that the Republican push for percentage hiring of blacks was motivated by something other than desire for civil rights. Asked to explain the "political aspect of this thing," Shultz deflected: "I really could not. I am not enough of an expert on this."[94]

The administration's decision to write off the Senate debate was correct, as the anti-Plan rider was accepted, despite the valiant efforts of Jacob Javits of New York to kill it. The debate alternated between the color-blindness issue and the separation of powers issue. Notable were the defenses of color blindness by southern senators, the attempts by most other rider supporters to dodge the civil rights issue, the general lack of participation by Democrats, and the discomfort of both union- supporting Democrats and many Republicans with the whole thing.[95]

Especially notable was Colorado Republican Senator Gordon L. Allott, whom history was quite simply leaving behind. It was Allott who had inserted into Title VII an amendment which became section 703 (j), forbidding the government to require hiring to correct racial imbalances. Allott had clearly felt very strongly on the issue in 1964. But in 1969, with his own party pushing something that, as Safire later admitted, "waddled and quacked enough like a quota for it to be so adjudged,"[96] Allott was strangely silent on the topic.

In fact, he deliberately dodged the whole issue, emphasizing instead that he was not anti-Nixon or anti–civil rights. Stating that he was in "support of what the President is trying to achieve" he added,

> The question here is not—and I want to make this clear—the correctness of the Philadelphia Plan. The question is whether we are going to permit the derogation and diminishment of the powers of the Comptroller General as an independent arm of Congress. As I say, it is unfortunate, that the particular area which would be immediately affected is one which, even at this moment, I feel so very strongly about.[97]

Despite such less-than-thumping support, the rider passed the Senate with a vote of 52–37. Affirmative action was on the ropes.

Nixon mobilized in preparation for the House vote. A press release on 19 December from Nixon emphasized tradition. Nixon explained that his position stressed deeds rather than words, and added, "Nothing is more unfair than that the same Americans who pay taxes should by any pattern of discriminatory practices be deprived of an equal opportunity to work on federal construction contracts." He went on to say that "[t]he Philadelphia Plan does not set quotas, it points to goals."[98]

In closed-door White House discussions of the Plan, its antiunion nature was increasingly salient. The Plan was discussed in an early morning meeting on 20 December with Ehrlichman, Nixon aids Bryce N. Harlow and Peter Flanigan, Shultz, and several GOP congressmen, including Gerald Ford, from Michigan. According to Ehrlichman's notes, the role of the comptroller general was emphasized, as well as standing up to the unions: "Construction: Tight union control of labor supply . . . The Plan challenges their control." Staats's view of the Civil Rights Act, that "you can't take notice of race" was seen to be (probably by Shultz, who used the same term in a press conference two days earlier) "very sweeping."[99]

A half hour later, the White House moved to another fight with the unions. Meany, as mentioned earlier, felt that the Nixon administration was at war with the unions. In fact, behind-the-scenes evidence suggests that Meany was exactly—literally—right. Nixon, Ehrlichman, and economic adviser Arthur Burns discussed the Davis-Bacon Act, which ensured that all construction done with public funds would pay the prevailing wage, guaranteeing high wages for unions (high wages were seen as exacerbating inflation). In Ehrlichman's scribbled handwriting, one finds, "Declare an 'emergency' & suspend the Act." Written ominously below is literal confirmation of Meany's suspicion: "war w/ trade unions."[100]

Later that day, the White House called another press conference. Shultz specifically pitted one soldier of the Democrats' coalition against another:

> The country's long established commitment to affirmative action for equal job opportunity has been gravely jeopardized by the United States Senate . . . the rider is part of an effort by some unions in the construction trades and supported vigorously by lobbyists for the AFL-CIO to block affirmative steps to open skilled and high-paying jobs to blacks and other minority groups.

Putting the Democrats on the spot, the secretary added, "I call attention to the impending vote on this bill in the House of Representatives; I hope it will be done on the record by roll call vote, so all Americans can know whether or not each member stands with the President for equal opportunity."[101] Pick your side, Shultz was saying to the Democrats, and let the country see which friend you have preferred.

Affirmative Action Triumphant: "Those Who Burn Are in the Coalitions"

In preparation for the 22 December House showdown on the anti–affirmative action rider, Nixon had called a breakfast meeting with Ehrlichman and Republican congressional leaders in the State Dining Room. According to Ehrlichman's notes, Senator Gordon Allott began by discussing his concerns with the "strong moral" and "religious" issues involved with the Plan—though, significantly, he did not stress this angle. Indeed, it appears that Allott had no problems with the quota issue, with the notes showing that he claimed he would "bow to no one" regarding civil rights, that the "Fletcher remarks [were] true" (Fletcher had been outspoken in equating the Plan with equal opportunity and justice).

Allott's position was pro-Plan *and* pro–comptroller general. But his primary allegiance remained with the comptroller general. Stating his position for the rider that would kill the Plan, Allott argued that the rider was not sweeping, that a 1921 law states the comptroller general's ruling binds the executive branch. Allott stated that the "real argument" was whether or not Congress was going to have its jurisdiction trampled by the executive branch and the attorney general, thus losing "our one independent arm"—the comptroller general, who has attorneys on his staff anyway. Rather than fighting for the cause of color blindness, his paramount principle only five years earlier, the notes show Allott summing up with the separation of powers issue: "Don't see that we're doing anything but protecting this cong[ressional] institution."

Senator Robert Griffin warned that Allott did not speak for the Senate as a whole, and argued that the rider delegated powers to the General Accounting Office in a way that was unconstitutional and "unproper" [*sic*]. Apparently citing a 1967 affirmative action court decision that he said was in line with the attorney general,[102] Griffin also argued that the Congress did not, in 1921, intend for the comptroller general to be the "last word," and that the Senate, in supporting the rider, violated this intention. After Nixon pointed out that he felt strongly on the constitutional implications and "on issues," Griffin reassured him that if the House debate went like the Senate debate, then some liberal Democrats "will sit silent." Griffin was clearly aware of the political conundrum that the Philadelphia Plan represented for liberal Democrats.

At this point, Nixon used the discourse of preemption politics to sell the Plan to his congressmen: "Make Civ. Rts [civil rights] people take a stand—for labor or for CR [civil rights]." According to Ehrlichman's notes, Arthur Fletcher, who was undoubtedly for the Plan for moral reasons, then said to Allott, "At grass roots—those who burn are in the coalitions." The notes continue menacingly, "See if we can't deliver." Nixon then officially ordered "The line," which would highlight the Democrats' troubles: "Dems [Democrats] are token oriented we are job oriented."[103]

Apparently, the GOP senate opponents of the Plan had more to say and sought to contact the president privately. On the day of the breakfast and House debate, a memo to Nixon from Bryce Harlow told of Senator Spessard Holland calling twice about the Philadelphia Plan. "He further stated," wrote Harlow, "that you once told him that he could talk with you anytime he really needed to. His point was that he really wants to talk with you." Bryce recommended "that you call Senator Holland today" and tell him that "the Administration's position is firm on this." Senators Allott and Robert Byrd had also tried to contact the president, with Byrd warning that the Senate would rule against Nixon.[104]

Meanwhile, administration officials scrambled to develop a scheme to "best exploit the situation—win or lose." In a great irony of affirmative action, the Nixon administration planned to lobby the civil rights leaders to support affirmative action. In an effort to "muster support," calls were made to Roy Wilkins and Clarence Mitchell, among others. If affirmative action was in the interest of the civil rights movement, its leaders would have to be told this by Republicans in the White House.[105]

The debate in the House was more spirited than the Senate debate, though it covered much of the same territory. New in the House debate were the Democrats' questions as to the sincerity of the Nixon administration's support for the affirmative action Philadelphia Plan. Again the pro-Plan/antirider forces seemed to have the safest claim to legitimacy, attesting to the legitimacy of civil rights and affirmative action and the illegitimacy of the anti–civil rights stance.[106] Republicans seemed to relish their role, rare in the post-Goldwater era, as civil rights saviors. Those attacking the Plan avoided attacking civil rights, and stressed constitutional issues. In the words of Representative George H. Mahon, a Texas Democrat, "The issue involved is the integrity of the House of Representatives . . . the issue here is the power of the Congress over the Federal purse."[107] Pro-Plan Representatives, such as Republican Frank T. Bow from Ohio, could retort that the comptroller general was an "unelected czar" with a fifteen-year term, and then set a match to the Democratic coalition tinder: "I definitely believe the Philadelphia Plan is a question of civil rights, and the question concerns a group of people who want to maintain complete control of labor and want to dictate who may and may not work." Stressing that the Plan involved goals and not quotas (no one ever attempted to question the repugnance of quotas), Bow concluded that the rider was meant to provide "equal employment opportunities in the city of Philadelphia, where it [*sic*] has been denied over the years."[108]

Loyal Nixonite Gerald Ford also read supportive letters, from Steven Horn, vice chairman of the U.S. Commission on Civil Rights, George Shultz, and Nixon himself. Nixon threatened, "To be quite candid, I share the Attorney General's serious doubts as to the constitutionality of this amendment and may have to withhold my signature from any legislation containing [the rider]." Ford also read the statement by Nixon which stressed the civil right to be a construction worker. The Nixon statement also repeated the now familiar goals-not-quotas mantra.

Gerald Ford (who in 1966 displayed his sensitivity to the plight of African-Americans by asking, "How long are we going to abdicate law and order—the backbone of any civilization—in favor of a soft social theory that the man who heaves a brick through your window or tosses a firebomb into your car is simply the misunderstood and underprivileged product of a broken home?"[109]) continued the attack on the Democratic coalition. Obviously relishing the moral high ground, Ford explained that the old civil rights laws were meaningless without jobs, and said,

> Those who vote "yea" in effect are saying all these other rights are fine but we are not going to help get you a job under Federal contracts. An "aye" vote will permit the kind of discrimination in employment that has existed in the past. An "aye" vote is going to mean you vote to perpetuate job discrimination in Federal contracts. A "nay" vote means that individuals will have the protection of the Federal Government in getting jobs. Minority groups will have an opportunity to earn a living so that they can enjoy the fruits of social legislation which the Congress has passed in the last two decades.

Finally, the Democrats were provoked. California Democrat Chet Holifield countered that the Philadelphia Plan "is advanced for political purposes." Insisting that the real issue was the separation of powers, he added that "[t]his is a real struggle for power and it is also a very clever little gimmick to put the liberals and the Democrats on the spot on this thing." James G. O'Hara of Michigan pointed out the inconsistency of the Nixon position, which had been against the granting of cease and desist orders for the EEOC, and that those supposedly for equal opportunity should be for cease and desist powers also. O'Hara and Roman Pucinski of Illinois resisted the methods of the Plan. O'Hara called for a color-blind America, where race has no meaning, and Pucinski, pointing out the percentage hiring called for by the Plan, stated bluntly, "If these are not quotas, then the English language has lost its meaning," and asserted that in advocating racial quotas, "They are turning back the clock."[110]

California Democrat Augustus F. Hawkins stated that he could not "in good conscience" believe that Nixon wanted the Plan for equal opportunity, and finally asked rhetorically, "Why should minority employment be limited in effect to a single industry? And, why only to certain cities in the first instance?" He pointed out the controversy with the Department of Defense awarding millions of dollars worth of contracts to textile firms judged discriminatory by the OFCC, and complained of a Nixon initiative in the politics of preemption in the area of EEOC reform. Instead of supporting cease and desist powers for the EEOC as liberals wanted, "The Administration . . . prefers to confuse the issue with a new and different approach unsupported by a single civil rights authority or organization." Hawkins offered some support for his suspicions by reading a letter to House Speaker John McCormack from Clarence Mitchell, director of the Washington Bureau of the NAACP, which stated:

> It is amazing that the same administration which has sought to destroy the voting rights bill, which is against strengthening existing equal employment opportunity legislation, which has been guilty of outrageous footdragging in school desegregation, now suddenly is on a great crusade to save the Philadelphia Plan. It is very odd that at the beginning of the year the administration was perfectly willing to let the textile industry continue employment discrimination by reaching a dubious unwritten agreement with the big employers of that highly discriminating industry, but now is enthusiastically cracking down on discrimination that involves labor unions.[111]

Democrat Frank Thompson from New Jersey proposed an amendment that would require a check for Title VII compliance in the textile industry: "I want the great friends of civil rights to be consistent," he scoffed. When Ford mentioned that he had just received a letter that afternoon from Shultz that the contracted textile firms are in written agreement with Title VII now and in full compliance, Thompson snapped, "I have a file here an inch thick showing noncompliance . . . This gentleman [Ford] should have no objection to my amendment if they are complying."[112] In a remark that highlighted the peculiar split of political forces in the debate, Republican John B. Anderson of Illinois, mentioning a recent article in which the black union leader Bayard Rustin trumpeted the old union/civil rights Democratic party coalition, said with apparent smugness, "[T]hat coalition has not served the black man very well on the floor of this House this evening."

As it turned out, the black man won, and the anti-Plan rider was defeated, 208–156. The House debate had Republicans siding with Nixon 3 to 1. The majority of Democrats voted against affirmative action, with 54 northern Democrats joined by 61 of the 67 southern Democrats to form the losing anti–affirmative action side, leaving 84 Democrats to side with Nixon. In New York

City, blue-collar representatives Mario Biaggi and Joseph Addabbo were the only ones in opposition to the Plan. Urban Pennsylvania Democrats were against it 7 to 1.[113]

In a hasty Senate debate, spiced with numerous references to the impending Christmas holiday (as well as assurances from pro-rider/anti-Plan Senators that they were not pawns of the labor lobby), the previous Senate vote was overturned, and the rider was defeated, 39–29. Antiquota stalwart Gordon Allott, who could not bring himself to vote for the Plan, also apparently could not bring himself to vote against Nixon, and did not vote at all. The Philadelphia Plan, and explicit, proportional race-conscious justice, became the official policy of the United States government.

The next day, Nixon and staff privately celebrated, but they were not celebrating a victory of every American's civil right to be in a construction union, or the victory of the principles of affirmative action or the moral worthiness of blacks for employment preference. Nixon seemed giddy that they had the lead in the war against the trade unions. This being a war, Nixon also kept score, remembered his losses, and caricatured his enemy. On 23 December, Ehrlichman's notes show a heading, "Beaten the unions"; underneath, he wrote, "Surtax, Philadelphia Plan v. They won Haynsworth." Poking fun at Meany's blue-collar background and vernacular, Nixon caricatured Meany talking to Shultz: "When I was a plumber, it never occoid to me to have niggers in the union."[114]

After the Nixon victory, Javits reportedly said to Nixon aid Len Garment, "You see now what we can do up here when the President gives some leadership. We can practically accomplish miracles." Indeed. Despite the labor lobby's confident efforts (top AFL-CIO lobbyist Andrew Biemiller reportedly said to a Nixon aid, "I'm sorry, I'm afraid we've got this one"), the Nixon forces came through, despite almost no help from the civil rights community, save for a few written statements coaxed from Roy Wilkins (who five months earlier said Nixon's civil rights policies almost made him vomit) and Whitney Young.[115] The pro–Philadelphia Plan lobby at the Federal level was the Nixon administration.[116] Robert B. Semple, Jr., reporting in the *New York Times* of 26 December openly discussed Nixon's instrumental machinations:

> Some of those who worked in the President's behalf say now that they were skeptical of his motives. They did not doubt, they say, his commitment to minority employment, but they have privately suggested that he might have sensed political profit in pitting the civil rights movement against its natural allies in the labor movement.[117]

Despite this comment, the usually press-suspicious Nixon loved Semple's article, which he saw as otherwise illustrating presidential leadership. He directed aids to tell Semple that "RN found this an exciting reporting job" and to distribute reprints to civil rights groups.[118]

On 29 December, the White House was still congratulating itself. With Nixon, Ehrlichman, press secretary Ronald Ziegler, and Henry A. Kissinger in the Oval Office, the atmosphere seemed rather like the winning team's locker room after a big game. They privately mused on the ingenuity of the whole affair. The bind that the union leadership was in with their own rank and file and the impossibility of compromise with the "civil rights people" were highlighted. Labor Secretary Shultz was approvingly characterized as "a bulldog."[119] (The "bulldog," in his memoirs, used a peculiar metaphor to refer to his justice initiative, referring to it as "a sledgehammer."[120]) Ehrlichman later recalled:

> Nixon thought that Secretary of Labor George Shultz had shown great style in constructing a political dilemma for the labor union leaders and civil rights groups. Shultz persuaded Nixon to declare himself in favor of "the Philadelphia Plan." . . . The NAACP wanted a tougher requirement; the unions hated the whole thing. Before long, the AFL-CIO and the NAACP were locked in combat over one of the passionate issues of the day and the Nixon Administration was located in the sweet and reasonable middle.[121]

"We Have a Distrust of the Present Administration"

The White House celebrations were short-lived, however. The logic of the Philadelphia Plan was that it could give Richard Nixon some of that creativity and originality that all presidents desire; he could preempt the liberal agenda by confounding the liberals with a new idea ("racial goals not racial quotas") that exacerbated tension within the Democratic coalition, and he could appeal to one part of that coalition and perhaps establish more desperately needed leadership backing. It was risky, but a president with such uncertain authority and electoral support, and angry anyway with the unions, had to take risks. In other words, the logic of an opposition president facing the assumed establishment dictates risk-taking.

Whatever the satisfaction of beating the unions, it was apparent that civil rights groups, though not complaining about gaining such a powerful tool as affirmative action, were not prepared to give Nixon the credit for it. This was apparent in some statements made during and directly after the House debate. Some black leaders, rather than rallying behind the newly supportive Nixon, accused the president of a nefarious instrumentalism. For example, Clarence Mitchell said the Plan was a "calculated attempt coming right from the President's desk to break up the coalition between Negroes and labor unions. Most of the social progress in this country has resulted from this alliance." Democratic Representative Augustus F. Hawkins declared, "Nixon's people are forcing employers to lay off workers and then telling them to put in a certain quota of blacks into these vacancies. It is a strategy designed to increase friction between labor and Negroes."[122] In January 1970 Pohl Hause of the NAACP Washington Bureau downplayed the overall significance of the Plan and hissed, "We have a distrust of the present administration. Period."[123]

In February 1970, while administrators in the OFCC, with Nixon apparently unaware, were gleefully expanding the effective and efficient affirmative action model from the Philadelphia Plan to *all* (including nonconstruction) federal contractors,[124] Moynihan sought outside consultants on the African-American question. Why was Nixon not getting any support from blacks? He invited four social scientists to a White House meeting to discuss with a frustrated Nixon (and Ehrlichman, Haldeman, Moynihan, and Garment) how the president could "improve his standing among black Americans," according to sociologist David Riesman, one of the guests, along with political scientists Charles Hamilton, James Q. Wilson, and Aaron Wildavsky. Riesman, Wilson, and Hamilton all believed that withdrawing the still- pending Supreme Court nomination of Harrold Carswell, whom Nixon had selected after Haynsworth had been defeated and whom many believed to be a racist, would be an important first step. Nixon appeared interested, but Wildavsky then forcefully argued, according to Riesman, that "if Nixon withdrew the Carswell nomination, the liberals would believe that they had him on the run." Haldeman agreed, and Nixon then seemed persuaded.[125] How to appeal to blacks, how to appear liberal without yielding to liberals, remained a puzzle in the winter of 1970.

Not that the administration did not try. The February meeting with the social scientists came in the midst of a big winter push to gain legitimacy in the black community. Officials arranged meetings for Nixon with a group of black lawyers and a group of black doctors.[126] In February, plans were made to split the black community, targeting the "black silent majority," or the "probably 30% who are potentially on our side."[127] In March, a meeting was arranged between Nixon and African-Americans hired in the administration to exchange views and "to get a photo of meeting."[128] By June, Bryce Harlow still considered relations with blacks "totally unacceptable," and in seeking advice around the White House on how to change this, he was told the basic problem stemmed from "an unstated attitude (almost a policy) of disregard toward blacks brought about by a political concern for white votes."[129] In other words, the perception in the White House was that Nixon's plan to simultaneously appeal to the black audience and the southern audience was failing.

Were there other possible sources of leadership legitimacy? One of Nixon's campaign advisers, Kevin Phillips, had seen the white working classes as potential GOP territory, and had dissuaded Nixon from any appeal at all to black voters, seeing that group as conspicuously absent from *The Emerging Republican Majority,* as he termed it in his 1969 book.[130] In 1969, however, future support from any group was still only conjecture. Many expected Wallace's American Independent party to return in the 1970 congressional race, and Wallace himself to return in 1972 and garner much of the disenchanted union support, with the Democrats getting the rest. At any rate, it was hard for Nixon to court the unions at this time. The lobbying power of the diabolical labor/civil rights coalition had greatly angered him during the humiliation of his first two, down-in-flames Supreme Court nominations (Haynsworth in December 1969 and Carswell in April 1970). Civil rights people might be expected to fight southern Supreme Court appointments tooth and nail, but labor, too? Here the strength of the liberal establishment was embarrassingly obvious. Nixon had, according to Ehrlichman's notes, seen the Haynsworth nomination struggle, which mostly coincided with the development of the Philadelphia Plan in the fall of 1969, as a "PR battle" which must be won. After Haynsworth and then Carswell crashed and burned, Nixon ordered that several Senators who had opposed him should never be invited to the White House again.[131] When Nixon finally nominated the more liberal Minnesotan Harry Blackmun, he was extremely concerned that Blackmun be seen as just as conservative as Haynsworth and Carswell, and called this "of the highest priority with our whole Congressional and PR staff."[132] After a year in office Nixon was used to seeing labor as an enemy on crucial issues.

A Better Idea

Serendipity seemed necessary to change the White House view. Nixon stumbled onto white working-class support on the merits of his foreign policy, specifically Vietnam. Ironically, this also happened at the time that the administration was struggling with the anti-union Philadelphia Plan, though the full realization of the situation did not hit until much later. In late November 1969, Nixon received "buckets and buckets of telegrams that had come from all over the country."[133] The mail was in response to Nixon's 3 November speech in which he asked for the support of the "silent majority" of Americans who disagreed with the radical Vietnam war protesters and who implicitly agreed with Nixon's position of settling the war rather than simply surrendering. Though the phrase "silent majority" had been used in the campaign and later, by both Nixon and Agnew, now it seemed to catch on.[134]

Still, in the affirmative action showdown month of December, despite the sense that the silent majority was with him, it was not entirely clear who these silent, "Middle Americans" were. Nixon asked Haldeman and Safire for ideas about "where we have succeeded, where we have failed, and what our goals should be during the next year."[135]

Then, in the spring of 1970, construction workers dramatically beat up anti-war demonstrators in New York. A few days later, on 20 May, one hundred thousand marched (in what was called the Hard Hat March, in reference to the thousands of helmeted construction workers who took part) in *support* of Richard Nixon and his Vietnam policies. Here was a better possibility than attracting blacks of disrupting the Democrats and establishing the legitimacy to lead that Nixon needed. White House aid Michael Balzano later called the march "an explosive moment in the creation of the New Majority."[136] The president quickly invited construction representatives to the White House in a much publicized visit (Nixon was even photographed wearing a hardhat; liberals criticized him for condoning mob violence).[137]

That summer, the White House heard new warnings of the vitality of the Wallace movement and his American Independent Party, which were seen as potential threats in the 1970 and 1972 elections—and not just in the South. "Need to handle Wallace," Nixon wrote to himself on 19 July 1970. This required securing the Democrats' northern working-class support. How to do this? Saddle the Democrats with the "race-liberal-student tag," Nixon wrote on his note pad. The notion that Nixon had gained support by being "more liberal on Race, welfare, environment, troop withdrawal" now seemed a terrible mistake.[138]

By September of 1970, preempting the liberal agenda with policies that courted organized labor became a major part of domestic strategy for the 1970 elections. On 8 September Haldeman was reporting to Colson that with regard to labor Nixon now felt "[t]here [was] a great deal of gold there to be mined."[139] On 6 October Colson sounded almost obsequious as he urged labor appeals: "As a follow-up to the development of some pro-labor legislation, we should be thinking about federal legislation that would obviate the need for major strikes, some form of 'voluntary' compulsory arbitration. This is something Meany is very interested in and would have broad general appeal as well as being strong in the labor area."[140] In Nixon's briefing at a meeting on the congressional campaign for that fall, speechwriter William Safire recalls Nixon's directions:

> Don't blame labor for inflation. Don't get an antilabor tag on any of our candidates. Here's the line: "Let's understand once and for all the candidates who say they are Democrats are not basically Democrats. They have broken away from the Democratic Party. These issues are bigger than Democrat or Republican. Vote against those who have deserted the principles of the Democratic Party.[141]

In fact, Nixon had blamed labor for inflation; this was the rationale behind suspending the Davis-Bacon Act, which had kept union wages at the highest prevailing wage. Now this was to be covered up in a flurry of olive branches.

In addition to legislative appeals to labor, the White House stepped up recruitment of white ethnics onto its team. According to Nixon assistant Michael P. Balzano, Jr., ethnic hiring after 1970 was intended to serve a political purpose, as Nixon tried to bring disgruntled Democrats into his administration.[142] By October 1971 Pat Buchanan told Nixon, regarding a new Supreme Court appointment, "[W]e ought to get the most brilliant and qualified Italian-American strict constructionist jurist . . . and then play up his Italian background—and let the Democrats chop him up if they want."[143] By 1972, as Balzano put it, "a series of agency directorships and assistant secretary positions began going to people whose names were difficult to spell and almost impossible to pronounce."[144]

In September of 1970, Nixon was very nervous about his early domestic program, where his probing for preemptive possibilities had taken him into some liberal policies in social issues—the kinds of things the white working-class voter hated. Of course this included race. In an "EYES ONLY" memo from John R. Brown III to Ehrlichman, Finch, and Haldeman, Brown related that the "September 5 News Summary" reported that "the majority of people in the West between the Alleghenies and the Rockies" had a whole series of beliefs about social issue politics, all basically conservative, such as, "The rebellious kids are both wrong and a menace," and notably, "Negroes have rights but forced integration will leave everybody worse off." (The memo did not specify the context of integration.) Brown continued,

> The President asked that you take note of this. He feels that we'd better shape up and quit trimming the *wrong* way. It is very late—but we still have time to move away from the line of our well-intentioned liberals on our own staff. It is dynamite politically and wrong usually on the merits [original emphasis].

The new reality of an obvious need to pander to middle America had Nixon scratching his head to understand what they were thinking in 1969. Brown went on, presenting Nixon's theory of the reason for those early liberal social issue policies:

> The president went on to say that he can't emphasize too strongly his concern that our Administration team—including White House staff—has been affected too much by the unreal atmosphere of the D.C. press, social, and intellectual set. Perhaps Cambodia and Kent State led to an overreaction by our own people to prove that we were pro students, blacks, left. We must get turned around on this before it

is too late—emphasize anti-crime, anti-demonstrations, anti-drugs, anti-obscenity. We must get with the mood of the country which is fed up with the liberals.[145]

Nixon was apparently quite worked up about these apparent 1969 political blunders, and a month later, he suddenly refused to see his domestic policy adviser Ehrlichman and would not answer his memoranda. After about a week, Nixon sent him a newspaper column, written by Kevin Phillips, which Nixon said was "a correct view" from which Ehrlichman had deviated. Phillips argued that the social issue, as defined by political observers Scammon and Wattenberg, was a Republican issue, but that Nixon had not properly exploited it. The Philadelphia Plan was specifically fingered, along with some other policy moves, as having "detracted from the Nixon administration's ability to use the 'social issue,' and lessened pro-Republican realignment." Ehrlichman wrote a detailed memo to Nixon, defending the domestic policy and reminding him why the administration supported the Plan a year before. He argued that the correct position on the social issue, and current policy, was not purely conservative, but contained some deliberate liberal "zigs" to go with the conservative "zags," just as Nixon had included liberal Pat Moynihan on his staff with the other more conservative members. Citing the Scammon and Wattenberg book, *The Real Majority,* which argued that Republicans must move ahead on civil rights but at a slow pace, Ehrlichman explained, "Our domestic policy job, as I have understood it up to now, was to insure some *balance"* (original emphasis). Following the logic of the politics of preemption, he wrote, "As we can . . . we will try to co-opt the opposition's issues." Defending the Philadelphia Plan, he wrote,

> While anti-labor and pro-black, the legislative battle drove a wedge between the Democrats and labor which has stretched the membrane. The Plan itself is not widely understood in non-labor circles, in my view. Labor understands it and hates it. In due time, if we administer it without undue zeal it can become a "slow and reasonable" approach to civil rights such as Scammon describes in his advice for Republicans.

This quiet, liberal "zig" was necessary and permissible if hidden from the national audience; on the other hand, in the area of suburban integration, there was "a serious Romney problem," a reference to liberal Housing and Urban Development Secretary George Romney, who "keeps loudly talking about [integration] in spite of our efforts to shut him up." Nixon remembered. Next to the description of the Plan as the politics of preemption, the president scribbled, "OK."[146]

In order not to offend the apparent new source of authority, who resisted anything other than color blindness, Nixon then backed away from the controversial, race-conscious hiring policy he had done so much to legitimate. Having rescued it from bureaucratic limbo (where it was not clear that the Democrats would ever have let such a controversial policy receive such a high profile, or even develop fully), and pushed it through Congress with zeal, the administration's support faded into ambiguity. As Safire recalled of the Plan, "[M]ost of the zip went out of that integration effort after the hardhats marched in support of Nixon and the war" (though Safire felt "we dropped our pressure on construction unions too soon").[147] Commenting on the weak enforcement of the Plan and other Nixon civil rights retreats, Leon Panetta winced, "Principles of equality . . . would fall before the needs of November."[148] The Philadelphia Plan was held in reserve in favor of the more flexible "hometown plans" (each city's unions and civil rights supporters were given an opportunity to work out an OFCC-approved construction industry agreement satisfactory to both sides; failing this, the federal government would impose a Philadelphia-style plan). Shultz was moved to the directorship of the newly created Office of Management and Budget. Arthur Fletcher was also moved outside of Labor (and wrote a book about his experiences, cynically titled, *The Silent Sell-Out*). The U.S. Commission on Civil Rights criticized the entire program as weakly enforced and ineffectual. In 1972 OFCC director George Holland resigned, complaining that efforts there were "largely cosmetic and illusory" and that there was no movement toward "the achievement of the reality of equal employment opportunity for all citizens."[149] Though the hometown plans were still based on an affirmative action model, civil rights groups saw them as another example of Nixon retreat. Due to a policy of criticizing nearly everything that Nixon did, civil rights groups and liberals were boxed into a pro-affirmative action position when their nemesis Nixon appeared to back away.

Meanwhile, the Office of Minority Business Enterprise, the tiny office with no budget, lost in the Department of Commerce, quickly became mired in bureaucratic red tape and squabbling, and became a lightning rod for criticism. Whitney Young said, "Black capitalism is a shambles." Darwin W. Bolden, a black businessman and OMBE insider said that the OMBE was "one of the poorest-managed federal agencies I know," a "tragic failure" that "cannot be saved."[150] Despite a tremendous growth in budget (up to $242.2 million in 1974) and some measurable growth in numbers of black businesses, doubts remained. "Its main purpose was political," complained one resigning OMBE assistant. While it seemed apparent all along that the project could build a Republican black middle class, there were complaints that grants were given only to declared minority Republicans and that phone calls soliciting political contributions would follow OMBE grants. According to historian Herbert Parmet, "The chairman of the Watts Labor Community Action Committee complained that the pressure on him 'was almost unbearable,' and that his failure to support Nixon's reelection effort in 1972 after warnings that he would not get any money unless he got 'in line' cost him a $1.5 million contract."[151]

Though most parts of the affirmative action model, including race consciousness, were now legitimate, and even a quota of sorts was institutionalized in the Plan, the specific issue of racial quotas remained a peculiar taboo to Americans. Nixon sought to rehabilitate his tarnished reputation while tagging the Democrats as the race party and the quota party. As if on cue, the Democrats clumsily embraced the quota concept at their 1972 convention. In a controversial move led by a small but energetic group of party liberals, the Democrats reformed their process for selecting convention delegates. Major new efforts were mandated to open up the delegate selection process and improve representation of minorities and women. When it became known that the Cook County, Illinois, delegation had been chosen by Chicago Mayor Richard Daley in closed meetings, and that these delegates did not reflect the correct percentage of blacks and women in that jurisdiction, the delegation was kicked out of the convention and replaced with one with the correct numbers. Not only was affirmative action the operating principle of the Democratic party, but it tacitly became the party's civil rights platform as well.[152]

Nixon could not have written a better script. Safire felt Democratic presidential candidate George McGovern was vulnerable to being labeled "the quota candidate," and Nixon quickly responded to the Democrats:

> In employment and in politics, we are confronted with the rise of the fixed quota system—as artificial and unfair a yardstick as has ever been used to deny opportunity to anyone.
>
> Again, as in many attacks on basic values, the reasons are often well-intentioned. Quotas are intended to be a short-cut to equal opportunity, but in reality they are a dangerous detour away from the traditional value of measuring a person on the basis of ability.
>
> You cannot have it both ways: You cannot be for quotas in limiting political opportunity and against quotas in limiting economic opportunity.
>
> The basic idea of quotas is anti-ability wherever it is applied.[153]

While Nixon officials in the fall of 1972 rehearsed answers to inevitable press questions about how the Philadelphia Plan fit in with Nixon's anti-quota diatribes (even the Nixon team had trouble understanding the difference between goals and quotas[154]), the graceless Democratic embrace of quotas at their 1972 convention allowed Nixon to paint them as advocating still- illegitimate quotas in all areas. Not surprisingly, Patrick Buchanan's purple prose was put to good use with this issue, as he contributed a special section of Nixon's Republican convention acceptance speech on the quota issue (paraphrasing Marx?):

Every man, woman, and child should be free to rise as far as his talents, and energy, and ambitions will take him. That is the American dream. But into that dream there has entered a spectre, the spectre of a quota democracy—where men and women are advanced not on the basis of merit or ability, but solely on the basis of race, or sex, or color, or creed. . . .

You do not correct an ancient injustice by committing a new one. You do not remove the vestiges of past discrimination by committing a deliberate [act] of present discrimination. You cannot advance the cause of one minority by denying the rights of another.[155]

All that remained was for America to forget that it was the Republican Nixon who pushed racial quotas through a formerly reluctant Congress.

Preemption Politics Revisited: Nixon and Affirmative Action in Context

We have already seen how the Philadelphia Plan bubbled up from the OFCC bureaucracy, and how its possibilities for preempting the liberal agenda were recognized. In previous chapters, we saw how taken-for-granted boundaries of legitimate action limited options and shaped political actors' interests. In the case of Nixon's support for affirmative action, the effect of context is perhaps best understood as shaping an interest in choosing from an ideologically wide range of policy possibilities. Nixon's affirmative action initiatives may seem risky, even foolish, in retrospect, but as Skowronek points out, an opposition president confronting an establishment still assumed to be powerful has to take risks. Only with bold new policies can he gain that crucial legitimacy in order to fashion a distinctive and history-making leadership project. Though Nixon and his administration were basically conservative, Nixon often exhibited a very open mind in pursuing the necessary political support. Recall his campaign, when he talked of positive rights and coalitions with black militants. His open-mindedness continued into his presidency.

The authority for a creative project was all the more important, Nixon felt, if he was going to be president during the bicentennial celebration in 1976. Writing notes to himself a month after the Philadelphia Plan congressional victory, Nixon felt that in his project there was a "[n]eed for a name": "Square Deal. Fair Deal, New Deal, New Frontier, Great Society." Nixon recounted past presidential leadership projects. At this point, he was unsure where he stood, liberal or conservative, or where he should be going.[156] But he wanted to go *somewhere*. It was a fundamentally cultural understanding of the presidency which led Nixon to take risks thought necessary to establish something for the history books.

The administration was therefore looking into all kinds of possibilities. Little seemed to be too off limits, or too obscure. For example, two weeks after the battle in the House over the Philadelphia Plan, Nixon learned of the popularity of auto racing, and the political support given him by "two of the greats of auto racing" (Andy Granatelli and Mario Andretti). As an opposition president with a weak electoral mandate, Nixon logically urged Haldeman and his staff to "think about a way to recognize auto racing as a sport, and Granatelli and Andretti particularly as a way for the President to identify with the millions of people who find this a happy way to spend their Sunday afternoons."[157] Even grasping at straws such as the racing enthusiast vote seemed worth the risk and the effort.

A similar broad vision and more willingness to take risks was shown by Buchanan, whose theme for the 1972 reelection campaign was Democratic division; virtually anything that would work to that end was on the table. As early as March, Buchanan had been pushing this line on Nixon, an "attack" that would "focus on those issues that divide the Democrats, not those that unite Republicans." This attack "should exacerbate and elevate those issues on which Democrats are divided—forcing [then-probable Nixon opponent Edmund] Muskie to either straddle, or come down on one side or the other." In July Buchanan suggested that Nixon "[m]aintain as guiding political principle that our great hope for 1972 lies in maintaining or exacerbating the deep Democratic rift." His ideas were detailed in a 5 October 1971 paper unabashedly called "Dividing the Democrats." One dividing strategy involved George Wallace. Though the administration, according to Jonathan Schell, had tried to avoid a 1972 confrontation with Wallace (by contributing four hundred thousand dollars to his Alabama gubernatorial primary opponent in 1970), Buchanan advised support for Wallace if he were to run in the Democratic presidential primaries, to produce a Democratic party rift. Buchanan also suggested promoting left-leaning or black Democrats, with the hope that a fourth party would drain away support for the Democrats: "There is nothing that can so advance the President's chances for reelection—not a trip to China, not four and a half per cent unemployment—as a realistic black . . . campaign." Alternatively, he added, "We should continue to champion the cause of blacks within the Democratic Party." If the Democrats themselves were the black party, this would also be good for Nixon.[158]

The scrupulous Buchanan also suggested setting up "an outside direct mail group" to send things to "columnists, editorial writers, and political writers in order to get all our negative propaganda into their hands." (Phony mail had long been an administration strategy for needling the media when it criticized Nixon, and praising it when support was given.) It would also be useful for Nixon to "get a poll" that showed Humphrey as the leading Democrat to frighten the left-leaning Democrats, causing dissension. Additionally, "we should have several divisive questions worked up and distributed at major press conferences of the leading Democrats." Would Buchanan go so far as to urge Nixon to make federal policy on the basis of its divisive instrumental potential with respect to the Democrats? In fact this gamble was to be the central technique. So, for example, if Nixon were to promise aid to Catholic schools (which he did in fact do), then "clearly this divides the Democrats who run the New York *Times* from the Democrats who run for office in Queens and the North Bronx." William Safire quotes a Buchanan memo (apparently the same one) in which he explains:

> When RN [Nixon] comes out for aid to parochial schools, this will drive a wedge right down the Middle of the Democratic Party. The same is true of abortion; the same is true of hardline anti-pornography laws. For those *most against* aid to Catholic schools, *most for* abortion, and an end to all censorship are the New York *Times* Democrats. And those most violently *for* aid to Catholic schools and *against* abortion and dirty books, are the Jim Buckley Democrats.[159]

Other possibilities included continuing to nominate southerners like Haynsworth to the Court, and dabbling with welfare policy. "Like other proposals," Buchanan explained, "the above calls for what the Vice-President termed 'positive polarization.' "[160] Clearly, civil rights was not the only area targeted for the politics of preemption.

While the logic of preemption politics led White House initiatives to go in a variety of directions, it also led to frequent support for an often liberal and prolific Democrat-controlled Congress. As political scientist David Mayhew shows, even Nixon initiated legislation with a liberal flavor: a tenfold increase in food stamp outlays resulting from a federalization of eligibility and benefits standards, expansion of unemployment benefit coverage, massive increases in funds for urban mass transit. "Nixon's $30 billion revenue-sharing plan to help fund state and local governments passed by way of an odd 1972 coalition that included many northern Democratic liberals." Despite the rightward shift in the Nixon position on the social issue after the Philadelphia Plan, Mayhew maintains, "In the regulatory area, Nixon's years produced more legislation than any period since the New Deal."[161] What this underscores is the expectations and importance of the liberal national audience that watched Nixon perform. In Mayhew's terms, "public moods," not simply public opinion but weighted toward elite views, intensity of opinion, and citizen action, was the force behind the productive Nixon years.[162] In other words, the audience or public took for granted a leftward political direction, and it could not be completely reversed without great risk. Nixon may have wanted to direct energies more to the Right, but he would almost certainly sacrifice authority to lead if he tried. Some years later, Ronald Reagan would encounter a very different public mood, and much greater authority to repudiate the liberals.[163]

Such a broad sweep of liberal initiatives would suggest that few areas would be spared attention. But liberal opinion was especially intense on the civil rights issue, where the civil rights tradition had made anti–civil rights positions of any kind likely to produce storms of protest. This made Nixon's southern strategy an especially uncomfortable one, once he assumed office. In other words, after working to slow civil rights (especially in the area of school integration), but encountering deafening cries of protest from civil rights liberals now used to success, the imperative of legitimacy required *something* for civil rights. The preemption strategy was to use these necessities as opportunities to disrupt the civil rights agenda. Both the Philadelphia Plan and black capitalism/minority enterprise had possibilities of disrupting the Democrats' coalition. The Plan would tie the tails of labor and civil rights quite directly. Labor opposed black capitalism, too, since it promised to link civil rights interests with business interests, rather than with unions. And by focusing on costless employment programs, Nixon could tell his conservative supporters that he was inexpensively mitigating the spread of welfare dependency, and tell civil rights supporters that he cared. If he were to yield to liberals, he later recounted, "I had to at least take positions that the liberals didn't like."[164]

One of the administration's liberals, Daniel Patrick Moynihan, certainly did not seem to like these policies. Moynihan's Democratic sensibilities had always led him away from race-targeted policies (though he was aware of race-based problems). On 8 October 1969 he sent to Nixon his thoughts on what Richard Nixon's first-year goals should be. In the area of civil rights, Moynihan wrote,

> *The growing antagonism between White and Black will have begun to recede.* At year's end the Administration will have succeeded in establishing bona fides with black America, while reassuring white America, especially the white working class, that an administration is in office which understands that gains for blacks must not be automatically translated into losses for whites. The ill informed, often insensitive, and frequently crude manner in which Administration officials have handled black issues in the early months of the Administration will have been succeeded by positive programs in the hands of positive men who understand, among other things, that the great need is for reassurance among *all* weak and exposed groups in the society [original emphasis].[165]

But a 1969 Republican's logic of preemption was precisely to *divide* the weak and exposed. Moynihan was ignored.

Two years after the Philadelphia Plan, some civil rights groups were still booing loudly. Bayard Rustin wrote,

> Why . . . would a President who has developed a "Southern strategy," who has cut back on school-integration efforts, tried to undermine the black franchise by watering down the 1965 Voting Rights Act, nominated to Supreme Court men like Haynsworth and Carswell, cut back on funds for vital social programs, and proposed a noxious crime bill for Washington, DC—which is nothing less than a blatant appeal to white fear—why indeed would such a President take up the cause of integration in the building trades?

Rustin argued that the Plan was pushed in the context of a concerted Republican attack on organized labor, and that "[i]t is designed primarily to embarrass the unions and to organize public pressure against them." The advantages of the Plan, according to Rustin, were corporate support, the value of the Plan as a cover for antiblack policies in the South, "and, above all, he weakens his political opposition by aggravating the differences between its two strongest and most progressive forces—the labor movement and the civil rights movement."[166]

Looking back decades later, during the eighth of what were to be twelve consecutive years of low-key-on-civil-rights GOP presidential politics, Nixon's assessment of his own civil rights record suggested a different picture—or perhaps just different goals: "Impeccable."[167]

8

Conclusion: Culture, Politics, and Affirmative Action

This book has sought to explain a remarkable transformation in American politics and political culture and the origins of a national controversy. In 1964 black Americans were having their race used to stop or hinder their employment or promotion in obvious ways. This undercut American moral leadership in front of an increasingly important world audience which was increasingly committed to principles of human rights. It was assumed that the poor showing of blacks in employment statistics was the result of this discrimination. When Congress moved to address the problem, the assumed counterprinciple to blacks having their race intentionally used against them was not having race used *for* them, but emphatically for race to be taken out of the model altogether, out of the daily practices of American employment. A line of sorts was drawn in the political culture of federal civil rights enforcement, following the principle of color blindness. What was ironic about this obsession with exclusive reliance on equal treatment was that unequal treatment of groups is characteristic of American politics and not uncommon in employment. But in the moral logic of American political culture, African-Americans were seen as deserving no more than a color-blind law. Not coincidentally, this is what civil rights groups demanded, and it was in fact a spectacular victory: most assumed that significant movement toward economic equality would naturally result from color blindness.

Though few could have predicted it in 1964, the boundaries which made racial preference a taboo in that year soon began to blur and move. It was not a self-interested civil rights lobby suddenly realizing that affirmative action was what they should have been fighting for all along, and suddenly aided by new material resources. In fact the civil rights lobby was falling into disarray. The moves to racial hiring were not ideological, not based on new beliefs in the justice of racial group rights or preferences. The driving force of the change came

from context-dependent, largely taken-for-granted logics of action, which simultaneously pointed differently situated actors toward an interest in affirmative action. Many of the most powerful people in the country, mostly white and
male, began to see specifically hiring black Americans as a sensible and appropriate thing to do.

One factor that made it safer to pursue and advocate affirmative action was
the perceived crisis caused by black rioting. The violence meant to many that
the country, or at least the cities, were falling apart. At the same time, the watchful eyes of a Cold War global audience were looking for moral leadership from
the United States, a moral leadership expressed in terms of the doctrine of human rights. The imperatives of crisis management and maintenance of legitimacy on the world stage shaped narrow order-restoring options. Simple repression was ruled out; getting jobs for black Americans was a quiet priority.
President Lyndon Johnson struggled to make color-blind Great Society programs restore order. Businesses threw out old ideas of merit and brought
African-Americans in. A best-selling government report proclaimed that the
members of white society were sinners and affirmative action was part of the
penance.

Meanwhile, officials working in the administrative agencies created to enforce the ostensibly potent color-blind model found it difficult to demonstrate
the model's potency. Administrators, not guided by ideological considerations
but by a logic of administrative pragmatism, sought demonstrable effectiveness
to avoid the humiliation of agency failure, and sought efficiency to make the
best use of meager budgets and staff. For an impatient audience of civil rights
groups and supporters that expected rationalized, calculable progress, affirmative action was constructed as a promising tool to maintain agency legitimacy.
Even those advocates outside of the government, such as the NAACP Legal
Defense Fund, were guided by a pragmatic logic in their support for affirmative
action. There was no ideological or ethical attachment to the affirmative action
model.[1]

As crisis managers and pragmatic administrators began unreflectively to redefine civil rights to mean the numbers-based, equal results of affirmative action, those accustomed to fighting for the civil rights tradition saw this as just
another part of the tradition. After all, equal results had been expected all along.
Consciously or unconsciously, they used the celebrated principles associated
with the color-blind approach as safe traditions in a discourse which suggested
nothing new was being advocated. Anyone who questioned the civil rights tradition risked their own legitimacy in that national context of the still-recent,
noble, and violent southern struggle and then of the burning ghettoes, and the
international context of newly independent, nonwhite countries and a Cold War
in which the enemies scored victories with every publicized denial of human

rights. Resistance to affirmative action was almost nonexistent. And, in this context, the courts, taking for granted their role as maverick minority protectors and pragmatic problem solvers, had no trouble in stretching other traditions to hide the novelty of affirmative action for African-Americans.

All that remained to legitimate a new civil rights policy for the Left was for a right-leaning president to enter the scene. Striving for a mark in the history books as presidents typically do, Nixon logically was attracted to the creative and liberal-confounding policy of affirmative action. Whatever the sympathies of those in the Labor Department on this issue, the policy gained White House support as a preemptive strike at the liberal agenda, chosen not to further any beliefs in compensatory justice, but to divide Democrats as part of a haphazard search for much-needed presidential authority in an inhospitable political climate. In December of 1969, Nixon spoke as if the goal of the civil rights movement, as if Martin Luther King's famous dream, had always been a peculiarly limited one: the right to be a construction worker.

Given the strong cultural rules against it, it is unlikely that affirmative action could ever have been forced onto the government by a well-organized interest group, or constructed from scratch in Congress or in a presidential leadership project. It had to happen incrementally, unintentionally, in behind-the-scenes meetings of White House officials and meetings of administrators, and in pragmatic, nickel-and-dime court decisions. It needed special circumstances, such as the crisis perceived in the cities, a Cold War moral struggle based on a global model of human rights, and a conservative President Nixon needing to confound a liberal establishment used to having its way. Yet in those five years between 1964 and 1970, the political culture changed, so that affirmative action could be safely propounded to a national audience (though usually called "civil rights" and "equal opportunity," less often called "affirmative action," and never called "quotas"), and by 1971 it could be sanctioned by the Supreme Court. The Left quickly forgot its old dream of full employment and rallied to defend the new policy, which promised to guarantee the even older dream of equal participation. In their commitment to criticism of Nixon's every move, liberals were boxed into the position of de facto affirmative action defenders when Nixon's support wavered. Exactly where it came from, how and why it emerged, did not matter in the crisis climate of turbulent 1960s America. Intellectual justifications for affirmative action based on a compensatory logic were quickly derived. Republicans loudly backed away from that which they made possible.

While the new boundary was redrawn well beyond simple color blindness, Nixon had discovered that, inexplicably, the progression had to stop: no quotas. Why rationalized race-reporting paperwork, the irrelevance of discriminatory intent, the obsolescence of traditional conceptions of merit, the bottom-line standard of numbers of minorities hired, and even the racial proportionalism suggested by Nixon's racial hiring "goals" would be accepted and yet quotas still remain a taboo is difficult to comprehend. The law said keep track of race, make sure your day-to-day activities do not harm certain racial groups, strive to hire certain percentages of these racial groups—but whatever you do in this race-obsessed culture, do not set hard and fixed quotas. That the boundary remained here and not somewhere else is another of the ironies of this strange story. Americans took the repugnance of quotas for granted, but rarely if ever did anyone explain why they were bad without also indicting the other, more accepted parts of affirmative action. In fact, rarely did anyone explain why quotas were bad.

Affirmative Action in the 1990s . . . and Beyond?

We have seen the history of affirmative action. What is the status and likely future of the controversial policy? To answer that question, we must first bring the story up to date. We saw that after 1964, few in the lawmaking arena, either legislators or lobbyists, wanted to be opposed to racial preference. In the Equal Opportunity Act of 1972, Congress had another chance to stop affirmative action dead in its tracks, to fulfill the late Senator Everett Dirksen's final crusade, and they did not do so. Senator Sam Ervin's anti–affirmative action amendments, one prohibiting "discrimination in reverse by employing persons of a particular race . . . in either fixed or variable numbers, proportions, percentages, quotas, goals or ranges," and another making Title VII's prohibition of preferential treatment applicable to executive orders, were voted down (22–44 and 30–60, respectively).[2] The lack of support for Ervin's amendments, which would seem to comport rather nicely with public opinion, underscored in 1972 the legitimacy of affirmative action and the illegitimacy, the great political risk, of challenging the civil rights tradition.

In 1978 the Supreme Court finally accepted a reverse discrimination case. In *Regents of the University of California v. Bakke,*[3] the Court did not speak with a commanding voice, but through a set of opinions it more formally retraced the strange boundary already negotiated in Congress. At issue was the claim of Alan Bakke, who had been denied admission to the University of California at Davis medical school for two consecutive years. The school had set aside sixteen of one hundred places for minority students, and Bakke's credentials were superior to those of many minority students who were admitted to fill these spots. Though Bakke claimed discrimination under the Fourteenth Amendment and Title VI of the 1964 Civil Rights Act, which states that programs receiving federal assistance cannot discriminate on the basis of race, it was clear that the case would have implications in the employment arena as well. Four justices ruled in favor of Bakke; the Davis plan was discriminatory and not permissible. Another four argued that racial classification schemes were constitutional, and that the Davis plan was acceptable. In the middle was Justice Powell, who announced the ruling: The Davis plan was an unconstitutional quota plan, but racial classifications were constitutionally permissible. In a remarkable compromise, Bakke was to be admitted, Davis had to move away from a fixed quota, but treating applicants with regard to race was acceptable.[4]

Eleven years after the Philadelphia Plan and nine years after the important *Griggs* decision, Ronald Reagan was elected president, promising to "get the government off the backs of the American people," and in civil rights he gave prominent support to the color-blind model. But there was no assault on affirmative action. He issued no anti–affirmative action executive orders, and instead weakly announced that smaller companies under contract with the United States government did not have to file written affirmative action plans. He proposed no new civil rights bill to protect whites from reverse discrimination. He did appoint color-blind supporters in strategic positions (Attorney General William French Smith, Assistant Attorney General for Civil Rights William Reynolds) who made some controversial statements but mostly worked behind the scenes to try to undo the behind-the-scenes developments that had (unintentionally) led to affirmative action. He appointed conservative Clarence Thomas to chair the EEOC, but no changes were made to the EEOC's *Guidelines on Affirmative Action*. Instead, Thomas *informally* told the general counsel not to approve agreements with goals and timetables in them. Informal changes at the Office of Federal Contract Compliance Programs also reduced pressure for racial goals and timetables, which officially were unchanged. Rather than launching the assault himself, Reagan also appointed conservatives to the Supreme Court, so that they could take the heat for rolling back affirmative action.[5] Reagan thus used affirmative action to exploit white resentment, but he actually did very little to eliminate it.

Eventually, the more conservative Supreme Court did roll back affirmative action. In 1989's *Wards Cove v. Atonio*,[6] the Court did an about-face on the race-conscious adverse or disparate impact theory that had been the legacy of *Griggs*. The plaintiffs had charged that statistical disparities between minority participation in skilled and unskilled jobs were enough to make a prima facie charge of discrimination; the Ninth Circuit Court of Appeals had agreed. The Supreme Court ruling narrowed the comparison so that it was necessary to show disparities between the racial composition of the relevant job and the racial composition of the *qualified* population in the corresponding labor market. In addition, alleged victims had to identify exactly which practice harmed them. Finally, the decision revised *Griggs* by ruling that to meet the business necessity standard, employers did not have to show that a practice causing a disparate impact was "essential" or "indispensable," but something more on the order of business convenience needed to be shown.[7]

The decision was arguably more in line with public opinion and at least with the Republican administration, now led in the White House by Reagan's former vice president, George Bush. Democrats, led by Massachusetts Senator Edward Kennedy, came up with a bill to undo the undoing of the *Wards Cove* decision, thus restoring *Griggs*. As Congress prepared to debate equal employment opportunity and affirmative action again, Bush defended that curious line of legitimacy: no quotas. He would veto any "quota bill," as he called it. The issue was thus defined *not* as racial targeting and preferences versus color-blind equal opportunity. but racial quotas versus no quotas, a negative position that was safely mute on what else would be acceptable. Though Bush's legitimacy would have been questioned if he vetoed a civil rights bill, it would likely be enhanced by vetoing a *quota* bill.

The first attempt, the Civil Rights Act of 1990, restored the business necessity standard, relieved plaintiffs from having to identify specific business practices which were discriminatory, and offered punitive damages to victims of discrimination. The bill made its way through Congress, only to be vetoed by Bush, who declared it a quota bill, believing the threat of punitive damages and the hassle of proving business necessity would lead employers to try to fill racial quotas to avoid liability.[8] Many Republican Congressmen apparently did not agree with him, but still the veto override was one vote shy.[9]

Following the national spectacle of the Supreme Court confirmation hearings for Clarence Thomas, who was accused of sexual harassment, Congress passed and Bush signed the Civil Rights Act of 1991, which contained provisions for victims of sexual harassment to receive damages. Affirmative action was upheld as an appropriate remedy, punitive damages were possible but limited, the premise of affirmative action as appropriate in cases of minority group underrepresentation was accepted, a commission was created to examine the underrepresentation of minorities and women in upper management jobs (the Glass Ceiling Act of 1991), but race-norming, or the practice of having job applicants who take qualifying tests compete only against members of their own race, was prohibited. Though the Glass Ceiling Act section quite clearly was based on the affirmative action model, the new act continued the tradition of congressional vagueness: Republican Senator Bob Dole of Kansas saw the new act as consistent with *Wards Cove*, while Democrat Edward Kennedy proclaimed that *Wards Cove* was overturned.[10]

The apparent victory of the Civil Rights Act of 1991 did not mean that liberals were marching around trumpeting their support for affirmative action. While the Left had always avoided advocating racial hiring per se or racial preferences, a strategy of avoiding talking about civil rights altogether seemed to promise political benefits. After twelve years of absence, a Democrat, Bill Clinton, captured the White House with what was by all appearances a deliberate strategy of avoiding the civil rights issue. In office, he followed the safe Nixon strategy of seeking to appoint minorities to government posts, while trying to be "low-key" on civil rights. He nominated a friend, University of Pennsylvania law professor Lani Guinier as Assistant Attorney General for Civil Rights, apparently without awareness of some of her legal writing. When it was learned that her writing seemed to advocate race-conscious reforms of the democratic process (her focus was on voting rights and not employment), she was labeled a "quota queen" by conservative critics, and Clinton reluctantly withdrew the nomination. Clinton knew that avoiding the quota tag was crucial for his authority to lead. The eventual appointee, Deval Patrick, had no paper trail leading to expressed advocacy of quotas. Patrick expanded on the Clinton approach used for government appointments, the promotion of racial or gender "diversity," which could logically benefit whites as well as blacks, depending on the context. Given the apparent stability of the construction of African-Americans as a group undeserving of preference in American political culture, the low-key promotion of diversity promised to be a less risky discourse of advocacy for the affirmative action model, since it redefines the issue not as a break for blacks but as a public good, suggesting the image of an integrated socioeconomic ladder. The Right immediately began to attack this position, however, considering it an "alarming prospect" that "any citizen . . . might be discriminated against for the sake of diversity."[11]

This was, of course, the sort of argument the Right had been making against affirmative action for decades. It always appealed to the majority of Americans, though it struck many civil rights leaders as disingenuous for reasons largely described in chapter 3. The reverse discrimination argument had never been strong enough to lead a movement to eliminate affirmative action entirely, though in early 1995 this suddenly changed. Despite the recent success of the 1991 Civil Rights Act, affirmative action—preferences and not just quotas— became the focus of a bold new attack. What happened?

First, events on the global scale made arguments against affirmative action more attractive. The United States is no longer in a moral competition with the Soviet Union to show the developed and developing nations which system is the most just and progressive. Support for equal opportunity, extraordinary measures to force the expected results of equal opportunity, as well as aid for the disadvantaged in general made historic gains in this special context. The Communists decisively lost the Cold War, while several formerly lesser developed nations, especially in Asia, found success in the capitalist system. Meanwhile, Africa has declined in strategic importance and remains marginal economically. Shortly after the end of the Cold War, movements to reform welfare gained new support in the United States, as it became increasingly unclear whether an America less sympathetic to the nonworking poor risked any loss of legitimacy in a world where capitalism reigned triumphant.

Another global development threatens affirmative action: Ethnic animosity is arguably, in the post-Communist era, the most serious source of conflict in the world. Some critics of affirmative action, such as Nathan Glazer, have long maintained (among other arguments) that affirmative action goes against the American pattern of declining salience of ethnic difference, and should be rejected on the ground that it forces America to be a race-conscious society.[12] In a context of global ethnic conflict, which in the early 1990s included an effort at "ethnic cleansing" in a civil war in Bosnia, as well as an ethnicity-based slaughter in Rwanda of historic proportions, supporting policies which reify racial difference may sound increasingly illegitimate, making it difficult to defend affirmative action from attack.

The immediate cause of the new attack on affirmative action was the political calculations of the congressional Republicans, GOP candidates for the presidency in 1996, and GOP strategists. Though the rout of the Democrats in the 1994 congressional elections and the following successful attack on government funding for the Congressional Black Caucus immediately suggested fewer affirmative action defenders on Capitol Hill,[13] affirmative action was actually not a part of the successful national campaign for a GOP takeover of the House of Representatives. The rallying cry was a vague demand for less government; the social issue focus was welfare. Succeeding by exploiting anger over the perceived failures of the rights revolution, however, made it certain the Republicans would use other rights issues to consolidate their successes. In the post–Cold War world, affirmative action, like welfare, was vulnerable. When a move to put an affirmative action referendum on the California ballot gained publicity, Republican presidential candidates began to compete with each other over who could make the most sweeping indictment of the policy. Affirmative action, Americans were told again, is not fair.

In the spring of 1995, some on the Left tried to save affirmative action. Their strategies showed that the Left was finally willing to yield to the American moral model rather than try to change it. If blacks were not seen as worthy of preferences, perhaps other groups, along with black Americans, could be the promoted beneficiaries of affirmative action. Civil rights activist and former presidential candidate Jesse Jackson led an effort to show that *women* benefitted from affirmative action; the hope was that women would be seen as more deserving and white males would not want to kill a policy that could benefit their wives, sisters, mothers, or daughters. What was astonishing about this effort was that it had to be made at all. Women benefitted from all EEOC pressures and the affirmative action requirement for government contractors was expanded to include women shortly after Nixon shepherded the Philadelphia Plan through Congress. One-half of the American population was eligible for preference and still the Right focused on, and the public only seemed to care about, *racial* preferences.

The other major effort on the Left in the spring of 1995 was to make affirmative action beneficiaries seem more worthy of preference by making affirmative action a class-based preference and not a racial preference.[14] The idea of a class-based affirmative action had nothing of the notion of an efficient and effective way to prevent discrimination and, in fact, promised to be an administrative nightmare, both for government agencies *and* employers. Class-based affirmative action had nothing at all to do with discrimination. It was compelling because it harkened back to the pre-affirmative action days, when civil rights leaders and liberals argued for coalition-sustaining, big-picture, color-blind attacks on the problem of opportunity. Though the poor in America have hardly been the beneficiaries of American munificence, the poor of all races would likely be seen as more deserving than blacks. In other words, putting a white male face onto affirmative action seemed even better than a white female face. Whatever its problems as a practical policy, it did have a suggestion of good preemption politics for President Clinton, if only because it could make Republicans the enemies of whites with high aspirations but stagnant incomes. The other possibility was that class-based affirmative action could simply prolong the Democratic blood-letting on the issue.

As early as the late 1980s and early 1990s, there were signs that liberal intellectuals might be less inclined to defend the policy. At the same time that the Right was fortifying its Washington establishment, some well-known figures identified with the Left, such as Arthur Schlesinger, Jr. and William Julius Wilson, gave prominent support to color-blind approaches. Wilson, who believed affirmative action had not appreciably helped the black poor, saw as the only politically and practically feasible solution to black disadvantage truly universal programs—programs that are both race-blind as well as class-blind. While not disavowing affirmative action, he emphasized that "the hidden agenda for liberal policymakers is to improve the life chances of truly disadvantaged groups such as the ghetto underclass by emphasizing programs to which the more advantaged groups of all races and class background can positively relate."[15]

By the summer of 1995, momentum to eliminate affirmative action was increasing.[16] The wild card in the future of affirmative action is the possibility of renewed urban black violence. No one has ever explained the wave of riots that rocked the United States in the 1960s, and there is no guarantee it may not happen again. A 1992 riot in predominately black south central Los Angeles turned out not to be a harbinger of a crisis, but it underscored the seriousness of obvious racial exclusion in America. Of course, in the 1990s it is not clear that urban rioting would be combated with job opportunities. The world may be less interested in how America manages mass disorder than it was in the late 1960s.

The Cultural/Institutional Foundations of Politics and Social Policy

Though the late 1960s were an extraordinary time in American history, the logics of action which created affirmative action were not themselves extraordinary, and have implications for future studies. What can the ironies of affirmative action tell us about how best to understand American politics and policymaking?

LEGITIMACY AND THE CONTINGENCY OF INTEREST

I have argued for a fundamentally cultural interpretation of politics, policy, and law, with a priority focus on what political actors take for granted. This means that studies of politics should begin with the legitimacy imperative, the idea that little can be gained in politics unless one plays by the rules, and with sensitivity to the resulting historical and cultural contingency of interest. This is the central insight of the new institutional approach in sociology. In contrast, the predominant ways of understanding social policy give primacy to the organization and to the resources of challenging interest groups and the state structures which shape their opportunities.[17] The main problem with interest-group approaches in understanding the ironies of affirmative action is that interest groups as traditionally understood, as economic or social groups such as business or civil rights organizations, played only supporting roles. Civil rights groups, quickly losing coherence, were in a haphazard fashion demanding more money for programs like those of the Great Society and strong enforcement of the color-blind model. They did not begin to demand affirmative action until after the government constructed it.[18]

In fact, if one would want to declare the civil rights groups winners in some interest-group struggle because the result was the legitimation of affirmative action, then one would have to explain why some of the most prominent players on the civil rights side were sabotaging the effort. Many actually opposed racially exclusive affirmative action. Some of the mainstream civil rights leaders, including Martin Luther King, Jr. and Bayard Rustin, believed in color blindness and, aware of the inconsistent American justice model, they also sensed that affirmative action would be counterproductive to the long-range goals of civil rights groups. Whites could not be left out of "compensatory" programs. King wrote, "It is my opinion that many white workers whose economic condition is not too far removed from the economic condition of his black brother, will find it difficult to accept a 'Negro Bill of Rights,' which seeks to give special consideration to the Negro in the context of unemployment, joblessness, etc. and does not take into sufficient account their plight [that of the white worker]."[19] King's comment meshes with the thinking of the lonely union man, N. P. Alifas, whom we met in Chapter 3, who was seen *in that context* as a fool for daring to resist veterans' preferences. The comment also meshes with the strategy we saw King pursue in chapter 4, in his testimony to the Kerner Commission. Liberal Martin Luther King and conservative Richard Nixon both knew that affirmative action for blacks would disrupt the liberal coalition.[20] For Eli Ginzberg, whom we saw at the Kerner Commission hearings, the relationship of whites to quotas was obvious: *"You obviously include poor whites also."*

Business groups, which have a history of fighting burdensome regulation, should presumably have had an interest in protecting their rights to hire, promote, and fire as they pleased. Yet, to the surprise of regulators, business groups were almost completely absent as opponents of affirmative action. In fact, as crisis managers, some business leaders were *advocates* of affirmative action. It was only unions, with strong, parochial beliefs in their trades as family property and little sense of responsibility for crisis management, who offered political resistance.[21]

Political group interests are best understood as socially constructed reflections of the institutional boundaries of legitimate action, not natural manifestations of objective material interests. Context is crucial. Frank Dobbin, in his cross-national study of industrial policy development, has shown that what economic groups fight for in the industrial policymaking of different countries varies, and he concludes that "if national context is needed to predict how 'objective' material interests will be perceived and pursued, then national context may deserve pride of place in theories of interest."[22] The ironies of affirmative action show that interests also vary by *historical* context. It was very risky if not impossible to advocate affirmative action in 1964 and retain legitimacy as a serious political actor. It was not then a question only of offending coalition partners—it was a question of the entire civil rights project going down in flames. This is a very real and fascinating part of politics, and our analytical frame must be able to account for it.

But there is more to the complexity of context than cross-national or historical variation. Those who were post-1964 affirmative action advocates were sometimes and sometimes not close to and concerned with the employment problems of black Americans. To understand this and to understand political change, we must refine our understanding of context.

EXPLAINING CHANGE: PATTERNED ANARCHY, DISCOURSE AS DATA, AND THE IMPORTANCE OF THE AUDIENCE

Another lesson of the ironies of affirmative action is that while institutional approaches have been the weakest thus far in explaining change,[23] we have seen that the focus on taken-for-granted rules can be essential to understanding political change. There are three important principles in explaining political change in institutional terms. First, to understand the kind of political change that made possible the legitimation of affirmative action, we must see that institutional contexts, the boundaries and logics of legitimate action, are cross-cutting and nested within each other.[24] We must see the "patterned anarchy" of "institutional frictions," as Karen Orren and Stephen Skowronek have argued.[25]

Second, to measure the boundaries of possibility, we must appreciate the importance of what the political actors themselves are usually very concerned with: their discourse, the patterns of argument with which they can safely advocate political change. The best data for an institutional approach to change is political talk, including public speeches, private memos and letters, court opinions, and so forth. Equally important to what political actors *do* say is what they *do not* say, what they take for granted as illegitimate. Carefully analyzing political discourse allows us to trace the boundaries of safe and legitimate political action and the varying effects of context.

Third, institutionalists are wont to reify political rules or boundaries unless they remember that *the key to understanding the logic of institutions and interests of political actors is the perceived audience and the assumed expectations of that audience.* It is the assumed expectations of the perceived audience which maintain the boundaries of legitimacy and thus the degree of risk associated with various borderline actions. Different political actors perceive different audiences, and their perceptions mark off potentially conflicting logics of action. Some audiences are parochial, such as the small communities of agency administrators and federal courts; others are global. The audience will always also include those who are doing the acting, and so self-understandings will be relevant in every case.

For example, in the late 1960s both administrative agencies and increasingly the courts understood themselves as problem solvers, coping with Congress's increasing tendency to pass vague social legislation, and taking for granted the modern West's project of progress and justice. The audience of the administrators consisted of themselves, frustrated civil rights groups, human resources and various legal specialists, the watchdog U. S. Commission on Civil Rights, and to a surprisingly limited extent, Congress and the president. Significantly, save for a few in Congress, almost all who cared considered the performance to be measured not by the *procedures* of administration but the *results* of administration. This audience demanded of legitimate administrators results that could be expressed in the rational language of numbers of blacks who were getting jobs. The Equal Employment Opportunity Commission was not created to investigate complaints of discrimination. It was created to help minorities get jobs by providing "equal opportunity." There was no audience prepared to applaud the simple but careful practice of the color-blind model. The administrators assumed this, and the logic of their action and interests was based on this assumption.[26]

Similarly, the basis of the logic of crisis management is not to be found in Lyndon Johnson's biography but in the expectations of the global audience. If the United States had not become a world power with a goal of beating out the Soviet Union as the model for developing nations, the global audience would not have been perceived as relevant. If the United Nations had not found consensus on the sacredness of the principle of human rights, and if new African nations had not been triumphantly achieving independence, the global audience may have expected efficient, state-of-the-art repression instead of the empowerment of disadvantaged black Americans. Certainly the state had the capacity to crush the insurgency, and this arguably could have produced political gains or consolidation of gains among white working-class voters. But the global audience was important and it expected the protection of human rights.[27] The courts' limited audience expecting problem solving and a discourse of tradition, the general public expecting only (but at least) a commitment to equal treatment/color-blind traditions, the 1969 audience of fellow Republicans and White House officials accepting the necessary, risky liberal policies only because these policies interrupted the liberal agenda and promised a history-making presidency—all of these cross-cutting logics and audiences are important to an understanding the political changes which legitimated affirmative action, and all are rooted in fundamentally cultural assumptions of the actors in this strange story.

The importance of the audience of political action and discourse invites the question of how this relates to public opinion and democracy. As mentioned in the introduction, the color-blind Civil Rights Act of 1964 had a national groundswell of public opinion support. In contrast, affirmative action has never had the support of public opinion. The institutionalization of a policy that the majority does not want would seem to be an example of democracy failing. But as we saw, it was not an example of special interests ramming a policy through, either. How do we explain controversial policymaking in front of an unsupportive national audience?

I have already described how some legitimate politics happens on the political margins. The ironies of affirmative action show how administrative agencies and the courts can be engines of controversial political change because, as

CULTURE, POLITICS, AND AFFIRMATIVE ACTION

235

they are not understood as democratic engines of policymaking, their audiences are insular and may have different standards of legitimacy than the national audience. Also, since the changes they produce are incremental and understood in the courts as fitting with precedent, significant changes in policy can occur over time.

For those government leaders beholden to the national audience, a variety of factors kept the majority from resisting affirmative action in those crucial years. The first factor was the riots. As discussed in chapter 4, a crisis generally allows for a relaxation of the boundaries of legitimate action, as the restoration of order becomes a paramount concern. Such an environment could allow for either repressive or empowering measures which under normal circumstances would provoke outrage. Another factor was the frequent use of the discourse of tradition. The Johnson administration kept safe, color-blind labels on programs and policies which were in practice targeted to African-Americans. Nixon took some risks and targeted his programs, but insisted that they were also a part of tradition—nothing radical. Other factors muting the resistance of the national audience were the distractions of the busing issue in civil rights and of Vietnam in foreign policy. The Nixon administration knew the nation, and especially the South, was more concerned about the more visible controversy surrounding the forced busing of school children to achieve integrated schools at this time, while domestic policy adviser Ehrlichman could tell Nixon that the Philadelphia Plan was "not widely understood in non-labor circles." And though Nixon was battling the trade unions in domestic policy, it was precisely these unions which went public in spectacular fashion in support of Nixon's Vietnam policy. When Congress was obliquely determining the fate of affirmative action in December of 1969, Vietnam was identified as the number one problem confronting the country.[28] This meant that it was the cheers and (mostly) jeers of the highly attentive, liberal civil rights establishment that were loudest to Nixon officials making employment policy.[29]

What is clear from the sometimes broad and sometimes narrow range of the audience for political action and discourse is that political scientists must be aware of the crucial importance of the social and cultural context of political action, and that it will not do for sociologists to study politics and law while neglecting the inner workings of political and legal institutions. Both disciplines have much to teach each other, and while it is fruitful to develop different lines of inquiry, rigid respect for disciplinary boundaries only inhibits the understanding of substantive research questions.

THE MORALITY OF POLITICS

The ironies of affirmative action also have another lesson for the study of American politics and social policy. Most political analysts, even those taking a cultural perspective, tend to leave out of the analysis the meaning of the entire political enterprise, which I argue is essentially moral in character. This means that policy and lawmakers must maintain a *moral* legitimacy.

An overlooked contribution to political sociology by John Meyer and his colleagues is that we gain insight by remembering what the heroes and villains of modern politics take for granted: politics is a part of the modern West's project of the pursuit of justice and progress. If we instead start with the assumption that the political landscape is filled with various self-interested groups differentially enabled and constrained by their resources and state structures, whose moral language is secondary at best to the material forces at work, then it becomes difficult to explain why these self-interested groups would almost never fail to give these moral justifications, and spend great amounts of time and money in formulating and disseminating their discursive strategies. Why bother? People bother because they take as given the moral aspirations of the Western project. Morality provides rules or boundaries, not just sugar coatings. The reason we can have an ordered politics is because we have shared understandings of the purpose of the entire enterprise. Without the collective understandings of what politics is *for,* originally brought from Europe, American political life would have been, to paraphrase Hobbes, nasty, brutish, and short. It may indeed be nasty and brutish sometimes, but the commitment to justice and progress, the most fundamental rules of the (modern) political game, keep it going. Different nations have their own versions of how this is to be understood and attained. Within nations, shared understandings of morality and justice—a moral model—define the basic boundaries of policy and lawmaking. Anyone wishing to pursue a material interest lessens the risk of illegitimacy by acting *within the boundaries* of what is considered by the significant political players and audiences legitimate political action.

A lesson of the ironies of affirmative action is that these boundaries can be quite specific. In many ways, as explored in chapter 2, the color-blind paradigm is the modern, American way. It is congruent with the modern ideals and institutions that Americans strongly identify with. But as we saw in chapter 3, there are so many contradictions to this model that its zealous standard in the affirmative action issue seems a curiosity. The key to understanding resistance to affirmative action, and to understanding all past policies toward African-Americans, is the peculiar meaning of race in America. The resistance to or uncomfortable acceptance of racial preferences does not result from the simple application of the rule of color/difference blindness, but from the rejection of an African-American claim for moral worthiness, for the status of being deserving. And though abstract individualism is seen as appropriate for *blacks,* this is only as inevitable as all the other contingent "exceptions" to the model stitched together and guiding the creativity of policy and lawmakers.

It should be emphasized that though our moral order is socially constructed, a pastiche of moral meanings and contexts linked and mutated by countless historical circumstances, this should not suggest that it is necessarily weak or *easily* changed. When people in a society take something for granted, when they institutionalize something, it can be as real to them as the earth they stand upon, no matter how illogical it may be to a stranger.

As I have argued, cultural approaches to politics which conceive of culture as values or as different strands of tradition are simply too vague. It will not do to say that America is a classically liberal society, but that there are "exceptions." The exceptions are just as real and just as constraining as the liberal parts of the model. The impact of culture can be more specific than traditions of values; its impact is seen on the level of meanings. Despite Meyer's contribution, the institutionalists have thus far avoided the study of moral rules, using their cultural approach to argue for the significance of the meaning of practices[30] or ontological definitions.[31] We need to realize that it is also the moral meanings of different groups that can become taken for granted—some are unreflectively considered worthy of special treatment, and others are not. This is necessary for understanding the politics of social policy.

Two influential books make a similar point but do not develop it into a theory of political understanding and explanation. Theda Skocpol's brilliant *Protecting Soldiers and Mothers* uses what she describes as a polity-centered approach. Her point is that the state should not be seen as simply responding to the naturally occurring claims of economic interest groups, but that the state is a force in its own right, and that the relationships between states and political parties, as well as the impacts of state and party organizations on the outlooks and capacities of politically active social groups, are the most important factors influencing which social policies are enacted.[32] She is careful to point out that both state and party structures (which, for example, could prohibit women from voting) as well as "socioeconomic relations and cultural patterns" will affect the politicized social identities and the capacities of these groups.[33] But Skocpol's book also demonstrates the moral foundations of politics, though this is not emphasized in the model. She shows the precocious social provisions supplied by the developing American state from the Civil War period through the Progressive Era for veterans and mothers, but it is crucial that it was men as *soldiers* and women (who could not even vote at this time) as *mothers* who were considered morally worthy and not men and women as simply men, women, citizens, workers or the poor. It is true that the Republican party made political gains by rewarding veterans, and the women's groups formed powerful lobbies, but it is not likely that this would have been possible without a *prior* set of shared understandings that these groups have legitimate claims to special desert. The crucial enabling and constraining force of shared moral understandings is clear in the empirical story; she remarks, "Institutional and cultural oppositions between the morally 'deserving' and the less deserving run like fault lines through the entire history of American social provision."[34]

Jill Quadagno's *The Color of Welfare* also puts culturally based group meanings at the center of the empirical story but not at the center of the theoretical model. Quadagno argues that the "motor of change" in American social politics is the "politics of racial inequality," and that the forces that change and alter institutional arrangements are rooted in "the contradictions between an egalitarian ethos and anti-democratic practices that reproduce racial inequality."[35] Race is thus (correctly) placed at the center of the story but we are not given guidance as to how to understand it. The subtitle suggests the key to understanding is "racism": *How Racism Undermined the War on Poverty*. But what is racism? Is it a psychological affliction? Clearly not, since it varies by nation and can change over time, and white Americans are not equally discriminatory to all nonwhite groups. Focusing on the taken-for-granted boundaries of political action and discourse, we see that it is the institutionalized moral worthiness or desert of different groups which is at the foundations of American social policy. Both Skocpol and Quadagno are on target, but the centrality of group meanings and the moral foundations of politics must be incorporated into our frameworks of understanding.

The fundamental importance of moral legitimacy in politics is not just limited to the differing worthiness of groups, however. The ironies of affirmative action also show that there is a *cumulative* moral effect in social politics and law. When the nation has followed a general course that is either Right or Left for some time and with continuing success, it is difficult for opposition leaders who manage to take power to repudiate this prevailing direction, as Stephen Skowronek has pointed out. But we must recognize that these limits on opposition are normative in character. Nixon, for example, wanted to turn the nation Right after eight solid years of untrammeled liberalism. However, in this context it is easy to understand that the greater the number of conservative policies he tried to implement, the greater the outrage of the liberal establishment, and the more his legitimacy as a leader was threatened. Nixon thus had liberal "zigs" to add to his conservative "zags," as his domestic policy adviser John Ehrlichman put it. Exclusively conservative moves would have risked his legitimacy. Similarly, Nixon nominated Chief Justice Burger to make the Supreme Court more conservative, especially on racial issues. Burger responded by promptly sanctioning fundamental affirmative action principles in an opinion (*Griggs*) for a unanimous Court. After decades of siding with black plaintiffs, an immediate about-face was out of the question. Even the tradition of unanimous decisions on important race cases remained intact.

ASSUMED CAUSAL MODELS IN SOCIAL POLICYMAKING

Shared understandings of the moral worthiness of groups also have an indirect effect which shapes policymaking. As we have seen, Americans also have a basic causal model or principle which is unproblematically assumed in some cases to bring about justice and progress. Insofar as this model specifies mechanisms of social change, it could be said to be an assumed sociological or social theory which can guide policymaking. When groups are assumed to be unworthy of special treatment, the sociological causal model that lies at the heart of the American dream and the color-blind model is invoked: free individuals, freely contracting, pursuing happiness, will naturally produce a just and equal society. This equal opportunity or natural society model does not guide all policymaking (the veterans, for example, were given direct preferences rather than a scheme of equal opportunity), but it is derived from the classically liberal tradition that Americans identify with, and it is assumed to be the general picture of the United States.

Though Americans almost never discuss it, the goal of color blindness and equal opportunity is to populate the lower rungs of the socioeconomic ladder *only* with the least talented and least ambitious among us, and not overrepresentations of any other identifiable groups. Assuming that true equal opportunity is possible, there is nothing in this model that is inconsistent with the notion that an integrated meritorious group will *always* be stepping over an integrated group of untalented, unambitious, and unlucky homeless people on their way to shopping malls, cinemas, and car dealerships. Without massive charity or government programs, inequality and poverty are *built into* the equal opportunity society. It was the great contribution of the civil rights movement to ensure that black Americans had a right to at least compete fairly (in 1945, only 43 percent of Americans believed in equal opportunity laws, and 44 percent opposed them, while in 1968, 83 percent approved, and 15 percent disapproved[36]). But after the Civil Rights Act of 1964, when the equal opportunity causal model was put into effect, an obvious racial exclusion, an identifiable group disproportionately represented on the lower rungs of the socioeconomic ladder, continued to exist in seeming refutation of the cherished model. It is the continued disproportionate group identifications of the poor (blacks and women) that fuels much of the desire—and discomfort—associated with affirmative action.

The ambivalence of many toward affirmative action was reflected by a Supreme Court justice, in H. W. Perry's study of that venerable institution. In a discussion of the effect of public pressure on the Court's willingness to take a case, Perry brought up the example of affirmative action and the Court's initial reluctance to take a reverse discrimination case. The anonymous justice responded:

> At times the Court may feel the public's demand on [affirmative action]. Though there may be a strong argument in favor of postponing it, because if it turns out to be that the Constitution should be color-blind, you could have allowed [affirmative action] to go on and not have to come to that decision. You might be able to bring about social change in the mean time.

Perry calls this statement "remarkable," pointing out the irony that a Justice would ignore for the common good a policy apparently perceived as impermissible; "the court would allow all this remedial work to go on before it was forced to declare the policy unconstitutional."[37]

The dilemma is that both racial inequality and exclusion *and* affirmative action are rejected for moral/cultural reasons, but many Americans came to believe the former cannot be rectified without the latter. For this Supreme Court justice, affirmative action is simply the lesser of two evils. The notion of equal opportunity, so pristinely undefined in much of American political discourse, has proven to be a problem of enormous complexity, linking virtually every institution in society: government, the economy, businesses, the family, and so on. It is easier simply to call the inequality "discrimination" and force the *expected* result of equal opportunity through affirmative action's racial hiring goals than to tackle the enormous complexity of the opportunity problem (something the early civil rights leaders used to discuss, as in Whitney Young's call for a "domestic Marshall Plan."). But to admit this is to admit the practical failure of a great American principle, or model, of bringing about justice—an embarrassment to everyone.

The tension that has existed in the affirmative action debate is analogous to a cultural contradiction which exists in many of our policy debates: Americans remain committed to the natural-society, invisible-hand causal model of bringing about justice *and* the equality and just results that it is supposed to produce. But when the invisible hand fails to perform its magic, we will sometimes comfortably, sometimes uncomfortably *force* it to do so. Americans have unproblematically used the state to provide schooling or to support farms or the timber industry, and few attack programs that help small businesses or provide federal emergency relief for victims of natural disasters. In other cases, there is great discomfort or resistance due to our taken-for-granted aversion to illegitimate "big government" or state meddling in what should be allowed to occur naturally. In the case of affirmative action, the early taboo and later extreme discomfort and resistance are due to the meaning of race. In every case, the meanings of the specific project or the beneficiary of state responsibility will be important to understanding the politics of the policymaking. There are insights to be gained from considering the policy options that policymakers *did not* consider and the strategies that advocates for one legitimate possibility use to define an opposing option as outside the boundaries.

EXPLAINING POLITICS AND EXPERIENCING POLITICS

A related parting note on the cultural approach to policy and lawmaking should be added. Steven Brint has commented that social scientists who try to explain policy outcomes rather than only interpret politics "may seem to sap the richness and texture from social and political life as it is actually lived."[38] My hope is that this study has shown that this does not have to be. The theoretical assumptions used in this book to explain the resistance to and rise of affirmative action are in harmony with the politics that we experience on the everyday level. We know that audiences are important: millions of dollars are spent in polling, focus groups, and the selling of candidates. The other side of the coin is that great efforts are made to cover up actions considered too risky or illegitimate. We also know that moral arguments are crucial. When challenging groups or business groups organize, they do not present to government officials or the national audience proof of their organizational skills or copies of their accountants' financial books. They use their organizational resources or points of access to the government to make arguments, and these arguments, to the extent that there will be a wide audience for them or for the actions they advocate, must be grounded in the shared understandings of what politics is all about. I do not mean to claim that moral meaning will be the determining factor in every case, but the ironies of affirmative action suggest that scholars should be aware of cultural meanings and audience expectations in all cases and at all levels of political action. The legitimacy imperative suggests that the moral forces that give passion to politics and create headlines and third-rail political issues are not so different from the forces usually understood as political structure by social scientists. If enough Americans, or at least enough of the powerful and politically active, believe that marital infidelity disqualifies one from being a legitimate statesman, then elected officials will be risking their legitimacy every time they enjoy a romantic tryst. Similarly, if enough political actors believe in the constraints of certain political "structures" or procedural rules, then crossing these boundaries will also risk an actor's legitimacy. The importance of the structure of legislation or law should never be seen as something different from culture, even if behind the scenes and away from the public view. The requirements and procedures which organize the federal government are not concrete entities which can be photographed; they are ritualized, taken-for-granted practices maintained by shared understandings of their legitimacy.[39] Power, resources, interests, and organization are important, but they only make sense within this framework of shared understandings of the purpose and practice of politics, of the moral and causal models which place limits on policy possibility and determine the degree of risk. That the moral considerations are inconsistent does not prove that they are irrelevant; it proves only that politics can be ordered by inconsistent rules of desert and procedure.

The story of affirmative action is a story filled with irony, though in this it is not distinct in American politics. What is distinctive is the emotion surrounding the issue and its ironies, an emotion based not on a passion for meritocratic hiring but on the meaning of race. For the Right, affirmative action has been convenient if unwanted, always available for execration before a cheering American majority, but remarkably resilient. For the Left, it has for just as long been unquestioningly, if uncomfortably, accepted and nurtured, an orphan justice born in a turbulent time.

NOTES

Chapter One

1. Much of the Right's position will be explored in the next two chapters. For a comprehensive collection of the positions of both Right and Left, see *Racial Preference and Racial Justice*, edited by Russell Nieli, (Washington, DC: Ethics and Public Policy Center, 1991). For the Left's position specifically, see, for example, Kathanne Greene, *Affirmative Action and Principles of Justice* (New York: Greenwood Press, 1989), and essays contained in Ronald Dworkin's books, *Taking Rights Seriously* (Cambridge, MA: Harvard University Press, 1978), chapter 9, and *A Matter of Principle* (Cambridge, MA: Harvard University Press, 1985), part 5.

2. Herman Belz's *Equality Transformed: A Quarter Century of Affirmative Action* (New Brunswick: Transaction Publishers, 1991), gives some historical account of affirmative action, but he is more concerned to argue against the policy than to show its formation. The benchmark evenhanded account is Hugh Davis Graham's *The Civil Rights Era: Origins and Development of National Policy, 1960–1972* (New York: Oxford University Press, 1990). Though this work is brilliantly researched, it pays little attention to the social and cultural context of the origins of affirmative action.

3. On the other hand, fair-minded observers have correctly seen that the intersection of race and politics in America is filled with irony. See Graham, *Civil Rights Era;* Paul Burstein, *Discrimination, Jobs, and Politics: The Struggle for Equal Employment Opportunity in the United States Since the New Deal* (Chicago: University of Chicago Press, 1985); Paul Sniderman and Thomas Piazza, *The Scar of Race* (Cambridge, MA: Harvard University Press, 1993).

4. Graham, *Civil Rights Era*, pp. 108–13.

5. See Frank Dobbin, *Forging Industrial Policy: The United States, Britain, and France in the Railway Age* (New York: Cambridge University Press, 1994), pp. 5–7 for a similar critique of interest accounts in political analysis. While basic pluralist accounts have become quite sophisticated, they still pay little attention to the social bases of group interest, especially regarding the content of interest. See, for example, Clarence N. Stone, "Group Politics Reexamined: From Pluralism to Political Economy," in *The Dynamics of American Politics: Approaches and Interpretations*, edited by Lawrence C. Dodd and Calvin Jillson (Boulder, CO: Westview Press), pp. 277–96.

6. Legal scholar Alfred Blumrosen argues that Title VII is color-conscious, since (1) employers must be race-conscious to give credence to a complaint of discrimination; (2) the House of Representatives debate on the records and reporting section of the title "demonstrates that the legislators knew that the records which would be kept would indicate the race of the applicants or employees"; and (3) proving discrimination in court requires race consciousness. Alfred Blumrosen, *Modern Law: The Law Transmission System and Equal Employment Opportunity* (Madison: University of Wisconsin Press, 1993), pp. 253–55. However, Title VII is still color-blind in that (1) whatever the machinery of complaint recognition or court strategies, it forces employers to be color-blind *in their daily hiring and promoting practices;* (2) the section of the title dealing with record keeping in fact makes no mention of *racial* record keeping. The race-conscious aspect of the racial reporting later required by the Equal Employment Opportunity Commission became the subject of some concern and debate.

7. *Congressional Record,* 88th Cong., 2d sess., 1964, 110, pt. 5:6549. For other comments on the color-blind model dominating Congress, see Michael Evan Gold, *"Griggs'* Folly: An Essay on the Theory, Problems, and Origins of the Adverse Impact Definition of Employment Discrimination and a Recommendation for Reform," *Industrial Relations Law Journal* 7 (1985): 429–598; Richard A. Epstein, *Forbidden Grounds: The Case against Employment Discrimination Laws* (Cambridge, MA: Harvard University Press, 1992); Nathan Glazer, *Affirmative Discrimination: Ethnic Inequality and Public Policy* (Cambridge, MA: Harvard University Press, [1975] 1987).

8. This point has been made by some on the Left, but it has never been developed in any systematic way.

9. On public opinion and the Civil Rights Act of 1964, see Burstein, *Discrimination, Jobs, and Politics,* chapter 3. For public opinion data on affirmative action, see Seymour Martin Lipset, "Two Americas, Two Value Systems: Black and White," in *Social Theory and Social Policy: Essays in Honor of James S. Coleman,* edited by Aage Sørensen and Seymour Spilerman (Westport, CT: Praeger, 1993), pp. 202–32.

10. In the study, some respondents were asked to answer the following question: "In a nearby state, an effort is being made to increase dramatically the number of blacks working in state government. This means that a large number of jobs will be reserved for blacks, even if their scores on merit exams are lower than those of whites who are turned down for the job. Do you favor or oppose this policy?" Respondents were then read various adjectives, such as violent, irresponsible, or lazy, and asked to choose a number between one and ten, with the higher number indicating that the adjective was a more accurate description of blacks. Sniderman and Piazza, *Scar of Race,* pp. 103–4. The researchers also found that holding negative stereotypes had no effect on attitudes toward affirmative action (p. 98).

11. Burstein, *Discrimination, Jobs, and Politics,* p. 122; see chapter 5 generally.

12. Belz, *Equality Transformed;* Robert R. Detlefsen, *Civil Rights under Reagan* (San Francisco: ICS Press, 1991).

13. See James E. Jones, Jr., "The Rise and Fall of Affirmative Action," in *Race in America: The Struggle for Equality,* edited by Herbert Hill and James E. Jones, Jr. (Madison: University of Wisconsin Press, 1993), pp. 345–69.

14. Peter Hall, "Policy Paradigms, Social Learning and the State: The Case of Economic Policymaking in Great Britain," *Comparative Politics* 25 (1993): 275–96.

15. From sociology, I rely on, generally, the essays collected in *The New Institutionalism in Organizational Analysis,* edited by Walter W. Powell and Paul J. DiMaggio (Chi-

cago: University of Chicago Press, 1991), especially Paul J. DiMaggio and Walter W. Powell, "Introduction," pp. 1-38; *Institutional Structure: Constituting State, Society, and the Individual,* edited by George M. Thomas, John W. Meyer, Francisco Ramirez, and John Boli (Beverly Hills: Russell Sage, 1987), especially John W. Meyer, John Boli and George M. Thomas, "Ontology and Rationalization in the Western Cultural Account," pp. 12-37; and *Institutional Patterns and Organizations,* edited by Lynne G. Zucker (Cambridge, MA: Ballinger, 1988); see also George M. Thomas and John W. Meyer, "The Expansion of the State," *Annual Review of Sociology* 10 (1984): 461–82; Frank Dobbin, *Forging Industrial Policy: The United States, France, and Britain in the Railway Age* (New York: Cambridge University Press, 1994); Yasemin Soysal, *Limits of Citizenship: Migrants and Postnational Membership in Europe* (Chicago: University of Chicago Press, 1994); John Boli, *New Citizens for a New Society: The Institutional Origins of Mass Schooling in Sweden* (New York: Pergamon Press, 1989). In political science, I rely on Karen Orren and Stephen Skowronek, "Beyond the Iconography of Order: Notes for a 'New Institutionalism'," in *Dynamics of American Politics,* pp. 311–30; Rogers M. Smith, "If Politics Matters: Implications for a 'New Institutionalism'," *Studies in American Political Development* 6 (1992), pp. 1–36; John Kingdon, "Agendas, Ideas, and Policy Change," in *New Perspectives on American Politics,* edited by Lawrence C. Dodd and Calvin Jillson (Washington, DC: Congressional Quarterly Press, 1994), pp. 215–29; James A. Morone, *The Democratic Wish: Popular Participation and the Limits of American Government* (New York: Basic Books, 1990); and Stephen Skowronek, *The Politics Presidents Make: Leadership from John Adams to George Bush* (Cambridge, MA: Harvard University Press, 1993).

16. For the notion of the "legitimacy imperative," see DiMaggio and Powell, "Introduction," pp. 12–13, 15.

17. On this point I have been aided by the work of Frank Dobbin. See, for example, Frank Dobbin, "Cultural Models of Organization: The Social Construction of Rational Organizing Principles," in *Sociology of Culture: Emerging Theoretical Perspectives,* edited by Diana Crane (New York: Basil Blackwell, 1994), pp. 117–53; Dobbin, *Forging Industrial Policy;* Frank Dobbin, "The Origins of Private Social Insurance: Public Policy and Fringe Benefits in America, 1920–1950," *American Journal of Sociology* 97 (1992): 1416–1450. On this point also see Peter Berger and Thomas Luckmann, *The Social Construction of Reality: A Treatise in the Sociology of Knowledge* (Garden City, NY: Doubleday, 1965). For the origins of the idea of interest-based action, see Albert Hirschman, *The Passions and the Interests: Political Arguments for Capitalism before Its Triumph* (Princeton: Princeton University Press, 1977).

18. Stephen E. Ambrose, *Nixon: The Triumph of a Politician, 1962–1972* (New York: Simon and Schuster, 1989), p. 193.

19. Meyer et al., "Ontology and Rationalization"; Thomas and Meyer, "Expansion of the State."

20. I thank Frank Dobbin and Stella Jeong for this point.

21. Boli, *New Citizens for a New Society.* Thus, advocacy of policy solely on the basis of fidelity to God's will is risky in American politics, probably illegitimate (though again, one can imagine contexts and audiences where such a discourse would be welcome).

22. Seymour Martin Lipset, *First New Nation: The United States in Historical and Comparative Perspective* (New York: W. W. Norton, [1963] 1979).

23. Alasdair MacIntyre, *Whose Justice? Which Rationality?* (Notre Dame, IN: University of Notre Dame Press, 1988), p. 2.

24. Bellah et al., *Habits of the Heart: Individualism and Commitment in American Life* (New York: Harper & Row, 1985).

25. Rogers M. Smith, "Beyond Tocqueville, Myrdal, and Hartz: The Multiple Traditions in America," *American Political Science Review* 87 (1993): 549–66.

26. I build on Boli's notion in *New Citizens for a New Society* of socially constructed basic models providing the logic for policymaking, though instead of stressing an ontological model as Boli does, I stress the complex moral model. On a plurality of justices, see Michael Walzer, *Spheres of Justice* (New York: Basic Books, 1983); also see MacIntyre, *Whose Justice?;* Alasdair MacIntyre, *After Virtue* (Notre Dame, IN: University of Notre Dame Press, 1984); and Jennifer L. Hochschild, *What's Fair? American Beliefs about Distributive Justice* (Cambridge, MA: Harvard University Press, 1981).

27. Among "new institutionalist" scholars, see Soysal, *Limits of Citizenship*. Others in sociology have called for increased attention to discourse. See, for example, Robert Wuthnow, *Meaning and Moral Order* (Berkeley: University of California Press, 1987); Joseph Gusfield, *The Culture of Public Problems: Drinking-Driving and the Symbolic Order* (Chicago: University of Chicago Press, 1981).

28. Kingdon, "Agendas, Ideas, and Policy Change," pp. 224–25.

29. This principle was attributed to the Hungarian sociologist Karl Mannheim by Louis Wirth in his introduction to Karl Mannheim, *Ideology and Utopia* (New York: Harcourt Brace Jovanovich, 1936), pp. xxii–xxiii. The new institutionalist embrace of this idea is based not on Mannheim but on Berger and Luckmann, *Social Construction of Reality*.

30. I borrow the phrase from Orren and Skowronek, "Notes for a 'New Institutionalism'."

31. For the importance of institutionalized causality principles, see Dobbin, *Forging Industrial Policy*.

Chapter Two

1. Daniel Bell, *The Coming of Post-Industrial Society* (New York: Basic Books, 1973), p. 425.

2. Ibid., p. 419.

3. See Seymour Martin Lipset, "Two Americas, Two Value Systems: Black and White" in *Social Theory and Social Policy: Essays in Honor of James S. Coleman,* edited by Aage Sørensen and Seymour Spilerman (Westport, CT: Praeger, 1993), pp. 209–32; Seymour Martin Lipset, *First New Nation* (New York: W. W. Norton, 1979), pp. xxxiv–xxxv; Seymour Martin Lipset, *The Continental Divide: The Values and Institutions of the United States and Canada* (New York: Routledge, 1990), p. 38.

4. Lipset, *First New Nation,* pp. xxxiv–xxxv.

5. Lipset, *Continental Divide,* p. 38.

6. Morris Abram, "Fair Shakers and Social Engineers," in *Racial Preference and Racial Justice,* edited by Russell Nieli (Washington, DC: Ethics and Public Policy Center, 1991), pp. 29–44, 33.

7. The book is Nathan Glazer, *Affirmative Discrimination* (Cambridge, MA: Harvard University Press, [1975] 1987). The quote is from Nathan Glazer, *Ethnic Dilemmas* (Cambridge, MA: Harvard University Press, 1983), p. 161. Both books contain a variety of arguments against affirmative action. Also see Thomas Sowell, *Civil Rights: Rhetoric or Reality?* (New York: Quill, 1984) for arguments emphasizing the illogic of affirmative action.

8. See Jonathan Rieder, *Canarsie: The Jews and Italians of Brooklyn against Liberalism* (Cambridge, MA: Harvard University Press, 1985), pp. 107–19.

9. William A. Gamson and Andre Modigliani, "The Changing Culture of Affirmative Action," *Research in Political Sociology* 3 (1987), pp. 137–79.

10. Ibid., pp. 145–47.

11. Ibid., p. 170.

12. Georg Simmel, *The Philosophy of Money* (Boston: Routledge and Kegan Paul, 1978), p. 443.

13. Ibid., p. 442.

14. Ibid., p. 297.

15. Peter L. Berger, Brigitte Berger, and Hansfried Kellner, *The Homeless Mind: Modernization and Consciousness* (New York: Vintage Books, 1973), pp. 52–53.

16. Ibid., p. 55.

17. Karl Marx, "The Manifesto of the Communist Party," in *The Marx-Engels Reader*, edited by Robert C. Tucker (New York: W. W. Norton, 1978), p. 475.

18. Ibid., p. 476.

19. On this point, see also Berger, Berger, and Kellner, *Homeless Mind*, "Excursus," and Robert Nisbet, *The Sociological Tradition* (New York: Basic Books, 1966), p. 43. On the general leveling effect of capitalism, see Bryan S. Turner, *Citizenship and Capitalism* (Boston: Allen & Unwin, 1986), p. 23.

20. In Gellner's words, race would have to be "entropy-resistant." Ernest Gellner, *Nations and Nationalism* (Ithaca: Cornell University Press, 1983), p. 35.

21. Ibid., p. 63.

22. Ibid., p. 64.

23. See T. H. Marshall's thoughtful discussion in his *Class, Citizenship, and Social Development* (Garden City, NY: Doubleday, 1964), pp. 65–122.

24. John Boli, "Human Rights or State Expansion?" in *Institutional Structure: Constituting State, Society and the Individual*, edited by George M. Thomas, John W. Meyer, Francisco Ramirez, and John Boli (Beverly Hills: Russell Sage, 1987), pp. 133–49; Marshall, *Class, Citizenship, and Social Development*, pp. 74–83.

25. Boli, "Human Rights," p. 135. See also Turner, *Citizenship and Capitalism*.

26. Philip Selznick, *Law, Society, and Industrial Justice* (New York: Russell Sage Foundation, 1969), p. 53.

27. A. V. Dicey, *Lectures on the Relation between Law and Public Opinion in England During the Nineteenth Century* (London: Macmillan, [1905] 1948), p. 151.

28. Turner, *Citizenship and Capitalism*, p. 18.

29. Alvin Gouldner, *The Dialectic of Ideology and Technology* (New York: Seabury Press, 1976), pp. 199–204.

30. Quote taken from Rogers Brubaker, *Citizenship and Nationhood in France and Germany* (Cambridge, MA: Harvard University Press, 1992), pp. 39–40.

31. There were exceptions to and creative applications of merit or utility as a basis of separating classes of people, and this is important, because it provided the justification for the marginalization of many groups in society, including, most obviously, blacks, children, and slaves, but many more. Martha Minow maintains that such groups were given special legal status because they were either in hierarchical relationships of dependency, or they were seen to lack the capacity to reason. Thus, while status and lineage were abolished as ways to maintain inequality, the new order still supported legitimate modes of exclusion. "The category of incompetent persons once included married

women and sailors and—for some purposes—aliens, persons born out of wedlock, servants, wards, Jews, Quakers, villeins, monks, clergy, excommunicates, lepers, and civil servants." Martha Minow, *Making All the Difference* (Ithaca: Cornell University Press, 1990), p. 127.

32. Orlando Patterson, *Ethnic Chauvinism* (New York: Stein & Day, 1977); See also John W. Meyer, John Boli, and George M. Thomas, "Ontology and Rationalization," in *Institutional Structure*, pp. 12–38.

33. Patterson, *Ethnic Chauvinism*, p. 221.

34. Ibid., p. 225.

35. Ibid., p. 226.

36. Meyer, Boli, and Thomas, "Ontology and Rationalization," in *Institutional Structure*, p. 28. See also Michael Mann, *Sources of Social Power*, vol. 1 (New York: Cambridge University Press, 1986).

37. Meyer, Boli, and Thomas, "Ontology and Rationalization," in *Institutional Structure*, p. 25.

38. Bernard Bailyn, *The Ideological Origins of the American Revolution* (Cambridge, MA: Harvard University Press, 1967).

39. See J. R. Pole, "Enlightenment and the Politics of American Nature," in *The Enlightenment in National Context*, edited by Roy Porter and Mikuláš Teich, (New York: Cambridge University Press, 1981, pp. 192–214, 195; and Gordon S. Wood, *The Creation of the American Republic, 1776–1787* (New York: W. W. Norton, 1969), chapter 1.

40. Yehoshua Arieli, *Individualism and Nationalism in American Ideology* (Cambridge, MA: Harvard University Press, 1964), p. 50.

41. Richard Hofstadter, *The American Political Tradition* (New York: Knopf, 1973), p. 9.

42. Knud Haakonssen, "From Natural Law to the Rights of Man: A European Perspective on the American Debates," in *A Culture of Rights: The Bill of Rights in Philosophy, Politics, and Law, 1791–1991*, edited by Michael J. Lacey and Knud Haakonssen (Washington, DC: Woodrow Wilson International Center for Scholars, and Cambridge: Cambridge University Press, 1991), pp. 19–61, pp. 48–49.

43. Quoted in Bailyn, *Ideological Origins*, p. 187.

44. Bellah et al., *Habits of the Heart: Individualism and Commitment in American Life* (New York: Harper & Row, 1985), p. 33. See also Arieli, *Individualism and Nationalism*, chapter 6.

45. Bellah et al., *Habits of the Heart*, p. 142.

46. Arieli, *Individualism and Nationalism*, p. 193.

47. Bailyn, *Ideological Origins;* Edwin Dorn, *Rules and Racial Equality* (New Haven, CT: Yale University Press, 1979); Louis Hartz, *The Liberal Tradition in America* (San Diego: Harcourt, Brace, 1955).

48. Samuel Huntington, *American Politics: The Promise of Disharmony* (Cambridge, MA: Harvard University Press, 1981), chapter 2.

49. Quoted in Arieli, *Individualism and Nationalism*, p. 91.

50. Quoted in ibid., p. 191.

51. The catch was that many Americans did not see blacks (or women, or a variety of other groups) as having that great equalizer, reason.

52. Arieli, *Individualism and Nationalism*, p. 24.

53. James E. Jones, Jr., "The Rise and Fall of Affirmative Action," in *Race in Amer-*

ica: The Struggle for Equality, edited by Herbert Hill and James E. Jones, Jr. (Madison: University of Wisconsin Press, 1993), pp. 345–59, 347.

54. Andrew Kull, *The Color-Blind Constitution* (Cambridge, MA: Harvard University Press, 1992), p. 20.

55. Arthur Earl Bonfield, "The Origin and Development of American Fair Employment Legislation," *Iowa Law Review* 52 (1967): pp. 1043–92, 1052.

56. Ibid., p. 1051.

57. Ibid., p. 1059.

58. Stanley Lieberson, *A Piece of the Pie* (Los Angeles: University of California Press, 1980); Theodore Hershberg et al., "A Tale of Three Cities: Blacks, Immigrants, and Opportunity in Philadelphia, 1850–1880, 1930, and 1970," *The Annals of the American Academy of Political and Social Science* 441 (1979): 55–81.

59. In 1944 the National Opinion Research Center asked white respondents, "Do you think Negroes should have as good a chance as white people to get any kind of job, or do you think white people should have the first chance at any kind of job?" Only 44 percent said that blacks should have an equal chance. In 1945 a Gallup poll asked, "Do you favor or oppose a law in this state which would require employers to hire a person if he is qualified for the job, regardless of his race or color?" Forty-three percent were in favor, 44 percent were opposed, and 13 percent had no opinion. In the Northeast, 58 percent favored the law, in the Midwest, 41 percent, in the West, 41 percent, and in the South, only 20 percent. See Paul Burstein, *Discrimination, Jobs, and Politics* (Chicago: University of Chicago Press, 1985), p. 44.

60. The case was *NLRB v. Jones & Laughlin Steel Corp.*, 301 U. S. 1, 49 (1937). See Bonfield, "Origin and Development" on this point; see also Burstein, *Discrimination, Jobs, and Politics,* chapter 2.

61. Quoted in Michael I. Sovern, *Legal Restraints on Racial Discrimination* (New York: The Twentieth Century Fund, 1966), p. 10.

62. Burstein, *Discrimination, Jobs, and Politics,* p. 37.

63. Sovern, *Legal Restraints,* p. 23

64. Graham, *Civil Rights Era,* p. 19.

65. Leon Mayhew, *Law and Equal Opportunity* (Cambridge, MA: Harvard University Press, 1968), p. 66.

66. Quoted in John L. Ansbro, *Martin Luther King, Jr.: The Making of a Mind* (Maryknoll, NY: Orbis Books, 1982), p. 73.

67. Martin Luther King, Jr., *Where Do We Go from Here: Chaos or Community?* (Boston: Beacon Press, 1967), p. 97.

68. Ibid., p. 84.

69. Lester A. Sobel, ed., *Civil Rights, 1960–1966* (New York: Facts on File, 1967), p. 227.

70. Bayard Rustin, "The Blacks and the Unions," *Harpers,* May, 1971, pp. 73–81. SNCC ignored Rustin's advice, and embraced black power ideology three years later.

71. Sobel, *Civil Rights, 1960–1966,* p. 350. This effort to expand the base also extended, on the part of some black leaders, to the linking of civil rights with the New Left anti-Vietnam War movement.

72. Graham, *Civil Rights Era,* p. 111.

73. Ibid., p. 112.

74. Whitney Young, Jr., and Kyle Haselden, "A Debate over 'Compensatory' Pro-

grams," in *Freedom Now!,* edited by Alan F. Westin (New York: Basic Books, 1964), pp. 279–89.

75. Whitney Young, *To Be Equal* (New York: McGraw-Hill, 1964), p. 29.

76. See chapter 3; see also Nathan Glazer, *Ethnic Dilemmas* (Cambridge, MA: Harvard University Press, 1983), pp. 160–62.

77. Young, *To Be Equal,* p. 57.

78. King, *Where Do We Go from Here,* pp. 196–99.

79. A curious and neglected aspect of Title VII is that Communists are explicitly not members of the protected classes. Section 703 (f) states, "As used in this title, the phrase 'unlawful employment practice' shall not be deemed to include any action or measure taken by an employer, labor organization, joint labor-management committee, or employment agency with respect to an individual who is a member of the Communist Party of the United States or of any other [related organization]." Sovern, *Legal Restraints,* p. 69. An attempt was also made in Congress to explicitly keep atheists off of the list of protected groups—an interesting note on how culture shapes moral reasoning.

80. The excerpts are contained in appendix 1, in Alfred Blumrosen, *Black Employment and the Law,* (New Brunswick, NJ: Rutgers University Press, 1971). The House report is from 88th Cong., 1st sess., H. Rept. 914, pt. 2, and the Senate report is from 88th Cong., 2d sess., S. Rept. 867.

Chapter Three

1. When respondents to a survey were told, "Everyone in America should have equal opportunities to get ahead," 98 percent agreed. Herbert McClosky and John Zaller, *The American Ethos: Public Attitudes toward Capitalism and Democracy* (Cambridge, MA: Harvard University Press, 1984), p. 83.

2. Harvey Mansfield, Jr., "The Underhandedness of Affirmative Action," in *Racial Preference and Racial Justice,* edited by Russell Nieli (Washington, DC: Ethics and Public Policy Center, 1991), pp. 127–40.

3. Thomas Sowell, *Civil Rights: Rhetoric or Reality?* (New York: Quill, 1984), p. 119.

4. Currently, a policy of affirmative action for veterans in the private sector is restricted to Vietnam veterans, and applies only to state contractors (*Vietnam Era Veterans Readjustment Assistance Act of 1974,* section 402).

5. The examinations were established in 1883 with the Pendleton Civil Service Reform Act, which was ostensibly designed to ensure the selection of the most able job applicants while guarding against chronic problems of patronage and preference (William Pyrle Dillingham, *Federal Aid to Veterans, 1917–1941,* [Gainesville: University of Florida Press, 1952]. See also Eugene B. McGregor, "Social Equity and the Public Service," *Public Administration Review* (January/February 1974): 18–29).

6. See Chester A. Newland, "The Politics of Civil Service Reform," in *The Promise and Paradox of Civil Service Reform,* edited by Patricia W. Ingraham and David H. Rosenbloom (Pittsburgh: University of Pittsburgh Press, 1992), pp. 63–96, pp. 73–74.

7. Dillingham, *Federal Aid to Veterans,* Dixon Wecter, *When Johnny Comes Marching Home,* (New York: Houghton Mifflin, 1944). On the development of Civil War veteran pensions, see Theda Skocpol, *Protecting Soldiers and Mothers* (Cambridge, MA: Harvard University Press, 1992).

8. Wallace Evan Davies, *Patriotism on Parade: The Story of Veterans' and Hereditary Organizations in America, 1783–1900* (Cambridge, MA: Harvard University Press, 1955).

9. Davies, *Patriotism on Parade,* p. 152.

10. It is notable that in Skocpol's description of the wide expansion of eligibility of veterans' pensions, some pretense of injury was maintained. Thus, old age was considered a disability. See Skocpol, *Protecting Soldiers and Mothers,* pp. 110–11.

11. Wecter, *Johnny Comes Marching,* p. 187.

12. Mark A. Emmert and Gregory B. Lewis, "Veterans Preference and the Merit System," in *Centenary Issues of the Pendleton Act of 1883,* edited by David H. Rosenbloom (New York: Marcel Dekker, 1982), pp. 45–62, 48.

13. Ibid., p. 48.

14. Dillingham, *Federal Aid to Veterans,* p. 186.

15. Emmert and Lewis, "Veterans Preference," p. 49.

16. Ibid., p. 48.

17. Katherine Mayo, *Soldiers What Next!,* (Boston: Houghton Mifflin, 1934), p. 115.

18. Nathan Glazer, *Ethnic Dilemmas* (Cambridge, MA: Harvard University Press, 1983), p. 176.

19. Dillingham, *Federal Aid to Veterans,* pp. 188–91.

20. Nathan Glazer, *Affirmative Discrimination* (Cambridge, MA: Harvard University Press, [1975] 1987), p. x.

21. Dillingham, *Federal Aid to Veterans,* p. 188.

22. Roy V. Peel, "The 'Separateness' of the Veteran," in *The Annals of the American Academy of Political and Social Science,* 238 (March 1945): 167–73.

23. I am indebted to Theda Skocpol for this point.

24. Drafts for the Civil War and afterwards actually did not rely on the obligation of citizens to do militia service, but on the authority of Congress to raise armies. However, though the citizen soldier principle would seem to make veteran demands illegitimate, some in the military seemed to subscribe to the notion of citizen soldier. General Lewis Hershey, head of Selective Service from its beginning in World War II through 1970 said, "[T]he militia system . . . is the ancestor of the Selective Service System and the direct descendant bears a very close resemblance to its illustrious forefather." See Eliot A. Cohen, *Citizens and Soldiers: The Dilemma of Military Service* (Ithaca: Cornell University Press, 1985), p. 125.

25. Davis R. Ross, *Preparing for Ulysses: Politics and Veterans During World War II* (New York: Columbia University Press, 1969) p. 13.

26. Ibid., p. 14.

27. Ibid., p. 18.

28. Ibid., p. 27.

29. In 1938, perhaps as an olive branch offering to veterans, Roosevelt signed an executive order which established a provision requiring personnel officers to state reasons for passing over an eligible veteran in hiring a nonveteran (if insufficient reasons were given, the veteran was hired). Dillingham, *Federal Aid to Veterans,* p. 193.

30. See Jerome S. Bruner, *Public Thinking on Post-War Problems,* (Washington, DC: National Planning Association Planning Pamphlets, no. 23, October 1943). The Gallup Poll did ask some questions about the treatment of veterans in the 1940s, and these also show wide support for veterans as a deserving group. For example, in January 1944 the Gallup Poll asked respondents if they approved or disapproved of a bill that would have the government give a "certain sum of money" to members of the armed forces when they leave the service. Eighty-eight percent of respondents approved of such a bill, 8 percent disapproved, and 4 percent had no opinion. In August of that year, the Gallup Poll

asked, "When the war is over and many soldiers return to civilian life, they may not find jobs. Do you think the Government should give soldiers money if they find themselves out of work after the war?" Eighty-three percent of respondents said yes to this question, with 13 percent saying no, and 4 percent having no opinion. The same poll also asked, "Should the Government give war workers money if they find themselves out of work when the war is over or nearly over?" Here Americans drew a sharp distinction. War *workers* deserved no special treatment: only 21 percent said yes, while 71 percent responded no, and 8 percent had no opinion. Finally, a 1945 poll found that 75 percent of Americans believed that income tax on armed forces service pay should be canceled, while 16 percent believed it should be paid, and 9 percent had no opinion.

It appeared that something about the experience of World War II had some effect on the meaning of the veteran status. For example, in 1946 the Gallup Poll asked, "Would you be willing to pay higher taxes to have your state government pay a bonus to war veterans at this time?" Excluding veterans, 52 percent said yes, while 39 percent said no, and 9 percent had no opinion. In 1935, the question had a 50-50 response. The Gallup Poll, *Public Opinion: 1935–1971* (New York: Random House, 1972); see vol. 1, 1935–1948.

31. *Congressional Record,* 78th Cong., 2d sess., 1944, 90, pt. 3:3501–2.

32. U.S. Senate Committee on Civil Service, *Preference in Employment of Honorably Discharged Veterans Where Federal Funds Are Disbursed: Hearings before the Committee on Civil Service,* 78th Cong., 2d sess., 1944, on S. 1762 and H. R. 4115, pp. 62–65.

33. Neither the Senate nor the House reports contained any significant discussions of equality of opportunity or justice in principle. See 78th Cong., 2d sess., 1944, S. Rept. 907, and 78th Cong., 2d sess., 1944, H. Rept. 1289.

34. *Congressional Record,* 78th Cong., 2d sess., 1944, 90, pt. 3:3502.

35. The law equally applied to female veterans, which was a novelty in veterans' preference law.

36. *Congressional Record,* 78th Cong., 2d sess., 1944, 90, pt. 3:3504. Though American legislators felt they could only persuade private employers, many were aware, from information given at the hearings, that other countries legislated preferences in industry, sometimes legislating veteran hiring quotas, as in France, Italy, and Poland. See "Statement from 1936 Hearings on Veteran Employment Laws in Other Countries," by Millard W. Rice, National Legislative Representative, Veterans of Foreign Wars, in Hearings on S. 1762 and H. R. 4115, p. 51 (see note 32 above).

37. No distinction in the Act was made between those who volunteered and those who were drafted. Interestingly, the fact that many of the soldiers volunteered was mentioned to underscore their worthiness. This may be surprising, since if someone volunteers for something, it can usually be assumed that they are aware of the consequences of their action (what was called "assumption of risk" in old workers compensation law). Thus, the *forced* economic servitude of slaves, and the depressed economic state that is its legacy, could count for more persuasive power in the rhetorical strategy of the legitimation of targeted social policies for African-Americans. In the United States, however, this has not been the case.

38. *Congressional Record,* 78th Cong., 2d sess., 1944, 90, pt. 3:3504.

39. The lone dissenter, Howard Smith (Republican of Virginia), gave no reason for his vote. Steven Lim, "The Effect of Veterans' Reemployment Rights, Veterans' Preference Laws, and Protective Labor Laws on the Status of Women Workers in the World War II Period," *Hofstra Labor Law Journal* 2 (1986): 301–54, p. 310.

40. 78th Cong., 2d sess., 1944, H. Rept. 1289, p. 5.

41. Gamson and Modigliani, "Culture of Affirmative Action," p. 147.

42. Samuel Ordway, Jr., "The Veteran in the Civil Service," in *The Annals of the American Academy of Political and Social Science* 238 (March 1945): 133–39, p. 138.

43. Ibid., pp. 138–39.

44. Peel, "'Separateness' of the Veteran."

45. Ibid., p. 170.

46. See Grace Blumberg, "De Facto and De Jure Sex Discrimination under the Equal Protection Clause: A Reconsideration of the Veterans' Preference in Public Employment," *Buffalo Law Review* 26 (1976): 3–82, p. 16; see also Lim, "Veterans' Reemployment Rights."

47. *Bateman v. Marsh*, 64 NYS 2d 678 (1946) at 684–5.

48. *Opinion of the Justices*, 166 MA 589 (1896) at 595.

49. *Mitchell v. Cohen*, 333 U.S. 411 (1948) at 418.

50. "Of the wisdom of such (preference) legislation, we are not made the judges" *Opinion of the Justices*, 166 MA 589 (1896) at 595; "Encouragement and reward of military service are [veterans' preference's] rational basis. If it is unwise and costly, this does not make it unconstitutional" *White v. Gates*, 253 F2d 868 (1958) at 869. In one case, the court even sought to limit a particularly strong state preference law. In 1887, there was passed a law in Massachusetts that actually exempted veterans from *even having to take* the civil service examination. A nonveteran who scored first on a police detective examination did not get the job, and filed a suit (*Brown v. Russell*, 166 MA 14, N.E. 1005 [1896]). The court determined that preference is legal if it is limited to candidates of equal qualification, but that it is in the public interest to have at least minimally qualified civil servants. The court also expressed concern that veteran status is closed to some through no fault of their own. See Blumberg, "De Facto and De Jure Sex Discrimination," p. 10.

51. *Commonwealth ex rel. Graham v. Schmid*, 333 PA 568 (1938) at 573. Similarly, *Opinion of the Justices*, 166 MA 589 (1896) at 595, reasoned that the Massachusetts legislature thought that a veteran "would be likely to possess courage, constancy, habits of obedience and fidelity, which are valuable qualifications for any public service or employment."

52. See Blumberg, "De Facto and De Jure Sex Discrimination"; Lim, "Veterans' Reemployment Rights"; Pat Labbadia, "The Veterans' Preference Statutes: Do They Really Discriminate against Women?" *Duquesne Law Review* 8 (1980): 653–82; Casenotes, "Absolute Veterans' Preference in Public Employment: Personnel Administrator of Massachusetts v. Feeney," *Boston College Law Review* 21 (1980): 1110–42.

53. 442 U.S. 256 (1979).

54. Ibid., at 277.

55. Ibid., at 265.

56. See note 50.

57. *Personnel Administrator of Mass. v. Feeney* at 280.

58. Ibid., at 281.

59. Ibid., at 274–75.

60. Ibid., at 286.

61. Ibid., at 287.

62. Ibid., at 287.

63. Blumberg, "De Facto and De Jure Sex Discrimination," p. 19.

64. EEOC Decision 74–64 (7 December 1973) 8 FEP Cases 557.

65. David H. Rosenbloom, *Federal Equal Employment Opportunity: Politics and Public Personnel Administration* (New York: Praeger, 1977), p. 45.

66. Bernard Rosen, "Affirmative Action Produces Equal Employment Opportunity for All," *Public Administration Review* 34 (May/June 1974): 237–39, 239.

67. Jean J. Couturier, "Civil Rights in Civil Service—The Winds of Change?" *Public Administration Review* 34 (May/June 1974): 243–45, 244.

68. For World War II rejection rates, see George Q. Flynn, *The Draft, 1940–1973* (Lawrence, KS: University Press of Kansas, 1993), pp. 31–33. Fifty percent were originally rejected, or one million of the first two million drafted, a figure found shocking and embarrassing to many concerned about the health of Americans. Most rejections were based on poor teeth, eyes, feet, or illiteracy. An effort was made to rehabilitate about 20 percent of those rejected. In the period between June 1948 and June 1955, 52 percent were rejected. If these statistics included all those who deferred or who fulfilled their military obligation through means other than the draft, 23.6 percent of American youth would be unfit to serve. Flynn, *The Draft*, pp. 152–53. Bruce K. Chapman maintains that the rejection rate fluctuates between 47 and 52 percent. Bruce K. Chapman, "Politics and Conscription: A Proposal to Replace the Draft," in *The Draft: A Handbook of Facts and Alternatives*, edited by Sol Tax (Chicago: University of Chicago Press, 1967), pp. 208–20, p. 216. See also Walter Y. Oi, "The Economic Cost of the Draft," in *The Military Draft: Selected Readings on Conscription*, edited by Martin Anderson (Stanford, CA: Hoover Institution Press, 1982), pp. 317–46.

69. David H. Rosenbloom, *Federal Service and the Constitution* (Ithaca: Cornell University Press, 1971), p. 136. Theda Skocpol points out that government largesse for Civil War veterans was unavailable to those who fought for the South, those who had been slaves not freed before the war ended, those potentially quite respectable citizens who chose not to serve, or those immigrants who came after the war. Skocpol, *Protecting Soldiers and Mothers*, p. 149.

70. Michael Walzer, *Spheres of Justice* (New York: Basic Books, 1983), p. 147.

71. 5CFR ch. 1, Sections 310.102, 310.103. Quoted in Bureau of National Affairs, *Corporate Affairs: Nepotism, Office Romance, and Sexual Harassment* (Washington, DC: Bureau of National Affairs, 1988), appendix C.

72. For example, the Pendleton Civil Service Reform Act of 1883 made it illegal for more than two people from the same family to work for the civil service. A civil service law directed at equal employment opportunity, designed to allocate jobs more evenly during the depression (by requiring that employed spouses of workers be dismissed before other persons), was passed (Act of June 30, 1932) as a rider to an appropriations bill, but was repealed five years later. See Joan G. Wexler, "Husbands and Wives: The Uneasy Case for Antinepotism Rules," *Boston University Law Review* 62 (1982): 75–142 and 85, n. 43.

73. See Daniel Bell, *The End of Ideology* (Cambridge, MA: Harvard University Press, [1961] 1988), chapter 2.

74. Perrin Stryker, "Would You Hire Your Son?" *Fortune*, March 1957.

75. Ibid., p. 220.

76. Ibid., p. 224.

77. 330 U.S. 552.

78. Ibid., at 556.

79. Ibid., at 563. See also Richard H. Fallon, Jr., "To Each According to His Ability,

from None According to His Race: The Concept of Merit in the Law of Antidiscrimination," *Boston University Law Review* 60 (1980): 815–77, 827–28.

80. *Kotch v. Board of River Port Pilot Commissioners* at 566 (1947).

81. Ibid.

82. Stryker, "Would You Hire?," p. 224.

83. Wexler, "Husbands and Wives."

84. David W. Ewing, "Is Nepotism So Bad?" *Harvard Business Review* (January/February 1965): 23.

85. Wexler, "Husbands and Wives," p. 79.

86. In this sense, it can be said that the color-blind model did construct group preferences, in that it deems some arbitrary cleavages of difference worthy of protection (the "protected classes") and others unworthy. Merit hiring is protected only for some. Title VII thus is a preference law not for blacks, but for all racial groups, including whites.

87. Bureau of National Affairs, *Corporate Affairs*, p. 32.

88. Protection from racial discrimination could conceivably have been interpreted as a protection from family discrimination, as we saw in *Kotch v. Board of River Port Pilot Commissioners.* While this may appear to be a stretch, certainly stranger interpretations have been made in American legal history. With respect to Title VII, much of the development of the law seems to go beyond the statute, as we will see. One related aspect of this development beyond the scope of the present study was that enforcement agencies for Title VII and Executive Order 11246, in developing the affirmative action model, had to determine what *race* meant and which racial groups were to be counted for affirmative action purposes with virtually no statutory guidance. For example, in one case, white Europeans from Spain were considered by the OFCC to be protected and recruited or hired as "Spanish-surnamed" people, while Thai-Americans were to be regarded as white and presumably unprotected and undeserving of preference. Glazer, *Ethnic Dilemmas,* pp. 198–201. Certainly this interpretation would be regarded as a deviation from the order. The rights of white people from Europe, whether from Spain or Slovakia, were almost certainly as far from President Johnson's mind as nepotism protections when he issued Order 11246.

On a related note, the EEOC ruled that discrimination on the basis of excessive weight or age also were not violations of Title VII. See "First Annual Digest of Legal Interpretations, 2 July 1965 through 1 July 1966," in *Civil Rights During the Johnson Administration, 1963–1969,* edited by Steve F. Lawson (Frederick, MD: University Publications of America, 1984), part 2: "EEOC Administrative History," Documentary Supplement, Reel 2, frame 0076.

89. *Gibson v. ILGWU, Local 40,* 13 FEP Cases 997, (9th Cir. 1976) at 1003.

90. *Sogluizzo v. Local 817, Teamsters,* 28 FEP Cases 534 (SNY 1981) at 535.

91. Bureau of National Affairs, *Corporate Affairs*, p. 12.

92. Ewing, "Is Nepotism So Bad?," p. 22.

93. See "Clifford Alexander Oral History," [1973], in *Civil Rights During the Johnson Administration, 1963–1969,* edited by Steven F. Lawson, part 3: "Oral Histories," reel 1, frame 0029.

94. Ewing, "Is Nepotism So Bad?," p. 36.

95. "Alexander Oral History," in Lawson, ed., *Civil Rights During Johnson,* part 3, reel 1, frame 0006.

96. The American Association of Collegiate Registrars and Admissions Officers and The College Board, *Undergraduate Admissions: The Realities of Institutional Policies,*

Practices, and Procedures: A Report on a Survey (New York: College Entrance Examination Board, 1980).

97. Robert Klitgaard, *Choosing Elites* (New York: Basic Books, 1985), p. 28.

98. Peter W. Cookson, Jr., and Caroline Hodges Persell, *Preparing for Power* (New York: Basic Books, 1985), p. 174.

99. Peel, "'Separateness' of the Veteran," p. 169.

100. Blumberg, "De Facto and De Jure Sex Discrimination," p. 65.

101. Preferences for women are rejected in about the same numbers as preferences for blacks. In response to the question "Laws requiring employers to give special preference to minorities when filling jobs are . . . ," only 10 percent said, "necessary to make up for a long history of discrimination," while 76 percent said they were "unfair to qualified people who are not members of a minority." When the question replaced "minorities" with "women," the percentages were 9 and 76, respectively. For both questions, 15 percent declined to choose. See Herbert McClosky and John Zaller, *The American Ethos* (Cambridge, MA: Harvard University Press, 1984), p. 93.

102. Boris I. Bittker, *The Case for Black Reparations* (New York: Random House, 1973), p. 69.

103. Ross, *Preparing for Ulysses*, p. 64.

104. Mark Granovetter, *Getting a Job* (Cambridge, MA: Harvard University Press, 1974), p. 22.

105. The American embrace of equal opportunity (98 percent agree with the statement, "Everyone in America should have equal opportunity to get ahead" (McClosky and Zaller, *The American Ethos*, p. 83) is also curious because although there are limitations on the government regarding how it can treat citizens, the bulk of law gives discretion to employers, to property rights. Employers are legally hemmed in only by notions of certain protected classes (race, gender, religion, national origin; more recently age and disability), not by any meritocratic fairness ideal, not by any true notion of giving everyone an equal chance to get ahead.

106. Richard Hofstadter, *The American Political Tradition* (New York: Knopf, 1973), p. 15. See also J. R. Pole, *The Pursuit of Equality in American History* (Berkeley: University of California Press, 1978).

107. See chapter 2, note 31.

108. Pole, *Pursuit of Equality*, p. 91.

109. "American history," Samuel Huntington has stated, "is the history of the efforts of groups to promote their interests by realizing American ideals." Samuel Huntington, *American Politics: The Promise of Disharmony* (Cambridge, MA: Harvard University Press, 1981), p. 11.

110. Quoted in Hofstadter, *American Political Tradition*, p. 131.

111. The American legal record regarding race is indeed a sorry one. Obviously, only blacks were enslaved. Despite the color blindness of the language of the Constitution, the Naturalization Law of 1790 said that only free white immigrants were eligible for citizenship. While the United States Constitution made no mention of race, some state constitutions, including those of Pennsylvania and New York, did mention race. In 1882, the Chinese Exclusion Act was passed, restricting immigration from China. The Chinese also could not own property in many states. Other immigrants were restricted on an ethnic basis in 1921. Japanese-Americans were rounded up in concentration camps during World War II. For a review of these and other sordid details of American racial history, see Ronald Takaki, "Reflections on Racial Patterns in America," in *From Different*

Shores, edited by Ronald Takaki (New York: Oxford University Press, 1987), pp. 26–37. See also Michael Omi and Howard Winant, *Racial Formation in the United States* (New York: Routledge, 1986), pp. 66–68, for a discussion of organization of politics in the United States along racial lines.

112. See Seymour Martin Lipset, "Two Americas, Two Value Systems: Black and White" in *Social Theory and Social Policy: Essays in Honor of James S. Coleman,* edited by Aage Sørensen and Seymour Spilerman (Westport, CT: Praeger, 1993), pp. 209–32; Seymour Martin Lipset, *First New Nation* (New York: W. W. Norton and Co., 1979), pp. xxxiv–xxxv; Seymour Martin Lipset, *The Continental Divide* (New York: Routledge, 1990), p. 38.

113. See Rogers M. Smith, "Beyond Tocqueville, Myrdal, and Hartz: The Multiple Traditions in America," *American Political Science Review* 87 (1993): 549–66, for a review. Even the perceptive sociologist John Boli does not see anything problematic in "exceptions" or "violations" to abstract individualism. (John Boli, *New Citizens for a New Society: The Institutional Origins of Mass Schooling in Sweden* [New York: Pergamon Press, 1989], pp. 259–60).

114. Alasdair MacIntyre, *Whose Justice? Which Rationality?* (Notre Dame, IN: University of Notre Dame Press, 1988), p. 2.

115. Smith, "Beyond Tocqueville," p. 550.

116. Theda Skocpol, *Protecting Soldiers and Mothers,* p. 149.

Chapter Four

1. I derive this definition from Jürgen Habermas and James O'Connor. Habermas traces the concept's origins to the practice of medicine, in the context of assessing whether or not a patient's self-healing powers will be enough to recover (Jürgen Habermas, *Legitimation Crisis* [Boston: Beacon Press, 1973], p. 1). Thus, identifying crisis as that which is experienced from the viewpoint of the sufferer, Habermas associates the term with the deprivation of "his normal sovereignty." Similarly, O'Connor identifies crises in traditional Marxism with those unpredictable historical moments when "capital loses its 'normal ideological sovereignty,' hence when there may occur a political vacuum in which political power is up for grabs." James O'Connor, *The Meaning of Crisis* (New York: Basil Blackwell, 1987), p. 114. In emphasizing the subjective element, O'Connor echoes the institutionalists in declaring, " 'Crisis' is also a 'subjective' historical process—a time when it is not possible to take for granted 'normal' economic, social, and other relationships; a time for decision; and a time when what individuals actually do counts for something" (ibid., p. 3). This definition would not include as a crisis the threat of being voted out of office. Politicians can sense a loss of control through a voter threat to remove them from office, but clearly this situation would probably not lead governing elites to reach beyond the boundaries of legitimacy to regain control, though they may reach beyond the party's previous platform or understandings.

2. From the perspective of advocates of radical change, a crisis can be understood as a *policy window,* to use political scientist John Kingdon's term, or "an opportunity for advocates of proposals to push their pet solutions, or to push attention to their special problems." (John W. Kingdon, *Agendas, Alternatives, and Public Policies* [Boston: Little, Brown, 1984], p. 173.) Not necessarily requiring a crisis, he explains that a policy window may open if there is a change in the "political stream," meaning a change in the executive administration or legislature, or a shift in the national mood, or "because a new problem captures the attention of governmental officials or those close to them." Clearly,

though, in Kingdon's scheme, a national crisis such as that caused by the urban riots can create a policy window—and open it wide.

3. Stephen D. Krasner, "Approaches to the State: Alternative Conceptions and Historical Dynamics," *Comparative Politics* 16 (1984): 223–46, 234. See also William A. Gamson, *The Strategy of Social Protest* (Homewood, IL: Dorsey Press, 1975), for the argument that a major crisis aids challenging groups whose struggles began before the onset of the crisis.

4. The term is from Peter Berger and Thomas Luckmann, *The Social Construction of Reality* (New York: Anchor, 1965).

5. See Frank Dobbin, "The Institutionalization of the State: Industrial Policy in Britain, France, and the United States," (Ph.D. diss.), Stanford University, 1987, chapter 6.

6. See Paul L. Murphy, *The Constitution in Crisis Times, 1918–1969* (New York: Harper & Row, 1972), chapter 7, p. 222.

7. Ibid., pp. 288–89. See also Lawrence M. Friedman, *The Legal System: A Social Science Perspective* (New York: Russell Sage, 1975), p. 298.

8. In *A Common Destiny,* edited by Gerald David Jaynes and Robin M. Williams, Jr. (Washington, DC: National Academy Press, 1989), p. 63.

9. For a survey of crisis discourse used by American presidents, see *The Modern Presidency and Crisis Rhetoric,* edited by Amos Kiewe (Westport, CT: Praeger, 1994).

10. See David J. Garrow, *Bearing the Cross* (New York: Vintage Books, 1986), pp. 276–86.

11. Lee Rainwater and William L. Yancey, *The Moynihan Report and the Politics of Controversy* (Cambridge, MA: The MIT Press, 1967), p. 11.

12. Bayard Rustin, "From Protest to Politics: The Future of the Civil Rights Movement," *Commentary* 39 (February, 1965): 25–31, 27.

13. Quoted in Rainwater and Yancey, *Moynihan Report,* p. 13.

14. See chapter 2.

15. Much of this factual review is taken from *Civil Rights, 1960–1966,* edited by Lester A. Sobel (New York: Facts on File, 1967). The quotation is from p. 254.

16. Robert M. Fogelson, *Violence as Protest* (Garden City, NY: Doubleday, 1971), p. 131.

17. Ibid., p. 131.

18. Sobel, *Civil Rights, 1960–1966,* pp. 254–56.

19. Fogelson, *Violence as Protest,* p. 137.

20. Sobel, *Civil Rights, 1960–1966,* pp. 261–62.

21. Ibid., p. 308.

22. Allen J. Matusow, *The Unraveling of America* (New York: Harper & Row, 1984), p. 361.

23. Ibid., pp. 196–97. See also Joseph A. Califano, *The Triumph and Tragedy of Lyndon Johnson* (New York: Simon & Schuster, 1991), pp. 59–62.

24. Fogelson, *Violence as Protest,* p. 137.

25. Doug McAdam, *Political Process and the Development of Black Insurgency, 1930–1970* (Chicago: University of Chicago Press, 1982), p. 182.

26. Michael Lipsky and David J. Olson, *Commission Politics* (New Brunswick, NJ: Transaction Books, 1977), p. 92. See also Benjamin Muse, *The American Negro Revolution: From Nonviolence to Black Power* (Bloomington, IN: Indiana University Press, 1968), chapter 19.

27. Garry Wills, *The Second Civil War: Arming for Armageddon.* (New York: New American Library, 1968).

28. Fogelson, *Violence as Protest.*

29. David J. Garrow, *Bearing the Cross: Martin Luther King and the Southern Christian Leadership Conference* (New York: Vintage Books, 1986), p. 571.

30. Clayborne Carson, *In Struggle* (Cambridge, MA: Harvard University Press, 1981), pp. 209–10. Garrow, *Bearing the Cross,* pp. 481–97.

31. Sobel, *Civil Rights, 1960–1966,* pp. 376–77.

32. *New York Times,* 22 July 1967. In the post-1964 period, change was fast-paced. One study in Los Angeles found that leadership there, regardless of power base, had become more militant since the Watts riot. Demands had become more based on economic welfare than symbols or integration. In 1963, the interracial United Civil Rights Committee was hailed as *the* unified coordinating agency in Los Angeles, a symbol of liberal unity. By 1966, even middle-class moderates condemned it, amid "increasing belief that decisions affecting Negroes ought to be made by Negroes." By 1968, the organization did not exist at all. Harry Scoble, "Effects of Riots on Negro Leadership," in *Riots and Rebellion,* edited by Louis H. Masotti and Don R. Bowen (Beverly Hills: Russell Sage, 1968), pp. 329–46, 339.

33. "James Farmer Oral History," [1966], in *Civil Rights During the Johnson Administration,* edited by Steven F. Lawson (Frederick, MD: University Publications of America, 1984), part 3: "Oral Histories," reel 1, frame 0997.

34. "Randolph Oral History," [1968], ibid., frame 0207. See also McAdam, *Political Process,* for an analysis which traces the decline of the movement by documenting the proliferation of groups and the proliferation of different goals.

35. Martin Luther King, Jr., *Where Do We Go from Here?* (Boston: Beacon Press, 1967).

36. "Marshall Oral History," [1968], in Lawson, *Civil Rights During Johnson,* part 3, reel 3, frame 0033.

37. Ibid., frame 0036.

38. Steven F. Lawson, "Civil Rights," in *Exploring the Johnson Years,* edited by Robert. A. Divine (Austin: University of Texas Press, 1981), pp. 93–125, 107.

39. "Katzenbach Oral History," [1968], in Lawson, *Civil Rights During Johnson,* part 3, reel 2, frame 0486.

40. "Memo from Harry McPherson to George Christian," 1 August 1967, in Lawson, *Civil Rights During Johnson,* part 1: "The White House Central Files," reel 3, frame 0717.

41. Opening Meeting, Wednesday, 1 June 1966, White House Conference, "To Fulfill These Rights," in *Civil Rights, The White House and the Justice Department,* edited by Michal R. Belknap, vol. 2, *Presidential Committees and White House Conferences* (New York: Garland, 1991), p. 153.

42. Ibid., p. 169.

43. "Thursday Banquet Session, 2 June 1966," ibid., p. 224.

44. Ibid., p. 231.

45. *Washington Post,* 29 July 1967.

46. *New York Times,* 22 July 1967.

47. *Time,* 11 August 1967.

48. Bayard Rustin, "Lessons of the Long Hot Summer," in Bayard Rustin, *Down the Line* (Chicago: Quadrangle Books, 1971), pp. 187–99, 191.

49. *Congressional Quarterly* 25, no. 36, (1967): 1774.

50. "Randolph Oral History," [1968], in Lawson, *Civil Rights During Johnson,* part 3, reel 3, frame 0211.

51. Alfred Blumrosen, *Black Employment and the Law* (New Brunswick, NJ: Rutgers University Press, 1971), p. 38.

52. McAdam, *Political Process*, p. 209.

53. Harris Wofford, *Of Kennedys and Kings* (New York: Farrar, Straus, Giroux, 1980), p. 5.

54. Quoted in Carl M. Brauer, *John F. Kennedy and the Second Reconstruction* (New York: Columbia University Press, 1977), p. 238.

55. See Herbert H. Haines, *Black Radicals and the Civil Rights Mainstream, 1954–1970* (Knoxville: University of Tennessee Press, 1988), pp. 158–63, for a discussion of the general crisis atmosphere and its effects on the Kennedy administration.

56. *Robert Kennedy: In His Own Words,* edited by Edwin O. Guthman and Jeffrey Shulman (New York: Bantam Books, 1988), pp. 182, 184.

57. Haines, *Black Radicals,* p. 164; Arthur M. Schlesinger, Jr., *One Thousand Days: John F. Kennedy in the White House* (Boston: Houghton Mifflin, 1965), pp. 966–67; Bruce Miroff, *Pragmatic Illusions: The Presidential Politics of John F. Kennedy* (New York: David McKay, 1976), p. 255. Kennedy had twenty-one meetings with over seventeen hundred people.

58. See, for example, G. William Domhoff, *The Powers That Be* (New York: Vintage Books, 1978).

59. In a memo to Kennedy from Lee White, on "Specific Requests that can be made of the Business Council Members," White was careful to stress this point: "The Federal government has not stated that Negroes should be hired or elevated simply because they are Negroes but has attempted to secure qualified Negroes for all positions including those at policy-making levels. Many corporations may be overlooking a source of talent for executive roles in automatically ignoring the qualified Negro executive." Memorandum from Lee White to the President, 11 July 1963, in Michal Belknap, *Civil Rights, the White House, and the Justice Department,* vol. 5, *Equal Employment Opportunity,* pp. 193–94.

60. "Memorandum to Members of the Business Council and Cover Note by L.F.O.," in ibid., pp. 195–202.

61. Margaret Weir, *Politics and Jobs* (Princeton, NJ: Princeton University Press, 1992), p. 68. A president's interest in a creative leadership project is itself a part of the institution of the presidency; this will be important in the affirmative action story, as we will see in chapter 7. See Stephen Skowronek, *The Politics Presidents Make* (Cambridge, MA: Harvard University Press, 1993).

62. James I. Sundquist, *Politics and Policy* (Washington, DC: The Brookings Institution, 1968), p. 111.

63. Matusow, *Unraveling of America,* pp. 124–26. Weir points out that the focus on job training and young people was the result of the power of the CEA to define policy ideas and goals, a power largely resulting from a lack of alternative ideas. In fact, the country did not previously have a poverty program; the word "poverty" did not even appear in the index of the *Congressional Record* or the *Public Papers of the Presidents* until 1964 (Weir, *Politics and Jobs,* p. 70, citing Sundquist, *Politics and Policy,* p. 111).

64. Daniel Patrick Moynihan, "The Negro Family: The Case for National Action," in Rainwater and Yancey, *Moynihan Report,* pp. 41–124, p. 43.

65. Ibid., p. 49.

66. See generally Rainwater and Yancey, *Moynihan Report,* for this fascinating part in the story of civil rights.

67. See, for example, McAdam, *Political Process*, pp. 192–97; Matusow, *Unraveling of America*, pp. 214–16; Havard Sitkoff, *The Struggle for Black Equality: 1954–1980* (New York: Hill and Wang, 1981), p. 222.

68. See Hazel Erskine, "The Polls: Recent Opinion on Racial Problems," *Public Opinion Quarterly* 31 (1968): 696–703.

69. Califano, *Triumph and Tragedy*, p. 212. On law enforcement-based antiriot measures, see Joe R. Feagin and Harlan Hahn, *Ghetto Revolts: The Politics of Violence in American Cities* (New York: Macmillan, 1973), pp. 226–33.

70. Seymour Martin Lipset and Earl Raab, *The Politics of Unreason* (Chicago: University of Chicago Press, 1978), p. 379.

71. Richard Nixon, *RN: The Memoirs of Richard Nixon* (New York: Grosset and Dunlap, 1978), pp. 353–54.

72. Sobel, *Civil Rights, 1960–1966*, pp. 312–13.

73. *Fortune*, January 1968, p. 160.

74. Lipsky and Olson, *Commission Politics*, p. 69.

75. Even King led some protests with such demands, but this was rarely a part of proposed national policy. Businesses did not like this pressure. See, for example, George Strauss, "How Management Views Its Race Relations Responsibilities," in *Employment, Race, and Poverty*, edited by Arthur M. Ross and Herbert Hill (New York: Harcourt, Brace & World, 1967), pp. 261–89, p. 272.

76. 12 June 1965.

77. Memorandum from Attorney General Nicholas Katzenbach to Joseph Califano, 13 December 1965, in Michal Belknap, *Civil Rights, the White House, and the Justice Department*, vol. 14, *Securing the Enactment of Civil Rights Legislation, 1965–1968*, p. 82.

78. Ibid., p. 84. "Affirmative action" here simply referred to any positive government activity, and was not restricted to the racial issue.

79. Sundquist, *Politics and Policy*, p. 284.

80. Quoted in James W. Button, *Black Violence* (Princeton, NJ: Princeton University Press, 1978), p. 24. Shriver and the civil rights leaders were not just trying to further a political agenda, strengthening the OEO's own programs. Jobs repeatedly were mentioned as the key issue in the rioting. For example, a study of the Omaha riots in 1966 included interviews with 147 of the 163 arrestees, asking questions about what prompted their active participation. Without qualification, 114 of them said that difficulty and repeated disappointment in finding satisfactory and lasting jobs was a primary reason (Harry W. Reynolds, "Black Power, Community Power, and Jobs," in Masotti and Bowen, *Riots and Rebellion*, pp. 237–60). Urban violence, then, and the threat of *more* urban violence, can be seen as contributing to a race-conscious poverty policy.

81. "Memo from Hubert Humphrey to President Lyndon Johnson," 27 July 1967, in Lawson, *Civil Rights During Johnson*, part 1, reel 3, frame 0663. Humphrey told Johnson that the group felt Johnson should address the nation on television and also talk more about Great Society programs which could alleviate the causes of the riots.

82. Letter to President Johnson from George E. Reedy, 25 July 1967, in ibid., frame 0639.

83. Memo from Harry McPherson to President Johnson, 8 August 1967, in ibid., frame 0660.

84. "Memo to Joe Califano from Fred Bohm, 24 August 1967," in ibid., frame 0201.

85. Memorandum from Larry Levinson to the President, 15 July 1967, in Michal Bel-

knap, *Civil Rights, the White House, and the Justice Department,* vol. 11, *Urban Race Riots,* p. 33.

86. *Washington Post,* 25 July 1965, in Lawson, *Civil Rights During Johnson,* part 1, reel 9, frame 0643.

87. "Memo from Hubert Humphrey to President Lyndon Johnson," 27 July 1967, in Lawson, *Civil Rights During Johnson,* part 1, reel 3, frame 0663; "Memo from Tom Johnson to President Johnson," 26 July 1967, ibid., frame 0652.

88. "To End Disorder: President Lyndon B. Johnson's Address to the Nation on Civil Disorders," in Lawson, *Civil Rights During Johnson,* part 1, reel 10, "Selected Civil Rights Files—Joseph A. Califano," frame 0211. Reflecting the desperation of the situation, Johnson pleaded for help from the highest authority—God Himself—in calling for a national day of prayer. Johnson said, "My fellow Americans: We have endured a week such as no Nation should live through, a time of violence and tragedy." (ibid., frame 0210).

89. Press conference, 11:20 a.m., 31 July 1967, in ibid., frame 0228.

90. Memorandum from Wally Baer to the Vice President, 17 July 1967, in Michal Belknap, *Civil Rights, the White House, and the Justice Department,* vol. 11, p. 39

91. Memorandum from Attorney General Ramsey Clark to the President, 21 July 1967, in ibid., p. 41.

92. "Letter to President Johnson from Kerner Commission," 10 August 1967, in Lawson, *Civil Rights During Johnson,* part 1, reel 10, frame 0237.

93. "Memorandum for Honorable Robert S. McNamara," 10 August 1967, in ibid., frame 0273.

94. The report from Cyrus Vance on the Detroit riots, cited earlier, also called for the integration of the National Guard and the local police forces.

95. Some social scientists claim that the Economic Opportunity Act was deliberately aimed at the Democrats' black constituency (Frances Fox Piven and Richard A. Cloward, *Regulating the Poor: The Functions of Public Welfare* [New York: Pantheon Books, 1971]). According to Margaret Weir (*Politics and Jobs*), however, concerns for blacks *evolved* to largely dominate the Act and the War on Poverty.

96. Piven and Cloward, *Regulating the Poor,* p. 261.

97. The figures are from Weir, *Politics and Jobs,* pp. 84–86. See also Button, *Black Violence.*

98. Button, *Black Violence,* p. 37.

99. Alfonso J. Cervantes, "To Prevent a Chain of Super-Watts," *Harvard Business Review* 45 (September/October 1967): 53–65, 56.

100. See also Strauss, "How Management Views Its Race Relations Responsibilities," p. 274: "It is thought that if business does not take the lead, then the government and civil rights groups will be able to place restrictions on business policy that business will never be able to remove."

101. For more on the Ad Council, see Domhoff, *Powers That Be.*

102. Glenn K. Hirsch, "Only You Can Prevent Ideological Hegemony: The Advertising Council and Its Place in the American Power Structure," *The Insurgent Sociologist* 5 (1975): 64–82; p. 76.

103. 18 March 1968, p. 61.

104. Quoted in Robert L. Allen, *Black Awakening in Capitalist America* (Garden City, NY: Doubleday, 1969), p. 190.

105. See Frederick E. Case, *Black Capitalism: Problems in Development* (New York: Praeger, 1972), p. 5.

106. Quoted in *U.S. News & World Report,* 30 September 1968, p. 65.

107. Quoted in *U.S. News & World Report,* 14 October 1968, p. 83.

108. *U.S. News & World Report,* 12 February 1968, pp. 61–62.

109. National Advisory Commission on Civil Disorders, *Report of the National Advisory Commission on Civil Disorders* (New York: Bantam Books, 1968), p. 152.

110. For example, at a follow-up meeting of the McCone Commission on 22 August 1967, McCone, according to a White House aid present, made several general points of conclusion on the riots, including that "[t]he problem of unemployment must be dealt with largely by encouraging private firms to begin training programs and hiring Negroes." "Memo to Joe Califano from Matt Nimetz on McCone Commission Meeting," in Lawson, *Civil Rights During Johnson,* part 1, reel 10, frame 0269.

111. Button, *Black Violence,* p. 40.

112. National Advisory Commission, *Report,* p. 154.

113. Califano, *Triumph and Tragedy,* pp. 225–26.

114. Lipsky and Olson, *Commission Politics,* p. 114.

115. Press conference, 11:20 a.m., 31 July 1967 in Lawson, *Civil Rights During Johnson,* part 1, reel 10, frame 0225.

116. Commission Meeting, 7 October 1967, in Lawson, *Civil Rights During Johnson,* part 5: "Records of the National Advisory Commission on Civil Disorders (Kerner Commission)," reel 4, frame 0380.

117. Ibid., frame 0430.

118. For example, see Nathan Glazer, *Affirmative Discrimination* (Cambridge, MA: Harvard University Press, [1975] 1987), pp. 69–70.

119. Commission Meeting, 7 October 1967, in Lawson, *Civil Rights During Johnson,* part 5, reel 4, frame 0401.

120. Ibid., frame 0403.

121. Ibid., frame 0408.

122. Author's telephone interview with Eli Ginzberg, 29 November 1994.

123. Commission Meeting, 7 October 1967, in Lawson, *Civil Rights During Johnson,* part 5, reel 4, frame 0406.

124. Ibid., frame 0504.

125. Ibid., frame 0526.

126. Ibid., frame 0550.

127. Ibid., frame 0551. This was not the first time that suspicions arose in a crisis context in the federal government that perhaps "merit" was really a mask for white, middle-class conceptions of justice. As early as 17 September 1965, this controversial idea was being discussed in the Report of the President's Task Force on the Los Angeles Riots. Options in the report that were suggested to gain control and order included "review and liberalization of rigid employment standards by industry and civil service which arbitrarily and permanently exclude otherwise able men because of police records, mixed employment experience, and limited formal education and training." "Report of the Task Force on the Los Angeles Riots," 17 September 1965, in Lawson, *Civil Rights During Johnson,* part 1, reel 10, frame 0337. These questions of the fairness of supposed standards of merit were later treated in the courts and the standards were found to be discriminatory (see chapter 6).

128. Hugh Davis Graham, *The Civil Rights Era* (New York: Oxford University Press, 1990), pp. 149–50. It should also be added that reevaluation of testing was urged on the Equal Employment Opportunity Commission (EEOC) by a group of academic specialists in the winter of 1965–1966. See "Recommendations on Research in Job Opportunities Made by the Ad Hoc Research Advisory Group," 2 February 1966, in Lawson, *Civil Rights During Johnson,* part 2: "EEOC Administrative History," Documentary Supplement, reel 2, frame 0664. Also see the EEOC's Office of Research and Reports' "Testing of Minority Group Applicants for Employment," in ibid., frames 0667–0699.

129. Commission Meetings, 7 October 1967, in Lawson, *Civil Rights During Johnson,* part 5, reel 4, frame 0537.

130. Commission Meeting, 23 October 1967, in Lawson, *Civil Rights During Johnson,* part 5, reel 4, frame 0949.

131. Ibid., frame 0955.

132. Ibid., frame 0960.

133. National Advisory Commission, *Report,* p. 294.

134. Ibid., p. 415.

135. Ibid., p. 416.

136. Ibid., p. 294.

137. Ibid., p. 10.

138. Ibid., p. 2.

139. This view began ascendance in the civil rights community in the aftermath of the Moynihan report, and was prevalent at the June 1966 White House conference, "To Fulfill These Rights," where one participant later maintained, "There was a total refusal by most of the Negroes [I heard] to discuss *anything* that might remotely imply that there was anything whatsoever that Negroes, individually or collectively, should be doing or needed to do. [One leader's] formulation, which was repeated *ad nauseam,* was that race is entirely a white man's problem that could only be solved by white men, and that it was intolerable that the government had all these white men sitting around discussing 'our problem.' They simply refused to discuss anything but what the government ought to be doing" (emphasis in the original). Rainwater and Yancey, *Moynihan Report,* p. 252.

140. "Media Reaction Analysis Report: Riots in U.S. Cities, Office of Policy Research," in Lawson, *Civil Rights During Johnson,* part 1, reel 3, frame 0649.

141. 11 March 1968, p. 39.

142. National Advisory Commission, *Report,* p. 316.

143. Ibid., p. 385.

144. Ibid.

145. Lyndon Johnson, *The Vantage Point* (New York: Holt, Rinehart and Winston, 1971), p. 173. Attorney General Ramsey Clark maintained that by 1968, Johnson shifted his "concerns and time so far toward Vietnam that his involvement in civil rights was very, very limited." Quoted in Steven F. Lawson, "Civil Rights," in *Exploring the Johnson Years,* edited by Robert A. Divine (Austin: University of Texas Press, 1981), pp. 93–125, p. 109.

146. Memorandum from Harry C. McPherson, Jr., to Joseph Califano, 1 March 1968, in Michal Belknap, *Civil Rights, the White House, and the Justice Department,* vol. 11, p. 230.

147. Kingdon, *Agendas, Alternatives, and Public Policies,* chapter 8.

148. Memorandum from Roy Wilkins to Harry C. McPherson, Jr., 4 April 1968, in

Michal Belknap, *Civil Rights, the White House, and the Justice Department,* vol. 11, p. 234.

149. Lipsky and Olson, *Commission Politics,* p. 154, n. 79.

150. Ibid., p. 144.

151. Fogelson, *Violence as Protest,* p. 158.

152. *US News & World Report,* 7 October 1968, p. 29.

153. Button, *Black Violence,* p. 48.

154. Quoted in Allen, *Black Awakening,* p. 193.

155. See Joe McGinniss, *The Selling of the President: 1968* (New York: Trident Press, 1969), pp. 248–49.

156. Graham, *Civil Rights Era,* p. 323.

157. Ibid., p. 334.

158. Ibid., p. 330.

159. Ibid., p. 540, fn. 36.

160. Ibid., p. 335.

161. *Congressional Record,* 91st Cong., 1st sess., 1969, 115 pt. 29:39, 966.

162. 302 F. Supp. 726, NJ (1969).

163. Ibid., at 732.

164. Ibid., at 733.

165. Ibid.

166. *Porcelli v. Titus* 431 F. 2d 1254, 2 FEP 1024 (3rd Cir. 1970), cert. denied, 402 U.S. 944 (1971).

167. Certainly some repression did occur. The National Guard was used on some occasions, as well as federal troops. Many people lost their lives. The federal government set up military training schools for the National Guard, the Army, and police specializing in riot control. The 1968 Civil Rights Act contained a section making it illegal to cross state lines to incite riots. The 1969 Omnibus Crime Act appropriated $4 million for the prevention, detection, and control of riots (Feagin and Hahn, *Ghetto Revolts,* pp. 227–33). It is also well known that Martin Luther King was under FBI surveillance, and the black nationalist leaders were hounded by the FBI as well as local police.

168. Rowland Evans and Robert Novak, *Lyndon B. Johnson: The Exercise of Power* (New York: New American Library, 1966), pp. 496–97; see also Julie Leininger Pycior, "Lyndon, *La Raza,* and the Paradox of Texas History," in *Lyndon Baines Johnson and the Uses of Power,* edited by Bernard J. Firestone and Robert C. Vogt (New York: Greenwood Press, 1988), pp. 129–47.

169. Quoted in William E. Leuchtenburg, *In the Shadow of F.D.R.* (Ithaca: Cornell University Press, 1983), p. 160.

170. Skowronek, *Politics Presidents Make,* p. 18.

171. Leuchtenburg, *In the Shadow of F.D.R.,* p. 142. See also Alfred Steinberg, *Sam Johnson's Boy* (New York: Macmillan, 1968).

172. An illustrative anecdote is provided by Califano, who had to rush his son to the hospital; the younger Califano had swallowed a bottleful of aspirin. Johnson, wishing to speak with his aid, tracked him down at the hospital. Califano recounts, "'What are you doing at the hospital?' [Johnson] asked. After offering to help, Johnson said he'd always worried about children getting into medicine bottles and hurting themselves. 'There ought to be a law that makes druggists use safe containers,' he said. 'There ought to be safety caps on those bottles so kids like little Joe can't open them.' That prompted the

proposal for the Child Safety Act, which Congress eventually passed in 1970, which is why it's so difficult for Americans to take the tops off pill containers." Califano, *Triumph and Tragedy*, p. 180.

173. Quoted in Doris Kearns, *Lyndon Johnson and the American Dream* (New York: Harper & Row, 1976), p. 305.

174. Califano, *Triumph and Tragedy*, p. 210. Johnson later maintained that a policy of empowerment had been a preconscious response: "When violence breaks out, my instinct is to ask: What caused it? What can I do about it? It is necessary to search for the deeper causes from which anger and tension grow, the privations and indignities and evidence of past oppression and neglect. In the 1960s that evidence was all too plentiful." Johnson, *Vantage Point*, p. 172

175. Califano, *Triumph and Tragedy*, p. 217.

176. Kearns, *Johnson and the American Dream*, p. 305.

177. *Newsweek*, 7 August 1967, pp. 31–32.

178. See James A. Morone, *The Democratic Wish* (New York: Basic Books, 1990), chapter 5, for history of organized labor, from repression to empowerment.

179. Erskine, "The Polls."

180. "Memo from Fred Panzer to President Johnson," 11 August 1967, in Lawson, *Civil Rights During Johnson*, part 1, reel 3, frame 0752.

181. *Newsweek*, 7 August 1967, p. 25.

182. "Memo from Marvin (Watson) to President Johnson," 20 July 1967, in Lawson, *Civil Rights During Johnson*, part 1, reel 3, frame 0624.

183. Quoted in Muse, *American Negro Revolution*, p. 311.

184. Earl Brown and George R. Leighton, "The Negro and the War," *Public Affairs Pamphlets*, no. 71, 1942.

185. See Yasemin Soysal's *Limits of Citizenship* (Chicago: University of Chicago Press, 1994), for an analysis of the transnational discourse of human rights and its effects on Western European policy regarding migrants. Soysal shows that while many guest workers in European nations were denied formal citizenship, limits to legitimate policy options were shaped by rules of human rights, precluding, for example, the simple repatriation of guest workers, and allowing for these populations to enjoy social and civil rights on the basis of universal personhood.

186. Quoted in Morone, *Democratic Wish*, p. 204.

187. Quoted in Rupert Emerson and Martin Kilson, "The American Dilemma in a Changing World: The Rise of Africa and the Negro American," *Dædalus* 94 (1965): 1055–84, p. 1063.

188. "U.S. Information Agency report, Foreign Reaction to Senate Passage of the Civil Rights Bill," in Lawson, *Civil Rights During Johnson*, part 1, reel 3, frame 0462.

189. See "Media Reaction Analysis Report: Riots in U.S. Cities, Office of Policy Research," and attached memo to Johnson from Leonard H. Marks (26 July 1967), in Lawson, *Civil Rights During Johnson*, part 1, reel 3, frames 0647–0650. While Johnson received his own report, other media brought the global view to the American people. Both *Newsweek* (7 August 1967) and *U.S. News & World Report* (7 August 1967) carried special reports on the view of the international press.

190. Johnson, *Vantage Point*, p. 170.

191. "Telegram to State Department," April 1968, in Lawson, *Civil Rights During Johnson*, part 1, reel 3, frames 0083–84.

192. Statistics from U.S. Department of Labor Bureau of Statistics, *Handbook of La-*

bor Statistics, Bulletin 2340 (Washington, DC: Government Printing Office, August 1989), p. 554. The rates were 4.5 percent in 1965, 3.8 in 1966, 3.8 in 1967, 3.6 in 1968, and 3.5 in 1969.

Chapter Five

1. The use of term *pragmatism* is an intentional reference to the ideas of truth associated with the writings of William James and John Dewey, which were influential in my formulation of the concept. See John David Skrentny, "Pragmatism, Institutionalism, and the Construction of Employment Discrimination," *Sociological Forum* 9 (1994): 343–69. See also William James, *Pragmatism* (Indianapolis: Hackett Publishing, 1981); and John Dewey, *Reconstruction in Philosophy* (Boston: Beacon Press, 1948).

2. This is similar to Mashaw's notion of bureaucratic rationality, where agencies are seen to pursue the primary goal of program implementation, emphasizing information processing and conditioned by the values of accuracy and efficiency. See Jerry Mashaw, *Bureaucratic Justice: Managing Social Security Disability Claims* (New Haven, CT: Yale University Press, 1983), pp. 25–31.

3. Gary G. Hamilton and John R. Sutton, "The Problem of Control in the Weak State," *Theory and Society* 18 (1989): 1–46, 27.

4. Ibid., p. 26; see also James O. Freedman, *Crisis and Legitimacy: The Administrative Process and American Government* (New York: Cambridge University Press, 1978), p. 4.

5. See, for example, Frank Bourgin, *The Great Challenge: The Myth of Laissez Faire in the Early Republic* (New York: Braziller, 1989); William R. Brock, *Investigation and Responsibility: Public Responsibility in the United States, 1865–1900* (New York: Cambridge University Press, 1984).

6. For the rise of administrative government, see Stephen Skowronek, *Building a New American State: The Expansion of National Administrative Capacity* (New York: Cambridge University Press, 1982); and Samuel Haber, *Efficiency and Uplift: Scientific Management in the Progressive Era, 1890–1920* (Chicago: University of Chicago Press, 1964).

7. James Q. Wilson, "The Politics of Regulation," in *The Politics of Regulation,* edited by James Q. Wilson (New York: Basic Books, 1980), pp. 357–94, 375.

8. See for example Herman Belz, *Equality Transformed: A Quarter Century of Affirmative Action* (New Brunswick, NJ: Transaction Publishers, 1991); and Robert Detlefsen, *Civil Rights Under Reagan* (San Francisco: ICS Press, 1991).

9. See Lawrence Friedman, *Total Justice* (New York: Russell Sage, 1985).

10. Philip Selznick, *Law, Society, and Industrial Justice* (New York: Russell Sage, 1969), p. 225.

11. United States Commission on Civil Rights, *Federal Civil Rights Enforcement Effort, 1971: A Report of the United States Commission on Civil Rights* (Washington, DC: Government Printing Office, 1971). Also see Michael I. Sovern, *Legal Restraints on Racial Discrimination in Employment* (New York: The Twentieth Century Fund, 1966), appendix G.

12. Louis Ruchames, *Race, Jobs, and Politics: The Story of FEPC* (New York: Columbia University Press, 1953), pp. 25–27.

13. Ibid., p. 33.

14. Ibid., p. 39.

15. Letter from James L. Houghteling to Donald S. Dawson, 6 June 1951, in *Civil*

Rights, the White House, and the Justice Department, 1945–1968, edited by Michal R. Belknap, vol. 4, *Employment of Blacks by the Federal Government* (New York: Garland, 1991), pp. 80–81.

16. Report from the Fair Employment Board to the Civil Service Commission, in ibid., pp. 85–91.

17. Unissued White House press release, 20 July 1961, in ibid., pp. 150–51. I could find no information as to why the press release was never issued. The minority census, however, was performed each year of the Kennedy administration. The 1963 study touted increased scope and precision, counting blacks, Mexican-Americans, Puerto Ricans, American Indians, and persons of Oriental origins working for the government in the United States and overseas. "Minority Group Study, June 1963," in *Civil Rights During the Johnson Administration, 1963–1969,* edited by Steven F. Lawson (Frederick, MD: University Publications of America, 1984), part 1: "White House Central Files," reel 7, frame 0313.

18. Memorandum from J. F. K. to the Vice President, 22 August 1962, in Belknap, *Civil Rights, the White House, and the Justice Department,* vol. 5, *Equal Employment Opportunity,* p. 109.

19. Hugh Davis Graham, *The Civil Rights Era* (New York: Oxford University Press, 1990), pp. 50–59.

20. Press Release on Resignation of Robert Troutman and His Attached Final Report on Plans for Progress, 23 August 1962, in Belknap, *Civil Rights, the White House, and the Justice Department,* vol. 5, p. 119.

21. Ibid., p. 121.

22. Ibid., p. 115.

23. For example, the New York agency moved to an industry-wide view rather than focusing only on complaints. See Ruchames, *Race, Jobs, and Politics,* p. 177.

24. See Leon Mayhew, *Law and Equal Opportunity* (Cambridge, MA: Harvard University Press, 1968); also Jack Greenberg, *Race Relations and American Law* (New York: Columbia University Press, 1959).

25. Herbert Hill, "Twenty Years of State FEPCs," *Buffalo Law Review* 14 (Fall 1964): 22–69, Ruchames, *Race, Jobs, and Politics,* p. 95.

26. Alfred Blumrosen, *Black Employment and the Law* (New Brunswick, NJ: Rutgers University Press, 1971).

27. Graham, *Civil Rights Era,* p. 20.

28. Sovern, *Legal Restraints,* p. 47.

29. "EEOC Administrative History," Appendix F [1 November 1968], in Lawson, *Civil Rights During Johnson,* part 2: "EEOC Administrative History," reel 1, frame 0356.

30. Mayhew, *Law and Equal Opportunity,* p. 192.

31. Alfred Blumrosen, "Strangers in Paradise: *Griggs v. Duke Power Co.* and the Concept of Employment Discrimination," *Michigan Law Review* 71 (1972): 59–111, 68.

32. But see note 79 in chapter 2.

33. Quoted in U.S. Commission on Civil Rights, *Enforcement Effort,* p. 94.

34. Quoted in Michael Evan Gold, "Griggs' Folly: An Essay on the Theory, Problems, and Origin of the Adverse Impact Definition of Employment Discrimination and a Recommendation for Reform," *Industrial Relations Law Journal* 7 (1985): 429–598, 506. Gold also quotes Senator Hubert Humphrey as explaining, "A new subsection 703(j) is added to deal with the problem of racial balance among employees. The proponents of

the bill have carefully stated on numerous occasions that Title VII does not require an employer to achieve any sort of racial balance in his work force by giving preferential treatment to any individual or group. Since doubts have persisted, subsection (j) is added to state this expressly" (p. 506, fn. 284, originally quoted in *Congressional Record,* 88th Cong., 2d sess., 1964, 110, p. 12,723).

35. U.S. Commission on Civil Rights, *Enforcement Effort,* p. 85.

36. Sovern, *Legal Restraints,* p. 74.

37. Ibid., p. 76. In addition, Section 707 declared that the Attorney General could initiate action when there was "reasonable cause to believe that any person or group of persons is engaged in a pattern or practice of resistance to the full enjoyment of any of the rights secured by this title, and that the pattern or practice is of such a nature and is intended to deny the full exercise of the rights herein described" (quoted in Sovern, *Legal Restraints,* p. 77). A pattern or practice meant that the same employer repeatedly, intentionally denied equal treatment to minorities. The 707 suits were not frequently utilized: of the 112 cases referred to the Justice Department between 1967 and 1969, only 12 resulted in a suit being filed. This was perhaps mainly due to the time lag which existed between the official complaint filing and the referral to Justice, which often involved several years and required reinvestigation by the Department of Justice (U.S. Commission on Civil Rights, *Enforcement Effort,* p. 109).

38. Sovern, *Legal Restraints,* p. 79.

39. Graham, *Civil Rights Era,* pp. 189–90.

40. U.S. Commission on Civil Rights, *Enforcement Effort,* p. 87.

41. Blumrosen, *Black Employment,* p. 55.

42. Graham, *Civil Rights,* pp. 179–80. President Johnson was disturbed and wanted an explanation (undated, handwritten note to Bill M. from Lyndon Johnson, in Lawson, *Civil Rights During Johnson,* part 2, reel 3, frames 0042–0043).

43. Blumrosen, *Black Employment,* p. 55.

44. U.S. Commission on Civil Rights, *Enforcement Effort,* p. 88.

45. Author's telephone interview with Alfred Blumrosen, 12 August 1992.

46. According to *Barron's National Business and Financial Weekly,* 17 July 1967, reprinted in Blumrosen, *Black Employment,* p. 378.

47. "EEOC Administrative History" [1 November 1968], in Lawson, *Civil Rights During Johnson,* part 2, reel 1, frame 0012.

48. This is perhaps standard in matters of the budget, and particularly among administrative agencies (James O. Freedman, "Review Boards in the Administrative Process," *University of Pennsylvania Law Review* 117 (1969): 546–77). However, in the case of the EEOC, as I will argue later, it had rather significant consequences.

49. "EEOC Administrative History," in Lawson, *Civil Rights During Johnson,* part 2, reel 1, frame 0106.

50. Senator John L. McClellan opened one budget meeting by saying, "I feel [the EEOC] is a useless agency, unnecessary, uncalled for. I want the record to show exactly how I feel." "EEOC Administrative History," in Lawson, *Civil Rights During Johnson,* part 2, reel 1, frame 0105. The negative feelings were mutual. See "Clifford Alexander Oral History," [1971], in Lawson, *Civil Rights During Johnson,* part 3: "Oral Histories," reel 1, frames 0018–19.

51. EEOC Annual Report 1967, quoted in Shirley M. Seib, ed., *Revolution in Civil Rights* (Washington, DC: Congressional Quarterly, 1967), p. 78.

52. The Legal Defense Fund certainly had an idea. The organization was responsible

for having 476 complaints filed on the day the law went into effect, and 374 more soon afterward. Jack Greenberg, *Crusaders in the Courts* (New York: Basic Books, 1994), p. 413.

53. "EEOC Administrative History," in Lawson, *Civil Rights During Johnson,* part 2, reel 1, frame 0122.

54. Graham, *Civil Rights Era,* p. 203.

55. Ibid., p. 235.

56. Richard P. Nathan, *Jobs and Civil Rights* (Washington, DC: Government Printing Office, 1969), p. 19.

57. See Equal Employment Opportunity Commission, *Making a Right a Reality* (Washington, DC: Equal Employment Opportunity Commission, 1990), pp. 14–15.

58. Freedman, *Crisis and Legitimacy,* p. 113.

59. "EEOC Administrative History," in Lawson, *Civil Rights During Johnson,* part 2, reel 1, frame 0123.

60. Graham, *Civil Rights Era,* p. 239.

61. Both quoted in Nathan, *Jobs and Civil Rights,* p. 46.

62. "EEOC Administrative History," in Lawson, *Civil Rights During Johnson,* part 2, reel 1, frame 0223.

63. U.S. Commission on Civil Rights, *Enforcement Effort,* p. 102.

64. Graham, *Civil Rights Era,* p. 235.

65. "EEOC Administrative History," in Lawson, *Civil Rights During Johnson,* part 2, reel 1, frame 0135.

66. See U.S. Congress, Senate Committee on Judiciary, *Hearings on Equal Employment Opportunity Procedures, before Subcommittee on Administrative Practice and Procedure, on S. Res. 39,* 91st Cong., 1st sess., 27 and 28 March, 1969, p. 10.

67. Memorandum from Acting Attorney General Ramsey Clark to Joseph A. Califano, Jr., and Attachments, undated, in Belknap, *Civil Rights, the White House, and the Justice Department,* vol. 14, *Securing the Enactment of Civil Rights Legislation, 1965–1968,* p. 176.

68. Ibid., p. 192.

69. Ibid., p. 200.

70. Ibid., p. 201.

71. Quoted in Robert C. Rooney, ed., *Equal Opportunity in the United States* (Austin: Lyndon B. Johnson School of Public Affairs, 1973), p. 122.

72. Charles Jencks, *The Language of Postmodern Architecture* (New York: Rizzoli, 1977), p. 9.

73. Blumrosen, *Black Employment,* p. 68. That firms on the "zero list" were actually "excluding" minorities does not necessarily follow. To interpret zero black employees in this way, however, had precedent from early antidiscrimination programs and suggests the devil-may-care search for effectiveness.

74. Graham, *Civil Rights Era,* p. 199.

75. "Report of the White House Conference on Equal Employment Opportunity," 19–20 August 1965, in Lawson, *Civil Rights During Johnson,* part 1: "The White House Central Files," reel 8, frame 0037. See also "EEOC Administrative History," in *Civil Rights During Johnson,* part 2 reel 1, frames 0068-0069.

76. Ibid., frames 0028, 0037. The Civil Service Commission had its own racial reporting controversy. In the 1940s, a successful effort forced the elimination of racial identification and photographs on the standard employment form. The NAACP and the

American Civil Liberties Union both resisted the move toward benign race identification in the middle 1960s. See U.S. Commission on Civil Rights, *Enforcement Effort*.

77. Blumrosen describes him as "supportive" but "not devoted." Blumrosen telephone interview, 12 August 1992.

78. "Letter from F. D. Roosevelt, Jr. to the President regarding the activities of the first 100 days of the EEOC," 29 October 1965, in Lawson, *Civil Rights During Johnson*, part 2, reel 1, frame 0904.

79. Ibid., frame 0912.

80. "EEOC Hearing on the Proposed Employer Reporting System," 16 December 1965, in Lawson, *Civil Rights During Johnson*, part 2, reel 2, frame 0433.

81. Ibid., frame 0439.

82. Ibid., frame 0470.

83. "A Study of Patterns of Discrimination in Employment for the EEOC," 19 September 1966, Institute of Labor and Industrial Relations, in Lawson, *Civil Rights During Johnson*, part 2, reel 1, frame 0471.

84. Ibid., frame 0717.

85. Ibid., frame 0721. Cousens also suggested the industry-wide, public-forums approach because, in the course of the study, it was learned that a great many employers did not even know that the EEOC existed, and the public forum would serve an educational function, as well as enhancing the agency's image in minority communities.

86. "EEOC Administrative History," in Lawson, *Civil Rights During Johnson*, part 2, reel 1, frame 0136.

87. "The Role of the EEO-1 Reporting System in Commission Operations," 27 May 1967, in Lawson, *Civil Rights During Johnson*, part 2, reel 2, frame 0634.

88. "EEOC Administrative History," in Lawson, *Civil Rights During Johnson*, part 2, reel 1, frame 0068.

89. Ibid., frame 0069.

90. Quoted in Nathan, *Jobs and Civil Rights*, p. 29.

91. Belz, *Equality Transformed*, p. 30.

92. "White Collar Invitational Letter," appendix J, "EEOC Administrative History," in Lawson, *Civil Rights During Johnson*, part 2, reel 1, frame 0444.

93. Quoted in Nathan, *Jobs and Civil Rights*, p. 30.

94. "Project Outline for FY 1968, of the Office of State and Community Affairs, EEOC, 'Eliminating Discrimination by Affirmative Government Action,'" in Lawson, *Civil Rights During Johnson*, part 2, reel 1, frame 0979.

95. Ibid., frame 0980.

96. Ibid., frame 0990.

97. Alfred Blumrosen, Hugh Davis Graham, and James E. Jones, Jr., point out that affirmative action law was little developed at the time, though largely taken from established labor law, and quite uncontroversial. It must be remembered that this was still the era of massive and obvious discrimination in the South. Graham also points out the novelty of requiring affirmative action, something normally reserved for those found guilty, in contract law, which is designed to enforce compliance and not find guilt. Graham, *Civil Rights Era*, pp. 40–43; Author's telephone interview with James E. Jones, Jr., 29 June 1994; Author's telephone interview with Alfred Blumrosen, 12 August 1992.

98. Nathan, *Jobs and Civil Rights*, p. 89–91.

99. U.S. Commission on Civil Rights, *Enforcement Effort*, p. 50.

100. Graham, *Civil Rights Era*, p. 283.

101. Nathan, *Jobs and Civil Rights*, pp. 134–35.

102. See note 97.

103. Quoted in Nathan, *Jobs and Civil Rights*, p. 93.

104. U.S. Commission on Civil Rights, *Enforcement Effort.*

105. Ibid., p. 53.

106. Ibid.

107. *United States v. Sheet Metal Workers Int'l Ass'n.*, 280 F. Supp. 719 (E. D. MO, 1968), *rev'd,* 416 F.2d 123 (8th Cir. 1969).

108. James E. Jones, "The Bugaboo of Employment Quotas," *Wisconsin Law Review* 34 no. 2 (1970): 341–403, 346.

109. Jones, "Bugaboo," p. 346; U.S. Commission on Civil Rights, *Enforcement Effort.*

110. Nathan, *Jobs and Civil Rights,* p. 109.

111. An official from the Department of Labor, testifying to the Kerner Commission, saluted the overtly race-conscious hiring of the Cleveland Plan, which forced contractors in Cleveland to present "good" manning tables (meaning tables of the numbers of African-American workers to be hired). "Immediately," he explained, "you had to have the supply of individuals who could be indentured as apprentices and be hired as journeymen available. So it has been a combination of these this [*sic*] has brought on what degree of success we have had." Commission Meeting, 7 October 1967, in Lawson, *Civil Rights During Johnson,* part 5: "Records of the National Advisory Commission on Civil Disorders (Kerner Commission)," reel 4, frame 0394.

112. Jones, "Bugaboo," p. 347.

113. Graham, *Civil Rights Era,* p. 290.

114. Quoted in Jones, "Bugaboo," p. 360.

115. 90th Cong., 2d sess., 28 June 1968, S. Rept. 1340, p. 3497.

116. Ibid., p. 3499. See also Jones, "Bugaboo," pp. 361–64.

117. Arthur Fletcher, *The Silent Sell-Out* (New York: The Third Press, 1974), p. 65.

118. The primacy of substantive justice in the courts is examined in the next chapter.

119. *United States v. Ironworkers Local 86*, 443 F. 2d 544, 551 [9th Cir. 1971], quoted in Marcy M. Hallock, "The Numbers Game: The Use and Misuse of Statistics in Civil Rights Litigation," *Villanova Law Review* 23 (1978): 6. See also David Copus, "The Numbers Game Is the Only Game in Town," *Howard Law Journal* 20 (1977): 374–419.

120. *Southern Illinois Builders Ass'n v. Ogilvie,* 471 F. 2d 680, 686, 5 F.E.P. 229, 234 (7th Cir. 1972), in Martin Slate, "Preferential Relief in Employment Discrimination Cases," *Loyola University Law Journal* 5 no. 2 (Summer 1974): 315–48, 321.

121. See Richard A. Posner, *The Federal Courts: Crisis and Reform* (Cambridge, MA: Harvard University Press, 1985), for the growth in court caseload and responses.

122. Cornelius J. Peck, "The Equal Employment Opportunity Commission: Developments in the Administrative Process, 1965–1975," *Washington Law Review* 51 (1976): 840–48, 840.

123. *Oatis v. Crown Zellerbach Corp.,* 398 F. 2d 496 (5th Cir. 1968).

124. Paul Burstein and Kathleen Monaghan, "Equal Employment Opportunity and the Mobilization of Law," *Law and Society Review* 20 (1986): 333–88.

125. Robert Belton, "A Comparative Review of Public and Private Enforcement of Title VII of the Civil Rights Act of 1964," *Vanderbilt Law Review* 31 (1978): 905–61, 932.

126. Ibid., p. 934.

127. Blumrosen telephone interview, 12 August 1992.

128. Alfred W. Blumrosen, *Modern Law: The Law Transmission System and Equal Employment Opportunity* (Madison: University of Wisconsin Press, 1993), p. 69.

129. Blumrosen, "Strangers in Paradise," p. 74.

130. Ibid., see also George Cooper and Richard Sobol, "Seniority and Testing under Fair Employment Laws: A General Approach to Objective Criteria of Hiring and Promotion," *Harvard Law Review* 82 (1969) 1598–1679.

131. Jack Greenberg, *Crusaders in the Courts* (New York: Basic Books, 1994), p. 462.

132. Glazer, *Affirmative Discrimination*, pp. xiv–xv.

133. Blumrosen, *Modern Law*, p. 73.

134. Lawrence M. Friedman, *Total Justice* (New York: Russell Sage, 1985), p. 59.

135. See Philippe Nonet, *Administrative Justice* (New York: Russell Sage, 1969).

136. *Scenic Hudson Preservation Conference v. FPC*, 354 F. 2d 608, 620 (2d Cir. 1965), quoted in Mashaw, *Bureaucratic Justice*, p. 39.

137. John Kingdon, *Agendas, Alternatives, and Public Policies* (Boston: Little, Brown, 1984), p. 97.

138. Max Weber, *Economy and Society* (Berkeley: University of California Press, 1978), p. 975. Similarly, organization theorists Jeffrey Pfeffer and Gerald Salancik write, "What factors may lead organizations to collect information on certain aspects of their environment or their operations? One is the sheer ease of collecting the information. . . . Another possible dimension is the ease of processing the information, or fitting it into a presentable and transmittable form. This would place a premium on information which is quantifiable and easily measurable." In the modern organizational climate, efficiency itself becomes a "valued, social ideal." Jeffrey Pfeffer and Gerald R. Salancik, *The External Control of Organizations* (New York: Harper & Row, 1978), pp. 76, 35. On the rationalized pursuit of justice as characteristic of modernity, see John W. Meyer, John Boli, and George M. Thomas, "Ontology and Rationalization in the Western Cultural Account," in *Institutional Structure: Constituting State, Society and the Individual*, edited by George M. Thomas, John W. Meyer, Francisco Ramirez, and John Boli (Beverly Hills: Russell Sage, 1987), pp. 12–37.

139. Quoted in U.S. Commission of Civil Rights *Enforcement Effort*, p. 58.

140. See Paul Burstein, *Discrimination, Jobs, and Politics* (Chicago: University of Chicago Press, 1985) for the effects of public opinion on Washington legislators.

141. Luther Holcomb, EEOC Vice Chairman, suggested to White House aid Jake Jacobsen in 1966 a "massive attack" on riot cities "in the form of a crash program . . . through an affirmative action program." "Memo from Luther Holcomb to Jake Jacobsen," 25 July 1966, in Lawson, *Civil Rights During Johnson*, part 2, reel 3, frame 0138.

Chapter Six

1. Richard Goodwin, *Remembering America: A Voice from the Sixties* (New York: Harper & Row, 1988), p. 273. There may be empirical support for the use of the discourse of tradition, at least as it refers to legal or political tradition, in propounding a new idea such as affirmative action. Sniderman and Piazza found that if respondents were told that "both the House of Representatives and the Senate have passed laws to ensure a certain number of federal contracts go to minority contractors," 57 percent of whites supported it, whereas if told "Sometimes you hear it said that there should be a law . . . ," only 43 percent favored the minority set-asides. Paul M. Sniderman and Thomas Piazza, *The Scar of Race* (Cambridge, MA: Harvard University Press, 1993), pp. 131–32.

2. In the minds of many supporters, affirmative action was entirely congruent with traditional ideas of civil rights and equality. For instance, black leaders polled in Sidney Verba and Gary Orren's study showed 75 per cent supporting quotas for blacks, and 86 per cent also professing to value equality of opportunity over equality of results (for comparison, 10 per cent of business leaders supported quotas for blacks, while 98 per cent supported equality of opportunity over equality of results). Sidney Verba and Gary Orren, *Equality in America* (Cambridge, MA: Harvard University Press, 1985).

3. The use of the concept of tradition in this chapter is largely based on Edward Shils, *Tradition* (Chicago: University of Chicago Press, 1981), and Samuel Huntington, *American Politics: The Promise of Disharmony* (Cambridge, MA: Harvard University Press, 1981).

4. Justice and fairness are traditional in the sense that they are part of the traditional cultural projects of modernity and America, as discussed in chapter 2, and that, in substance, they are learned and founded on faith rather than reason. See Alasdair MacIntyre, *After Virtue* (Notre Dame, IN: University of Notre Dame Press, 1984).

5. Quoted in Michael I. Sovern, *Legal Restraints on Racial Discrimination in Employment* (New York: The Twentieth Century Fund, 1966), p. 10.

6. See Hugh Davis Graham, *The Civil Rights Era* (New York: Oxford University Press, 1990), p. 10.

7. Louis Ruchames, *Race, Jobs, and Politics: The Story of the FEPCs* (New York: University of Columbia Press, 1953), p. 23.

8. "Press and Radio Conference #51," in *Civil Rights, the White House, and the Justice Department, 1945–1968,* edited by Michal R. Belknap, (New York: Garland, 1991), vol. 1: *Attitudes, Goals, and Priorities,* pp. 11–13.

9. *Five Years of Progress, 1953–1958: A report to President Eisenhower by the President's Committee on Government Contracts,* (Washington, DC: U.S. Government Printing Office, 1958).

10. Huntington, *American Politics,* p. 27.

11. "Telegram from Thurgood Marshall to the President," in Belknap, *Civil Rights, the White House, and the Justice Department,* vol. 1, p. 119.

12. I borrow this concept from Paul Starr, who defines cultural authority as "the probability that particular definitions of reality and judgements of meaning and value will prevail as valid and true." The concept is a useful one for the study of the legitimation of affirmative action, since we are not concerned here with the power of government leaders to force anyone to obey a command, but rather the power of government leaders and officials to propound an idea as legitimate. See Paul Starr, *The Social Transformation of American Medicine* (New York: Basic Books, 1982). Some may consider the inclusion of authority under the concept of tradition to be a stretch, but I believe it is helpful in that it stresses the constructedness of social life. To some extent all authority is traditional. Rational-legal authority is not traditional, relative to monarchical or patrimonial societies, but in the modern West, rational-legal authority has itself become a tradition (or institution), something taken for granted. Shils is worth quoting at length on this point. Though Weber does discuss traditional authority as a separate category, "The other types of authority were also bound by tradition . . . The rational-legal type of authority—bureaucracy—was encased in the tradition of its own particular form of legitimacy. In a rational-legal order, as understood by Max Weber, rules are derived from and subsumed under other rules, in an ascending pyramid. At the pinnacle stand the most general laws, written constitutions, fundamental principles, unspoken postulates—the things which

are unquestioned. These fundamental principles and postulates of any legitimate political order, even a rational-legal order, are ultimately charismatic, but they are transmitted and received as traditions compelling respect both for their sacred properties and for their traditional givenness (Shils, *Tradition*, p. 186)."

13. "A Report to the President and the Cabinet of the Work of the President's Committee on Government Employment Policy," in Belknap, *Civil Rights, the White House, and the Justice Department,* vol. 4, *Employment of Blacks by the Federal Government,* p. 129.

14. Graham, *Civil Rights Era,* p. 75.

15. Ibid., p. 78–79.

16. Ibid., p. 95. See also Paul Burstein, *Discrimination, Jobs, and Politics* (Chicago: University of Chicago Press, 1985), pp. 103–9.

17. Excerpts are contained in appendix 1, in Alfred Blumrosen, *Black Employment and the Law* (New Brunswick, NJ: Rutgers University Press, 1971).

18. EEOC, *Making a Right a Reality: An Oral History of the EEOC, 1965–1972* (Washington, DC: 1990), p. 10.

19. "Johnson used his legislative skills to get Congress to act, but then assumed somewhat of a laissez-faire attitude in which he allowed enforcement to proceed without his help or hindrance." (Allan Wolk, *The Presidency and Black Civil Rights* [Rutherford, NJ: Fairleigh Dickinson Press, 1971], p. 247.

20. Lee Rainwater and William L. Yancey, *The Moynihan Report and the Politics of Controversy* (Cambridge, MA: The MIT Press, 1967), p. 14; Goodwin, *Remembering America,* p. 343.

21. Foreword, "EEOC Administrative History," [1968], in *Civil Rights During the Johnson Administration, 1963–1969,* edited by Steven F. Lawson (Frederick, MD: University Publications of America, 1984), part 2: "EEOC Administrative History," reel 1, frame 0003.

22. "Transcript of Proceedings, Department of Health, Education, and Welfare, Joint Federal Agency Meeting with Executives of the Pharmaceutical Industry," in ibid., frame 0924.

23. Ibid., frame 0928.

24. Nathan Glazer, *Affirmative Discrimination* (Cambridge, MA: Harvard University Press, [1975] 1987), pp. x–xi.

25. See Burstein, *Discrimination, Jobs, and Politics,* chapter 5, for discussions of the lack of lobbying against the Civil Rights Act's Title VII. Burstein maintains that it remains a mystery why there was so little lobbying against the Civil Rights Act (p. 107).

26. This will be discussed later in the chapter.

27. Gunnar Myrdal, *An American Dilemma* (New York: Harper & Brothers, 1944).

28. Ibid., p. 1009.

29. Ruchames, *Race, Jobs, and Politics,* pp. 94–95.

30. "Letter from Charles H. Houston to Harry S. Truman," in Belknap, *Civil Rights, the White House, and the Justice Department,* vol. 4, pp. 3–4.

31. "Letter from Harry S. Truman to Lester B. Granger," in ibid., p. 19.

32. Hubert H. Humphrey, *Beyond Civil Rights: A New Day of Equality* (New York: Random House, 1968), p. 37.

33. *Equal Employment Opportunity: A Report by the President's Committee on Government Contract Compliance,* (Washington, DC: U.S. Government Printing Office, 16 January 1953, pp. 4–5.

34. Quoted in Carl M. Brauer, *John F. Kennedy and the Second Reconstruction* (New York: Columbia University Press, 1977), pp. 221–22. Johnson sounded similar in a meeting with defense contractors in 1961, explaining that "[i]t is very easy in this troubled world to find reasons of self-interest for a program of non-discrimination." Among the reasons offered: "It is obvious that our 'national image' will be promoted throughout the world if we do not discriminate." Johnson ended this message by declaring (and citing the Golden Rule), "But I believe—and I think that all of you believe—that these arguments are secondary to an overriding proposition. It is that treating people alike— and as we would have them treat us—is the right thing to do." "Statement by the Vice President to Group of Defense Contractors," May 2, 1961, in Belknap, *Civil Rights, the White House, and the Justice Department,* vol. 5, *Equal Employment Opportunity,* p. 62.

35. This occurred in Birmingham, Alabama, on 15 September 1963.

36. Brauer, *Second Reconstruction,* p. 239.

37. This was mitigated somewhat by the image of blacks as rioters and black power advocates rather than peaceful demonstrators.

38. For a discussion of the cultural role of the courts, particularly the Supreme Court's role as legitimizer, see Walter F. Murphy, *Elements of Judicial Strategy* (Chicago: University of Chicago Press, 1964), pp. 17–19.

39. Lawrence M. Friedman, *The Legal System* (New York: Russell Sage, 1975), p. 255.

40. John Brigham, *The Cult of the Court* (Philadelphia: Temple University Press, 1987), p. 170.

41. Murphy, *Judicial Strategy,* p. 30.

42. David W. Rohde and Harold J. Spaeth, *Supreme Court Decision Making* (San Francisco: W. H. Freeman, 1976), p. 34.

43. Richard Posner, *Problems of Jurisprudence* (Cambridge, MA: Harvard University Press, 1990), p. 92.

44. S. F. C. Milsom, *Studies in the History of the Common Law* (London: Hambledon Press, 1985), p. 150. Historical context is almost certainly a relevant factor here. For example, when American law was undergoing great transformation in the pre–Civil War period, to the benefit of an emerging business class, the doctrine of precedent was considerably deemphasized. After the law was thus remade, legal formalism set in to protect against change. See Morton J. Horwitz, *The Transformation of American Law, 1780– 1860* (Cambridge, MA: Harvard University Press, 1977), p. 259.

45. Posner, *Problems of Jurisprudence,* p. 95.

46. Philip Selznick, *Law, Society, and Industrial Justice* (New York: Russell Sage, 1969), p. 53.

47. See, generally, Posner, *Problems of Jurisprudence,* and Richard A. Posner, *The Federal Courts: Crisis and Reform* (Cambridge, MA: Harvard University Press, 1985).

48. Barbara M. Yarnold, *Politics and the Courts* (New York: Praeger, 1992), p. 4; see also Rohde and Spaeth, *Supreme Court.*

49. K. N. Llewellyn, "The Constitution As An Institution," *Columbia Law Review* 34 (1934): 1–40, p. 23.

50. 279 F. Supp. 505, E. D. VA (1968).

51. Ibid., at 517.

52. Ibid., at 516.

53. The Burger Court overturned the opinion ten years later, but not until after it

played an important role as a tradition in civil rights law during that time. See Jack Greenberg, *Crusaders in the Courts* (New York: Basic Books, 1994), pp. 416–18.

54. 238 N. E. 2d. 839, C. P. (1968).

55. Ibid. at 844.

56. 314 F. Supp. 160, S.D. IN (1969).

57. 433 F. 2d. 421 (8th Cir. 1970).

58. 416 F. 2d. 123 (8th Cir. 1970).

59. 416 F. 2d. 980 (5th Cir. 1969).

60. 292 F. Supp. 413, S. D. OH (1968). See Owen M. Fiss, "A Theory of Fair Employment Law," *University of Chicago Law Review* 38 (1971): 235–314, 272.

61. "[W]here employer action was 'inherently destructive' of workers' rights, proof of intent was unnecessary under the NLRA [National Labor Relations Act] (*NLRB v. Erie Resistor Corp.; NLRB v. Great Dane Trailer, Inc.*)." Alfred W. Blumrosen, *Modern Law: The Law Transmission System and Equal Employment Opportunity* (Madison: University of Wisconsin Press, 1993), p. 109. *Quarles* was one of the few affirmative action opinions to look to the employment tradition, using a case dealing with discrimination against nonunion members (*Central of Georgia Railway Co. v. Jones* 229 F. 2d. 648 [5th Cir. 1956], cert. denied, 352 U.S. 848, 77 S. Ct. 32, I. L. Ed. 2d, [1956]) to assert that unions have a duty to fairly represent workers.

62. Glazer, *Affirmative Discrimination*, p. 51.

63. Thomas Sowell, *Civil Rights: Rhetoric or Reality?* (New York: Quill, 1984), p. 54.

64. 304 F. 2d 583, 586 (5th Cir. 1962).

65. 433 F. 2d 421 (8th Cir. 1970).

66. 443 F. 2d 544, 551 (9th Cir. 1971).

67. 311 F. Supp. 468, 471, S. D. OH (1970).

68. 301 F. Supp. 97, M. D. NC (1969).

69. 332 U.S. 463 (1947).

70. 316 U.S. 400 (1942).

71. 294 U.S. 587 (1935).

72. 452 F. 2d 315 (8th Cir. 1971).

73. 225 F. Supp. 353 (1963).

74. *Carter v. Gallagher* at 330.

75. Ibid., at 331.

76. 402 U.S. 1 (1971).

77. In this opinion, the Supreme Court stated, "Independent of student assignment, where it is possible to identify a 'white school' or a 'Negro school' simply by reference to the racial composition of teachers and staff, the quality of school buildings and equipment, or the organization of sports activities, a prima facie case of violation of substantive constitutional rights under the Equal Protection Clause is shown." *Swann v. Charlotte-Mecklenburg Board of Education,* at 18.

78. 442 F. 2d 159 (3d Cir. 1971).

79. Ibid., at 173.

80. 302 F. Supp. 726 (D.N.J. 1969), aff'd, 431 F. 2d 1254 (3d Cir. 1970).

81. The appeal opinion stated unequivocally, "State action based partly on considerations of color, when color is not used per se, and in furtherance of a proper governmental objective, is not necessarily a violation of the Fourteenth Amendment. Proper integration of faculties is as important as proper integration of schools of themselves, as set forth in

Brown v. Board of Education, 349 U. S. 294, 295, 75 S. Ct. 753, 99 L. Ed. 1083 (1955), the thrust of which extends to the selection of faculties." *Porcelli v. Titus*, 431 F. 2d 1254 (3d Cir. 1970) at 1257.

82. 395 F. 2d 920, 931 (2d Cir. 1968).

83. 378 F. 2d 22, 24 (2d Cir. 1967).

84. In *Offerman v. Nitkowski,* at 23, the court cited the *Brown v. Board of Education* case of 1955, and argued that "states necessarily based their desegregation plans on racial classification and the courts have uniformly held such classifications constitutional." Several school cases were cited.

85. *Carter v. Gallagher* at 325.

86. *Dobbins v. Local 212* at 445.

87. 401 U.S. 424 (1971).

88. Herman Belz, *Equality Transformed* (New Brunswick: Transaction Publishers, 1991), p. 51.

89. *Griggs v. Duke Power Company,* 420 F. 2d 1225 (4th Cir. 1970) at 1237.

90. Ibid., at 1235.

91. Ibid., at 1233.

92. Ibid., at 1235.

93. Petitioner's brief, pp. 9, 16.

94. Ibid., p. 24, *Wall Street Journal,* 9 February 1965.

95. Petitioner's brief, p. 25. The respondent's brief in opposition argued that these cases are irrelevant, because in voting, school, and jury cases, "it can be presumed or assumed that a significant number of the group involved have the necessary qualifications"; however, in employment, qualifications cannot be assumed without evidence.

96. Petitioner's brief, p. 29.

97. Petitioner's brief, p. 19.

98. One brief was supplied in support of Duke by the Chamber of Commerce of the United States of America, which explained that the organization wanted to preserve the employer's right to use ability tests.

99. 311 U.S. 128 (1941), at 132.

100. *Griggs v. Duke Power Co.,* 401 U.S. 424 (1971) at 429.

101. Ibid.

102. Ibid., at 432.

103. 395 U.S. 285 (1969).

104. *Griggs v. Duke Power* at 431.

105. Michael Evan Gold, "*Griggs'* Folly: An Essay on the Theory, Problems, and Origin of the Adverse Impact Definition of Employment Discrimination and a Recommendation for Reform," in *Industrial Relations Law Journal* 7 (1985): 429–598, 587.

106. Blumrosen, *Modern Law,* p. 280.

107. Biographical information on federal circuit and district judges is not easy to find. Some of the judges who ruled in the cases cited in this chapter have some information provided on them in the *Almanac of the Federal Judiciary* (Prentice Hall Law and Business, 1992). John D. Butzner, for example, who ruled on the influential Quarles case, was a Johnson appointee and is described as "somewhat liberal" by the *Almanac.*

108. For discussions of legislation as based on problem solving, see David Mayhew, *Divided We Govern* (New Haven, CT: Yale University Press, 1991), pp. 130–31; John W. Kingdon, *Agendas, Alternatives, and Public Policies* (Boston: Little, Brown, 1984), Chapter 5.

109. Donald L. Horowitz, *The Courts and Social Policy* (Washington, DC: The Brookings Institution, 1977), p. 5.

110. Ibid., p. 7.

111. Ibid., p. 10.

112. Graham, *Civil Rights Era*, pp. 366–70; Richard L. Pacelle, Jr., *The Transformation of the Supreme Court's Agenda* (Boulder: Westview, 1991), pp. 164–65.

113. 304 U.S. 144 (1938), 152–53.

114. Robert M. Cover, "The Origins of Judicial Activism in the Protection of Minorities," *Yale Law Journal* 91 (June 1982): 1287–1316, p. 1293.

115. Quoted in Alpheus T. Mason, *Harlan Fiske Stone, Pillar of the Law* (New York: Viking Press, 1956), p. 515. See also Cover, "Protection of Minorities," p. 1293.

116. Cover, "Protection of Minorities," pp. 1296–97.

117. Pacelle, *Supreme Court's Agenda*, p. 191.

118. Ibid., chapter 6.

119. On the role of the Burger Court in continuing and changing the direction of the Warren Court, see Stephen L. Wasby, *Continuity and Change: From the Warren Court to the Burger Court* (Pacific Palisades, CA: Goodyear Publishing, 1976); and Paul Brest, "Race Discrimination," in *The Burger Court: The Counter-Revolution That Wasn't,* edited by Vincent Blasi (New Haven, CT: Yale University Press, 1983), pp. 113–31.

120. An interesting discussion of Footnote Four is in John Hart Ely, *Democracy and Distrust* (Cambridge, MA: Harvard University Press, 1980).

121. Quoted in Greenberg, *Crusaders in the Courts,* pp. 164–65; Author's telephone interview with Jack Greenberg, 27 June 1994.

122. On this point, see also Richard A. Posner, *The Federal Courts: Crisis and Reform* (Cambridge, MA: Harvard University Press, 1985).

123. Horowitz, *Courts and Social Policy,* pp. 265–66.

124. Blumrosen telephone interview, 12 August 1992.

125. For an authoritative history of the *Brown v. Board of Education* case, see Richard Kluger, *Simple Justice* (New York: Vintage Books, 1977). Glazer focuses on the later history (Glazer, *Affirmative Discrimination,* chapter 3).

126. 372 F. 2d 836 (5th Cir. 1966) at 847.

127. *U.S. v. Jefferson County,* at 887.

128. Ibid.

129. Ibid.

130. Horowitz, *Courts and Social Policy,* p. 266.

Chapter Seven

1. Herbert S. Parmet, *Richard Nixon and His America* (Boston: Little, Brown, 1990), p. 597.

2. Charles V. Hamilton, "Blacks and Urban Affairs: Saying Is Not Doing," in *What Nixon Is Doing to Us,* edited by Alan Gartner, Colin Greer, and Frank Riessman (New York: Harper & Row, 1973), pp. 84–93.

3. A. James Reichley, *Conservatives in an Age of Change* (Washington, DC: The Brookings Institution, 1981).

4. Stephen E. Ambrose, *Nixon: The Triumph of a Politician* (New York: Simon & Schuster, 1989), p. 407.

5. Parmet, *Nixon and His America,* p. 600.

6. Eleanor Holmes Norton, "Civil Rights: Working Backward," in Gartner, Greer, and Riessman, *What Nixon Is Doing to Us,* pp. 201–15, 204.

7. Michael A. Genovese, *The Nixon Presidency: Power and Politics in Turbulent Times* (New York: Greenwood Press, 1990), p. 83.

8. Hugh Davis Graham, "The Incoherence of the Civil Rights Policy in the Nixon Administration," in *Richard M. Nixon: Politician, President, Administrator,* edited by Leon Friedman and William F. Levantrosser (New York: Greenwood Press, 1991), pp. 159–72.

9. Tom Wicker, *One of Us: Nixon and the American Dream* (New York: Random House, 1991), p. 411.

10. Leon Panetta and Peter Gall, *Bring Us Together* (Philadelphia: J. B. Lippincott, 1971), pp. 335, 371.

11. Quoted in William Safire, *Before the Fall* (New York: Da Capo Press, 1975), p. 544.

12. Quoted in Stephen Skowronek, *The Politics Presidents Make* (Cambridge, MA: Harvard University Press, 1993), p. 18.

13. "Memo to John Ehrlichman from The President," 13 March 1969, in *From: The President,* edited by Bruce Oudes (New York: Harper & Row, 1989), pp. 19–20.

14. Skowronek, *Politics Presidents Make,* p. 18.

15. See Everett Carll Ladd, Jr., and Charles D. Hadley, *Transformations of the American Party System* (New York: W. W. Norton, [1975] 1978), chapter 1, for a review of the competing interpretations prevailing at the time.

16. Stephen Skowronek, "Notes on the Presidency in the Political Order," *Studies in American Political Development* 1 (1986): 286–302, 298.

17. Ibid., p. 298.

18. Ibid.

19. See Edward G. Carmines and James A. Stimson, *Issue Evolution: Race and the Transformation of American Politics* (Princeton, NJ: Princeton University Press, 1989), p. 54.

20. Ambrose, *Triumph of a Politician,* p. 220; Parmet, *Nixon and His America,* p. 528.

21. Ambrose, *Triumph of a Politician,* p. 221.

22. John R. Petrocik, *Party Coalitions* (Chicago: University of Chicago Press, 1981), p. 89.

23. The AFL-CIO's Committee on Political Education spread the leadership orthodoxy, with 115 million leaflets, 24,000 union members at 638 telephone banks, 72,000 door-to-door campaigners, and 95,000 volunteers on election day. AFL-CIO head George Meany explained the AFL-CIO position on the 1968 election at a union convention: "The question we face as trade unionists in this coming election is, do we want to continue this forward march or do we want to accept a fellow like Richard Nixon to lead us? . . . Then there is another fellow [Wallace], who is waging a campaign of hate and fear, who promises the American people a police state. . . . We are not going to have him, but we can't afford to have Nixon, either. I tell you that a vote for Wallace is a vote for Nixon" (Archie Robinson, *George Meany and His Times* [New York: Simon & Schuster, 1981], pp. 278–79).

24. Richard M. Scammon and Ben J. Wattenberg, *The Real Majority* (New York: Coward-McCann, 1970), pp. 38–39.

25. Seymour Martin Lipset and Earl Raab, *The Politics of Unreason: Right-Wing Extremism in America, 1790–1977* (Chicago: University of Chicago Press, 1978), p. 342.

For examples of Wallace's campaign pitch, later to become the language of the Republicans in the 1980s and 1990s, see ibid., pp. 344, 349; Scammon and Wattenberg, *Real Majority*, p. 62; Thomas Byrne Edsall and Mary D. Edsall, *Chain Reaction: The Impact of Race, Rights, and Taxes on American Politics* (New York: W. W. Norton, 1992), p. 78. On the frustration of the white working-class voter, see Nathan Glazer and Daniel P. Moynihan, *Beyond the Melting Pot* (Cambridge, MA: The MIT Press, 1970), p. xxxv.

26. Carmines and Stimson, *Issue Evolution*, p. 188; Edsall and Edsall, *Chain Reaction*, chapter 2.

27. Edsall and Edsall, *Chain Reaction*, p. 37. See also Carmines and Stimson, *Issue Evolution*, for the change in the Republican party regarding the race issue.

28. Edsall and Edsall, *Chain Reaction*, p. 35. For Goldwater's position on civil rights, see James C. Harvey, *Civil Rights During the Johnson Administration* (Jackson, MS: University Press of Mississippi, 1973), p. 16.

29. Reichley, *Conservatives*, p. 54. The Nixon quotes are from this page. It is notable that Nixon's "thoughtful critics" are attributed authorship of Johnson's famous Howard University speech, later thought to justify affirmative action.

30. Ambrose, *Triumph of a Politician*, pp. 141, 193.

31. See Edsall and Edsall, *Chain Reaction*, p. 75. Studies of public opinion support this strategy. Polls show Americans support civil rights in principle in great numbers, but support declines when questions focus on specific policies or implementation issues. See Howard Schuman, Charlotte Steeh, and Lawrence Bobo, *Racial Attitudes in America: Trends and Interpretations* (Cambridge, MA: Harvard University Press, 1985), pp. 195–97.

32. Edsall and Edsall, *Chain Reaction*, p. 76.

33. Ibid., p. 164.

34. Ambrose, *Triumph of a Politician*, pp. 162–63.

35. See *Five Years of Progress, 1953–1958: A Report to President Eisenhower by the President's Committee on Government Contracts*, (Washington, DC: U.S. Government Printing Office, 1958). This seems to be the basis of the claim of Joan Hoff, another Nixon scholar, that there is a "consistency of Nixon's views on civil rights over his entire political career as well as his success where Johnson had failed to implement the Philadelphia Plan" (Joan Hoff, *Nixon Reconsidered* [New York: Basic Books, 1994], pp. 91–92). Hoff's position is problematic, and not just because Johnson is considered to have "failed" on this issue, since Johnson was more concerned with color-blind approaches anyway and never seemed to even be aware of the Philadelphia Plan. Nixon's support of equal employment opportunity in the 1950s and earlier as a senator or vice president is no explanation of his support for affirmative action in 1969 as president. By this logic, Nixon should have supported busing because he earlier supported school desegregation.

36. Ambrose, *Triumph of a Politician*, p. 125.

37. Quoted in Maurice H. Stans, "Nixon's Economic Policy Toward Minorities," in *Politician, President, Administrator*, edited by Leon Friedman and William F. Levantrosser, pp. 239–46, 239–40.

38. Rowland Evans, Jr., and Robert D. Novak, *Nixon in the White House* (New York: Random House, 1971), p. 137.

39. Ibid., p. 134.

40. Jonathan Schell, *The Time of Illusion* (New York: Vintage Books, 1975), p. 26.

41. *The Nixon Presidential Press Conferences*, edited by George W. Johnson (New York: Earl M. Coleman Enterprises, 1978), p. 16.

42. Ambrose, *Triumph of a Politician,* p. 248.

43. Richard Nixon, *RN: The Memoirs of Richard Nixon* (New York: Grosset & Dunlap, 1978), p. 436.

44. John Ehrlichman, *Witness to Power: The Nixon Years* (New York: Simon and Schuster, 1982), p. 224.

45. Quoted in Genovese, *The Nixon Presidency,* p. 85.

46. "Memo to Mr. Haldeman, Mr. Ehlrichman, Dr. Kissinger from The President," 2 March 1970, in Oudes, *From: The President,* p. 101.

47. Ehrlichman, *Witness to Power,* pp. 224, 228.

48. Notes of Meetings with the President, in *Papers of the Nixon White House,* edited by Joan Hoff-Wilson (Bethesda, MD: University Publications of America, 1989), part 3, "John Ehrlichman: Notes of Meetings with the President," Fiche #7, 3-7-E08.2

49. Quoted in Reichley, *Conservatives,* p. 184.

50. This review is largely taken from Congressional Quarterly, *Nixon: The First Year of His Presidency* (Washington, DC: Congressional Quarterly, 1970), pp. 49–52.

51. Letters were sent to Representatives Adam Clayton Powell, John Conyers, Louis Stokes, Robert Nix, Charles Diggs, Augustus Hawkins, and Shirley Chisolm from Nixon's assistant, Bryce N. Harlow, on 11 April 1969; see *Civil Rights During the Nixon Administration, 1969–1974,* edited by Hugh Davis Graham (Bethesda, MD: University Publications of America, 1989), part 1, "The White House Central Files," reel 1, frames 0819–0842. James E. Jones, Jr., associate solicitor in the Department of Labor, wrote that this embarrassment garnered much attention from the media and loud outcries from the civil rights community, putting significant pressure to act positively for equal employment opportunity (James E. Jones, Jr., "The Genesis and Present Status of Affirmative Action in Employment: Economic, Legal, and Political Realities," *Iowa Law Review* 70 [1985]: 901–44, 912).

52. Congressional Quarterly, *Nixon: The First Year,* p. 87.

53. Robinson, *Meany,* p. 288.

54. Schell, *Time of Illusion,* p. 82.

55. Robinson, *Meany,* pp. 288–89.

56. In Bayard Rustin, "The Blacks and the Unions," *Harpers,* May 1971, p. 80.

57. "Memo to the President from Robert J. Brown," 11 July 1969, in Graham, *Civil Rights During Nixon,* part 1, reel 1, frame 0043.

58. "Memo to President Nixon from Harry S. Flemming," 19 September 1969, in Graham, *Civil Rights During the Nixon,* part 1, reel 18, frame 0729.

59. Ibid., frame 0809. If groups were hired or used for political gain, Nixon seemed to have a distinct lack of grace in the effort. In a meeting of President-elect Nixon and AFL-CIO leader George Meany, which was very brief, Nixon introduced his secretary, Rose Mary Woods, and said, "She's a Catholic, too, George." Meany later wrote about the incident, "What the hell was that? As if that was important to me! What did I care what she was?" (Robinson, *Meany,* p. 279). Ethnicity also seemed a worthwhile topic at White House meetings. At a 15 December 1969 meeting with Nixon, Ehrlichman, Ronald Ziegler, and Bob Haldeman on an upcoming state of the union address, the conversation turned to a recent Bob Hope television special and some of the women guests. Ehrlichman wrote, "Miss World—Gold Diggers—Connie Stevens is Sicilian—Negro girl—something to see." "Notes of Meetings with the President," in Hoff-Wilson, *Papers of the Nixon White House,* part 3, fiche #7, 3-7-E08.2.

60. Stans also maintains that Nixon was pessimistic about winning votes with the program but was nevertheless compelled to action. Despite the OMBE having no funding, Nixon allegedly said to Stans, "This is something long overdue and I want you to give it a high priority. Politically, I don't think there are any votes in it for us, but we'll do it because it is the right thing to do" (Maurice H. Stans, "Nixon's Economic Policy toward Minorities," in *Politician, President, Administrator,* edited by Leon Friedman and William F. Levantrosser, pp. 239–46, pp. 240–41).

61. *Wall Street Journal,* 6 March 1969.

62. *Wall Street Journal,* 12 March 1969.

63. Hugh Davis Graham, "Incoherence," in *Politician, President, Administrator,* edited by Leon Friedman and William F. Levantrosser, p. 166.

64. Arthur I. Blaustein and Geoffrey Faux, *The Star-Spangled Hustle* (Garden City, NY: Doubleday, 1972), p. 58.

65. James E. Jones, Jr., "The Genesis and Present Status of Affirmative Action in Employment: Economic, Legal, and Political Realities," *Iowa Law Review* 70 (1985): 901–44, 912.

66. "Note to BH (Bob Haldeman)," 26 March 1969, in Graham, *Civil Rights During Nixon,* part 1, reel 1, frame 0735.

67. See U.S. Senate Committee on Judiciary, *Hearings on Equal Employment Opportunity Procedures, before Subcommittee on Administrative Practice and Procedure, on S. Res. 39,* 91st Cong., 1st sess., 27 and 28 March 1969.

68. Author's telephone interview with James E. Jones, Jr., 29 June 1994.

69. Safire, *Before the Fall,* pp. 266, 585. The self-help justification is so surprising because the quotas were later attacked by Nixon and other Republicans for violating meritocratic principles. It is also surprising that this argument was used, and that it transfixed the cabinet, since if quotas (and thus outside, government help) can be seen as self-help, then any government action, such as welfare benefits, can also been seen as self-help.

70. Arthur Fletcher, *The Silent Sell-Out: Government Betrayal of Blacks To the Craft Unions* (New York: The Third Press, 1974), p. 65.

71. Hugh Davis Graham, *The Civil Rights Era* (New York: Oxford University Press, 1990), pp. 326–27.

72. J. Larry Hood, "The Nixon Administration and the Revised Philadelphia Plan for Affirmative Action: A Study in Expanding Presidential Power and Divided Government," *Presidential Studies Quarterly* 23 (1993): 145–67, 150–52.

73. Ibid., p. 153.

74. "Memo to President Nixon from John Ehrlichman," 26 August 1969, in Graham, *Civil Rights During Nixon,* part 1, reel 18, frame 0713.

75. Nixon, *RN,* p. 438. Dirksen and fellow Republican Paul Fannin had objected on the Senate floor to the direction the OFCC was headed in February (Hood, "Expanding Presidential Power," p. 152).

76. Senate Committee, *Equal Employment Opportunity Procedures,* pp. 22–23.

77. Letter to Democratic Study Group (Donald M. Fraser, Chairman, John Brademas, Vice Chairman, James C. Corman, Secretary-Chief Whip, Don Edwards, Task Force on Civil Rights) from Bryce N. Harlow, 13 August 1969, in Graham, *Civil Rights During Nixon,* part 1, reel 2, frames 0056–0060.

78. Evans and Novak, *Nixon in the White House,* p. 137.

79. Richard P. Nathan, *The Plot That Failed: Nixon and the Administrative Presidency* (New York: John Wiley & Sons, 1975), p. 16.

80. *New York Times,* 24 September 1969.

81. Congressional Quarterly, *Nixon: The First Years,* p. 27-A.

82. Nixon, *RN,* p. 437.

83. Quoted in William B. Gould, *Black Workers in White Unions: Job Discrimination in the United States* (Ithaca: Cornell University Press, 1977), p. 52.

84. Quoted in Hood, "Expanding Presidential Power," p. 150.

85. Meany later explained, "I never trusted Nixon. He was very clever, and just an opportunist. I don't think he was ever sincerely anti or pro anything" (Robinson, *Meany,* p. 280).

86. Skowronek, *Politics Presidents Make,* pp. 44–45.

87. *Hearing on the Philadelphia Plan and S. 931 Before the Subcommittee on Separation of Powers of the Senate Committee on the Judiciary,* 91st Cong., 1st sess., 1969, p. 70.

88. This strategy was apparent early on, as a memo, dated 2 October, from Richard Blumenthal to White House consultant Daniel Patrick Moynihan reveals. The memo showed black numerical underrepresentation in the unions, explained Staat's opinion, and then explained that "The Attorney General, John Mitchell, has formally advised Secretary of Labor George Schultz (*sic*) that the so-called 'Revised Philadelphia Plan' is legal, since it involves the use of *ranges of goals* rather than *'quotas'*" (original emphasis). In Graham, *Civil Rights and the Nixon Administration,* part 1, reel 18, frame 0721. National Labor Director for the NAACP Herbert Hill also testified at the hearings, emphasizing pragmatic arguments.

89. S. 931 Hearing, p. 111.

90. Ibid., p. 132.

91. Ibid., p. 136.

92. Ibid., p. 134.

93. *New York Times,* 26 December 1969.

94. Press Conference, in Graham, *Civil Rights and the Nixon Administration,* part 1, reel 20, frames 0083–0086.

95. 115 *Congressional Record,* 91st Cong., 1st sess., 18 December 1969, pp. 39,950–39,966.

96. Safire, *Before the Fall,* p. 571.

97. 115 *Congressional Record,* 91st Cong., 1st sess., 1969, pp. 39,961–39,962.

98. Press Release, in Graham, *Civil Rights and the Nixon Administration,* part 1, reel 20, frame 0081.

99. Notes of Meetings with the President, in Hoff-Wilson, *Papers of the Nixon White House,* part 3, fiche #7, 3-7-F06.

100. Notes of Meetings with the President, in Hoff-Wilson, *Papers of the Nixon White House,* part 3, fiche #7, 3-7-F11.

101. Quoted in Hood, "Expanding Presidential Power," p. 158.

102. The notes here read, "*Rhodes*—A conferee took AG's argument." This may refer to *Ethridge v. Rhodes* (268 F. Supp 83, S. D. Ohio, 1967), actually a Fourteenth Amendment case, dealing explicitly with state responsibility regarding discrimination in unions. The court ruled that Ohio state contracts with discriminating unions were in violation of Fourteenth Amendment responsibilities. This section of the notes may also refer to a comment from Arizona GOP Representative John Rhodes.

103. Notes of Meetings with the President, in Hoff-Wilson, *Papers of the Nixon White*

House, part 3, fiche #7, 3-7-G02. Safire (*Before the Fall,* p. 316) reports that campaign strategy for 1970 was also discussed at this meeting, though he does not report a divide-the-democrats approach being discussed at this time.

104. Memo to President Nixon from Bryce Harlow, 22 December 1969, in Graham, *Civil Rights and the Nixon Administration,* part 1, reel 18, frame 0823.

105. Memo for John Price from John Campbell, 22 December 1969, in Graham, *Civil Rights During Nixon,* part 1, reel 2, frame 0266.

106. Even Elmer Staats felt it was necessary to tell Ehrlichman that his opposition to the Plan did not "revolve around the civil rights issue." Letter to John Ehrlichman from Elmer B. Staats, 22 December 1969, in Graham, *Civil Rights During Nixon,* part 1, reel 2, frame 0832.

107. 115 *Congressional Record,* 91st Cong., 1st sess., 23 December 1969, pp. 40,903.

108. Ibid., pp. 40,904–40,905.

109. Edsall and Edsall, *Chain Reaction,* p. 51.

110. 115 *Congressional Record,* 91st Cong., 1st sess., 23 December 1969, pp. 40,907–40,908.

111. Ibid., p. 40,917.

112. Ibid., p. 40,918.

113. Parmet, *Nixon and His America,* p. 600; Graham, *Civil Rights Era,* p. 340.

114. Notes of Meetings with the President, in Hoff-Wilson, *Papers of the Nixon White House,* part 3, fiche #8, 3-8-A05. The ten percent "surtax" on income tax was originally imposed by Johnson to help pay for the Vietnam War. Nixon pushed its continuation through a reluctant House, where both liberals and conservatives opposed it, on the belief that it would help check inflation, a growing problem (Reichley, *Conservatives,* pp. 90–91).

115. *New York Times,* 26 December 1969.

116. This is not too say, however, that there was no civil rights support for the Plan. At the local level, CORE and the NAACP worked with a coalition of churches in support of the Plan. A leaflet was distributed in the spring of 1969 in the Philadelphia African-American community which said: "DEMONSTRATE TO SUPPORT THE PHILA-DELPHIA PLAN! END BIAS IN THE CONSTRUCTION TRADES. Only one-half of 1 percent of the workers in these trades are Black: IRON WORKERS, ELECTRICIANS, STEAMFITTERS, PLUMBERS, ROOFERS, ELEVATOR CONSTRUCTORS, SHEET METAL WORKERS. THE PLAN WORKS. Last year it put 1,400 minority group workers on jobs in the Philadelphia Area. This year, with the Plan in abeyance, 1,400 workers have lost their jobs! Voluntary programs do not work. Only government action can deal with this deep-rooted racial exclusion." In Herbert Hill, "A Critical Analysis of Apprenticeship Outreach Programs and the Hometown Plans," Howard University Institute for Urban Affairs and Research Occasional Paper, vol. 2, no. 1 (1974), p. 75. See also chapter 5.

117. *New York Times,* 26 December 1969.

118. See memo to Ron Ziegler from John R. Brown III, 29 December 1969, in Graham, *Civil Rights During Nixon,* part 1, reel 18, frame 0830; memo to Herb Klein from John R. Brown III, 29 December 1969, in ibid., frame 0828.

119. Notes of Meetings with the President, in Hoff-Wilson, *Papers of the Nixon White House,* part 3, fiche #7, 3-7-C08. The notes here are not very clear. The actual text is as follows:

unions—rank and file wont (*sic*) let leadership go—Civ Rts people (unintelligible) to realize they couldn't compromise on this fundamental issue

View for 15 yrs—Chrmn of K Comm. (probably Chairman of Kerner Commission, possibly the Nixon Oval Office was thinking in terms of preventing further racial violence) Schultz (*sic*)—a bulldog.

120. George P. Shultz, *Turmoil and Triumph* (New York: Charles Scribner's Sons, 1993), p. 1110.

121. Ehrlichman, *Witness to Power,* p. 228.

122. Congressional Quarterly, *Congress and the Nation,* (Washington, DC: Congressional Quarterly, 3, 1973), p. 711.

123. Quoted in Hood, "Expanding Presidential Power," p. 161.

124. OFCC administrators had predictably pounced on the wonderfully practical affirmative action model after the Nixon administration had revived it and began preparing for its expansion at least as early as November of 1969. In "Order No. 4," contractors with at least a $50,000 contract and more than 50 employees were to "correct any identifiable deficiencies" in the utilization of minorities. Utilization was "having fewer minorities in a particular job class than would reasonably be expected by their availability." Racial hiring goals and timetables, roughly based on "the percentage of the minority work force as compared with the total work force in the immediate labor area" were now required. Quoted in Graham, *Civil Rights Era,* pp. 342–43.

Though this was a *major* expansion of the affirmative action model, there is virtually no record of anyone in the administration being aware of its existence. Though Shultz signed off on it on 3 February, there are no internal memos giving it more than a passing mention, and Shultz, Nixon, and Ehrlichman (as well as Safire, in his memoirs, *Before the Fall*) invariably refer to the Philadelphia Plan when discussing civil rights in employment, though Order No. 4 was obviously more far-reaching (Joan Hoff credits Nixon with the expansion but presents no evidence of his involvement. See Hoff, *Nixon Reconsidered,* p. 92).

The only evidence I have been able to find that anyone other than Shultz was aware of it is a memo of 10 June 1970, from Ehrlichman to Nixon, briefing Nixon of an impending meeting with Meany. Ehrlichman did not know Meany's purpose, but recommended to Nixon that if Meany complained about the Philadelphia Plan, Nixon should say, "The fact is that the Labor Department is demanding no more from the construction industry than from any other industry." In Hoff-Wilson, *Papers of the Nixon White House,* part 2: "The President's Meeting File, 1969–1974," fiche #70-6-7: A09.

125. Author's personal correspondence with David Riesman, 1 July 1994.

126. Memo for the President, 20 January 1970, in Graham, *Civil Rights During Nixon,* part 1, reel 2, frame 0288.

127. Memo to Jeb Magruder from John R. Brown III, 3 February 1970, in ibid., frame 0300; Memo to John R. Brown III from Jeb Magruder, 16 February 1970, in ibid., frame 0344.

128. Memo for the President, 15 March 1970, in ibid., frame 0371.

129. Report: Blacks, to Bryce Harlow from Lamar Alexander, 17 June 1970, in ibid., frame 0765.

130. Kevin Phillips maintained that "the GOP can build a winning coalition without Negro votes. Indeed, Negro-Democratic mutual identification was a major source of Democratic loss—and Republican or [George Wallace's] American Independent Party profit—in many sections of the nation" (Kevin Phillips, *The Emerging Republican Majority* [Garden City, NY: Anchor Books, 1970], p. 468).

131. John Robert Greene, *The Limits of Power: The Nixon and Ford Administrations* (Bloomington, IN: Indiana University Press, 1992), p. 40; Ehrlichman, *Witness to Power,* p. 126.

132. Memo to Bob Haldeman from the President, 13 April 1970, quoted in Oudes, *From: The President*, pp. 114–15.

133. Charles W. Colson, "Discussant: Charles W. Colson," in *Politician, President, Administrator*, edited by Leon Friedman and William F. Levantrosser, pp. 275–78, p. 275.

134. Safire, *Before the Fall*, p. 175.

135. Ibid., p. 179.

136. Michael P. Balzano, Jr., "The Silent vs. the New Majority," in *Politician, President, Administrator*, edited by Leon Friedman and William F. Levantrosser, pp. 259–74, p. 264.

137. Ambrose, *Triumph of a Politician*, p. 359; Parmet, *Nixon and His America*, p. 594.

138. Parmet, *Nixon and His America*, p. 602.

139. Memo to Mr. Colson from H. R. Haldeman, 8 September 1979, quoted in Oudes, *From: The President*, p. 158.

140. Memo to Henry Cashen from Charles W. Colson, quoted in ibid., p. 162.

141. Safire, *Before the Fall*, p. 320.

142. Michael P. Balzano, Jr., "The Silent vs. the New Majority," in *Politician, President, Administrator*, edited by Leon Friedman and William F. Levantrosser, p. 270.

143. Quoted in Greene, *The Limits of Power*, p. 67.

144. Balzano, "Silent vs. New Majority," in *Politician, President, Administrator*, edited by Leon Friedman and William F. Levantrosser, p. 270.

145. Memo to Mr. Ehrlichman, Mr. Finch, and Mr. Haldeman from John R. Brown III, 8 September 1970, in Oudes, *From: The President*, pp. 156–57.

146. Ehrlichman, *Witness to Power*, pp. 212–20. The entire photocopied Ehrlichman memo is included in the text, complete with Nixon's scribbled comments on the memo. The zig-zag model was apparent in Nixon's campaign speeches, as noted earlier, and was also advocated by Len Garment, who said, "Change requires a certain amount of zigging and zagging. The great trick is to keep operations directed at change within the law, while at the same time preventing those antagonistic to change from becoming too enthusiastic in their antagonism. What is needed is to maintain enough balance to keep going." Quoted in Reichley, *Conservatives*, p. 190.

147. Safire, *Before the Fall*, pp. 585, 572.

148. Panetta and Gall, *Bring Us Together*, p. 370.

149. Quoted in Norton, "Working Backward," pp. 206–7; see also Graham, *Civil Rights Era*, pp. 343–44, 446–47.

150. Graham, *Civil Rights Era*, p. 316.

151. Parmet, *Nixon and His America*, p. 601. For a discussion of OMBE budget and successes (for example, 30 of the top 100 black businesses in 1981 had begun between 1969 and 1971), see Hoff, *Nixon Reconsidered*, pp. 96–97.

152. Edsall and Edsall, *Chain Reaction*, pp. 93–95. The persons responsible for the new guidelines, adopted in November of 1969 (a month before the congressional debate on the Philadelphia Plan), largely adopted the pragmatic language of the administrative agencies. The "Official Guidelines of the Commission on Party Structure and Delegate Selection to the Democratic National Committee" professed classical liberal ideals from the 1964 Democratic National Convention, such as the prohibition of "discrimination in any State Party affairs on the grounds of race, color, creed or national origin . . ." The document also required that "State parties overcome the effects of past discrimination by

affirmative steps to encourage minority group participation, including representation of minority groups in the national convention delegation in reasonable relationship to the group's presence in the population of the State." A footnote in the text added weakly, "It is the understanding of the Commission that this is not to be accomplished by the mandatory imposition of quotas." Quoted in chapter 1, Appendix, in Nelson W. Polsby, *Consequences of Party Reform* (New York: Oxford University Press, 1983); see chapter 1 generally for the origins of the change.

The pragmatic language reflected not just a borrowing of language from the administrative agencies but also a pragmatic logic which led to the changes. The Democratic Party had great difficulty in knowing whether or not Southern states were complying with party antidiscrimination measures, as representation of blacks remained low in some of the Southern states (Denise L. Baer and David A. Bositis, *Elite Cadres and Party Coalitions: Representing the Public in Party Politics* [New York: Greenwood Press, 1988], p. 63). Debates over the guidelines also reflected political and moral motivations for the change, according to William J. Crotty. See Crotty, *Decision for the Democrats: Reforming the Party Structure* (Baltimore: Johns Hopkins University Press, 1978), p. 62.

153. Safire, *Before the Fall*, p. 571. The references to political quotas are swipes at the Democrats' use of quotas at their 1972 convention.

154. There were comical document exchanges, including Memo to Ken Cole from John Evans, 24 October 1972, and attached "Q & A," in Graham, *Civil Rights During Nixon*, part 1, reel 19, frames 0257–0258; Memo to John Evans from John Campbell, 23 October 1972, in ibid., frame 0259, Memo to Ken Cole from John Evans, 9 October 1972, and attached Leonard Garment article in ibid., frames 0260–0269; Letter to Philip E. Hoffman of the American Jewish Committee from President Nixon, 11 August 1972, in ibid., frame 0271; Memo to John Ehrlichman from William Safire, 6 September 1972 and attached "grilling of [press secretary Ron] Ziegler re the Philadelphia Plan and quotas." Safire asked Ehrlichman, "Could the Domestic Council come up with a clear definition of what was done in the Philadelphia Plan, what will continue to be done, and how different this all is from the quota system we oppose?" In ibid., frames 0274–0277.

155. In Hoff-Wilson, *Papers of the Nixon White House*, part 7: President's Personal Files, 1969–1974, fiche 402, 0003.

156. Parmet, *Nixon and His America*, p. 560.

157. Memo to Jeb Magruder from H. R. Haldeman, 9 January 1970, quoted in Oudes, *From: The President*, p. 87.

158. Schell, *Time of Illusion*, pp. 180–81.

159. Safire, *Before the Fall*, p. 556.

160. Schell, *Time of Illusion*, pp. 181–84. See also Parmet, *Nixon and His America*, p. 605, for Buchanan urging "a wedge between the liberal elite and (their) former working class allies."

161. David Mayhew, *Divided We Govern*, (New Haven, CT: Yale University Press, 1991), pp. 82–85.

162. Ibid., pp. 166–77.

163. Skowronek, *Politics Presidents Make*, chapter 8.

164. Quoted in Parmet, *Nixon and His America*, p. 560.

165. Memo to the President from Daniel P. Moynihan, 8 October 1969, in *From: The President*, p. 57.

166. Rustin, "The Blacks and the Unions," p. 79.

167. Quoted in Parmet, *Nixon and His America*, p. 560. Parmet interviewed Nixon in 1988.

Chapter Eight

1. Several years later, Vernon Jordan, former director of that National Urban League, expressed this spirit, declaring, "Black people are not wed to any given political philosophy. Our needs are not bounded by liberal dogma. We are pragmatic. We want results, and if conservative means will move us closer to equality we will gladly use those conservative means." Quoted in *A Common Destiny*, edited by Gerald David Jaynes and Robin M. Williams, Jr. (Washington, DC: National Academy Press, 1989), p. 210.

2. 118 *Congressional Record*, 92d Cong., 2d sess., 28 January 1972, pp. 1661–1662. It is hard to see what Ervin hoped to accomplish with the latter of these amendments described, as Title VII was regularly being interpreted to involve preferential treatment by this time. Glazer quotes an EEOC staffer allegedly saying in 1970, "The anti-preferential provisions (of Title VII) are a big zero, a nothing, a nullity. They don't mean anything at all to us," in Nathan Glazer, *Affirmative Discrimination* (Cambridge, MA: Harvard University Press, 1987 [1975]), p. 53.

3. 438 U. S. 265 (1978).

4. On the complex Bakke case, see, among others, Jack Greenberg, *Crusaders in the Courts* (New York: Basic Books, 1994), pp. 464–66; Herman Belz, *Equality Transformed* (New Brunswick: Transaction Publishers, 1991), pp. 148–55.

5. Norman C. Amaker, *Civil Rights and the Reagan Administration* (Washington, DC: Urban Institute Press), pp. 110, 117, 119–20; Alfred W. Blumrosen, *Modern Law: The Law Transmission System and Equal Employment Opportunity* (Madison: University of Wisconsin Press, 1993), pp. 270–74; Robert R. Detlefsen, *Civil Rights Under Reagan* (San Francisco: ICS Press, 1991), pp. 2–3; Steven A. Shull, *The President and Civil Rights Policy: Leadership and Change* (New York: Greenwood Press, 1989), pp. 69, 88, 96, 170.

6. 490 U. S. 642 (1989).

7. Blumrosen, *Modern Law*, p. 278; Herman Belz, *Equality Transformed*, p. 228; Detlefsen, *Civil Rights Under Reagan*, pp. 198–202.

8. Blumrosen, *Modern Law*, pp. 282–83; Richard A. Epstein, *Forbidden Grounds: The Case Against Employment Discrimination Laws* (Cambridge, MA: Harvard University Press, 1992), pp. 234–236.

9. Andrew M. Dansicker, "A Sheep in Wolf's Clothing: Affirmative Action, Disparate Impact, Quotas and the Civil Rights Act," *Columbia Journal of Law and Social Problems* 25 (1991): 1–50, p. 2.

10. "Note: The Civil Rights Act of 1991: The Business Necessity Standard," *Harvard Law Review* 106 (1993): 896–913; Blumrosen, *Modern Law*, p. 284.

11. I quote Terry Eastland's opinion piece in the *Wall Street Journal*, 2 November 1994, p. A15.

12. See Glazer, *Affirmative Discrimination*, chapter 1.

13. There were other signs affirmative action might have fewer defenders in Congress. In a television commercial aired in Boston in the summer of 1994 supporting liberal Democratic Senator Kennedy's reelection campaign, various accomplishments of the senator were recounted with accompanying visuals. When the Civil Rights Act of 1991 came up, the narrator mentioned Kennedy's struggle to protect against discrimination in the workplace, but only white women were shown.

14. See, for example, Richard Kahlenberg, "Class, Not Race," *New Republic*, 3 April 1995.

15. William Julius Wilson, *The Truly Disadvantaged* (Chicago: University of Chicago Press, 1987), p. 155. See part 2, generally, for Wilson's critique of the affirmative action approach, both in terms of its gains for blacks as well as its political liabilities. Also see Arthur M. Schlesinger, Jr., *The Disuniting of America* (New York: Norton, 1992).

A color-blind approach (in that it enforces employers to see job applicants as abstract individuals) that was used by civil rights groups and has been tried by some state anti-discrimination commissions in recent years may gain more support. It is basically a sting operation, where the commission will send two identically qualified applicants to apply for jobs at a firm. One applicant is black and one is white. If they are treated differently, a charge of discrimination may be brought against the firm, or there may be at least some unfavorable publicity. The approach is inexpensive and promises demonstrable results as rates of differential treatment can be tracked both over time and across geographical areas. It is unclear whether the public will support such a technique, however, and it is also unclear, given the complexity of the problem of "equal opportunity," whether or not this would have much impact among those who most need it. Still, this technique could be used not to make formal charges of discrimination but to measure how much discrimination is actually occurring. Rather than inferring discrimination from the statistics of minorities actually employed in a given industry, one could collect statistics of the number of qualified candidates who were denied opportunity where other white candidates were not.

16. For example, the University of California voted in July of 1995 to eliminate affirmative action by 1997.

17. See the excellent reviews in Theda Skocpol and Edwin Amenta, "States and Social Policies," *Annual Review of Sociology* 12 (1986): 131–57; Jill Quadagno, "Theories of the Welfare State," *Annual Review of Sociology* 13 (1987): 109–28; Theda Skocpol, *Protecting Soldiers and Mothers* (Cambridge, MA: Harvard University Press, 1992), Introduction.

18. Where civil rights pressure was organized, as in the Legal Defense Fund's effort in the courts, the construction of affirmative action was fumbling and pragmatic, driven by no direct interest in the development of the affirmative action model or racial proportionalism as matter of ideology.

19. Quoted in David J. Garrow, *Bearing the Cross: Martin Luther King, Jr., and the Southern Christian Leadership Conference* (New York: Vintage Books, 1986), p. 312.

20. Similarly, Alfred Blumrosen, in recounting his experience in the early days of working at the EEOC, explains how he told civil rights groups that there was precedent in the labor law of seniority systems that would allow moving qualified black workers immediately up to the "white jobs" that had been denied them for years, even moving out white employees who had been promoted after the Civil Rights Act went into effect. To his surprise, the civil rights leaders did not want to use this tradition, explaining that labor would not have supported Title VII if it would have resulted in this sacrifice (Blumrosen, *Modern Law: The Law Transmission System and Equal Employment Opportunity* [Madison: University of Wisconsin Press, 1993], p. 76).

Political scientists Edward Carmines and James Stimson (*Issue Evolution: Race and the Transformation of American Politics* [Princeton: Princeton University Press, 1989]) show the powerful effects that "race" has had on American politics since the 1960s, though by simply labeling the issue "race," they seriously confuse the issue. It is not "race" that Americans have reacted to abstractly, but specific *policies,* such as affirmative action and busing. For the unique effects of affirmative action on beliefs on race, see Paul M. Sniderman and Thomas Piazza, *The Scar of Race* (Cambridge, MA: Harvard University Press, 1993).

21. A 1963 letter from a trade union member to the *New York Times* goes a long way to understanding the resistance to affirmative action in unions: "Some men leave their sons money, some large investments, some business connections and some a profession. I have none of these to bequeath to my sons. I have only one worthwhile thing to give: my trade. I hope to follow a centuries-old tradition and sponsor my sons for apprenticeship. For this simple father's wish it is said that I discriminate against Negroes. Don't all of us discriminate? Which of us when it comes to a choice will not choose a son over all others? I believe that an apprenticeship in my union is no more a public trust, to be shared by all, than a millionaire's money is a public trust. Why should the government, be it local, state or Federal, have any more right to decide how I dispose of my heritage than it does how the corner grocer disposes of his?" Quoted in Benjamin J. Wolkinson, *Blacks, Unions, and the EEOC: A Study of Administrative Futility* (Lexington, MA: Lexington Books, 1973), p. 13.

22. Frank Dobbin, *Forging Industrial Policy: The United States, Britain and France in the Railway Age* (New York: Cambridge University Press, 1994), p. 220. On the point of critiquing "interests" as naturally occurring phenomena, see also Frank Dobbin, "Cultural Models of Organization: The Social Construction of Rational Organizing Principles," in *Sociology of Culture: Emerging Theoretical Perspectives,* edited by Diana Crane (New York: Basil Blackwell, 1994), pp. 117–53; Frank Dobbin, "The Origins of Private Social Insurance: Public Policy and Fringe Benefits in America, 1920–1950," *American Journal of Sociology* 97 (1992): 1416–50; Peter Berger and Thomas Luckmann, *The Social Construction of Reality* (Garden City: Doubleday, 1965); Albert Hirschman, *The Passions and the Interests* (Princeton: Princeton University Press, 1977), and *The Power of Public Ideas,* edited by Robert Reich (Cambridge, MA: Harvard University Press, 1988).

23. Paul J. DiMaggio and Walter W. Powell, "Introduction," in *The New Institutionalism in Organizational Analysis,* edited by Walter W. Powell and Paul J. DiMaggio (Chicago: University of Chicago Press, 1991), pp. 1–38, pp. 30–31.

24. See, for example, Yasemin Soysal, *The Limits of Citizenship: Migrants and Postnational Membership in Europe* (Chicago: University of Chicago Press, 1994), pp. 6–8.

25. Karen Orren and Stephen Skowronek, "Beyond the Iconography of Order: Notes for a 'New Institutionalism,'" in *Dynamics of American Politics,* edited by Lawrence C. Dodd and Calvin Jillson (Boulder, CO: Westview Press, 1994), pp. 311–30, pp. 328, 321.

26. Career interests made agency illegitimacy a terrible thing, but in no way should "career" be considered unproblematic and natural. Administrators do not in all places and at all times put their career interests first. Of course, it was Max Weber who pointed out this basic idea in *The Protestant Ethic and the Spirit of Capitalism* (New York: Scribner, 1952). It should also be added that many, if not most, of the administrators were also motivated by a culturally constructed concern for the fulfillment of the American justice project.

27. One may add that Lyndon Johnson had staked his presidential leadership project on aiding black Americans, so he risked leadership legitimacy by repressing the rioters for this reason, also.

28. For civil rights concerns relative to other concerns at this time, see Doug

McAdam, *Political Process and the Development of Black Insurgency, 1930–1970* (Chicago: University of Chicago Press, 1982), pp. 197–99.

29. The unequal influence of different parts of the public opinion on law and policymaking is well known. See, for example, Lawrence M. Friedman, *The Legal System: A Social Science Perspective* (New York: Russell Sage, 1975), pp. 163–64. See also, David Mayhew, *Divided We Govern: Party Control, Lawmaking, and Investigations, 1946–1990* (New Haven, CT: Yale University Press, 1991), pp. 171–72.

30. For example, Dobbin, *Forging Industrial Policy.*

31. For example, John Boli, *New Citizens for a New Society: The Institutional Origins of Mass Schooling in Sweden* (New York: Pergamon Press, 1989).

32. Skocpol, *Protecting Soldiers and Mothers,* p. 41; Theda Skocpol, "The Origins of Social Policy in the United States: A Polity-Centered Analysis," in *Dynamics of American Politics,* pp. 182–206, p. 191.

33. Skocpol, *Protecting Soldiers and Mothers,* p. 48.

34. Ibid., p. 149.

35. Jill Quadagno, *The Color of Welfare: How Racism Undermined the War on Poverty* (New York: Oxford University Press, 1994), p. 188.

36. Paul Burstein, *Discrimination, Jobs and Politics: The Struggle for Equal Employment Opportunity in the United States since the New Deal* (Chicago: University of Chicago Press, 1985), p. 57.

37. H. W. Perry, *Deciding to Decide: Agenda Setting in the United States Supreme Court* (Cambridge, MA: Harvard University Press, 1991), p. 259, n. 30. Interestingly, Bob Woodward and Scott Armstrong's earlier journalistic account of the Supreme Court shows the same reasoning. The authors describe the Justices' consideration of an early reverse discrimination case, *DeFunis v. Odegaard* (416 U.S. 312 [1974]). Allegedly, the Justices at conference expressed a desire to avoid the issue. Woodward and Armstrong noted, "The Court would have several more years before another reverse discrimination case worked its way up through the courts. In the meantime, affirmative action programs could continue to bring about more educational and employment equality" (Woodward and Armstrong, *The Brethren: Inside the Supreme Court* [New York: Simon and Schuster, 1979], p. 282). On American ambivalence to different justice ideals, see Jennifer L. Hochschild, *What's Fair? American Beliefs about Distributive Justice* (Cambridge, MA: Harvard University Press, 1981), chapter 8.

38. Steven Brint, "Sociological Analysis of Political Culture: An Introduction and Assessment," *Research on Democracy and Society* 2 (1994): 3–41, p. 22.

39. See the arguments in Dobbin, *Forging Industrial Policy;* see also William H. Sewell, Jr., "A Theory of Structure: Duality, Agency, and Transformation," *American Journal of Sociology* 98 (1992): 1–29. In an interesting essay, Sven Steinmo criticizes naive culturalist interpretations of American political change which argue for the importance of values. Steinmo instead shows the importance of a "labyrinth" of political institutions (for example, congressional committees) which require reformers to design their policies "to cater to the objections and desires of a huge number of interest groups and congressional constituencies." Though Steinmo tends to reify these institutions in his description, he also admits that policies developed in another way, such as by a small group of welfare state elites, "would be inimical to the twentieth century American system of government. Such a system would undermine America's system of 'checks and balances.'" He thus implicitly shows that cultural understandings of procedural justice are crucial in shaping welfare state policy. Though he does not recognize this as cultural, his imagina-

tive analysis emphasizes the taken-for-granted legitimacy of this fragmented and un-
wieldy American government "labyrinth." Sven H. Steinmo, "American Exceptionalism
Reconsidered: Culture or Institutions?" in *The Dynamics of American Politics: Approaches and Interpretations,* edited by Lawrence C. Dodd and Calvin Jillson (Boulder,
CO: Westview Press, 1994), pp. 106–31, pp. 126–27.

Index

Abel, I. W., 92

Abernathy, Ralph, 188

ability, test-measured. *See* test-measured ability

Abram, Morris, 21

abstract individualism: in American ideology, 26–28, 112; and bureaucracies, 23; color-blind model justified by, 7, 19; in contract law, 24; in Enlightenment project, 25; in modern citizenship, 23–24; nepotism as affront to, 53; in Stoic philosophy and Christianity, 25; theory versus practice of, 61; in tort and workmen's compensation law, 142–43; veterans' preference and, 42

Ad Council, 90

Addabbo, Joseph, 208

Addonizio, Hugh J., 88, 100

administrative pragmatism, 111–44; affirmative action at EEOC as, 127–33; affirmative action solution recurring, 113–20; color-blind model subverted by, 113, 127, 129, 130, 141–42; in courts, 139–41; Democrats borrow language of, 287n. 152; Dirksen's opposition to, 196; at EEOC, 125–33; at Office of Federal Contract Compliance, 133–39; Shultz's defense of, 201

adverse impact theory of discrimination, 97, 159, 169, 170, 226–27

Aerojet-General, 84

affirmative action, 6–8; administrative pragmatism and, 111–44; advocated by centers of American power, 67; affirmative action model in the courts, 139–41; alternatives to as pragmatic solution, 141–44; arguments for, 1; as arising before civil rights movement, 117; as arising from color-blind model, 15, 158; black poor not appreciably helped by, 230; for blacks as based on ascribed trait, 50, 51; business supporting, 89–91, 232; in Civil Rights Act of 1991, 227; civil rights goals linked to, 146, 274n. 2; civil rights organizations not responsible for, 5, 58, 112, 231, 290n. 20; civil service as slow to implement, 49; class-based, 230; classical liberal model's failure and, 113–20; coexisting with color-blindness in civil rights law, 8; Cold War as moral context of, 14, 107, 111, 158, 174, 223, 228; Congressional support for declining, 229, 289n. 13; constructed as in American tradition of rights and equality, 14; crisis management through, 67–110; debate as between fair-shakers and social engineers, 21; debate as between individualism and egalitarianism, 20; and equity, 6; in Executive Order 10925, 7; in Executive